THE SALVATION ARMY

Origins and Early Days: 1865–1900

The Salvation Army

Origins and Early Days: 1865–1900

GLENN K. HORRIDGE

AMMONITE BOOKS
GODALMING

First published 1993
© Glenn K. Horridge 1993

Ammonite Books
58 Coopers Rise
Godalming
Surrey GU7 2NJ

ISBN 1 869866 07 X

Printed and bound in the United Kingdom by
Staples Printers Rochester Limited
Neptune Close, Medway City Estate, Frindsbury
Rochester, Kent ME2 4LT

To my parents,
with grateful thanks.

CONTENTS

TABLES

MAPS

ILLUSTRATIONS

APPENDICES

ACKNOWLEDGEMENTS

To the three people most closely associated with the work on the original thesis and this book I have a deep sense of gratitude. My Ph.D. supervisor, Professor Roderick Floud, then Dean of Birkbeck College, London University and now Provost of City of London Guildhall University, was ever ready to advise and point out new avenues of research. My parents, Charlotte and Kenneth Horridge, were unstinting in their constant encouragement and general support.

In any large venture one receives help from many people. I found that the staff of the various Local Studies sections of the libraries visited in relation to the case-studies were extremely kind. In particular, Mr. John Janaway and Mr. Duncan Mirylees of the Surrey Local Studies Library in Guildford were generous in their support. Staff at London University Library, The Public Record Office, The Salvation Army International Heritage Centre, the British Museum Reading Room and the British Museum's National Newspaper Library at Colindale also rendered considerable assistance.

At various times throughout the research I have valued discussion of aspects of the work with friends and fellow historians. Foremost amongst these are Mr. Tony Kirby M.A. of Anglia Polytechnic University, Cambridge and Professor Norman Murdoch of the University of Cincinnati. Others to be thanked for their valuable comments and ideas are Doctor Pat Thane of London University, Doctor Hugh McLeod of Birmingham University and Professor Sir David Williams, Vice-Chancellor of Cambridge University.

Last but by no means least, a number of people played important parts in the production process and my thanks also go to them: Christopher and Freda Dragon for looking after me so well during much of this research; Marjorie Holmes for her care and attention with the typing; and Jan Lever for her cartographical skills.

INTRODUCTION

The Salvation Army today has an international reputation as a Christian organisation which attempts to put into practice what it preaches. Beyond some basic facts, however, nothing is widely known about its origins and development. There has, up to the present day, been no serious investigation into the Army's birth and early years. Nevertheless, this 'Church Militant' had a far-reaching religious, social, political and legal effect on late nineteenth century Britain and its message of Salvation by faith and works quickly echoed around the world.

There has been a great deal written on aspects of the Salvation Army but this has been done with either the aim of proselytising or providing a popular history. The very few published histories of the Movement certainly fall into the latter category. All the material produced has been based upon the assumption that the Army grew rapidly from 1878, that it had some impact and that working–class officers converted large numbers of their own class. Each of these broad assertions needs not only to be verified but also explained. Indeed, the origins of the Army's success lay not in 1878 but in the 1860s and even before, in the early lives of William and Catherine Booth. Whilst the Victorian society of the early 1860s might have been conducive to any number of missions to improve church membership and minister to the poor, the factors creating the Christian Mission and Salvation Army were brought together by the tireless efforts of this dedicated couple. Their single-minded fight to save the world inspired tens of thousands to join and support them. This was no mean achievement in a Christian nation more apparent than real.

Victorian Britain was amused and perhaps a little frightened by the advent of the Salvation Army which, after years of labouring, suddenly reared up in 1878. For a decade or so thereafter it built up an increasing momentum of religious revival and then, throughout the 1890s, settled to a slower but nevertheless still steady progress. Its growth is the history of autocratic leadership and selfless devotion to duty, the latter by all ranks but particularly by the officers. Where the Church and Chapel could not or would not go, the Army was found and its work usually quickly earned it praise and recognition. There were, of course, setbacks and corps closed but the Movement rolled relentlessly forward, adapting where necessary but always preaching its message of Salvation at every opportunity.

This book looks critically at why the Movement grew and in what locations. The socio-religious environment; the patterns of, and reasons for, station and corps geographical advancement; and the Movement's impact are all examined in detail. Moreover I felt that the use of case-studies enhanced the history and tested the ideas of the earlier chapters. Thus, Poplar, Manchester, Guildford, Honiton and Wales give their own local histories and thereby provide the opportunity to examine the Army at close quarters.

This history of the Salvation Army is based on as wide a selection of sources as possible. Despite the wholesale destruction of much primary material during the Blitz, the evidence presented here has been gleaned from what survived at the Salvation Army's International Headquarters in London and from libraries across the country. It is hoped that this study will enable historians and others to see the Army as the important contribution to late Victorian and Edwardian socio-religious life that it undoubtedly was. I hope also that it is seen as a statement of faith of thousands of Christians whose sole thought was the Salvation of Mankind.

CHAPTER ONE

THE VICTORIAN RELIGIOUS AND SOCIAL ENVIRONMENT

I. THE RELIGIOUS ENVIRONMENT

The Church of England

The *Religious Census* of Great Britain, conducted on Sunday 30 March 1851, was the only official investigation into patterns of religious worship ever attempted in Britain. It produced numerical and geographical evidence which destroyed the widely held but complacent view that the Church of England's membership figures were higher than the Nonconformists, with a small number of non-attenders deliberately staying away. Not only was the Church of England's position weaker than the Nonconformists *en masse* but the non-attenders were in the majority. The population of England and Wales at the time of the *Census* was 17,927,609. Even generously allowing 5,378,283 to be unavoidably absent (sick, too young or old, working or travelling)

> "It is tolerably certain that the 5,288,294 who every Sunday, neglect religious ordinances, do so of their own free choice, and are not compelled to be absent on account of a deficiency of sittings."[1]

The immense geographical dislocation of large numbers of people during the early Industrial Revolution resulted in ancient parishes being denuded of people while large, previously scantily occupied parishes, became immense towns within a decade or so. Leeds had a population of over 70,000 in 1831 yet was served by only one parish church and two chapels of ease. Generally there was little or no town planning as part of this rapid transition from an agrarian to an urban-based population. The cities were ill-equipped to cope with the flood of immigrants. As with all other aspects of urban life, religious provision did not expand before 1850 to keep up with town growth, even assuming a desire, by no means certain, on behalf of the population for such provision. It is not surprising therefore that the large towns in 1851 recorded the lowest religious attendance figures.

The *Religious Census* was intended to provide only a general picture of religious practice and as such was based on those who attended church or chapel. It made no attempt to gauge Christian belief or knowledge, yet it is probable that while few of the ever increasing masses physically went to what churches there were, a mixture of religious belief and knowledge existed. This mixture could however act in a negative way against religion; for example, a limited know-ledge might result in confusion such as was found with Henry Mayhew's costers in London in 1851.[3] 'Knowledge', not only about religion *per se* but about the aura surrounding it, caused many to stay away from anything to do with organised worship. Psychological and physical reasons were intertwined. Even when religious accommo-dation was sufficient, especially in the south and west of England, it was not used to capacity. The lack of churches and chapels was therefore only a part of the reasons for absence of obvious religious activity. Psychology or 'knowledge' was the church's main problem, due especially to popular and sometimes very real ideas regarding the cost of church going and the idea of respectability.

For the Church of England, the now out-moded parochial system and the retention of a mainly aristocratic image both hindered would-be church goers. This was most visible in pew-rents which formed an effective barrier to attendance. This fact was not generally accepted until the mid-nineteenth century, for pew-rents had been a custom of the Church for hundreds of years. Indeed in certain cases, such as churches built under the Act of 1818, the endowment of clergy came from pew-rents. This practice was also common in several Nonconformist chapels. Many of the upper working-class appeared to feel a definite boost to their status by renting a seat, thus reinforcing the views of respectability and unattainability held by what Bishop Selwyn called in 1854 ". . . the dark masses of our uninstructed people."[4]

The damage to the Established Church caused by pew-rents was hidden by the obvious abuses, which were gradually being eradicated in the early industrial society, of absenteeism and pluralism. By 1851, but for a very few anachronisms, these had gone and many of the clergy then turned against the practice of appropriated seating. It took several decades to achieve abolition because of the near obsessional debates on ritualism and the theoretical arguments aimed at how to recoup the 'lost masses' in the town. Clearly the Church suffered from psychological indecisiveness. Before 1851,

"For many years the Church of England had only infrequently and partially seen itself as a proselytising organisation."[5]

It was part of the Church's readjustment to industrialisation and the dense urban populations that its psychology had to change. Instead of being one half of the Squire-Church dual centrality of agricultural England, it had become by 1837 a minor part of the infrastructure of town life and, because towns after 1851 dominated Victorian England, a minor part of English life. Its one hope lay in convincing the working-class that the Church could benefit them. However where the urban denizens congregated most, the Church rarely penetrated. It particularly did not see the need to go to the people on the streets but took the view that the people must go to it. Only gradually did 'slum parsons' become active in the nineteenth century for the Church regarded the towns as missionary areas, its own home being the countryside and especially the south of England.

After 1851, the Church of England launched into a more rapid building plan than in the preceding fifty years, building on average 53.96 churches per annum before 1851 and 69.42 churches after. Many of the latter were in the industrial centres. In the 1860s and 1870s the Church was therefore beginning its recovery in buildings and more slowly in congregations but it became increasingly obvious that to succeed, it had to envelop evangelism. The Archbishop of York, William Thomson, expounded this theory to workmen in 1878

> "The Church of England must either come into closer contact with the working classes of the country, or else her national position will suffer, and her leading position perhaps be ultimately lost."[6]

The establishment of the Church Army, in imitation of William Booth's Movement, gave an impetus to the Church of England's evangelism. Combined with an increasing determination to 'go to the people', by 1914, the Church had succeeded in improving its quantitative position within English society.

The Nonconformists: The Methodists

There is little doubt that the numbers in the main Nonconformist denominations, measured by active involvement (becoming a member), increased more rapidly during the nineteenth century than those of the Church of England, whose figures were often based on attendance (and towards the end of the century, communicants on the day of highest attendance in the year). The numerical pattern of Nonconformist membership relative to population was an increase in the first half of the nineteenth century, a levelling out in the third quarter and a slow decline in the fourth quarter.

While it is true that throughout England and Wales Nonconformity was of considerable importance to the life of a large number of people, this has to be seen in numbers, denominations and geography. Just as the Church of England responded only slowly to industrialisation, John Wesley and his successors filled some of the religious void.

"The distribution pattern of Methodism which emerged in the nineteenth century was largely determined by the geographical variations in the Church of England's ability to maintain a proper pastoral oversight of the people in the eighteenth century."[7]

From its institution in 1740 Methodism concentrated on the areas of urban growth where industrialisation was creating a religious and social gap. It also gained a foothold in the non-industrialising areas such as those with grievances against the Church of England, for example, where agricultural improvements were initiated and friction over tithes worsened; wherever Squire-Church roles were weak or absent; in market towns with decaying industries; and in settlements on parish boundaries. This also applied to other Nonconformist denominations, mainly in the north and west.

The Methodist movement, despite an increasing number of schisms, grew numerically until the mid-nineteenth century but thereafter suffered a stagnation relative to population growth in the third and fourth quarters. The stagnating figures are in fact worse than at first appears, for many of those joining in the various denominations were in fact rejoining, and the Methodist movement as a whole was clearly no longer catering for the urban or rural poor as it had done between 1740 and the 1840s. After 1855 the Methodists were recovering from the disastrous consequences of the Fly Sheet controversy[8] and by 1860 had recovered large numbers. More importantly the 'Hungry Forties' and the 1850s crystallised a class distinction. Although very few of the upper-class were of Nonconformist persuasion, so were increasingly fewer of the lower working-class. The divisions within the working-class, although generally seen on an occupational basis, were reinforced by Chapel attendance. The poor of the 1860s onwards were absent from the Chapels while new members or those rejoining were increasingly from the middle and upper working-class. Many of these joined because it was consistent with the symbolism of respectability. The social status of Methodist families was also creeping upwards as they imbibed the doctrines of thrift and industry. Often an unintentional bar was put on the poor attending by the adoption of pew-rents by some Methodist Chapels. No longer were Methodists being recruited from a wide spectrum of society; instead it had become associated with shopkeepers and artisans.

The gap between the Methodists and the poor was freely admitted by the former in the 1850s when they initiated a variety of programmes such as the 'Home Mission and Contingent Fund' to evangelise among the slums. Even the Primitive Methodists, the closest counterpart of

4

the Salvation Army and the denomination claiming to be both for and of the working-class, noted at their conference of 1872

> ". . . that intelligence, wealth and respectability are becoming increasingly characteristic of us as a community."[9]

This was perhaps hardly surprising when charging pew-rents had earlier become a common practice with them. However, there is no doubt that with 200,000 members by 1900, the Primitive Methodists were the most successful of all nineteenth century religious denominations in reaching the working-class.[10]

The New Dissent

All other Nonconformist denominations can be grouped under the New Dissent, Old Dissent, the New Presbyterianism, and minor Victorian sects, with the Roman Catholics being a small but increasingly important factor in the nineteenth century religious environment. The New Dissent, made up of Congregationalists, Particular Baptists and New Connexion General Baptists all emerged from the splintering in the second half of the eighteenth century of the original Dissenting tradition. These former denominations had a geographical and numerical pattern of growth analogous to that of Methodism with a stagnation and gradual decline in membership relative to population after the 1850s. Their loss can again be explained partly by their failure to reach the poor, although the Baptists in particular were essentially a rural movement. The two Baptist denominations were concentrated by 1851 in the block of counties stretching from the East Midlands to the coast of East Anglia. Despite this rural emphasis, some industrial areas had a small though sometimes important number of Baptists, especially after 1850.[11] As with other denominations, herein lay their inherent weaknesses. They could not attract the working-class due to lack of chapels in the industrial cities and to their respectability.

The Congregationalist Chapels were found in increasing numbers of industrial centres in the late eighteenth and early nineteenth centuries but their failure to attract lower working-class membership was almost entirely due to an apparently in-built bias against such people. Those ". . . who found it hard to raise money for food" could not afford to support an unashamedly middle-class church.[12] It was openly stated by one minister that the Congregationalist Chapels were not for the poor. In addition, in 1848 the Rev. Thomas Binney told the Congregationalist Assembly:

> "Our special mission is neither to the very rich nor to the very poor."

5

Their chapels did however set up preaching stations in the poorer districts in an attempt to combat the lack of religion in the slums and achieved some success.[13]

The Old Dissent

The denominations making up this originally sixteenth century grouping were Quakers, English Presbyterians, most General Baptists and the Unitarian movement. All these stagnated and lost considerable numbers relative to population growth in the late eighteenth and early nineteenth centuries. They did not just fail to attract new members; many of their existing ones went to New Dissent denominations, although, during the last quarter of the nineteenth century, a partial recovery was evident in both the Society of Friends (Quakers) and Unitarian numbers. The Unitarians grew at this time by absorbing many English Presbyterian and General Baptist traditions and therefore members into its doctrines and congregations.

The major characteristic of the Old Dissent was that its groups

> ". . . tended to remain exclusive and elitest. . . . They abhorred the 'enthusiasm' of the new Dissent. . . and its evangelical preoccupation with expansion."[14]

Possibly because of this tendency and due to the smallness of their congregations of well-educated people, after about 1790 the Quakers and Unitarians in particular became represented, quite disproportionately to their size, in the upper middle-classes,

> ". . . among the wealthier merchants and manufacturers of industrial England, and within the radical municipal oligarchies which emerged after the Municipal Corporation Act of 1835 to challenge the traditional Tory-Anglican urban elites."[15]

However, at best, the Old Dissent could only attract a very few of the upper working-class because of the former's respectability, pew-rents and general level of learning conferred on its congregations.

The New Presbyterianism

During the early nineteenth century absorption of the original English Presbyterians into the Unitarian denomination, a new English Presbyterian Church came into being. It was extraneous to England being of Scottish origin. Not surprisingly, therefore, the strongest Presbyterian areas in 1851 were in the most northern counties, particularly Northumberland, Cumberland and Durham. These counties employed large numbers of Scotsmen and wherever a sufficiently sizeable group found themselves, a Presbyterian Church was established.

Both Scottish and the remnant English Presbyterians enjoyed a steady if relatively very small growth in Victorian England before and after their union in 1876. Even this must be seen against the continual migration of Scottish (and some Welsh and Irish) workers. It was essentially the foreignness of Victorian English Presbyterianism which stopped any sizeable growth and neither the separate parts nor the unified whole made any impression on the working-class as a group or the lower stratum and poor in particular.

The Roman Catholics

The Roman Catholic Church, with its apparent 'foreign Papist' traditions, was treated with suspicion by the majority of Englishmen. It therefore made only limited progress in converting the indigenous population, yet during the Industrial Revolution its numbers grew rapidly. By the end of the Victorian period, Catholicism had grown faster than any other denomination. This paradox of growth yet minimal native recruitment is explained by the tremendous influx of Irish workers attracted by work, an influx strengthened in the 1840s by the horrendous impact of the potato famine. The Irish were however distinctly foreign and tended to group themselves into poor, closely settled industrial communities. This proved to serve the dual purpose of stopping the dilution of their religious beliefs, which might have been expected to happen within a dispersed émigré population, while allowing their easy reclamation by the Roman Catholic Church. It also effectively stopped the transmission of their beliefs to large numbers of Englishmen who generally appeared to dislike and distrust 'the Papists'.

By the 1890s the Roman Catholic Church had long realised that it was making few inroads into the unaligned working-classes. In 1891 the *Catholic Times* gave the following reasons for their failure

"There can be no doubt that our poverty and want of social union are very serious sources of weakness."[16]

The Victorian Sects

Although the *Religious Census* revealed the extent of non-attendance at religious services, the ensuing debate and attempts to reach the masses would have achieved little had not the country been swept by revivalism in 1859 and throughout the 1860s.[17] It has not yet been appreciated just how significant the impact of this revival was. Some historians have suggested that numerically, few converts were gained by the various Churches and Chapels.[18] This may be true but religious impact should never be measured in purely numerical terms. In times of crisis or revival, many temporarily attach themselves to a denomination and upon leaving, carry away some belief or knowledge of Christianity. It is certainly possible for a denomination to have a far-reaching impact despite relatively small numbers, mainly due to a large turnover of membership and to high publicity. This appears to be the case with the Salvation Army. In addition, these historians fail to take into account small but generally persistent movements such as the Church of Jesus Christ of Latter Day Saints (Mormons), Seventh Day Adventists, Christian Scientists and Coaklers.[19] The very fragmentary nature of such unattached and small group efforts at evangelism often defies quantification.

Although the Salvation Army became the most well known mission of the 1880s and 1890s, it grew out of the increasingly popular Home Mission Movement of the 1860s. The 1859 religious revival rapidly spread over England. Large meetings led by famous preachers reinforced the momentum. As a result, there was a substantial rise in the founding of non-denominational mission halls, often with lay preachers to man them. There was also a practical willingness to put the physical needs of the poor before preaching religion. Many chapels and churches benefited from this renewed interest, including that of the Rev. William Booth. He was a Methodist New Connexion minister in Gateshead (Durham) and the mixture of the revivalistic mood and his personal oratory earned his Chapel the nickname of 'The Converting Shop'.[20] This type of 'success' was repeated many times over throughout the country.

The rather cautious and conservative attitude to revivalism, especially as displayed by the Anglican and Methodist Movements, only served to reinforce the working-class interest in the Home Mission Movement. Preachers were either individual evangelists or groups and came from all social levels, although rarely from the very poor who were the main object of attention. Of the wealthy, Brownlow North (grandson of a previous Bishop of Winchester) and Reginald Radcliffe, a prominent Liverpool solicitor, became two of the best known. From the working-class, an illiterate Staffordshire collier, Richard Weaver, became very prominent. He and a friend toured the countryside, often having their work reported in an evangelical journal, *The Revival,* which commenced publication in 1859.

Various denominations were making available funds and manpower to minister to the poor. The Methodist 'Home Mission and Contingent Fund' is one example of several. Some previously itinerant preachers were settling into slum locations and joined others in establishing missions such as the South London Mission, the Walworth Gospel Mission, the Gospel Mission Institution, the Spitalfields Gospel Mission, and the Christian Revival Association (later renamed the Salvation Army). These new missions augmented the work of the few other groups established for the same purpose before 1859.[21]

The hallmarks of these missions were locations in the poorest areas, some form of food relief, and open-air evangelism. Certain particular aspects of the Home Mission Movement became permanent such as the work of William Booth's one time helper, Dr. Barnardo, amongst children and the Blue Ribbon Movement for temperance. However, although the work of such missions was directed at the poor and some of the lower working-class did become leaders,[22] at best evangelism and religiously inspired social relief was tackled in a spasmodic and geographically imbalanced way.

II THE SOCIAL ENVIRONMENT

The Home Mission Movement grew out of both a religious revival and a social awareness of the abject poverty found in the heart of the industrial cities. Poverty and its alleviation had been a factor of English society at least as far back as Tudor times. During the early phases of the Industrial Revolution, a constantly shifting population hid the extent of poverty from what little real interest there was in it. The 'Hungry Forties' triggered off Victorian philanthropy because of the obvious distress and the writings of observers such as Tristan, Faucher, and Engels. The distress resulted in considerable working-class agitation as well as a clarification of class stratification.

England was by 1851 neither a rural nor urban country but an equal mixture of both.[23] This had not stopped her becoming a class-conscious country. At its simplistic level, the distinction in Benjamin Disraeli's terminology (1845) was between the rich and poor. This masks the stratification that had taken place and was continuing in the second half of the nineteenth century. Bearing in mind that England rapidly became more urbanised and that local circumstances affect generalisations, no matter what the division of the class system, alongside the concentration of industrialisation came a deepening in numbers and condition of the poor. By 1890 the term 'submerged tenth' was being used to indicate at least a tenth of an industrial community's population living below the level of subsistence, that is, people living on the streets or at best in very overcrowded insanitary conditions.

There is little doubt that the overall standard of living after 1851 improved but this did not apply to everyone. Generally those in skilled occupations gained most. Their wages rose both in money and in real terms; thus, as prices dropped, their situation improved. With this often came new or newer houses in specific 'better areas' of the towns, sometimes a servant or two, and frequently that stamp of respectability, religious affiliations. Those in regular employment in factories, mines, on farms, in domestic and ancillary services, and in the armed forces also benefited from a slow but consistent rise after 1851 in their economic situation.

Those who did not benefit were the poor, variously estimated during the second half of the nineteenth century as making up from ten to forty percent of the working-class. Some were the old and the sick or those thrown temporarily into poverty by the vagaries of the world economies such as the cotton famine caused by the American Civil War. The majority were either in short-term work, looking for odd jobs, or those engaged in sweated trades such as sewing and match-making.[24] Those who were not actually living on the streets congregated in often hastily and poorly built insanitary and over-crowded houses. Such accommodation was usually found in particular areas of town; for example, in London the East End was synonymous with slums for much of the nineteenth century.

The poor could afford only bad to moderate quality food which was often adulterated. They were also easy prey to disease. Evidence presented to mid-century Government Commissions gives many examples of their conditions; one privy to forty overcrowded houses was common in large towns in Lancashire, six to eight people shared beds, and piped water was available for only one hour a day. From other cities came similar evidence as well as reports of overcrowded cemeteries and of sewage openly collecting in streets.[25] Such conditions were only ameliorated to a small degree by the 1890s. While some of the major and most obvious abuses were eradicated (such as enclosing sewers, having piped water all day and better quality food), surveys by Charles Booth[26] and Seebohm Rowntree in the 1880s and 1890s still showed a large percentage of the very poor living below the subsistence level, in unhealthy surroundings and with little income and no savings.

The condition of the poor certainly resulted in the majority rejecting any type of religious commitment. Finding money for food, heat and the rent as well as in many cases some form of relaxation, (mainly drink), was the main focus of attention. Few were in any sort of trade union or friendly society; many used the very cheap drink as a means of escapism. Hence it was easy to criticise the 'idle poor' but, although a small number of the poor could be expected to have reached their 'station in life'[27] through their own actions, the majority could not help themselves.

Apart from Benthamite self-help, the temperance movement formed the basis of much Victorian philanthropy. The various agencies of the Home Mission Movement frequently had a temperance facet to their operations. Alongside and sometimes intertwined with the missions and temperance lay a host of other charities. In London alone 144 charities had been founded in the 1850s. These ranged from religious missions to housing charities, money for distressed gentlefolk, and the

R.S.P.C.A. The causes of such a proliferation of charity were fourfold. First, there was the desire to avert any form of social unrest. The theory of a transition to an orderly urban society in mid-Victorian Britain has been expounded by a number of historians, but popular disturbances did continue in and out of towns for political, social and religious reasons.[28] Both voluntary and legislative 'goodwill' was a way of pacifying the masses.

A second cause was genuine humanitarian concern for suffering. Here the religious stimulation came to the fore with the denominations, unattached missions and individuals all attempting to alleviate personal poverty for Biblical reasons. Many philanthropists were of non-Christian persuasion but believed in helping their fellow men for its own sake. Politically in the 1880s this belief often became espoused as Socialism.

The purely intrinsic attraction of slumming was another cause of charitable relief. Slumming could relieve monotony, frustration or, as has been suggested in the case of Gladstone, be a way of overcoming internal tension. The psychology of giving, of charity through committees, and as a mark of respectability must have had an added stimulus. Published subscription lists were a hallmark of Victorian charities and again provided a certain prestige of intrinsic satisfaction for the giver. Although these reasons suggest more ulterior motives for philanthropy than the Christian or social philanthropic ideals, most of those 'guilty' of such motives were probably unconscious of them.

The final motive was to educate the poor to be grateful and civilised. Such exponents as Octavia Hill and C. S. Loch felt that indiscriminate charity with no quantifiable aim or result was wasted; the moral improvement of the poor was the key. Thus in 1869 the Charity Organisation Society was formed to organise all relief, to identify areas of need (geographical and psychological), and to instil in the recipients virtues of self-help. Much of this philanthropy generated an increased period of investigatory work into the cause and effect of poverty and thus the last two decades of the nineteenth century saw a variety of 'revelations'.[29] Such work added to the demand for social reform which resulted in the increasing state intervention of the twentieth century.

CHAPTER TWO

THE CHRISTIAN MISSION

I. THE BACKGROUND OF THE CHRISTIAN MISSION

The apparent domination of the Salvation Army by the Booth family and in particular by its autocratic head, William Booth, had its origins more in the early lives of William and Catherine Booth than in the founding of the Christian Mission in 1865 or the Salvation Army in 1878. Several biographies have been written on both figures but a résumé of their lives before 1865 is necessary for a complete understanding of their later actions.

William Booth was born in Sneinton, Nottingham, on 10 April 1829, the third of five children.[1] The family was not well-off and at the age of thirteen Booth was apprenticed to a local Unitarian pawnbroker. The squalor William Booth daily witnessed in the shop, with people pawning their Sunday clothes to live for another week, produced a profound psychological effect. This took the form of a frustrated desire to help those suffering such economic and social privations. The poverty around him in Nottingham during the 1840s was exacerbated by the depressed economic condition of the lace market. Other local industries suffered too in a decade which later became known as the 'Hungry Forties'.

The death of William's father on 23 September 1843 pushed the family into further economic distress. They were forced to move and William's mother Mary took a small shop in a poor part of Nottingham. Here she eked out a precarious existence with William's six shillings per week as their sole regular income. Not only his poverty and that around him but aspects of life in Nottingham provoked his interest. In 1842 he became a strong supporter of the Chartists. His friend of later years, W. T. Stead, wrote in 1891 that

> "Young William Booth grew up in an atmosphere of unrest, in a hotbed of quasi-revolutionary discontent. The poverty that he saw on every side filled him with a spirit of passionate revolt against constituted authority ... He went to their meetings, he cheered their speeches, he subscribed to the Charter, and, if need had arisen, he would have been disappointed if he could not have shouldered a pike or fired a musket ... 'The Chartists were for the poor', so the boy reasoned, 'therefore I am a Chartist.'"[2]

12

This style of writing, which perhaps befits the editor of a 'popular' London evening newspaper,[3] nevertheless portrays a depth of feeling in Booth regarding the Chartists which is also commented on by other writers.

Although nominally Church of England, William became a regular attender at Broad Street Wesleyan Chapel and became 'converted' to Christianity in 1844, just before his 15th birthday.

The Chartists attracted William Booth because of Feargus O'Connor's oratory but the choice between politics and religion was ultimately decided by the Rev. James Caughey. This American evangelist visited Nottingham in 1846.

> "William Booth caught fire from the flame of this revivalist's oratory. He was deeply and pervasively influenced by the uncompromising realism of the American preacher."[4]

Caughey and other evangelists encouraged William Booth to start street meetings and work for the conversion of others. Thus on one Sunday

> "He marched his first regiment of the ragged and neglected into the aisles of this (Wesleyan Chapel) most respectable Temple, conducted them into the best pews he could find, and sat among them."

For this he was cautioned by the Elders and told to bring such people in only by the back door and sit them in the seats reserved for their class.[5]

Such an attitude did little to dampen William Booth's enthusiasm, but a year of unemployment between 1848 and 1849 made him severely question his future. Having completed his apprenticeship and with no prospect of another job in Nottingham, William followed his now married older sister to London in the autumn of 1849. He again worked at pawnbroking and, rejected by his sister's family because of his religious views, spent what little spare time he had in work for the Wesleyan Chapel which he attended. His interest in open air work, however, made him a victim of the Methodist vicissitudes so prevalent during the nineteenth century and especially in the 1840s and 1850s. He was suspended from his Chapel on the grounds of being a Reformer.

With the support of Mr. E. H. Rabbits, a local Reformist shoe manufacturer, Booth resigned from his pawnbroking post and became a preacher in the Reform Movement on 10 April 1852. The next month he became engaged to another Reformer, Catherine Mumford, but could not marry because of the uncertain future. Booth rapidly found it difficult to settle under the strict control of the local Reformist committee at Walworth. His initial three month contract with them was therefore not renewed by mutual agreement. In a search for security, Booth joined the Congregationalists in the expectation of training as a minister. However, disagreeing with certain aspects of their doctrines, he resigned shortly before entering their seminary. In November 1852 Booth accepted charge of a religious circuit at Spalding, controlled by a splinter group of the Reformers. He was never really happy there feeling

> "... that unless the Reform Movement became organised and set up a central authority he would have to leave it and attach himself to some Church that possessed these essentials of stability." [6]

As no organisation was forthcoming and as

> "... I could not approve of the ultra-radicalism that prevailed ... I looked for a Church nearer my notions of system and order, and ... I chose the Methodist New Connexion." [7]

William was accepted in 1854 by the Connexion's Annual Conference and appointed to evangelise in London. On 16 June 1855 William and Catherine were married. In 1857 he and his wife were transferred to the Brighouse (near Halifax) Circuit and, between 1858 and 1861, they served so successfully at Gateshead that their Chapel became known as 'The Converting Shop'. The spiritual revival of 1859 onwards helped the Booths in this and future successes. Failure of the 1861 Annual Conference to return them to evangelistic work was due partly to internal jealousy, but more so to the anti–revivalist conservatism prevalent in the Established Church and in the denominations of the time. The result was William Booth's resignation, presented to the 1862 Conference.

Between 1861 and 1865 the two evangelists toured the countryside owning no allegiance to any denomination. Despite being shut out of many Methodist Chapels by order of the 1862 Annual Methodist Conference, William and Catherine were particularly successful in the West Country and the provinces where William developed his working-class oratory using easily understandable images and ideas. He also instituted the practice of having people come out to the front of the meeting (communion rail in Church or Chapel or mourner's bench in Camp Meetings) to be saved, and initiated a 'Hallelujah Band' of working-men who were travelling preachers. In 1865 William Booth and his family (Appendix 1) returned to London to work as part of the Home Mission Movement. In July, as he was about to leave London for an evangelistic tour of Derbyshire, he was asked to conduct a week's services in Whitechapel. This Booth did and was so successful in attracting large numbers that he was asked to take charge of this undenominational group who met in

> "A dilapidated tent in a one-time (Quaker) graveyard off a Whitechapel by-street!"

The tent was run by the East London Special Services Committee which had been founded in 1861 by William Booth's acquaintance,[8] Reginald Radcliffe, with the aim of promoting evangelism in the East End. Booth at first considered his stay in London as only part of his transitory evangelism, but within six weeks he announced in a letter to *The Revival* his intention of remaining to work in the East End of London and that

> "We propose to establish a Christian Revival Association, in which we think a hundred persons will enrol themselves at once."[9]

Catherine Booth was to be of great importance in the formulation of William's ideas concerning the Sacraments, women's role in the Mission/Army, and education. She was born in 1829 in Ashbourne, Derbyshire. Her childhood was spent in reading religious books and she was educated, with one brief exception, at home due to illness. Like William she was expelled from the Methodists in London on the grounds of being a Reformer. By the time of their marriage in 1855, her views on religion were very set, as is shown by her control over the Gateshead New Connexion Circuit in 1860 when she took over owing to her husband's illness.

II. THE CHRISTIAN MISSION

Growth

Between August 1865 and May 1878, the Christian Revival Association changed its name five times[10] as the scope and geography of its work expanded. The increasingly damaged tent, which had been used in other localities in previous years and at least once had had its ropes cut while Booth was inside preaching, was in such poor condition that on 3 September 1865, Booth

> "... commenced Sabbath services in a large dancing room, 23 New Road, Whitechapel,"[11]

(Professor Orson's Dancing Academy). From here open-air work continued.

> "This we regarded at the outset, and consider still (1868), our special sphere."[12]

By the end of the first year,

William Booth preaching outside 'The Vine' public house, Mile End Waste,
5th July 1865.

William Booth preaching in the Effingham Theatre (later rebuilt and renamed the
East London Theatre), Whitechapel Road, London.

". . . after twelve months unflagging work, his remaining supporters tallied only sixty."[13]

Booth had therefore not achieved his hundred persons enrolling but he had changed his ideas over the year from having "no definite plans for the future" to believing that it might be their work to

". . . consolidate a mammoth working men's society just there in the East End, and with smaller branches all around."[14]

Various rooms had been taken as preaching stations by early 1867. Some of these had only a brief tenancy, but stations were established in Shoreditch, Poplar and Cambridge Heath as well as in other East End localities.

"It was not, however, until they took the Effingham Theatre (1867) that they considered their work as firmly rooted with some prospects of permanence."[15]

These stations were made more secure by more people joining the Mission than leaving. Booth had abandoned the second of his initial aims of getting people saved and sending them to the churches.

"This (latter part) at the outset proved impracticable.
1st. They would not go when sent.
2nd. They were not wanted.
And 3rd. We wanted some of them at least ourselves, to help us in the business of saving others.
We were thus driven to providing for the converts ourselves."[16]

By September 1867 the Christian Revival Association had become the East London Christian Mission, and from the base of the Effingham Theatre the work continued to expand. In February 1868 the Mission was regularly using 11 halls providing accommodation for 7,000 people.

"One hundred and twenty services outdoor and in are held weekly, at which the Gospel is preached on an average to 14,000 people."[17]

The *Christian Mission Report of 1867* stated

"That this is a true Home Mission: a mission to the heathen of London. . . They will not come to us, we must go to them."[18]

In addition to the preaching and, in true Home Mission style, the East London Christian Mission began poor relief almost from its beginnings. In 1866, a cholera epidemic and increasing unemployment forced the Mission to open a soup kitchen and to distribute food and clothing. Stations were continually encouraged to operate classes, food distribution, maternal societies, Bible studies, savings banks and various educational, usually Biblically-orientated, activities.

News of the Mission's work was transmitted in a monthly magazine, *The East London Evangelist,* which was commenced in October 1868. The magazines were also available in bound annual editions. From these it is evident that in September 1868 and August 1869, the Mission had ventured to establish footholds in Upper Norwood and, linking with another mission, in Edinburgh. Neither of these was successful. In the first case, William and Catherine had been asked by a wealthy citizen of Upper Norwood to establish a station for a recently formed colony of working people living on Gypsy Hill, Upper Norwood. The benefactor had built a hall for them but only a few attended. Mrs. Booth and then the East London Christian Mission improved the numbers, but the originator resumed control. In the second case, Mr. P. Stuart of Edinburgh visited East London to conduct meetings at the Mission. From February 1869, *The East London Evangelist* carried reports of his work in Edinburgh. The Booths visited there in July 1869, and union followed in the August. However, thirteen months later it was announced that

> "Financial considerations have compelled us to remove Brother and Sister Tidman from this station. (The reason being) we could not consistently send funds to Edinburgh given for the East of London had we possessed them, which indeed we do not."[19]

Mrs. Booth's public speaking from 1860 attracted many and while William conducted campaigns in the East End of London from 1865, Mrs. Booth did the same, often over several weeks' duration, in the West End with much success. She had also preached in the Croydon Public Hall in 1866. In May 1869, *The East London Evangelist* reported that "Mrs. Booth is now preaching at the Public Hall, Croydon."[20] This campaign reached an end on 27 June 1869 after an apparently spiritually successful twelve weeks. Because

> ". . . a few friends who had . . . become anxious for the continuance of meetings of a similar character but still more adapted to reach the crowds of working people who never attended any place of worship"

approached William Booth, a branch mission was established in Croydon.[21] This was the first successful extension of the East London Christian Mission outside the East End and caused the change of name to the Christian Mission in 1870. This was to be, with very few exceptions, the pattern of station (after 1878 corps) advancement adopted. If Catherine Booth or any missioners/officers preached in an area in halls and in the open-air and received enough local support, a branch mission (station/corps) would be established. (As the Movement grew, new areas to 'attack' were chosen with greater care.) Frequently that branch would be used as a 'springboard' for opening corps in smaller or other towns nearby. The earliest example of this is Bromley, six miles from Croydon, which opened in October 1870.

In December 1869 a branch mission was established at Brighton and work there proceeded well until the following year, when the evangelist in charge and the treasurer decided to become independent of the Booths. William Booth wrote

". . . this branch of the Mission . . . (has) *very unwisely* and, we may add, *very ungraciously,* separated from us."[22]

In September 1870, Mrs. Booth visited Hastings with a daughter for the latter's health. While there, she took the opportunity to preach and was well received. Following open-air work and a campaign, (a series of religious meetings), a station was opened there on Christmas Day 1870. Financial support had been promised for the venture from local "brethren of different denominations."[23] By December 1870, the state of the Mission was that there had been good progress in East London, Croydon, Bromley and Hastings. On the other hand, the Christian Mission had withdrawn from association with the Edinburgh Mission, and Upper Norwood and Brighton had seceded.

Although campaigns of meetings were held in several areas, no new permanent stations were opened during 1871 and 1872. This was due mainly to the fact that both Catherine and William were ill and that no suitable leaders could be found. During 1873 stations were opened at Wellingborough, Portsmouth, Chatham, Plaistow and Kettering with some smaller towns such as Tunbridge Wells being consolidated. Stockton and Cardiff were added in 1874 with Middlesborough listed for 1875. Appendix 2 lists all Mission stations in operation during the years 1868 to 1878. Geographically the sphere of operations spread south to 1870 and north-east thereafter. No plan of advancement has ever been found and the work appears to have spread either by the 'springboard' effect; by personal invitation;[24] or by Mrs. Booth and/or missioners preaching in randomly selected areas. The 'springboard' method was the most effective in spreading the work: a station was opened with outposts which were then reliant on the mother station until they could become self-sufficient. All were mutually supportive. A typical example was Hastings where the Mission began work in January 1871. By 1874 the Christian Mission was at work in nearby Ninfield, Boreham, Rye, New Romney and St. Leonards. In addition to Hastings, five other mother stations can be identified in 1875:

Portsmouth:	Buckland and Southsea;	
Cardiff:	Canton;	
Chatham:	New Brompton, Strood, Rochester, and Beacon Hill (Luton);	
Croydon:	Penge, Bromley, and Carshalton;	
Hammersmith:	Fulham.	

From 1875 the stations penetrated further north. "In 1876 we took our stand in Leeds, Leicester, and Hartlepool (East)."[25] The following year saw advances in West Hartlepool, Bradford and Whitby. Table 2.1 shows the steady growth of numbers of stations. By the end of

TABLE 2.1

Christian Mission Stations in Existence between 1868 and 1878

Year	Number of Corps	Geographical Concentration New Corps
1868/9	16	East London
1870	18	East London
1871	22	East London
1872	19	East London
1873	27	London/South
1874	31	London/South
1875	39	Midlands
1876	38	North
1877	31	North
1878	57	North

Sources: *The East London Evangelist.* 1868, 1869.
The Christian Mission Magazine. 1870–1878.

1877 and a few months before the Christian Mission adopted the title of the Salvation Army, there were 31 stations in operation. 9 of these were in East London, 4 in other parts of the capital, 1 in Wales, 7 in the south, and the remainder mainly in the large towns of the north-eastern Tees (Map 2.1). The evidence from *The Christian Mission Magazines* suggests that there were a number of areas other than those recorded above where the Mission attempted to establish itself and (sometimes only temporarily) failed. References to 'failed' or abandoned stations are however rare. The growth in the number of stations between 1865 and 1878 had mainly been founded on the hard work and increasing reputation of the Booths, with their strong working-class appeal in language and actions plus their use of female preachers, many of whom were placed in sole charge of stations from 1875. The impetus for extensive growth in 1878 and thereafter was also due to the Christian Mission's unequivocal organisation as an army under the leadership of General William Booth.

Control

Over the twenty-one years from his first open-air service in Nottingham until the founding of the Christian Revival Association in August 1865, William Booth's personal experiences of the religious diversities of different denominations and of poverty enabled him to develop a charismatic oratory and a fixed view of saving souls, no matter what the financial or personal cost. Combined with the intellectual power of an even more single-minded wife, Booth formed the Christian Revival Association with the aim of converting people and passing them on to churches. His success made this impracticable as converts frequently felt something akin to hero-worship.

Booth's independent spirit and rigid religious views forced many preachers and members to resign from the Association; this was the major cause of the slow development in the early years. Theologically the Association and its successors were basic and primitive. Booth

> ". . . believed in God, he believed in Satan; he believed in Heaven, he believed in hell; he believed that Christ had died to save sinners, he believed that without conversion no sinner could be saved — and there his theology stopped."[26]

This simplicity, the use of the 'penitent-form' which was used by people coming from the congregations to ask publicly for forgiveness and spiritual refreshment, and the incessant and often derided marches, open-air and indoor meetings held several times weekly, left Booth with a corps of 60 like-minded evangelists and followers after his first twelve months. He was in sole charge, for the East London Special Services Committee had apparently disbanded in October 1865. In the same month, Booth was rescued from the imposing financial restrictions and near poverty which he and his family were facing by the intervention of Mr. Samuel Morley M.P. Morley, a generous Nottingham philanthropist, was impressed with William Booth's work and invited the preacher to see him. The result of the meeting (perhaps encouraged by both men sharing the same birthplace) was personal financial aid of £100 per annum to the Booths.

William Booth required converts to the East London Christian Revival Society to sign a 'pledge'. This was done after acceptance of a printed card bearing the beliefs of the Society, (Appendix 3). The card was divided into two halves, seven Articles of Faith and a five part Bond of Agreement, much of it based on John Wesley's original ideals.[27] The Society's and Booth's subsequent actions were ruled by the first of the Articles:

Map 2.1

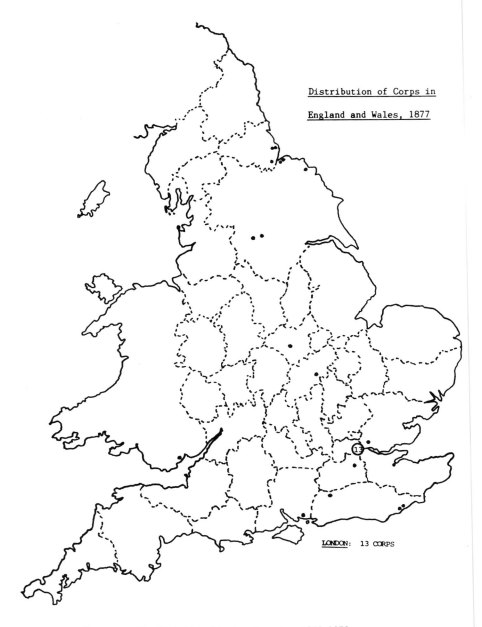

Distribution of Corps in
England and Wales, 1877

LONDON: 13 CORPS

Sources: The Christian Mission Magazine 1868-1878

22

"We believe that the Scriptures of the Old and New Testament were given by inspiration of God, and are the only rule of Christian faith and practice."

In Booth's terms this meant that the Bible and therefore religion was inviolable and that it was approachable direct and not only through an organised Church or Chapel service. Wesley had believed the same: Scripture, reason, experience. William Booth's thoughts were thus based in simplistic but forceful Protestant declarations. He also knew that the best chance of the work surviving was to organise it, therefore the latter half of the document desired a commitment from all in time, energy and money.

William Booth had realised from his founding of the 'Hallelujah Band' in early 1863 and his previous experiences with the Reformers that organisation was crucial. As the Christian Revival Association expanded slowly, both numerically and geographically, over the first five years, it was natural to utilise the Methodist traditions of an Annual Conference and a properly ratified constitution. The first Conference of evangelists, elected by the Elders of their respective stations,[28] was recorded in *The Christian Mission Conference Minute Book* as being held at The People's Mission Hall, 272 Whitechapel Road, London, on the 15, 16 and 18 June 1870. November is however the actual month according to *The Foundation Deed of 1875* and Booth was certainly away from London throughout June. *The Constitution* (extracts in Appendix 4) was written by Booth and clearly expressed his interpretation of the duties of members and evangelists.

The one major difference from any other previous religion or denomination was the equality shown to women as expressed in the quite revolutionary Section XII of *The Constitution*

"Section XII. *Female preachers* — 'As it is manifest from the Scripture of the Old and especially the New Testament that God has sanctioned the labours of Godly women in His Church; Godly women possessing the necessary gifts and qualifications, shall be employed as preachers itinerant or otherwise and class leaders and as such shall have appointments given to them on the preacher's plan; and they shall be eligible for any office, and to speak and vote at all official meetings."[29]

At the Annual Conference six out of thirty-four delegates were women. The idea of a mixed Conference was very unusual for the 1860s and 1870s or before, but one where women were held to be on an equal footing with men was unheard of and, in religious circles, generally considered heretical.[30]

The strong personal influence of William Booth over the Christian Mission can clearly be seen within this *Constitution*. Under Section III, Article I, it stated:

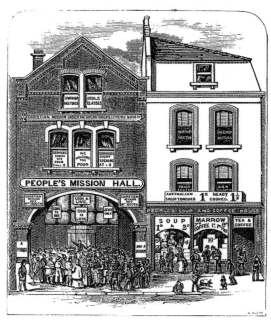

The People's Mission Hall, 272 Whitechapel Road, was opened on 10th April 1870. It also served as Booth's headquarters and, later, as part of the 'city colony'.

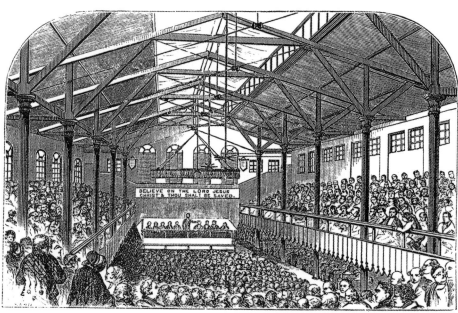

The interior of the People's Mission Hall. The premises cost, including alterations, well over £3,000 and the annual ground rent amounted to £135.

"The Mission shall be under the superintendence of the Rev. William Booth who is spoken of hereafter as the General Superintendent."

Article 2 of the same Section confirmed Booth's autocracy.

"The General Superintendent shall possess the power of confirming or setting aside the decisions and resolutions of any of the official society, or other meetings held throughout the mission, which in his judgement may be in any way prejudicial to the object for which the mission was first established."[31]

In addition, William Booth presided over any meetings he wished to attend. Further Sections provided for a number of committees, an Annual Conference and, most importantly for Booth's autocracy, a Conference Committee.

"Section XXIII. *The Conference Committee*
1. The Conference Committee shall consist of the General Superintendent, the Secretary of the Conference and five members of the Mission, appointed at each Annual Conference and to represent as far as possible the entire Mission.
2. The duty of the Committee shall be to take the oversight, promote the interests and conduct the general business of the Mission during the year.
3. The Committee shall meet every month or more frequently if required."[32]

In March 1867, three years before the first Annual Conference, a Christian Mission Committee was announced by the Mission's honorary legal adviser, Mr. Frederick Whittaker of Gray's Inn. This gentleman was to act as secretary. The Committee was an advisory body of philanthropists concerned mainly with the financial affairs (income and at first expenditure) of the Christian Mission. It became known as the Council in 1874 to avoid confusion with the separate Conference Committee. The makeup of the Council changed between 1867 and the last known list of 12 members (including William Booth) in 1876. At first the Council consisted of five London-based philanthropists and William Booth. It gradually evolved to include by 1876 W. S. Allen, M.P. for Cheadle in Staffordshire, and other close and nationally important friends of the Booths. Changes in membership usually came about either because William Booth would not be directed as to the Mission's expenditure or over a question of doctrine. Those on the Council by 1876 were therefore philanthropists concerned more with raising than spending money. Other philanthropists associated with the Mission, but not as members of the Council, ensured the Booth family's financial stability. The two most important examples were Henry Reed and Samuel Morley. Morley's annual contribution to Booth was supplemented by Reed, who set up a Trust

Fund of £5,000. For both Reed and Morley, William Booth insisted that he be put under no obligation to the giver as to the control of the Mission, particularly its or his finances. This desire for independence became stronger throughout the 1870s and some would-be philanthropists refused him aid because of it. The Council though appears to have fulfilled its role and provided the financial backing which enabled Booth and his close advisers to expand the work. The Council existed at least until the Christian Mission became the Salvation Army in 1878 and possibly thereafter although as with the Conference Committee, no minutes of their meetings remain. Few of those on the Council attended any Conference, thus by the Conference of 1870, William Booth had established a financial Council and a legislative Committee with himself as the pivot. He was therefore in control of "a respectable Council and a submissive Committee".

The General Superintendent's autocratic power is only tacitly acknowledged in Salvation Army historiography. General Frederick Coutts hinted at it by describing *The Constitution* as

> ". . . a voluminous document . . . The thirty-four octavo pages of closely printed type were divided under thirty-eight headings, ranging from the work of the Exhorter's Society to the use of unfermented wine at the monthly observance of the Lord's Supper and the holding of quarterly fasts. Eighteen conditions of membership were laid down which — among other things — called for regular attendance at class meetings but forbad the sale or perusal of such publications as the *London Journal* or the *Family Herald*".[33]

The Army's official historian believed that

> "The first constitution of The Christian Mission (1870) was a self-denying ordinance on the part of William Booth. By it Conference was made the final authority in the affairs of The Christian Mission".[34]

Yet *The Constitution* stated that William Booth, the General Superintendent, was able to confirm or set aside any decision or resolution which he felt was". . . prejudicial to the object for which the mission was first established". Although the Annual Conference theoretically had the right to control the Mission, the day-to-day running was left to the General Superintendent and his six very close advisers. A. M. Nicol, writing about the years immediately preceding the first conference stated

> "At last the Rev. William Booth was in command of his own, or within grasp of that despotic power which he always describes as benevolent in intention, practice and aim."[35]

The details of *The Constitution* as ratified by the 1870 Annual Conference which has not been previously published, seemingly confirm William Booth in an unassailable position.

There was much detail that had to be defined over the next few years such as the Mission's position on baptisms. Most of the definition was left to the Conference Committee. For the time being however

> "It was resolved that the Conference Committee select from the rules those which are to be considered the fundamental rules of the Mission and present them to the people."[36]

These previously unpublished rules are printed in Appendix 5.

There are two schools of thought as to how the General Superintendent used and retained his power. Salvation Army historians, as exemplified by Railton, Sandall and Coutts, maintain that any autocratic control was used in a benevolent way. The opposing idea, exemplified by Watts and Nicol, is that the General Superintendent was an increasingly tyrannical zealot. The former writers were Salvation Army officers serving or retired. The latter were ex-Mission/Army officers. All however agree that the Reverend William Booth was an autocrat. Evidence from both schools and from other previously unpublished material suggests that the truth falls between the two.

There was no mention of the First Annual Conference in *The Christian Mission Magazine* of 1870 but throughout that decade these magazines

> ". . . showed very clearly that the Rev. William Booth as superintendent was the life and essence of the organisation."[37]

Further evidence of Booth's control comes from the minutes (or lack of them) from the Annual Conferences. In 1871 the Conference made only slight amendments to certain rules. In 1872 William Booth was too ill to attend the Conference and it was cancelled. This raises the very important question as to why Booth did not appoint another person to preside in his place as he was eligible to do according to Section III, Article 3, of *The Constitution*. It is likely that he alone knew the daily routine of the Mission and as Mrs. Booth, probably his closest adviser, was also ill, there was no one who could ensure that the Conference would be guided along William Booth's lines. Clearly even the Committee were not going to be allowed to act as substitute for the General Superintendent. This suggests that his control of the Mission was so great that he alone ruled and that his organisation continued to be autocratically controlled. His influence must certainly have been powerful for his wife wrote at the time

"It would be too much to say that the work has not suffered in consequence of Mr. Booth's absence."[38]

This statement is supported by a number of instances, for example the failure of Mission Stations in several places such as Wapping. Other Stations reported that there was ". . . not a single case of conversion worth relating."[39]

Although Catherine Booth had taken control of the Mission during her husband's protracted illness, William decided in October 1872 that

"Though far from well and advised by the doctors to remain away . . . I have returned to my post."[40]

He therefore attended the 1873 Conference, held between 30 June and 1 July. The major change to occur here was a revision of the qualifications of membership to the Mission. Now, as with Mission Officers, the members were not allowed to use intoxicating liquor except under medical advice or for sacramental purposes. Tobacco also came under this ban.

The 1874 Conference took place on 22–24 June and was concerned mainly with the day-to-day running of the Mission and the

". . . great deal of hard toil to consolidate the fruits of the former year's vigorous advances."[41]

On the 14 June, at the opening morning meeting of the three-day 1875 Conference, William Booth presented to the gathering a *fait accompli* with regard to a significant reinforcement of his control. He as Chairman, George Scott Railton as the Secretary, and the Committee, had agreed a document known as *The Foundation Deed Poll*, enrolling it in Chancery of 5 June 1875. This was just nine days before the Conference met and they were not asked to ratify the action but told to accept. The report of the Conference in *The Christian Mission Magazine* stated that the *raison d'etre* of *The Foundation Deed Poll* was, because of some desertions and secessions, to

". . . render the use of any of our halls for other than a purely evangelistic purpose, utterly impossible."[42]

However it also served a number of other uses, not least to enshrine in a legal document the rules and operations of the Mission. When the document is closely inspected, it is clear that the position of General Superintendent was considerably reinforced.

"That the said Christian Mission is and shall be hereafter for ever under the oversight direction and control of some one person who shall be known as the General Superintendent.

1. . . . The said William Booth is and shall continue to be for the term of his natural life the General Superintendent of the Christian Mission.
2. The said William Booth . . . shall possess the power of confirming or setting aside all or any of the decisions and resolutions of any Conference. . . .
4. The said William Booth shall have power to appoint his successor."[43]

Whether there had been a Conference or not, the Christian Mission had grown between 1865 and 1875 (Table 2.1) due to the increasing reputation of the Booths, the financial work of the Council, and the Conference Committee. Until 1875 Conferences appear to have been of use mainly as disseminators of William Booth's ideas and for providing the ratification of his decisions regarding the running of the Mission. This was perhaps to be expected because as the Mission had grown, so the decisions needed became more urgent. It would therefore be unrealistic to suggest that Booth should wait for the Annual Conferences. He acted and his actions were later ratified. The 1875 *Foundation Deed Poll* now put this on a legal footing. It confirmed the power of the Conferences in certain matters such as annually to

". . . appoint to the respective Districts, to arrange, and finally adjust the appointments of the Evangelists."[44]

Yet in practice William Booth often decided on the appointments to Stations. He had overall power which was confirmed and guaranteed in *The Second Schedule* Rule 14,

". . . (the Conference may not do anything whereby) . . . the position or office of the aforesaid William Booth as General Superintendent of the said Christian Mission or the powers of the said William Booth as herein before set forth shall be in any way impaired or destroyed."[45]

What constituted impairing or destroying Booth's powers was decided by Booth himself.

Despite the detailed affirmation of Booth's power, within three years a new *Deed Poll* replaced its predecessor. The reason was that

"This period was a period of disintegration. Many of the workers in the Mission, between 1875 and 1878, left William Booth."[46]

From August to December 1875, William and Catherine were unable to take a full part in the Mission's activities, he because of a road accident and she because of a heart attack. The work was however continued by their eldest son, Bramwell Booth and the very able George Scott Railton. Booth himself made only the important decisions. When in December 1875 William Booth resumed full daily command, it was clear that a new element was needed in the control of the Movement to avoid the increasingly evident decline. The dual remedy came from the redefinition of Booth's control over everything and a renewed determination to go out onto the streets.

The causes of the decline were extremely diverse but cumulative. By 1875 Conference had become unrepresentative. Many members found it impossible to travel from or leave their Stations for Conferences of around three days. Certain aspects of the work and some geographical areas were therefore neglected. As it was the older experienced evangelists who staffed the larger, distant Stations, some expertise was lost in advisory government.

Conference was so ordered and convened that it spent much of its time in argument, debates and discussions. Talk permeated all of the Mission's activities, particularly Conference. In his opening address to the June 1877 Conference, William Booth stated

> "It became evident to me that we (the Conference) were drifting in a wrong direction . . . I launched the Conference on a sea of legislation and it all came to nothing."[47]

Debates and discussions took up an increasingly disproportionate amount of time.

> "Even members of Conference who had not had earlier experience of like procedure quickly developed an avid appetite for it. (There developed a) . . . plethora of discussion."[48]

The organisers of the Christian Mission were apparently the worst offenders.

> "These men were for rule and order. . . . An hour was a small thing to spend in discussing the precise minute at which an open-air meeting ought to be commenced or concluded,"

and meetings for various purposes were seemingly always being held, for example

> "Oh, those elders' meetings! . . . — prolonged till midnight many a time."[49]

It was little wonder that new members were not coming forward. They had to face a variety of committees to test the depth of their conviction and to see their progress after a set period. Committees had to be faced if members wanted to exhort or give out tracts or aid in 'social' work. Committees and discussions were of over-exaggerated importance and it seems clear that preachers were recording converts who soon became backsliders, possibly because of the bewildering array of interviewing groups.

It had become apparent by late 1876 that the number of backsliders was increasing. Of the 2,455 members in 1876, considerably fewer were found a year later. Part of the reason for this may have been that the Christian Mission officers had previously exaggerated the number of converts. The other reasons for the decline, apart from the unrepresentative Conferences and the committees, were the appointment of women over men which many felt to be non-Biblical; the exacting demands Booth made on his helpers; the Holiness Meetings which were objectionable to some people because of the excitement they engendered; and the schisms which occurred such as at Leicester (late 1876) where, as in a similar case at Portsmouth in 1875, the evangelist in charge abruptly resigned from the Christian Mission. This had also happened in 1870 at the Brighton Christian Mission Station where the evangelist in charge had been offered the financial backing to establish his own mission. In the cases of Portsmouth and Leicester, Booth decided to exert his legal authority in an attempt to avoid further losses of members and support. He went to court to establish his ownership of the Mission properties involved, sent his best evangelists to the towns to continue Christian Mission work, and therefore succeeded in keeping both Stations open.

The love of talk, the unrepresentativeness of Conference, the decline in membership and the schism at Leicester were used by William Booth and his Committee to do away with any pretence of democracy through the Conference. By a new *Deed Poll* of 1878, the old

> ". . . REPRESENTATIVE CHARACTER WAS DONE AWAY WITH and Mr. Booth became the "General", with sole control, etc., in this country or any other where it might spread."[50]

'Character' is the important word here because nowhere does Watts suggest that the Christian Mission was ever actually democratic or representative.

The action of ending the Conferences was originated when

> "Railton, Bramwell Booth, Dowdle, Ridsdell, Corbridge and other ardent spirits grew tired of attempted government by Conference and the slowing down of progress . . . (and protested to William Booth) . . . "We gave up our lives to work under you and those you should appoint, rather than under one another."
> "You tell us what to do", said Ridsdell, "and we'll do it."

This was alleged to have taken place in late 1876.[51] Certainly Railton and others were keenly aware that

> "As each Conference came round, it became more and more evident to everyone that what was done or not done during the year had little or no connection with any resolution of the Conference itself."[52]

Their feelings were exacerbated by the Leicester revolt. William Booth therefore called an extraordinary Conference for the end of

1876 but, with several of his key staff ill, the Conference was delayed until 23 and 24 January 1877. Booth chaired the Conference of 36 men and women evangelists and read to them the letter of resignation from Lamb, the Leicester evangelist.

> "Having got the conference thoroughly worked up over Lamb's insolent letter, Booth developed the traditional arguments in favour of one-man responsibility. Would anyone think of entrusting the conduct of the Russian war to a committee? In the war against the devil it was even more necessary to have the power to act promptly and decisively. Booth did not put any resolutions affecting his powers to this meeting. His object was to prepare their minds for the vital proposals which would come before the Annual Conference."[53]

A contemporary's view of the Extraordinary Conference stated that William Booth addressed the assembly on 'The Constitution and the future of the Mission'. Booth put forward

> ". . . in the plainest English his conviction that the time had come for a complete change of *regime*."[54]

In addition to the reference to the Russian War, Booth commented that every time a major theological, personnel or tactical decision was wanted, he was expected to give it and Conference was bypassed.

> "The conclusions reached, without a dissenting voice, were that government by committees was too slow and roundabout; that decisions were continually required upon important matters; that their's was a war, anyway; that the annual Conference should be continued, but as a council of war and not a legislative assembly."[55]

By the time the Conference met in June, the changes had been well discussed, formulated and presented for confirmation as recorded by *The Christian Mission Magazine* for July 1877. At the Conference of 11 to 14 June, Booth clearly expressed his view in the Opening Address, that". . . we must return to our practice at our earliest gatherings." This was that brethren were taken on

> ". . . upon the distinct understanding that they should labour under my superintendence . . . counsel and direction, . . . (particularly) understanding that I should direct them."

The Conference is then justified as important to". . . receive information and counsel from all" and would therefore continue as a Council of War. The Conference Committee was to be discontinued.

> "This is a question of confidence as between you and me, and if you can't trust me it is no use for us to attempt to work together. *Confidence in God and in me are absolutely indispensable both now and ever-afterwards*."[56]

The Minute Book recorded that

"The morning session was principally occupied with the delivery of the president's opening address after which it was resolved.
That this conference heartily endorsing the principles laid down in the President's address advises that the rules or resolutions of previous conferences respecting the mode of conference procedure shall not be allowed to interfere with the adoption of the programme he has set forth for the conduct of the present and future conferences.
Railton-Lamb."[57]

The result of the June Conference of 1877 was therefore that the Conference Committee was to be abolished, but an annual gathering for meetings was to continue; that Booth would make all the decisions and appoint the evangelists personally to stations; that instead of allowing complicated organisation, legislation would be simplified; that teetotalism would be universal for all members of the Mission; and Sunday Schools would be temporarily abandoned, as would soup-kitchens and food shops.

Such was now the power of the Mission that in the same Conference address and perhaps as a final psychological 'push' to any delegates who still had doubts, Booth stated that

"During the year we have relinquished nine stations . . . I wonder how many similarly circumstanced societies or organisations would dare to abandon as many stations, including the loss of 610 members, 72 of whom were public speakers, without fear of consequences."[58]

The evangelists left the 1877 Conference with the knowledge that they were under an autocratic leadership. William Booth was ". . . now the autocrat of all the Salvationists."[59] A. M. Nicol believed that Booth had at last got his long-intended way over the Mission and committees.

"His committee, or conference, bored him. Like Mark Twain, he was longing for a committee of one, and he, the boss of the show, to be that one."[60]

Apart from Booth's redefinition and formal tightening of his control, two other factors became apparent ". . . during those hard and difficult years of 1877 and 1878"[61] and perhaps contributed to the success of the Movement and the new style Annual Conferences known as War Congresses. One was the increasing persecution of the Mission in various parts of the country. The other was the militaristic talk sweeping England and being utilised by the Christian Mission. The possibility that Great Britain was about to enter a war against Russia meant that militarism was the theme of topical conversation. Missioners such as George Scott Railton and Elijah Cadman 'The Converted Chimney Sweep' used military terminology, the former as early as January 1873 when he wrote to William Booth addressing him as "My dear General" and signing himself "Your ever-to-be-faithful Lieutenant." Cadman in 1877 used posters written in military language to attract people to the Mission. On these he called himself Captain. Although such open cohabitation between religious and military phrases alienated some, it may have appealed to others.

By late 1877, converts were being appointed by the 'General' to aid preachers and organise various activities within a station. He could also have anyone removed and this ensured the lessening of diversity of thought. In March 1878, William Booth found a new resource of leadership and attraction in the use of women preachers working without male aid. This idea was first used in Felling-on-Tyne and proved to be very successful.

The name 'Salvation Army' was adopted almost accidentally. Railton, with William and Bramwell Booth, were

> ". . . drawing up a brief description of the Mission (at the latter's home, 3 Gore Road, Hackney), and, wishing to express what it was in one phrase, I (Railton) wrote, "The Christian Mission is a volunteer army of converted working people." "No," said Mr. Booth, "we are not volunteers, for we feel we must do what we do, and are always on duty." He crossed out the word, and wrote "Salvation." The phrase immediately struck us all, and we very soon found it would be far more widely effective than the old name."[62]

The name was quickly taken up and promoted by the evangelists and converts alike. William Booth may also have objected to the word 'volunteer' because after the 1863 reorganisation, 'The Volunteers' were a subject of considerable music hall and public fun.

The 'War Congress' of 1878 met from 3–8 August and was the largest ever seen. After a weekend of services, Monday morning was taken up by a prayer, song and march period followed in the afternoon by 'war memories', (testimonies). On Tuesday morning in front of nearly 200 people,

> "The greater part of the morning session was occupied with an address from the General Superintendent on the Past of the War, the afternoon session with his address on the Future of the War and accounts of the work at various stations."[63]

In his address in the early afternoon the General stressed that a military system of government was the best for the salvation of souls. In the evening there was a Holiness Meeting. The vital part came on Wednesday morning when

> "Mr Booth, with the unanimous and hearty concurrence of the Conference, executed a legal document"[64]

34

to scrap *The Foundation Deed Poll* and substitute another, this time changeable only through Parliament. This was to be done the following day with the registration of *The Deed of Annulment* in Chancery and, at the same time, the registration of *The Deed of Constitution*. The main provisions of the latter *Deed* were that William Booth, the General Superintendent for life, should exercise oversight, direction and control of the Mission alone; he had the power to appoint his successor by placing his or her name in a sealed envelope; he had the power to acquire or dispose of property and to set up or revoke trusts; and

> "The General Superintendent shall have power to expend on behalf of The Christian Mission all moneys contributed for the general purposes of the said Christian Mission or for any of the special objects or operations thereof but he shall annually publish a Balance Sheet (duly audited) of all such receipts and expenditure".[65]

It was also hoped that *The Deed of Constitution* would

> ". . . destroy the influence of those slanderers who, taking advantage of the fact that the supreme governing power in the Mission rests in the hands of the General Superintendent, have pretended that he could apply the property of the Mission to his own personal purposes."

The Christian Mission solicitor explained that

> ". . . any power over property and funds possessed by the present or any future Superintendent was solely and legally confined by this deed to the employment of it for the purposes and advantages of the Mission, and that only."

The final meeting of this National War Congress, (additional regional Annual Councils of War were to take place from 1879), was a musical service and whole night of prayer.[66]

Arthur W. Watts, who left the Mission some time after attending the War Congress and after an illness, later claimed that on the Tuesday night

> ". . . many of the delegates had returned to their stations thinking there was no more business of importance to be done"

and that few knew the extent of the changes being proposed or what the statutory majority of seventy-five percent of the delegates had passed.[67] However, the "many delegates" could not have numbered more than 45 of the nearly 200 attending because otherwise the statutory majority would not have been present. It is also unlikely that such a number would leave with a full day's business, evening concert and all night prayer meeting still to come. Finally the results and views of the two Conferences of 1877 must have caused considerable interest within the Movement, and so delegates would have been expecting to hear of the legal changes. However, Watts' general view that this *Deed of Constitution* placed Booth in an unassailable autocratic position appears justifiable.

Another critic of General Booth, A. M. Nicol, commented on *The Deed of Constitution*:

> "He (William Booth) saw, or thought he saw, that it would be in the best interests of the Mission for the present and the future that a people, moulded in his groove, should have a Constitution that gave the General for the time being unlimited powers, and that settled, once for all, the doctrines that should be taught and the objects that should be furthered by the Army. Such a Constitution, he believed, would avoid the questions on which other denominations had split."

Nicol goes on to draw out the very important point that William Booth, unable to follow the dictates of any other church, had in 1878 drawn up a constitution for an organisation that gave him

> ". . . authority to do with flesh and blood practically what he liked, send them where he thought best, dismiss them when he chose, and not even promise to give them any remuneration, and a host of other drastic things."[68]

This was the paradox of the new Movement, but was something noted only by Nicol and W. T. Stead. The latter believed that William Booth was continually against constituted authority in religion, yet he became a legally constituted authority. He who was so much against the restraints imposed by religious elders within societies to which he had once belonged, now imposed restraints on people under him. It could be argued however that Booth had to adopt a radical autocratic system of government in order to avoid the Movement making the same mistakes of time-wasting and indecision seen in the histories of all other denominations and churches.

General Booth's actions were open to misinterpretation and a popular music hall song of 1878 had for its chorus

> "General Booth sends round the hat;
> Samson was a strong man
> But he wasn't up to that."[69]

Regardless of this, the idea that William Booth was after personal financial gain appears to be refuted by the terms of *The Deed of Constitution*. Booth's gain was in wielding alone an increasingly large organisation. This power was achieved by his continual redefinition of his legal rights. From the first Conference in 1870 he dallied with democratic government but without any real desire to lose control.

Consciously or not, he was in fact tightening his control, as can be seen from the Conference Committee, Council and the cancelling of the 1872 Annual Conference. *The Foundation Deed Poll* of 1875 legally established what was already evident, that day-to-day control by a constitutionally established head rather than the Annual Conferences or monthly Committee meetings was necessary to create and continue a vibrant movement. In addition, he clearly needed to have written rules regarding new contingencies such as secession and therefore loss of property. Finally in 1878, *The Deed of Constitution* allowed Booth to do away with any pretence of democracy and to return to full autocratic control. It simplified but strengthened the rules regarding the General's power. There appears to have been whole-hearted support from the two 1877 Conferences for this move, although any dissent would not have been recorded. Certainly several people resigned from the Mission between 1877 and early 1878. Clearly though, by August 1878, William Booth was the undoubted head of potentially the strongest and nationally the fastest growing revivalistic force in nineteenth-century England.

CHAPTER THREE

THE GROWTH AND ORGANISATION OF THE SALVATION ARMY

I. GROWTH: NUMERICAL AND GEOGRAPHICAL

During the six years of 1878 to 1883, the newly-formed Salvation Army expanded more rapidly than at any other time in its history. Table 3.1 shows the massive annual growth with the peak for the new corps openings occurring in 1882. In addition to the 519 corps in England and Wales by December 1883, there were a further 37 in Scotland and 17 in Ireland.[1] Thereafter growth within England and Wales continued but at a slower rate.

From 1878 the Salvation Army kept up the process of the last years of the Christian Mission by opening most new corps in the north of England (Table 2.1). Of these openings, the majority occurred in Tyneside, South Yorkshire, central Lancashire and — the main exception to the rule — in the coal-mining communities of South Wales. All apart from the latter were centred in major conurbations and most had corps already established nearby. Thus the 'springboard' policy, first tried in the Christian Mission, continued to be used by Booth,

TABLE 3.1

**Growth and Total Number of Salvation Army Corps
in England and Wales, 1878–1883**

Year	Number of New Corps in the Year	Total Number of Corps by December
1878	26	57
1879	47	104
1880	55	159
1881	75	234
1882	153	387
1883	132	519

*Sources: The Christian Mission Magazine. 1878.
Pocket Book 1884.*

providing that there was a large number of the working-class in any new area.

Sunderland was apparently chosen in 1878 for these two reasons. It was reasonably near the two large Mission stations of East and West Hartlepool so that assistance could be rendered when necessary, and Sunderland itself was a

> ". . . seaport and garrison town of some hundred thousand inhabitants."[2]

This sentence from *The Christian Mission Magazine* gives an idea of the type of audience that Booth hoped to attract and in what conditions he felt the work could grow. In turn, the growth from Sunderland to Felling-on-Tyne was aided by a contact of General Booth's in the latter place lending a hall for evangelical use. The working-classes were in the vicinity and the Sunderland Mission Station (Corps) was within easy supporting distance. The contact made easy the usually difficult task of locating a large cheap building. This loan proved to be the starting point of an evangelical revival which spread along Tyneside, thanks largely to the 'Hallelujah Lasses'. These were such a great attraction that other young girls were sent as evangelists to open more corps in the same area. Within twelve months the Tyne District consisted of 22 stations, 37 officers and ". . . a long way on for 3,000 members."[3] Not all the stations survived but over 13 of the original 22 were still in existence in 1884.[4]

A similar revival to that in Tyneside took place in South Wales where the first town to be occupied (after Cardiff in 1874) was Merthyr Tydfil. Again, young female officers were sent and were accorded considerable respect by large crowds.

In South Yorkshire and Lancashire, more mature evangelists were sent from London to the major conurbations. There appears to have been no real overall national strategy of 'attack', but towns were often reconnoitred as to suitability. In 1879 the borders of Birmingham were 'attacked' via West Bromwich and Wednesbury. Corps were opened in Birmingham itself in the following year alongside a large number in Nottinghamshire and Derbyshire. Throughout 1879 and 1880 the work continued to give priority to areas of readily accessible, densely-packed populations or to small 'captive'[5] communities such as mining or coastal villages with their relatively little contact with the larger conurbations. The majority of both large and 'captive' communities were in the Midlands, the north, and South Wales so it was in those areas that the Army tended to concentrate.

In the south, east and west, little happened between 1878 and 1880. A few corps were opened in Cornwall during 1879[6] but these remained isolated for many months. Cheltenham and Gloucester had

TABLE 3.2

The Number of Urban Sanitary Districts with Salvation Army Corps, 1883

Population	Number of Urban Sanitary Districts	Number of Salvation Army Corps by end of 1883
Under 3,000	—	156
3,000– 10,000	467	160
10,000– 20,000	160	84
20,000– 50,000	96	75
50,000–100,000	28	24
100,000 Plus	20	20

Sources: *Census of England and Wales. 1881. Report.*
Pocket Book 1884.

both been opened in that year and in 1880, a corps was opened in Bristol. The Movement soon took hold in the latter town as in Wales, just across the River Severn. By 1884 there were seven corps in the city and a number of others on the outskirts.

In 1881 corps were opened from Cirencester to Reading and in the south-west, in both north and south Devon. Between 1882 and 1883 more corps were opened in London, the work spread deep into Devon and Cornwall, stations were opened on the east and south coasts, and the north was further consolidated.

Map 3.1 shows the geographical distribution of corps at the end of 1883. The Army had expanded to cover the majority of population centres and was not, like its nearest parallel, Primitive Methodism, confined to particular areas. Table 3.2 provides further evidence which confirms this growth within cities. The number of Urban Sanitary Districts (hereafter U.S.D.'s) of each size is compared with the number of Salvation Army corps in that same District. The Salvation Army's main advance was in the large towns of over 10,000 inhabitants. Out of 304 such towns, the Army had corps in two-thirds (203). In the 467 smaller towns of 3,000 to 10,000 inhabitants, there were corps in just over one-third (160). In the Districts covering under 3,000 people but with a combined population of nine million people, the Army had 156 corps. Thus the stronghold of the Army was in the town.

The difficulty for the Army in the countryside and in the predominantly agricultural counties was transport. The population was very widespread, sometimes over extremely large distances. Therefore although there were fewer corps per head of population in the densely packed towns and cities, some of which had very high corps-population ratios such as Liverpool at 1 to 92,084 and Birmingham at 1 to 80,154,[7] the Salvationists had an easier task of bringing the

Army to more people's attention. In addition the Salvation Army *per se* was only five years old by the end of 1883 and so to have 519 centres in England and Wales was a considerable achievement.

After 1884 the Army continued to expand nationally but at a much slower rate; however the Movement was spreading internationally at a rapid speed. Few corps were ever acknowledged as having closed but the lack of certain corps' reports in the *War Cry* suggests that a number did close. This was despite careful reconnaissance[8] and perhaps a trial 'attack' from a possible 'mother' corps. The loss of corps can best be shown by Table 3.3. Between 1883 and 1905 the Army lost 95 corps. A third of these were in the industrial north but the general pattern is of an even distribution. Conversely over the same period the Army gained 627 corps plus 78 Circle Corps, (a number of villages and hamlets under the command of one person), thus making a total gain of 705. A third of these were in the industrial north, with Lancashire gaining the most with a total of 86, approximately three new corps a year. Unlike the losses, the gains were mainly concentrated in certain areas, namely the industrial north, London and the counties immediately surrounding it, the Home Counties, East Anglia, and South Wales. Several counties, most notably the entire south-east, remained fairly static (Map 3.2). The evidence indicates that nationally the Salvation Army was a strong and growing denomination at a time when

> ". . . the figures show that the churches failed markedly to keep pace with the rise in people."[9]

II. RECRUITMENT: THE SUPPLY AND DEMAND EQUATION

Supply: Militarism

The Salvation Army could neither have grown nor been sustained without a large number of recruits. These were possibly attracted and certainly after 1878 greeted by a tripartite religious experience of autocracy, persecution and militarism. General Booth's autocratic power was firmly established in law by the time of the War Congress of August 1878. His desire for orderliness was well known to his missioners/officers and members. The persecution of the Army gathered rapid momentum parallel to the Movement's growth. Serious persecution occurred only in certain geographic areas but perhaps served nationally to create an interest in the Salvation Army and encouraged people to attend their open-air and indoor meetings.

Map 3.1

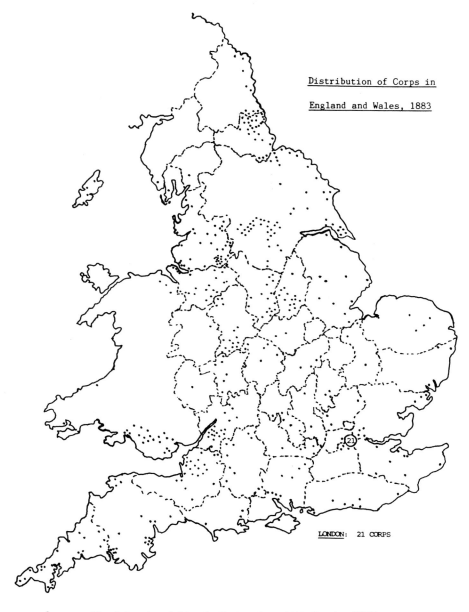

Distribution of Corps in

England and Wales, 1883

LONDON: 21 CORPS

<u>Source</u>: <u>The Salvation Soldier's Pocket Book 1884</u> (London 1883)

Map 3.2

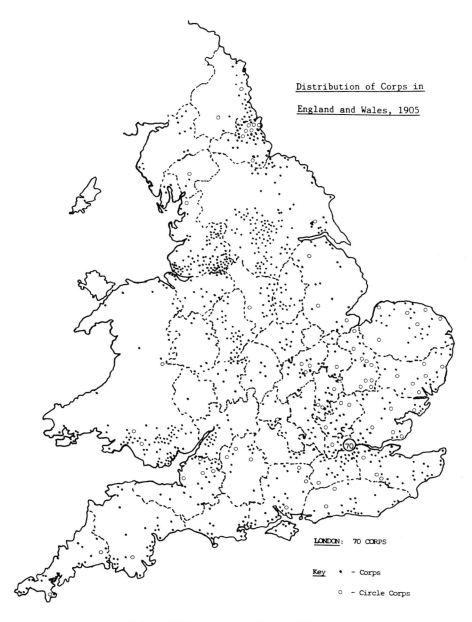

Distribution of Corps in

England and Wales, 1905

LONDON: 70 CORPS

Key   •   - Corps

      ○   - Circle Corps

Source: Index of Salvation Army Corps, 1905

TABLE 3.3

County Table of Corps' Growth including the Numbers of Gains, Losses and Circle Corps

County	December 1878	December 1883	December 1905	Lost	Gained	Circle Corps
1. Lancashire	5	45	124	5	84	2
2. West Riding of Yorkshire	7	43	90	6	53	—
3. London	7	26	69	1	44	—
4. South Wales	5	22	64	—	42	2
5. Durham	13	30	45	2	17	7
6. Kent	2	12	38	2	28	3
7. Hampshire	1	11	35	3	27	2
8. Norfolk	—	5	30	2	27	6
9. Somersetshire	—	22	27	7	12	4
= 10. Devonshire	1	20	26	2	8	1
= 10. Essex	—	8	26	—	18	6
11. North Riding of Yorkshire	5	11	24	3	16	—
12. Cheshire	—	16	23	4	11	1
= 13. Cornwall	—	19	22	4	7	3
= 13. Northumberland	2	11	22	1	12	2
= 13. Suffolk	—	3	22	—	19	5
= 13. Sussex	3	7	22	2	17	2
= 14. Gloucestershire	—	22	21	5	4	—
= 14. Surrey	—	4	21	—	17	1
= 14. Lincolnshire	—	13	21	2	10	3
= 15. Nottinghamshire	—	12	17	3	11	—
= 15. Derbyshire	—	16	17	7	8	1
= 15. Northamptonshire	1	7	17	3	13	3
16. Cambridgeshire	—	2	15	—	13	9
17. Wiltshire	1	15	14	7	6	3
= 18. East Riding of Yorkshire	—	13	13	6	6	1
= 18. North Wales	—	3	13	—	—	1
= 18. Hertfordshire	—	5	13	1	9	3
= 19. Cumberland	—	3	12	—	9	—
= 19. Warwickshire	1	10	12	1	3	—
= 19. Middlesex	1	2	12	—	10	1
= 19. Bedfordshire	—	3	12	1	10	3
= 20. Dorsetshire	—	2	11	—	9	—
= 20. Worcestershire	—	8	11	4	7	—
= 20. Staffordshire	1	16	11	6	1	—
= 20. Leicestershire	1	2	11	—	9	—
= 20. Monmouthshire	—	9	11	—	2	—
= 21. Oxfordshire	—	4	9	2	7	1
= 21. Buckinghamshire	—	2	9	1	8	—
22. Shropshire	—	1	8	—	7	—
23. Berkshire	—	6	7	2	3	—
= 24. Westmorland	—	2	3	—	1	1
= 24. Huntingdonshire	—	1	3	—	2	1
25. Herefordshire	—	1	1	—	—	1
26. Rutlandshire	—	—	—	—	—	—

Note: 1. The 1905 Corps totals have been taken to decide the order of counties.
    2. 495 corps are recorded in the above 'December 1883' column. There were an additional 24 corps in the Welsh countryside, other than in Monmouthshire, South Wales and North Wales.

Sources: The Christian Mission Magazine 1878.
    The Salvationist 1879.
    Pocket Book 1884.
    Index of Salvation Army Corps, 1905. (Hereafter Corps Index 1905.)
    Printed list marked "Confidential".

The two most recent historians to write on the Salvation Army put some stress on the fact that the militarism of the Army was both in keeping with the time and appealing to the people.[10] Their work is based on two articles which appeared in different journals in 1971. The first, by Olive Anderson, saw the Crimea War and American Civil War as influencing the British population into accepting military speech and references into everyday language. In particular, the influence of the American preachers who often used military analogies and words in their usually successful missions to Great Britain in the late 1860s and 1870s, was strong.[11] Likewise, H. Cunningham wrote about the impact of jingoism on British society in 1877–8. In particular he noted the strength of jingoism, it being early 1878,[12] (around the time of the change of name by Booth to Salvation Army). However, both Anderson and Cunningham based their work on limited and selective primary evidence and, equally of importance, both say that the militarism and jingoism were limited in geographical extent.[13]

Despite suggesting that there is little evidence to support the view that the militarism of the Salvation Army was such an important factor in attracting members, it may still be useful to identify what made up the militarism. Twenty different facets of it are apparent, any one or combination of which might appeal. These facets were: uniforms, flags, bands, songs, mass-rallies, the novelty of being an identifiable religious Army, simple and broad-based theological message, use of working-class rhetoric, names of people (nicknames), being identified as working-class, names of buildings, corps (having a distinct local headquarters), style of meetings, posters, clear way to gain more converts (person to person), young people's work, no Sunday work, women's equality, organisation, and discipline.

Armies were identified by their clothing and the evangelists of the Christian Mission had worn what might be termed a uniform of frock coats, tall hats, black ties; when conducting open-air meetings or marches, they were usually armed with an umbrella. Captain Cadman's speech at the War Congress of 1878 presented the first public demand for a Salvation Army uniform, albeit initially for the officers.

> "God bless all the captains of the Salvation Army. I would like to wear a suit of clothes that would let everybody know I meant war to the teeth and Salvation for the world."

The first venture at being identified as a Salvationist was crude badges attached to hats or arms in late 1878. In 1880, an attempt to regularise the increasing variety of military uniform for officers and soldiers was made through the *War Cry*. On 16 June 1880, the Army's black straw bonnets first appeared in public on the heads of twenty-five women cadets. General Booth believed the uniform

"... to be very useful, attracts attention, gives opportunity for conversation, gathers people at the open-air demonstrations, excites respect in the rowdy population, indicates not only connection with the Army, but the person's position in it, and is a safeguard against conformity to the fashions of the day."

Uniform was also classless and this helped social assimilation between soldiers in an age when dress frequently denoted one's station in life.

As a natural corollary to military style uniforms, flags were adopted. The first evidence of a flag comes from the cover of the first *Report of the Christian Mission* in 1867 where a picture of the Mission's Headquarters shows a flag bearing the words "East London Christian Mission". No other flags are known to have been used but discussions as to the nature of a symbolic flag took place between members of the Booth family in 1874 and 1876.[14] However it was not until 1878, in the month after the War Congress, that the first Army flag was presented. Mrs. Booth arranged the ceremony at Coventry in September 1878. Thereafter flags became prolific and served as a very useful rallying point with their crimson for the blood of Christ, blue for purity and the sun in the centre for light and heart. The motto 'Blood and Fire' was placed around the sun.[15]

"The use of flags has done more than any one could have imagined to bind all our soldiers together, and to encourage and develop the spirit of enterprise and resolution."[16]

No army marched without music so General Booth was not against its use as another means of attracting crowds. On Monday 5 August 1878, during the War Congress

"Processions led by a band of musical instruments will march to and from Fieldgate after the morning and afternoon meetings, and before the evening meeting."[17]

Shortly after, Booth heard that Salvationists in Salisbury were aided by a Methodist family. Charles Fry and his three sons had been invited by A. W. Watts, a Mission Evangelist, to play their brass instruments in an effort to stop the mob who

"... had taken to singing popular songs to drown the voices of the Salvationists."[18]

Despite some internal opposition within the Army to band music, the family were encouraged to become Salvationists and accompanied the General on various campaigns. This quickly stimulated the desire of other corps[19] to follow Salisbury's example. Bands of various combinations and sizes became common after the General allowed the establishment of the first official corps band at Consett in December

MRS. GENERAL WILLIAM BOOTH
THE MOTHER OF THE SALVATION ARMY.

Trade band in 1895.

1879. Ballington Booth, the General's second son, had however established his own 'Hallelujah Brass Band' nine months earlier in Manchester.

Music for popular use was of little practicality without words and although the Christian Mission adopted the hymns current in the Victorian churches and chapels of the 1860s and 1870s, it published certain hymns relating to its theological message of conversion and renewal. The first known example, entitled 'The Swelling of Jordan', had as its opening verse:

"Poor Christian, look up to the joys set before thee,
And haste on thy way to the regions of glory.
A crown and a kingdom thy faith may discover,
Thy troubles are great, but they soon will be over,
For Jesus has suffered, thy soul to deliver,
And light up thy passage through Jordan's dark river."[20]

Within a decade of its origin, the Christian Mission had selected and printed in its magazine similar simple songs and those with a popular militaristic flavour, such as, with its typical recruiting cry, "*Who'll be the next* to follow Jesus?"[21] In 1879 the Salvation Army published its own songbook of 532 pieces with a supplement of 101 others, all in one volume. The first volume of original Salvation Army songs (as all hymns were now called) and music was published in 1883 under the title of *Salvation Music Volume II.* The majority of songs were sung to popular secular tunes such as 'Storm the Forts of Darkness' which was sung to 'Here's to Good Old Whisky.' It was the words which were of importance and the stress on battle, victory, a soldier's life, suffering and above all Holiness (leading a converted Holy Life) became the focal point of the Movement's *raison d'être.*

The aim behind the important militaristic factors of uniform, flags, bands and songs was, like the processions and rallies, initially to attract attention. From the first War Congress of 1878, area War Congresses were held in every district where the Salvation Army was in existence. The huge rallies served to encourage the soldiers and provide large demonstrations of mass support, even if much of it was passive rather than active (merely going to services to witness the scenes rather than taking a part). In addition to area (Divisional) War Congresses, all possible occasions were used for rallies, be they weddings, important regional holidays such as the Northern Wakes, or funerals. When asked about such tactics, William Booth stated that

"They are all explained by the first necessity of the movement, which is TO ATTRACT ATTENTION. If the people are in danger of the damnation of Hell, and asleep in the danger, awaken them — "to open their eyes". These and other methods attract their attention, secure a hearing for the gospel, and thousands repent, flee to Christ from the wrath to come, and are saved. Many of the objections have been made to the using of a drum in our processions; but there cannot certainly be anything more objectionable in our calling the poor people into our Theatres and Halls by beating a drum than in other Christians calling their congregations by beating a bell: no principle is involved in either case."[22]

General Booth was playing on the novelty of his organisation. It attracted people because it was identifiably different from any other form of religion. It was also somewhere to go and something to do, a relief in the often drab monotony of life whether in the industrial, mining or agricultural communities. Its simple theological message, based on the General's own belief of Heaven and Hell, God and Satan, was preached with rhetoric and with stories that were easily understood. The speakers themselves were usually working-class and their converts were immediately expected to stand up and become, effectively, lay-preachers of mini-sermons, testifying how they became converted. Many of these people as well as the preachers took names related to their past professions which were readily identifiable by others as belonging to the working-class. Amongst those chosen were the Blood Washed Collier; the Hallelujah Fishmonger; the Milkman who has not watered his milk since he was saved; the Saved Railway Guard; and Happy Eliza.

The language and officers were of the people and the message was taken directly into the streets where the lowest stratum lived. Meetings were held as easily in the open-air as in theatres or music-halls. There was no bar on entry, no pew-rents and no need to change into Sunday clothes. The Army deliberately chose non-Church-like names for their buildings such as Salvation Army Barracks, Salvation Stores or Salvation Warehouse. Booth's justification was

"It is well known that there is a strong prejudice existing in the minds of the vast majority of the population against Churches and Chapels, and that on no account will they enter them. By calling our places Barracks, Factories, Stores, and the like, we avoid this prejudice, and obtain the attendance of the people; and when we add the word Salvation, we make known in the simplest and plainest manner possible that the meetings that are to be held there, will be for the purposes of salvation. Some people have strongly denounced these names but we think them simple and useful and no more objectionable than 'Christ Church', 'Jesus College', and the like."[23]

Each building was designated as a corps on the official records and given a specific number with the oldest, Whitechapel, being number 1. The corps building provided a distinct local headquarters. Generally the officer's living quarters were nearby in the poorest areas.

"It was a duty to secure lodgings in the toughest quarter of a town, simple rooms furnished with plain rush-bottomed chairs."[24]

The regular weekday and Sunday in and out-door meetings were conducted in a very different style from any other denomination. There was a freedom of worship reminiscent of the Hallelujah Bands.

> "My farm-lad Dick used to attend regularly. 'It's as good as a "theayter"' he told me. 'You can go in when you like, and if you want a drop or a smoke in the middle, why, out you come, just as you please.'"[25]

Intertwined with this ran an intensive neo-charismatic excitement which apparently did not always last long with individuals, some of whom left the Movement soon after joining. It was however an excitement approved of by William Booth:

> "... it is impossible for any war to be carried out without much excitement, especially this war. Men cannot find out that they are terrible rebels against God — every moment in danger of the damnation of Hell — without being excited; and soldiers of the cross cannot look on their fellow-creatures laughing, dancing, sleeping, cursing, and swearing on the verge of the horrible gulf, without being moved to their very depths; nor can they rush in upon them with the offer of mercy, awake them from their slumber, drag them away from the burning gulf, and see them plunge in the fountain of mercy, without being themselves excited. There never was a real work of God without excitement. Read the accounts of Old Testament revivals as well as those since Pentecost. Excitement is allowed and welcomed in every other domain; in business, politics, music, and pleasure; in war it is deemed a necessity, and it is so here."[26]

All the excitement was fostered by other facets of militarism in addition to those identified above. These were the judicious use of posters, designed to be read by the lowest of the working-class with the aim of attracting them to the meetings; the genuine desire to wear the uniform and talk directly to neighbours, friends and strangers at every opportunity; Booth's demand was that anyone associated with the Movement should not work on Sundays and, if their job demanded it, they should change their position. Connected with this was the desire to see all shops closed on a Sunday, and the respect and encouragement shown to young people. Officers as young as fifteen years of age evangelised at corps and, within corps, young people were given the same tasks as their elders.

Probably the most unusual aspect of the Salvation Army was the position of women within its ranks. Even before 1878, women had been given equality with men in the Christian Mission. Once the Salvation Army became publicly prominent, it was this facet which attracted considerable interest. Booth exploited the novelty and began sending young girls in pairs to take command of corps. The first of these left London on Saturday 30 March 1878 for Felling-on-Tyne. Within a year other young 'Hallelujah Lasses' were

50

READER,—If you are not SAVED, you will go to HELL!
'Believe on the Lord Jesus Christ and thou shalt be saved.'

SALVATION ARMY!

ATTERCLIFFE.

BLOOD AND FIRE!

LOOK OUT! LOOK OUT! LOOK OUT!

CAPTAIN MORRELL

And SOLDIERS of the 37th Corps (Regulars) will challenge the DEVIL for War
and make a SPECIAL ATTACK on his Territory,

ON SUNDAY, SEPT. 19th.

Guns loaded at 7 a.m.; First Volley fired at 10 a.m., NEWHALL ROAD.

Musical Instruments in the Battle Field. Wounded picked up as we go along, and handed over to THE GREAT PHYSICIAN.

CAPTAIN MORRELL

(Better known as the DEVIL DRIVER), from Leicester, letting the enemy have it right
and left. Barracks at 11, with a garrison kept by Capt. Morrell.

A HOST OF DARE DEVILS!!

Will repeat the firing on the Battle-field.

Again at PINFOLD LANE, at 2 p.m., right in front of the Enemy,
And from thence march off to the VESTRY HALL, where they will arrive at 3 o'clock p.m.

The HALLELUJAH CHORISTERS, or POP-GUNS,

Will be going off in all directions, also a Band of the Devils who used to be, will testify as to what the GENERAL has done for
them since they enlisted in this great and glorious Army.

Skirmishing at 5.30 at AMBERLEY SQUARE and VESTRY HALL, at 6 p.m. when the Devil Driver will Sing and Speak!
Subject—PULLING THEM OUT OF THE FIRE!

51

". . . ministering to a crowded congregation, which they had themselves collected out of the streets, and (were) building up an aggressive church militant out of the human refuse which other churches regarded with blank despair. They had come to the town without a friend, without an introduction, with hardly a penny in their purses. They had to provide for maintaining services regularly."[27]

Upon the farewell of the female officers from Darlington after six months, the *Darlington and Richmond Herald* noted:

"It is incredible that two girls without friends, without learning, without any of the elaborate machinery which the church regards as almost indispensable for its operations . . . should raise out of the gutter and dram shop a vigorous working church of nearly 200 members. The Bishop of Durham could not do it! All the ministers of the town could not do it."[28]

Female ministry had therefore proved its worth as a means of gaining more officers, in tapping a hitherto unused source of understanding for half the population, and as a novelty in a period when women in positions of equality and responsibility were rare.

Supply: Control

None of the aspects of militarism could have been effective without the organisational abilities of the Booths. Organisation and discipline formed the dual means of control deemed so necessary by William Booth. The control did not come in the form of formal corps worship but in the resources, rules and discipline which ensured a similarity with other corps throughout the country. General Booth had experimented using theatres and the open-air instead of chapels and once had used a uniformed group. The latter had been a tenuous act which he initiated but did not fully oversee. The lessons learned however were very important, particularly regarding the use of non-church like buildings and discipline. William Booth stated at the 1877 Annual Conference:

"Many year ago I and my dear wife were holding a series of spiritual services at Walsall. We had a measure of success but, anxious more effectively to move the crowd, we got together what I fancy was the first hallelujah band . . . (containing) . . . Jim Cleaver, the Birmingham rough, and other worthies of the same character . . . It was the common people's movement in every respect . . . They were not troubled with any scruples about vulgarity . . . All (wore) red shirts."[29]

This uniformed group met with considerable success[30] and hallelujah bands with their freedom of worship, jumping, catchy hymns and very short sermons became a common sight, especially in the north of England during the 1860s. William Booth however did not have the time to form a central core to the bands and nor did he accompany the original group on their tour of the Black Country. The movement died out by the early 1870s for three reasons, "There was no organisation, no discipline, and no management."[31] Only their memory remained and this was later connected by the *Midland Free Press* to William Booth's evangelists returning to the area "in their grand old style."[32]

General Booth had defined and redefined his power base between the Annual Conference of 1875 and the War Congress of 1878. To maintain his control he had to ensure both supplies and discipline. Arrangements concerning resources and supplies were formalised from Headquarters as the need arose. Two examples were the Training Department for officers, which was instituted in May 1880, and a Music Editorial Department, 1883. The Christian Mission Headquarters at the People's Mission Hall was first occupied in April 1870. In August 1881 much larger premises were taken at 101 Queen Victoria Street and were called the International Headquarters. In the previous January, the work had been departmentalised and William Booth's eldest son, Bramwell, made Chief of the Staff. It was in this capacity that he issued the first general order which

> ". . . required the regular preparation by treasurers and secretaries of corps of statements of corps accounts for public reading, forbade the dismissal of members (soldiers and recruits) by corps officers without observance of the proper procedure, and the assembly of soldiers for any purpose at officers' quarters. Long sermons were deprecated."[33]

The procedure mentioned in the above quotation had been adopted to ensure that William Booth's control foresaw an answer to every possibility. Booth had made a close study of Field Marshal Lord Garnet Wolseley's *Soldiers' Pocket Book* and had then directed Railton to use it as a base to prepare the *Orders and Regulations for the Salvation Army*. The first part was published in October 1878. Booth wrote in the introduction:

> "It is a remarkable fact that our system corresponds so closely to that of the Army and Navy of this country that we have been able to use even the very words of many of their regulations."

Detailed regulations and explanations were given governing all conceivable aspects of life such as dress, marriage, 'attacking' a town, conditions of membership, and duties of the various ranks. Booth also made it clear how the government of the Movement was to be conducted.

> "Only with this absolute power over men can there be any regularity

The International Headquarters from where the Salvation Army's growing international work and some domestic activities were co-ordinated after August 1881.

Clapton Congress Hall, previously the London Orphan Asylum, was opened by General Booth on 13th May 1882. The conversion cost £23,000.

... This is militarism — a settled, absolute, regular system of using men to accomplish a common settled purpose."[34]

Despite the book being publicly denounced in a pamphlet by La Comtesse De Gasparin, who saw Booth as a second Ignatius de Loyola,[35] 25,000 copies were quickly sold.

As the Movement and thus organisation rapidly grew in the early 1880s, it became necessary for General Booth to issue further detailed Orders and Regulations applicable to certain sections of the Army. In 1881 'General Orders for Little Soldiers' Meetings' were published in *The Little Soldier.* In 1885 a 600 page book entitled *Orders and Regulations for Field Officers* was printed by order of the General. Bramwell wrote about this book:

> "My father was really less an organizer than a legislator; he was a whole legislature in himself. He laid down the law in every detail, thinking of everthing, and left others to organise the machine. I think he gave more attention to the *Orders and Regulations for Field Officers* than to anything else he wrote. His anxiety was to compile in that book a set of regulations which would perpetuate the Salvation Army, and preserve it from the mistakes and confusions which had befallen so many other societies in the religious sphere."[36]

Five years later, *Orders and Regulations for Soldiers* was published ". . . at the people's favourite price of one penny."[37] Again William Booth laid down laws in minute detail.

Further and more elaborate editions of the various Orders and Regulations were published over the succeeding years, while other books gave explicit details on various aspects of life such as *The Training of Children* (1888). In addition to these writings and perhaps as an indicator of his love of legislation or, more likely, his desire to control all possibilities, Booth realised that

> "The Deed Poll declaring the doctrines and constitution of the Salvation Army does not provide any method for the appointment of a General in the event of a Generalship becoming vacant through unforseen contingencies which may nevertheless possibly arise."

This section of a previously unpublished letter from William Booth to Bramwell was written in January 1896.[38] It was however eight years before the problem was resolved in the form of a *Supplemental Deed of Constitution, (1904).* This sets out provision for a High Council and what it should do in the event of any General being permanently incapacitated through such mental or physical infirmity as necessitated removal; it could declare any General unfit to continue in office for certain specified reasons and elect a new General should a successor not have been named.

Most important to Booth's control of the newly-created Salvation Army was not only the theoretical organisation and laws but the maintenance of discipline throughout the Movement. This is clearly outlined in the *Orders and Regulations for Salvation Soldiers* under the sections of Government, Leadership, and Obedience.[39] He was prepared to do away with anything or anyone who hindered or disagreed with the Salvation Army. Thus the abandonment of both relief work such as soup-kitchens and Sunday Schools was deemed necessary to enable the Army to concentrate on its main task of expansion to new areas. Poor relief was abandoned from 1875 and resumed in 1888 although social work efforts such as rescue of prostitutes had been organised before this date. Sunday Schools had been closed in 1877 and Booth stated at that year's Annual Conference:

> "But we have not as yet any real plan to propose for dealing with the children. So far as our experience of Sunday-schools has gone, they have been an injury to the Mission wherever they have existed. There are only three left, I believe, and, with regard to these, we have no present intention of doing anything.
> But it must be distinctly understood that no new school must be commenced — in fact, no new plan of any kind must be adopted anywhere without my consent."[40]

The Sunday School restarted on 30 July 1880 at Blyth in Northumberland although it was unofficial at first.

Any person found or believed to be passively or actively hindering the advancement of the Salvation Army was summarily dismissed. There was no redress for soldiers or officers. On most occasions General Booth acted on the evidence of any person senior to the one being 'reported'. There are only two references in official Army writings to this formal procedure/system of reporting. One was in the first general order, issued in 1881. It stated that soldiers and recruits could not be dismissed by corps officers ". . . without observance of the proper procedure." The other, written in 1932, noted that

> "A system of reporting and inspection, which enabled the General to know how far his instructions were being obeyed, was devised."[41]

No explanation nor date is given of this system but the latter quotation clearly includes officers. The effectiveness of adverse reports is shown in the examples of courts-martial noted in respective issues of the *War Cry*. These however were not many, at least in public, for the *Orders and Regulations for Salvation Army Soldiers* stated that such proceedings were a discredit to the Army

> ". . . (and are to) be kept as secret as possible, and never held unnecessarily."[42]

The number or percentage of soldiers voluntarily or forcibly giving up the Salvation Army is difficult to estimate, but there was a high turnover in numbers of officers. This included some of General Booth's own children who rebelled against his tight control. Regardless of this, William and Catherine Booth believed such strong control was necessary to avoid any possibility of the Movement failing.

III. DEMAND

The progress of the Salvation Army could not have been achieved unless there was a need for such an organisation. This need could have sprung from one or varying combinations of the type of occupational structures within an area, from the socio-economic climate, and from the state of local religious provision.

Correlations between the Geographic Areas of Growth of the Salvation Army and the Occupational Structure

Correlations between the geographic areas of Salvation Army growth and occupational structure can best be shown in tabular and cartographic form. Table 3.4 demonstrates the relative strength of the five major occupational categories, county by county, within Great Britain in 1881. Table 3.5 has the same county order (chosen from highest to lowest numbers of corps) and demonstrates corps seating capacity. The evidence is strongly in favour of seeing the Salvation Army as establishing itself in industrial areas. Map 3.2 confirms this, showing that by December 1883, four distinct regions of corps density were apparent: the Durham/Northumberland border area; an area running from Lancashire, Cheshire and the West Riding of Yorkshire, through Staffordshire, Derbyshire, and Nottinghamshire and into the northern tip of Warwickshire and Worcestershire; London; and in the south-west, mainly around Somerset and Gloucestershire and including South Wales. Table 3.5 shows the counties with the highest to lowest number of corps plus their seating capacity in numbers and as a percentage of the respective county population. However when using this Table it must be remembered that although some corps have only one entry in *The Salvation Soldier's Pocket Book for 1884,* they frequently used two or more buildings every night in different parts of the town. This was often in addition to a building on Sundays as well as open-air work. For example Bolton had only one entry but two halls in continuous use. Also the seating capacity figure and percentage was worked out by the addition of the seats in the town for one meeting.

The tabular evidence suggests that in those counties where the Salvation Army was strongest, any of the five major occupational

TABLE 3.4

The Percentage of the Five Major Occupational Categories in Counties — 1883

Registration County	Corps	Agric.	Tex.	I + S	Mining	C
1. Lancashire	45	—	29.55	2.39	3.63	0.94
2. West Riding of Yorkshire	43	4.55	27.58	3.09	5.71	—
3. Durham	30	2.40	3.32	7.54	20.08	5.00
4. London	26	—	5.80	—	—	—
= 5. Gloucestershire	22	10.77	12.31	—	1.73	—
= 5. Somersetshire	22	19.15	12.54	1.06	2.40	—
= 5. South Wales	22	24.27	3.77	3.84	13.88	2.12
6. Devonshire	20	18.08	10.98	1.20	—	4.02
7. Cornwall	19	20.73	7.72	1.58	10.74	6.61
= 8. Staffordshire	16	5.24	5.94	9.60	9.16	—
= 8. Cheshire	16	8.29	20.51	1.51	1.42	—
= 8. Derbyshire	16	7.97	11.85	4.72	10.70	–
9. Wiltshire	15	27.86	8.67	1.17	—	—
= 10. East Riding of Yorkshire	13	12.89	5.86	—	—	4.86
= 10. Lincolnshire	13	29.92	5.97	2.68	—	2.33
= 11. Kent	12	16.86	4.52	1.05	—	2.23
= 11. Nottinghamshire	12	8.90	26.61	1.19	9.57	—
= 12. Hampshire	11	13.05	6.48	—	—	5.41
= 12. Northumberland	11	7.27	3.68	3.07	11.89	4.58
= 12. North Riding of Yorkshire	11	18.88	6.63	8.74	5.58	1.35
13. Warwickshire	10	5.18	7.98	1.87	—	—
14. Monmouthshire	9	7.72	3.15	8.45	15.82	1.73
= 15. Essex	8	17.26	6.72	—	—	3.24
= 15. Worcestershire	8	11.97	10.41	8.55	1.19	—
= 16. Sussex	7	16.91	1.38	0.89	—	—
= 16. Northamptonshire	7	17.62	26.53	—	0.89	—
17. Berkshire	6	22.08	5.60	1.07	—	—
= 18. Hertfordshire	5	19.60	13.75	0.94	—	—
= 18. Norfolk	5	24.46	11.24	1.25	—	1.51
= 19. Surrey	4	9.49	4.78	—	—	—
= 19. Oxfordshire	4	26.16	8.50	—	—	—
= 20. Suffolk	3	27.60	8.28	1.28	—	2.77
= 20. Cumberland	3	16.74	7.99	4.55	10.42	—
= 20. North Wales	3	22.80	4.95	—	5.88	1.54
= 20. Buckinghamshire	3	21.86	9.94	—	—	—
= 21. Middlesex	2	4.28	3.61	—	—	—
= 21. Bedfordshire	2	21.58	34.04	0.97	—	—
= 21. Cambridgeshire	2	35.67	6.24	—	—	—
= 21. Dorsetshire	2	23.36	10.17	1.18	—	1.34
= 21. Leicestershire	2	10.60	32.33	—	2.49	—
= 21. Westmorland	2	26.09	9.53	1.02	—	—
= 22. Huntingdonshire	1	36.28	7.78	1.09	—	—
= 22. Herefordshire	1	32.02	6.56	1.37	—	—
= 22. Shropshire	1	24.07	5.59	1.52	3.68	—
23. Rutlandshire	0	35.12	4.52	1.09	—	—

Key: Agric. = agriculture
Tex. = textile
I + S = iron and steel
Mining = mining
C. = coastal

Note: 1. As the five columns of occupational percentages are calculated from the National *Census of 1881*, the order of the counties has been decided by county totals from the chronologically nearest corps list, that of December 1883.
2. 495 corps are recorded in the above 'Corps' column. There were an additional 24 corps in Wales. See above, Table 3.3, Note 2.

Sources: *Census of England and Wales. 1881. Occupations.*
Pocket Book 1884.

TABLE 3.5

Number of Corps Seating Capacity per Registration County
done in high to low numerical ordering

Registration County	Corps	Seating Capacity	%[1]
1. Lancashire	45	47300	1.35
2. West Riding of Yorkshire	43	72500	3.29
3. Durham	30	44300	5.06
4. London	26	35617	0.93
= 5. South Wales[2]	22	16220	1.84
= 5. Somersetshire	22	15470	3.15
= 5. Gloucestershire	22	18770	3.57
6. Devonshire	20	15800	2.59
7. Cornwall	19	9750	2.98
= 8. Derbyshire	16	13850	3.58
= 8. Cheshire	16	22100	3.55
= 8. Staffordshire	16	20540	2.04
9. Wiltshire	15	7500	3.01
= 10. East Riding of Yorkshire	13	17700	4.88
= 10. Lincolnshire	13	10770	2.31
= 11. Nottinghamshire	12	11600	2.64
= 11. Kent	12	10930	1.54
= 12. Northumberland	11	10850	2.49
= 12. North Riding of Yorkshire	11	14500	6.18
= 12. Hampshire	11	9900	1.72
13. Warwickshire	10	7700	1.05
14. Monmouthshire	9	6450	2.75
= 15. Worcestershire	8	6950	1.81
= 15. Essex	8	4950	0.89
= 16. Northamptonshire	7	5500	2.00
= 16. Sussex	7	4650	0.94
17. Berkshire	6	3800	1.53
= 18. Norfolk	5	4700	1.04
= 18. Hertfordshire	5	2950	1.45
= 19. Oxfordshire	4	2200	1.21
= 19. Surrey	4	4900	1.06
= 20. Bedfordshire	3	2400	1.55
= 20. North Wales	3	2850	0.16
= 20. Cumberland	3	4650	1.85
= 20. Suffolk	3	1150	0.32
= 20. Buckinghamshire	3	1300	0.83
= 21. Leicestershire	2	1950	0.59
= 21. Dorsetshire	2	2100	1.13
= 21. Cambridgeshire	2	850	0.44
= 21. Westmorland	2	1850	2.87
= 21. Middlesex	2	1200	0.31
= 22. Shropshire	1	950	0.35
= 22. Herefordshire	1	1500	1.26
= 22. Huntingdonshire	1	400	0.75
23. Rutlandshire	0	0	0

[1] Per respective county population.
[2] Because the respective Welsh counties contain so few corps, it is here justifiable to include North and South Wales *en bloc*. There were an additional 24 corps in other Welsh counties. See above, Table 3.3, Note 2.

Source: Pocket Book 1884.

categories could have exerted an influence. The occupational percentages fluctuate considerably throughout Table 3.4. Only one occupation can effectively be isolated to measure its importance relative to the Salvation Army, namely, agriculture. This on its own clearly tended not to produce growth areas for the Army for in the 30 counties where agriculture was the largest occupation, 20 counties had eight corps or less. Table 3.4 does however demonstrate that in the top 21 counties with 10 or more corps, other industrial activity was diverse or there was a leading local economic sector such as mining in Durham. The Table also shows that, apart from London, most of the 21 counties were in the industrial north, the generally old industrial south-west, and South Wales. Counties with nine or less corps tended to have considerable non-industrial diversity, especially a lack of iron and steel, mining, and coastal activity. They had a very mixed occupational structure, or were mainly agricultural, thus further suggesting that agriculture alone was not a powerful factor in Salvation Army development.

Further evidence confirms that the Army grew fastest not only in counties with industrial diversity but also in areas with a strong local leading occupational, usually industrial, economic sector. Such a local sector could take the form of agriculture but generally was connected to textiles, iron and steel, mining or the coast. Only 4 of the 48 U.S.D.'s of over 50,000 people had not been penetrated by the Salvation Army by 1884. These were Bury, West Ham, Aston Manor and Ipswich. All had no leading economic sector and were very widely diversified in occupations. Bury, despite an unusually extreme broad base of occupations, also had considerable involvement in textiles and this does make it something of an enigma. The evidence suggests therefore that although diversity could provide a base for Salvation Army growth, it could not be too wide or non-industrial diversity.

Clearly, the Salvation Army grew in the mining and coastal villages as well as the larger centres. Although perhaps the small and insular communities of miners and seamen might seem improbable ground for religious development, the Army's working-class appeal, and the neglect of the churches, plus the very fact of the communities being close-knit, eased the Army's growth. This is apparently not true in the dispersed mining communities of Shropshire, but it is true in the concentrated Northumberland and Durham border coalfield. Certainly in South Wales, the close-knit coal-pit and iron-work areas such as Ebbw Vale aided the Army's success.[43] There were many instances in South Wales of the Salvation Army growing rapidly within weeks of its arrival because of the support from the community and of it quickly spreading by word of mouth from one community to another. There was also a rapid extension of the South Wales coalfield from 1880[44] and this must be seen as a contributory factor to the growth of the Movement. The close-knit 'captive' audiences of the coastal and mining villages spread the revivalism engendered by the Army and, combined with the success in the leading sector or industrially diverse towns of the north and south (Table 3.4), the Army was able to grow.

The Socio-Economic Climate and Industry

Apart from identifying the occupational factors of industrial diversity or a leading local sector being of importance to the Salvation Army's expansion, there were other equally tangible factors underlying this growth. These factors were density of population, the standard of living, and wages. Table 3.4 demonstrates that the centres containing the largest number of Salvation Army corps in 1883 were mainly those having densely populated towns or small mining or coastal communities. From the early 1800s the population was increasing in most of these counties due to high birth-rates and migration. The increasing level of industrial development was labour-intensive and thus migration took place on a large-scale. This was particularly true for Northumberland and Durham as well as in Lancashire, Cheshire and the West Riding of Yorkshire where the Army had four out of its top ten major growth areas, (Table 3.5).

Any discussion on standard of living in the second half of the ninteenth century must take into account that

"Historians and contemporary sources are in agreement about the existence of dramatic contrasts in the economic experience and standard of living of different wage groups."[45]

The standard of living did improve from the 1850s but not just for the supposedly separate stratum at the top of the working-class hierarchy. Indeed, it is no longer feasible to use Professor Hobsbawm's narrow wage, respectability and politically moderate criteria to identify such a stratum. Hobsbawm's view, even if accurate measurement of his criteria were possible, relies on seeing the working-class as a fixed and unchanging social entity with well defined cultural divisions. However such divisions are actually hard to find.[46] In actuality, those who benefited from the improved standard of living not only varied over time but also between areas.

A large number of the working-class did benefit from the improving standard of living, much due to the fact that

"... the third quarter of the nineteenth century was a period when...real wages rose substantially, though the benefits seem to have accrued disproportionately to certain groups of skilled workers."[47]

61

Certainly improvement was not the lot of everybody and tens of thousands were still living in extreme poverty due to industrial and personal circumstances. Poverty remained immovable in London and the large industrial cities and for those suffering from it, trade union membership and church membership was out of the question on financial and perhaps psychological grounds.

Apart from this 'base' of poverty, between the years 1873 and 1896

"... there were also periods of very high unemployment which exacerbated the problem of chronic low wages and underemployment."[48]

Different industries and areas were affected at different times. Shipbuilding shifted geographically during this period, away from London and the Thames estuary and to the northern yards on the Clyde, Tyne, Wear and Tees. This was mainly due to iron, steel and coal being more readily accessible in the north, and to the fact that the organisation of the industry in London pushed up production costs. Employment in shipbuilding on the north-east coast steadily increased throughout the last quarter of the nineteenth century.[49]

Geographically the distribution of the textile industries changed very little but a relative decline in importance set in from the 1850s. Their share of total employment almost halved between 1851 and 1911.[50] Much of this was perhaps due to the transformation of most sections of the textile industries from domestic crafts to a factory-based activity. The fact that geographically the old–established textile industries tended to remain dominant hides the fact that much misery must have been caused as the process went on. Not everyone could move to take up a job in a factory which anyway needed fewer personnel due to improved technology and greater concentration of the work force than under the old system. Gradual unemployment then was exacerbated by sudden vagaries in the industry such as The American Civil War (1861 to 1865) causing a cotton famine from which the industry, although diversifying its sources in later years, never really recovered in terms of failure to recapitalise. This, plus the effects of foreign competition and the new factories often causing displacement of labour, combined to make the areas surrounding the major centres of the industry (south Lancashire, north-east Cheshire and the West Riding of Yorkshire) good ground for Salvation Army activity.

Undoubtedly the most rapid period of growth in the coal industry took place in the second half of the nineteenth century when the industry's labour force grew by nearly one million between 1850 to 1913.[51] Output from the English fields rose from 48 million tons in 1854 to 185 million tons in 1913.[52] However, although this was a successful industry, the massive increase in male employment in it magnified the appalling working conditions and the social problems of labour. One result was the spread of trade unionism. It is noticeable that all along the coalfields, including the little researched Somerset coalfields with their small settlements, many having the same dreary uniformity which typified the industry, the Salvation Army took hold. It can be suggested perhaps that marked discontent from poor conditions, apparent in many bitter worker/owner struggles in the latter half of the nineteenth century, fed not only trade unionism but also what was arguably the religion of the working-class, the Salvation Army.

As far as the iron and steel industries are concerned, the 'end of the Iron Age' came by the latter part of the 1880s. Although the quantity of iron, particularly pig-iron rose from 1.5 million to 8 million tons between 1855 and 1913, the period was characterised by changes in location. By the end of the nineteenth century, Teeside was the most successful of the new areas while Staffordshire and West Yorkshire suffered rapid decline. All these places were ones of rapid Salvation Army growth. In the steel industry

> "The calm tones of the British steel manufacturers in the mid-1880s were succeeded by deep alarm within a reasonably short space of time." [53]

Certain areas fared worse than others during the slack period of the late 1880s and early 1890s. Worst hit, mainly because of the more favourable conditions of foreign competitors, appear to have been Lancashire and South Wales. When the return to prosperity came for the industry, other areas, especially on Teeside, benefited dramatically at the expense of the original areas.

What does this examination of the major industries tell us about the growth of the Salvation Army in relation to the geographical distribution of corps by 1883? In textiles, south Lancashire, north-east Cheshire and the West Riding of Yorkshire, where the Army took firm hold from 1878, were areas of decreasing and geographically changing employment, often in a situation similar to the economic decay of south-western towns. In coal, the living and working conditions experienced by an increasing number of men and their families from mid-century helped breed a dissatisfaction with their surroundings, including the established churches and chapels. The majority of the mining communities were small and often isolated, thus their populations were both 'captive' audiences and usually genuinely interested in anything new or different. The Salvation Army, with its novel methods of preaching and working-class appeal was thus able to take root all along most of the coal areas down to and including the Somerset coalfields. This evidence supports the above theory that the Army thrived in areas with diverse industrial activity or where there was a leading economic sector. The dissatisfaction regarding the harsh life in the mining communities also helped the Army as people could give public vent to their feelings either with or against the Movement. Finally, in the iron and steel industries, Staffordshire and West Yorkshire were hit by relocation of the former industry while Lancashire and South Wales were hit a little later by decrease in the latter industry. Conversely the very diversity of Teeside's occupational structure allowed the Army to grow in the large conurbations. This survey confirms that given a reasonably concentrated base of population, the Army grew either in areas of industrial diversity, one leading sector, or areas of decaying industries. Whatever their nature, all these areas fall precisely in the three main regions of rapid and concentrated Salvation Army growth.[54]

Religion

The relative divisions of the Christian churches and chapels, their growth and religious impact in the second half of the nineteenth century, have been examined earlier in the book. What has not been ascertained in detail is their geography and the answer to the question — did the Salvation Army take over from other denominations or break fresh ground? Table 3.6 shows the strength of each denomination within England, relative to its performance nationally. The five gradings of 1 to 5 reflect a high to low performance while the '0' indicates non-existent or barely perceptible activity. The first county, Northumberland, therefore had little Church of England, Methodist, Baptist and Congregationalist activity relative to their performance in the rest of the country. The Roman Catholics, Presbyterians and Salvation Army were however thriving in this county. The gradings are not indicative of comparitive strength within English counties but are of use as an indicator of where each denomination had strength and weakness.

Table 3.6 shows that the Army was strongest in the industrial centres of England, such as Durham and Lancashire, whereas the older churches and chapels were often concentrated in other parts of the country. This is particularly evident with the Established Church whose strength lay in the southern half of England, below a line from Shropshire to the Wash. Within the other denominations, the Roman Catholic Church was gaining strength, due mainly to Irish immigrants settling in those counties containing large towns and seaports nearest Ireland; the Methodists had their strength in Cornwall but also found considerable support in Bedfordshire and in parts of the north-east; the Baptists were strong in the Home Counties; the Congregationalists had considerable strength in East Anglia and throughout much of the

TABLE 3.6

Denominational Strength per County in the Third Quarter of the Nineteenth Century

County	C. of E.	R.C.	M.	B.	C.	P.	S.A.
Northumberland	5	3	5	5	5	2	2
Durham	5	3	4	5	5	3	1
Cumberland	5	4	5	5	5	3	4
Westmorland	4	5	5	5	5	4	2
North Riding of Yorkshire	4	3	2	5	5	4	1
East Riding of Yorkshire	5	4	2	5	4	4	1
West Riding of Yorkshire	5	4	3	3	4	4	2
Lancashire	5	2	5	5	4	4	1
Cheshire	4	3	4	5	4	4	3
Staffordshire	5	3	4	5	5	5	4
Derbyshire	5	4	3	4	4	0	2
Nottinghamshire	4	4	3	4	4	0	2
Lincolnshire	4	5	1	4	5	0	3
Shropshire	3	5	4	5	4	0	5
Herefordshire	3	5	5	4	5	0	4
Worcestershire	4	4	5	4	5	5	4
Warwickshire	4	3	5	4	5	5	5
Leicestershire	3	4	4	2	4	0	5
Rutlandshire	1	0	5	2	4	0	0
Northamptonshire	1	5	4	2	2	0	4
Huntingdonshire	2	0	4	1	3	0	5
Cambridgeshire	3	5	4	1	3	0	5
Norfolk	3	5	4	4	5	0	5
Suffolk	1	5	5	2	1	0	5
Essex	2	5	5	3	1	0	5
Hertfordshire	2	5	5	2	2	0	4
Bedfordshire	2	5	2	1	5	0	4
Buckinghamshire	2	5	4	1	3	0	5
Oxfordshire	2	5	5	4	4	0	4
Berkshire	2	5	5	4	3	0	5
Middlesex	3	5	5	4	3	0	5
London	5	2	5	4	4	4	5
Surrey	2	5	5	4	4	0	5
Kent	2	5	5	4	4	0	4
Sussex	2	5	5	4	4	0	5
Hampshire	2	5	5	4	2	0	4
Wiltshire	1	5	4	2	2	0	3
Gloucestershire	3	4	5	3	2	0	2
Somersetshire	2	5	5	4	3	0	2
Dorsetshire	1	5	4	5	1	0	4
Devonshire	2	5	5	4	3	0	3
Cornwall	5	5	1	5	5	0	3

Key: C. of E. = Church of England
R.C. = Roman Catholic
M. = Methodists
B. = Baptists
C. = Congregationalists
P. = Presbyterians
S.A. = Salvation Army

Sources: Gay, J. D. *The Geography of Religion in England.* (London. 1971). Indices of Attendance accompanying each map of denominational distribution. *Pocket Book 1884.*

south-west; the Presbyterians were strongest only in Northumberland with a weak following in the surrounding English counties.

The Table is interesting for identifying where both the Army and one or more other denominations were strong. In each of the three Ridings of Yorkshire, the Salvation Army and Methodists were strong relative to their national position. The Army's strength came from their concentration on the industrial centres and mining communities within the North and West Ridings. The East Riding of Yorkshire remained static at 13 corps from 1883 until after 1905,[55] (Table 3.3). During the time it established itself in the harsh industrial communities of Yorkshire, the Army showed much of the original appeal of early Methodism. The Movement was not tied by buildings already owned nor was it reliant on already established congregations. The Army rented accommodation or, particularly in smaller mining communities, waste-ground upon which to erect cheap iron huts. The Methodists kept their strongholds of fifty years earlier but made fewer inroads than the Army into the fast growing conurbations or the coastal and mining communities.

In Derbyshire, Nottinghamshire and Lincolnshire, the Army and Methodists were again strong, the latter particularly in Lincolnshire. Derbyshire and Nottinghamshire had heavy concentrations of textile and mining communities and it was in these, which were generally less than fifty years old, that the Army flourished. As in the three Ridings of Yorkshire, the then avowedly working-class Methodists had established a number of strongholds several decades earlier. It was the retention of these rather than new church growth that they concentrated on. Within the predominantly agricultural Lincolnshire, the Methodists again had some long established chapels in the market towns and small textile areas. The Army rented or erected halls in the same towns and relied on its novel methods of preaching to appeal to the working-class.

Wiltshire, Gloucestershire and the south-west generally had strong Church of England, Congregationalist and Army congregations although there were certain exceptions. The most notable of these was the extreme weakness of the Church of England in Cornwall while it was one of only two major strongholds of Methodism. The appeal of the Salvation Army and Nonconformity in general, alongside a general retention of Church of England congregations, was due to conservatism in the south maintaining the Established Church while pockets of industrial activity, (such as the development of the Somerset and Gloucestershire coal-seams), and the decaying areas of the older industries, welcomed Nonconformity.

TABLE 3.7

**Lancashire and Cheshire Urban Sanitary Districts
and Salvation Army Corps, 1883, 1905**

	1883				1905			
Size of Town	Number of towns	Number of towns with S.A. Corp(s)	Total No. of S.A. Corps	Seating capacity as % of pop.	Number of towns	Number of towns with S.A. Corp(s)	Total No. of S.A. Corps	Seating capacity as % of pop.
LANCASHIRE								
Under 3,000	16	—	—	—	10	5	5	7.14
3,000–10,000	63	6	6	4.93	47	15	15	4.20
10,000–20,000	34	5	5	4.46	40	18	18	2.23
20,000–50,000	23	10	10	3.07	34	23	25	2.06
50,000–100,000	5	5	7	2.52	9	8	16	2.00
Over 100,000	6	6	18	1.66	7	7	46	1.42
CHESHIRE								
Under 3,000	8	—	—	—	6	1	1	10.86
3,000–10,000	10	3	3	5.02	11	4	4	4.75
10,000–20,000	5	4	4	8.42	7	7	7	3.47
20,000–50,000	4	3	5	7.51	5	4	5	2.40
50,000–100,000	2	2	3	5.22	2	1	3	2.37
Over 100,000	—	—	—	—	1	1	2	0.9

Sources: *Census of England and Wales, 1881. Population.*
Ibid. 1901.
Corps Index 1905.

An Analysis of the Salvation Army in Lancashire and Cheshire

An analysis of the Salvation Army in Lancashire and Cheshire will
yield detailed information regarding conditions suitable for the
Movement's growth. Maps 3.3 and 3.4 show the geographical distribution of corps in 1883 and 1905 respectively, the latter map clearly
indicating the substantial growth of the Army. Both maps and Tables
3.7 and 3.8 establish that the strength of the Salvation Army in the
two counties lay in the major towns. This confirms the findings from
the rather broad Table 3.2. In the smaller towns there was clearly less
chance of an 'invasion' by Salvationists. By 1905 the Army had
increased the number of smaller towns 'invaded' whilst retaining and
often increasing the number of corps in the towns of over 50,000
inhabitants. Only in two of these towns did the Movement not have
corps in 1905, Bootle in Lancashire and Wallasey in Cheshire. There
are no apparent reasons for this except possibly both had extremely
broad based local economies.

It is perhaps conceivable that recent town growth may have attracted
the Army but there is no evidence that this in itself was the case.
Many of the fastest growing towns in percentage terms were small

TABLE 3.8

Lancashire and Cheshire Towns Containing one or more Salvation Army Corps, 1883, 1905

Size of Town (by Population)	Percentage of Towns With One or More S.A. Corp(s)			
	Lancashire		Cheshire	
	1883	1905	1883	1905
Under 3,000	—	50	—	17
3,000–20,000	11	38	47	61
20,000–50,000	54	70	83	92
Over 50,000	100	94	100	67

Sources: Census of England and Wales, 1881. Population.
Ibid. 1901.
Pocket Book 1884.
Corps Index 1905.

in actual numbers of inhabitants (under 10,000 in Cheshire and 20,000 in Lancashire) and Table 3.7 shows that by 1883, the Army had 'invaded' very few of these communities. Even by 1905, the Movement was in less than half of them in the respective counties. What happened in the very largest towns was that as they expanded between 1883 and 1905, the Army increased its numbers of corps, for example in Manchester (7 corps to 15) and Liverpool (5 corps to 14).

The expansion of the Salvation Army into more towns did not mean that the Movement retained its seating capacity to population percentage at the 1883 level. Table 3.7 makes it clear that in all sizes of towns by 1905, the Army had lost seats in relation to population. This is however not so significant when the Army's priority was not building massive centres of worship but to open corps in more towns and in areas of high population density in towns already 'invaded'. The fact that this occurred in quite considerable numbers in Lancashire and to a smaller degree in Cheshire indicates some success. The Army's aim was to reach as many people as possible. The Movement was a high profile denomination which spent much of its time in the open air. Its meeting hall was the streets and waste land near the corps and frequently the largest buildings available were hired for special meetings. Its effect therefore should not be measured purely in the number of seats it provided.

Table 3.7 also shows that the smaller the town, the greater the seating capacity. The Army often hired or built large halls seating between 250 and 1,000 people. While these might give a low seating capacity in towns of 20,000 to 50,000 inhabitants, in smaller towns the corps could hold relatively large numbers of people. Overall by 1905 the total seating capacity to total county population dropped in percentage terms for both Lancashire and Cheshire from 1.35 and 3.55 to 1.04 and 2.95 respectively. At the same time the Movement reached more people by expanding into new geographical areas, thus fulfilling its basic aim of going to the people.

To consider the question of seating capacity in a wider context, in a sample of five counties taken from Table 3.5, seating capacity between 1883 and 1905 dropped in percentage terms in Devonshire (2.59 to 1.84) and Nottinghamshire (2.64 to 1.70), remained steady in Durham (5.06 to 5.00) and Essex (0.89 to 0.92), and grew slightly in Suffolk (0.32 to 0.51). The common factor between the last three counties' corps is that they were in the top five for having the most 'Circle Corps' (Table 3.3). One reason for the 'growth' therefore is that the buildings used in each visit to a village were counted as seating capacity although they were not in full use by the Army. This makes the figures slightly misleading if they are taken to indicate Salvation Army work throughout the week. However meetings were held by an officer or soldier every week so as strictly seating capacity they may be included.

Having shown that the Salvation Army sought to establish themselves in the largest towns first, it is pertinent to see if the Movement was attracted by any particular industry or industries. Table 3.9 identifies the top three occupations for men and women in each of the thirteen major Lancashire and Cheshire U.S.D.'s. Just under two-thirds of the U.S.D.'s have 'Cotton, Cotton goods, Manufacture' as their leading occupations for both men and women. This is usually followed by 'Iron and Steel Manufacture', 'Coal Mining', or another textile related occupation for the men, and 'Domestic Indoor Servant' or 'Milliner, Dressmaker, Staymaker' for the women. As corps were established in all but one of these U.S.D.'s by 1883, it may be conjectured that the Army found considerable support from the workers in these occupations. Additional evidence for this comes from the fact that a relatively large number of male and female officers were recruited from the occupations named above.

Taking the top occupations of Lancashire and Cheshire combined, after 'Cotton, Cotton goods, Manufacture' came 'Coal Mining' for men and 'Domestic Indoor Servant' for women.[56] Clearly the Salvation Army attracted a degree of support from those employed in the manufacture of cotton. The majority of towns with a contemporary reputation for cotton manufacture had Army corps in 1883 for example, Ashton-under-Lyne, Bolton, Burnley, Bury, Chorley, Manchester and Oldham in Lancashire and Knutsford, Nantwich and

Map 3.

Distribution of Corps in Lancashire

and Cheshire - 1883

Source: The Salvation Soldier's Pocket Book for 1884 (London 1883)

Map 3.4

Distribution of Corps in Lancashire

and Cheshire - 1905

Source: Index of Salvation Army Corps, 1905 (London 1905)

TABLE 3.9

The Leading Occupations in the Major Urban Sanitary
Districts of Lancashire and Cheshire, 1883

U.S.D.	Male	Female	No. of S.A. Corps
LANCASHIRE			
Blackburn	Cotton Manuf., Iron/Steel Man., Carpenter/Join.	Cotton Manuf., Dom. In. Serv., Milliner, Dress.	1
Bolton	Cotton Manuf., Iron/Steel Man., Cott./Cal. Dyer	Cotton Manuf., Dom. in Serv., Milliner, Dress.	1
Bury	Cotton Manuf., Iron/Steel Man., Cott./Cal. Dyer	Cotton Manuf., Dom. in. Serv., Milliner, Dress.	—
Burnley	Cotton Manuf., Coal Miner, Iron/Steel Man.	Cotton Manuf., Dom. in. Serv., Milliner, Dress.	3
Liverpool	Harbour/Seaman, Comm. Clerk, Mess./Porter	Dom. in. Serv., Milliner, Dress., Charwoman	5
Manchester	Comm. Clerk, Mess./Porter, Cotton Manuf.	Cotton Manuf., Dom. in. Serv., Milliner, Dress.	7
Oldham	Cotton Manuf., Iron/Steel Man., Coal Miner	Cotton Manuf., Dom. in. Serv., Milliner, Dress.	1
Preston	Cotton Manuf., Iron/Steel Man., Carpenter/Join.	Cotton Manuf., Dom. in. Serv., Milliner, Dress.	1
Rochdale	Cotton Manuf., Wool Cloth Man., Iron/Steel Man.	Cotton Manuf., Wool Cloth Man., Dom. in. Serv.	1
St. Helens	Glass Manuf., Coal Miner, Manuf. Chemist	Dom. in. Serv., Glass Manuf., Milliner, Dress.	1
Salford	Iron/Steel Man., Comm. Clerk, Cotton Manuf.	Cotton Manuf., Dom. in. Serv., Milliner, Dress.	2
CHESHIRE			
Birkenhead	Harbour/Seaman, Comm. Clerk, Iron/Steel Man.	Dom. in. Serv., Milliner, Dress., Schoolmaster	2
Stockport	Cotton Manuf., Wool Cloth Man., Carman, Carter	Cotton Manuf., Dom. in. Serv., Hatter, Manuf.	1

KEY

Carman, Carter	Carman, Carrier, Carter, Haulier
Carpenter/Join.	Carpenter/Joiner
Charwoman	Charwoman
Coal Miner	Coal Miner
Comm. Clerk	Commercial Clerk
Cotton./Cal. Dyer	Cotton, Calico-Printer, Dyer, Blender
Cotton Manuf.	Cotton, Cotton goods, Manufacture
Dom. in. Serv.	Domestic Indoor Servant
Glass Manuf.	Glass Manufacture
Harbour	Harbour, Docks, Wharf, Lighthouse Service
Hatter, Manuf.	Hatter, Hat Manufacture (not straw)
Iron/Steel Man.	Iron and Steel Manufacture
Manuf. Chemist	Manufacturing Chemist
Mess./Porter	Messenger, Porter, Watchman (not Railway or Government)
Milliner, Dress.	Milliner, Dressmaker, Staymaker
Seaman	Seaman (Merchant Service)
Schoolmaster	Schoolmaster
Wool. Cloth Man.	Woollen Cloth Manufacture

Note: 1. Birkenhead's leading occupation came out equally between Harbour and Seaman.
Source: Manuscript Analysis of *Census. 1881.* Table 10. pp.53–67.

Stockport in Cheshire.[57] The coalfields were bounded roughly by St. Helens, Manchester, Oldham, Burnley, Blackburn and Chorley, thus taking in Wigan and Bolton. All these towns had a Salvation Army corps by 1883 and many had added a second corps by 1905. Oldham in fact had three corps by this later date, possibly because of its extensive cotton and mining industries. Certainly two of the corps were established well within the town while the third and most recent lay a little way outside amidst a relatively new coal-mining community. This does suggest that once firmly rooted, Salvation Army corps were prepared to spread themselves to newly growing communities in the 'springboard' effect. Certainly several of the corps listed in 1905 were along the coal-seams extending from Lancashire, into Cheshire and the West Riding of Yorkshire.

Although it might be suggested that most of the nine Lancashire and Cheshire corps known to have closed between the end of 1883 and 1905 (Table 3.3) might have been within coal communities that contracted as some coal resources became worn out, they were in fact equally spread between the old seams (as at Over Darwen), manufacturing towns (such as Milnrow), and large conurbations (for example Liverpool). A mixture of factors may therefore have forced the closure of corps. One factor may have been economic as each corps was self-financing. Another may have been the difficulty in finding suitable property. However, causes are difficult to ascertain. Equally difficult to determine is the impact of the female Domestic Indoor Servant on the Salvation Army. Nationally a considerable number from this occupational group did become officers (Table 3.12) and this suggests that they formed a large volume of support within Salvation Army corps.

Five U.S.D.'s differ from the pattern established above. Liverpool and Birkenhead both had 'Seaman (Merchant Service)' and 'Harbour, Dock, Wharf, Lighthouse Service' as their leading male occupations. This is not surprising as Liverpool's 203 acres of dockland made it England's second largest port and as Birkenhead lay opposite, just across the River Mersey. 'Commercial Clerks' and 'Messengers, Porters and Watchmen' were also employed in large number, usually in port related activities. Even in Birkenhead though, iron and steel manufacturing still figured prominently. In Manchester and neighbouring Salford, 'Commercial Clerks' were the first and second most labour intensive occupations respectively. Again however, 'Cotton, Cotton goods, Manufacture' is prominent. Finally as regards male occupations in the five U.S.D.'s, St. Helens is rather unusual in that 'Glass Manufacture' came first followed by 'Coal Mining' and 'Manufacturing Chemist'. For female occupations, 'Domestic Indoor Servant' was either first or second in the occupational lists generally accompanied by 'Cotton, Cotton goods, Manufacture', and 'Milliner,

73

Dressmaker, Staymaker'. Perhaps not unexpectedly, 'Glass Manufacture' among women was strong in St. Helens.

It is clear that the Salvation Army established itself and grew in the largest towns, apparently enjoying the support of at least some of the workers from occupations identified in Table 3.9. Salvation Army membership in the two counties increased from 7,297 soldiers in 1883[58] to 14,200 in 1905. It is however interesting to ask why those joining the Salvation Army had either not been attracted to, or had abandoned, other religious denominations. It is clear that in 1851 both Lancashire and Cheshire were poorly equipped to deal with the spiritual needs of the increasing number of people. In percentage terms, Lancashire had one of the lowest totals of religious accommodation per head of population in the country.[59] From the 1840s the Church of England was only just beginning to fill the religious vacuum created by recently established textile, mining, and iron and steel communities in the north of England. It was in such communities that the Nonconformists had striven, not always successfully, to establish chapels. For the Church of England, even in the 1870s, dozens of parishes encompassed 30,000 acres or more, for example the Parish of Lancaster stretched for 66,100 while that of Oldham was 58,620. Despite this, with the increasing numbers of new church buildings and, perhaps more importantly, the combination of Nonconformists (particularly Methodist) strongholds and the evangelical zeal of certain denominations such as the Primitive Methodists, an ever growing number of people had at least the opportunity to worship.[60]

A survey of churches and chapels listed in town directories for 1883 was carried out to see if the Salvation Army became established in areas of low or imbalanced religious provision. All towns of over 20,000 inhabitants were examined and a division made between those of 20,000 to 50,000 and those of 50,000 plus. In both categories of towns there was seating accommodation for 50 percent or more of the inhabitants and in purely percentage terms, the Church of England took the lead in this provision. In actual numbers of buildings used for worship, the Nonconformists had more in total than the Church of England, thus perhaps indicating the former's strength. The Methodists, in particular the Wesleyans and Primitive Methodists, appear quite strong if numbers of buildings are taken as a guide. However, must importantly for this study, the religious provisions within these towns did not vary significantly between the two categories nor within them. The establishment of the Salvation Army was therefore not dependent on the type of religious provision already in existence for it became established in some towns and not in others equally alike in religious accommodation. A sample of 15 Lancashire and Cheshire towns of under 20,000 inhabitants was taken to establish what, if any, were the religious differences from the larger towns. In fact, the above pattern remained similar but on a much smaller scale and often with less denominational choice. Occasionally in the smallest communities the nearest registered[61] Church or Chapel was in the next village but this appears to be only for the newest of them. These communities of under 20,000 inhabitants were not immediately attractive to the Salvation Army in the two counties for there were larger towns with more people and therefore a broader social spectrum awaiting 'invasion'. The larger the town, the seemingly higher chance there was of a corps supporting itself and the Army being accepted.

The considerable number of chapels must however have had some effect in acquainting people's minds with the idea of Nonconformity, if only from a distance. Possibly some corps may have started in small villages such as those found around the coalfields where the Methodist fervour, often found soon after their arrival, was still relatively fresh.[62] Also, some people may well have seen the Army as an echo of the early days of the Primitive Methodists. Records from village corps are rare and many corps, especially those commenced during the 1880s and early 1890s in communities based on dwindling coal resources, may not have survived for long. Another factor which may have helped the Salvation Army, particularly in Lancashire, was that it was a distinctly Protestant Movement. Echoes of the considerable 1850s and 1860s Protestant and Roman Catholic antagonism still rumbled on in many towns, especially where the Irish had large communities such as in Manchester. However, it was apparently not so much religious factors but the size of town and the support of the workers that were of primary importance to the Salvation Army. Without such continuous support this Movement, financed entirely by voluntary contributions, could not have survived and certainly could not have grown as it did.

IV. WILLIAM BOOTH'S OFFICERS

William Booth's thirteen years from 1852 to 1865 as a Methodist minister and itinerant evangelist gave him the opportunity to learn the most effective methods of reaching the masses with religion. Upon taking charge of the Christian Revival Association in 1865, he used his experience and employed where possible members of the working-class. He considered these the most likely to gain a hearing from their fellow-men.

The use of working-class ministers was however not a new concept in the nineteenth century. The Nonconformist denominations had for many decades accepted such ministers in considerably varying numbers and Church, Chapel and independent City Missions were often led by men of working-class origin. Table 3.10 analyses the social status

TABLE 3.10

The Social Structure[1] of Ministers and Officers[2], 1870–1899

							S.A.	
Class	Cong. %	Bap. %	Unit. %	Prim.M. %	Wes. %	S.A. %	Male %	Female %
I	22	16	20	15	28	1	1	—
II	25	16	31	25	24	4	2	2
III	34	39	22	44	22	81	49	32
IV/V[3]	5	4	2	12	2	12	8	4
Unspec.[4]	13	25	25	4	24	2	2	—
Sample of	116	118	49	52	89	506	314	192

Key: Cong.   = Congregational Ministry
       Bap.   = Baptist Ministry
       Unit.   = United Methodist Ministry
       Prim.M.   = Primitive Methodist Ministry
       Wes.   = Wesleyan Ministry
       S.A.   = Salvation Army

[1] K. D. Brown classified all occupations as for the *Census of England and Wales. 1951.*
[2] Based on one Salvation Army sample only (1883).
[3] In the *Census of 1951*, classes IV and V contained relatively few jobs in total and all were working-class.
[4] Mainly students.

Sources: Brown, K. D. *A Social History of the Nonconformist Ministry in England and Wales 1800–1930.* (Oxford. 1988). Tables 1.1, 1.5, 1.6, 1.7, 1.8. pp.20, 24.
          The Appointments of Officers 1883.

of Nonconformist ministers and Salvation Army officers recruited between the years 1870 and 1899. Despite the generally small numbers of ministers in the sample, it appears that at the very least just under a quarter of them were from the working-class (Classes III to V). For some denominations the figure was much higher. Clearly ahead of all others in percentage terms, the Primitive Methodists and Salvation Army had their greatest success amongst these people. In fact, the Salvation Army gained 93 percent of its officers from this class. As the dates of the Army's officer sample were 1878 to 1883, which coincided with the most rapid period of the Movement's expansion, it could be argued that the Army was reaching larger numbers of the working-class than any other denomination. However, an accurate figure would rely on material no longer extant and certainly by the end of the century, the Primitive Methodists had twice as many members as the Salvation Army. If these were spread in accordance with Table 3.10s recruitment of Primitive Methodist ministers (56 percent working-class), it would mean that numerically they were considerably stronger than the Army within this class. The Primitives were then and are still considered the most

"... thoroughly working class of major religious denominations in nineteenth-century England."[63]

One point that is clear is that both denominations were strong within the working-class. Also, there were few Salvation Army officer recruits coming from Classes I and II. This resulted in less middle-class domination and therefore social division between officers and people in the Army compared with that found in the majority of Churches and Chapels.[64]

Booth had been acutely aware of the frequently apparent social divide since the incident in his teens when he encouraged a group of destitutes and roughs to attend his Wesleyan Chapel. Not only their visit but their sitting in a conspicuous position greatly offended the elders and congregation and Booth was cautioned against a repetition. This and similar acts made him unpopular in the Chapel

"But the incident marked the point at which Booth began to diverge from the ways of the conventionally-religious."[65]

As William Booth felt himself to be of the poor, he believed that he could attract the poor and that preachers should preach to their class. Thus in 1870, when he was asked where his preachers for the Christian Mission would come from, he replied

"We shall get them from the public-houses. Men who have felt the fire will be the best men to rescue others, and we shall never fail in getting the right men."[66]

Two years later he wrote a book entitled *How to Reach the Masses with The Gospel*. In it he outlined his reasons for using the working-class and stated that those wholly employed in the Mission

"... may lack the human polish and refinement which education gives ... (but they) ... are genuine working men. One has been a blacksmith, another a navvy, another a policeman, another a sailor, and the remainder have been engaged in similar callings. Consequently, they can speak to the working man as belonging to the same class, illustrating their exhortations with their own experience. They know the life of a working man; they understand the temptations."[67]

These members of the working-class were instructed to preach to all people whether they would listen or not. Booth felt that the vast majority of ministers hindered themselves in reaching the people by not making them listen.

"The great blunder of ministers of the Gospel is that they are sent to minister to a certain set of people who wish to hear them. Whereas it has always been God's plan to send his agents to a place or places where they were to speak in His name to all alike, whether they would hear or whether they would forbear — in fact, TO MAKE THEM HEAR, whether they would obey or not."[68]

The Christian Mission

The autocratic control and organisational abilities of William Booth meant that, from 1865 to mid-1878, the Christian Mission grew from a single tent to 31 stations. *The Christian Mission Magazines* record between 1868 and 1878 a growing number of paid evangelists or missioners. By 1878 the figure was approximately 60. Around a third of the names appear to change annually thus indicating a relatively high turnover of staff. Some evidence suggests that this was due to disagreement with either the Annual Conference, William or Catherine Booth, members of the station, or to ill-health. Of the leaders who remained in 1878, 22 among those of at least one year's service have known previous occupations (Table 3.11). One third of the Table and half of the 60 evangelists of that year were converted in the Mission, but although many were to varying degrees dissolute in their pre-conversion life, they were not yet being gathered from the lowest stratum of society. The Booths equated drink and drunkenness with the nadir of sin and so were happy to see these people abstain and become converted and useful to the Mission. However, two questions remain: Of what class were they and why did they join?

The broad-based occupational classification of Table 3.11, Booth's writings (1872) and magazine reports show that the evangelists came from a wide social range spread throughout the working-class. It is probable therefore that the remaining 38 evangelists whose occupations are unknown reflect a similar occupational picture.

The success of the Christian Mission was in the hands of these men and women and therefore their reasons for joining are important. Their reports and biographies reveal a common conviction of having a 'cause' which was probably inspired by their background and experiences. Of the 60, 17 are known to have had some previous experience of church or chapel. The majority of these had Methodist connections and appear to have been attracted by Booth's Methodistic approach, by his previous reputation in the chapels and by his present success. Five of his staunchest and most prominent evangelists were Methodists, namely, Eliza Collingridge, Wesleyan; William Pearson, Primitive Methodist; William Corbridge, William Ridsdel, and Elijah Cadman, all Primitive Methodist local preachers. Occupational and religious evidence suggests that only about 15 of these evangelists were women but the Home Mission Movement and Methodism were essentially male-biased.[69] Many women showed support for the

TABLE 3.11

Known Occupations of Christian Mission Evangelists in 1878

Classification		Sex	Detail	Total
Professional	I. 1. 2.	M	Timekeeper. Local Gov't	
	I. 3. 1.	M	Evangelist	
	I. 3. 1.	M	Evangelist	
				3
Domestic	II. 4. 2.	M	Stablehand	
	II. 4. 1.	F	Servant	
	II. 4. 1.	F	Servant	
				3
Commercial	III. 6. 1.	M	Station Checker	
	III. 6. 1.	M	Railway Guard	
	III. 6. 3.	M	Sailor	
	III. 6. 3.	M	Bargeman	
	III. 6. 5.	M	Porter	
	III. 6. 5.	M	Docker	
				6
Agricultural	IV. 7. 3.	M	Gardener	
				1
Industrial	V. 16. 3.	M	Baker	
	V. 16. 3.	M	Grocer's assistant	
	V. 22. 2.	M	Navvy	
	V. 22. 2.	M	Factory Worker	
	V. 22. 2.	M	Factory Worker	
	V. 22. 2.	M	Labourer	
	V. 22. 2.	M	Labourer	
	V. 23. 1.	M	Sweep	
				8
Unoccupied	V. 24.	F	Housewife (married)	
				1
				22

Sources: *Census of England and Wales.* Vol. III. Table 10. Occupations. pp. 140–147.
The Appointments of Officers 1883.
The East London Evangelist. 1868–1869.
The Christian Mission Magazines. 1870–1878.
Booth, W. *How to Reach the Masses with The Gospel.* (London. 1872).

Christian Mission and after the first few years joined in increasing numbers, no doubt inspired by the writings and leadership shown by Catherine Booth.

The evidence above suggests that the long-serving evangelists had a determination to work hard regardless of their pre-Mission 'dissolute' days.[70] After conversion this determination became imbued as the Protestant work ethic — hard work to get a reward, in this case translated into spiritual terms. Long hours were spent preaching and 'saving souls' for a heavenly reward. In some cases, the possibility of a regular salary and certainly the respectable status of an evangelist was a lure, but arguably the main reasons for their joining were a determination to work hard in a cause they passionately believed in. Their moderate success was due to their sober, literate, combined and supported zeal.

The Salvation Army

The Army's most rapid growth in England and Wales took place in the period from the War Congress of 1878 to the end of 1883. A total of 519 corps had been successfully established by the latter date. Each corps needed at least one officer to command it yet little is known about the total number of officers, their names, or which corps they commanded. Only three complete lists of officers and their corps survive from the late 1870s and 1880s but from these and the mass of biographical material printed in increasing volume, it is possible to detect certain trends. By August 1880, the balance between numbers of male and female officer entrants was almost equal and was to remain so into the twentieth century. There was also a high number of resignations due perhaps to the youthfulness of the officer corps, geographical mobility and the Army's autocracy.

The most important surviving officer list is *The Appointments of Officers 1883*. This contains the names of 723 male and 746 female officers together with personal information. An analysis of this shows that in the years before 1883, the largest numbers of women came from the 17 to 21 age-range (with two girls as young as 14 recorded) while for the men, the largest numbers came from the 20 to 23 age-range. A decade later, this age-range had risen by two years for the women while many more men than before were in their late 20s and 30s.[71] This is perhaps indicative of the greater respect with which the Army was held in by the 1890s.

In the early 1880s, the vast majority of the female officer entry were single and only one-fifth of the men were married. This latter fact is important because as wives were expected to at least help run the corps (but their names were absent from the officer list), the Army had nearly 100 more officers than previously realised. By the 1890s, more officer entries were married but as the average entry age had risen, this is not surprising. General Booth had an active policy of encouraging officers to intermarry. *The Appointments of Officers* lists 36 couples who did so, the women resigning their own rights of officer-ship to become a joint officer with her husband. Two couples were however subsequently expelled.

80

The loss of women officers' rights when marrying contradicts the constant statement regarding equality.[72] The Army were clearly not so radical as to lose the concept of man's conjugal superiority. They also carried this social policy into pay; the husband, as head of the household, received the pay for the couple. This policy and the idea that single female officers could manage on less money than their male counterparts has been abolished since the Second World War. The pay scale in force in mid-1882 was

"... married men, 27s. (for each child under 14, 1s per week); single man-captain, 21s.; man-lieutenant, 18s; women-captain, 15s; and woman-lieutenant, 12s."[73]

Clearly not only was there a disparity of six shillings per week, (men therefore getting a third more than women), but women captains received less than men lieutenants.

Geographically the largest numbers of male and female officers came from the industrial cities and London. Thus it is not surprising to find that by 1883, as Table 3.12 shows, the Army recruited 64.8 percent of its officers from the Industrial Class. A heavy reliance on this Class continued for the remainder of the century. Table 3.12 in fact provides a detailed analysis of pre-Salvation Army officership

TABLE 3.12

**Breakdown and Comparison of Occupations, Nationally
and for Salvation Army Officers, Early 1880s**

Occupation	Nat. Total	M	F	S.A. Officers	M	F
I PROFESSIONAL CLASS						
1. *Government*						
1. National Govt.	50859	46506	4353	1	1	—
2. Local Govt.	53493	50476	3017	3	3	—
3. Colonial	240	240	—	1	1	—
2. *Defence*						
1. Army	87185	87168	17	1	1	—
2. Navy	37395	37362	33	1	1	—
3. *Professional*						
1. Clerical	51120	43958	7162	5	4	1
2. Legal	43641	43541	100	4	4	—
3. Medical	64548	26638	37910	9	—	9
4. Teachers	171831	47836	123995	6	1	5
5. Lit./Science	8394	7780	614	1	1	—
6. Engineers	14809	14809	—	4	4	—
7. Artists	58517	40164	18353	—	—	—
8. Exhib./Shows	5034	4477	566	4	3	1
Class Total[1]	647075 (5.8%)	450955	196120	40 (7.9%)	24	16

81

TABLE 3.12—*continued*

Occupation	Nat. Total	M	F	S.A. Officers	M	F
II DOMESTIC CLASS						
4. *Domestic*						
1. Domestic	1502676	244391	1258285	71	6	65
2. Other serv.	301134	14117	287017	7	2	5
Class Total	1803810 (16.1%)	258508	1545302	78 (15.4%)	8	70
III COMMERCIAL CLASS						
5. *Commercial*						
1. Merchants	285138	277000	8138	5	4	1
2. Money deal	16659	16570	89	—	—	—
3. Insurance	15068	14821	247	2	2	—
6. *Conveyance*						
1. Railways	139408	138760	648	13	13	—
2. Roads	167232	165854	1378	8	8	—
3. Canals etc.	183984	183034	950	10	10	—
4. Storage	32026	27847	4179	3	2	1
5. Messenger	140613	136775	3838	12	12	—
Class Total	980128 (8.8%)	960661	19467	53 (10.5%)	51	2
IV AGRICULTURAL CLASS						
7. *Agriculture*						
1. Fields	1196836	1135763	61073	3	3	—
2. Woods	8151	8151	—	—	—	—
3. Gardens	73637	70539	3098	2	2	—
8. *Animals*						
1. Animals	104560	103891	669	2	2	—
Class Total	1383184 (12.3%)	1318344	64840	7 (1.4%)	7	—
V INDUSTRIAL CLASS						
9. *Books Etc.*						
1. Books	98321	82722	15599	7	7	—
2. Prints/Maps	6721	6408	313	1	—	1
10. *Machines*						
1. Machines	160797	159735	1062	18	18	—
2. Tools	48556	39631	8925	2	1	1
3. Clocks	32064	30848	1216	—	—	—
4. Surgical	1511	1181	330	—	—	—
5. Arms	8227	8003	224	1	1	—
6. Musical	9249	9008	241	—	—	—
7. Type, Dies	2708	2623	85	—	—	—
8. Sport	4864	2965	1899	—	—	—
11. *Houses*						
1. Houses	666738	665350	1388	18	18	—
2. Furniture	101066	89197	11869	12	12	—
3. Decorations	18856	13736	5120	12	12	—
12. *Carriages*						
1. Carriages	63308	62861	447	1	1	—
2. Harness	23866	21831	2035	1	1	—
13. *Ships*						
1. Hull	45671	45632	39	2	2	—
2. Masts	8409	8335	74	1	1	—
14. *Chemicals*						
1. Colouring	3261	2715	546	—	—	—
2. Explosives	3616	1607	2009	—	—	—
3. Drugs	36138	34275	1863	1	1	—

TABLE 3.12—*continued*

Occupation	Nat. Total	M	F	S.A. Officers	M	F
15. *Tobacco*						
1. Tobacco	22175	12862	9313	—	—	—
16. *Food/Lodge*						
1. Board	115655	67392	48263	—	—	—
2. Drinks	65052	60177	4875	7	6	1
3. Food	448664	375775	72889	24	21	3
17. *Textiles*						
1. Wool	233256	108371	124885	5	2	3
2. Silk	63577	21455	42122	3	1	2
3. Cotton	586470	231147	355323	16	3	12
4. Hemp	22471	14070	8401	1	1	—
5. Mixed/Unspec.	147874	87981	59893	6	3	3
18. *Dress*						
1. Dress	981105	364680	616425	78	22	56
19. *Animal Subs.*						
1. Grease	10401	9266	1135	—	—	—
2. Skins	39748	34262	5486	2	2	—
3. Hair	18053	10036	8017	—	—	—
20. *Veg. Subs.*						
1. Oils	20509	16639	3870	—	—	—
2. Cane	17909	15334	2575	—	—	—
3. Wood	75338	71417	3921	—	—	—
4. Paper	52989	27190	25799	—	—	—
21. *Mineral*						
1. Miners	441272	435497	5775	17	17	—
2. Coal	58044	56734	1310	2	2	—
3. Stone	193083	189783	3300	1	1	—
4. Earthenware	74407	52917	21490	1	1	—
5. Salt	2982	2823	159	—	—	—
6. Water	2673	2653	20	—	—	—
7. Prec. Metals	29632	23622	6010	1	1	—
8. Iron/Steel	361343	348029	13314	21	20	1
9. Copper	7348	7298	50	1	1	—
10. Tin/Zinc	39188	34633	4555	1	1	—
11. Lead	2460	2319	141	1	1	—
12. Other/Unspec.	65160	56183	8977	3	3	—
22. *General/Unspec.*						
1. Makers/Deal	121407	76118	45289	25	18	7
2. Mech./Labour	694836	677167	17669	35	21	14
23. *Refuse*						
1. Refuse	14339	12685	1654	1	1	—
Class Total	6373367 (57%)	4795178	1578189	328 (64.8%)	224	104

VI NO SPECIFIC OCCUPATION

24. *No Spec. Occup.*						
1. No spec. occup.	14786875	4856256	9930619	—	—	—
Class Total	14786875	4856256	9930619	—	—	—

[1] Class totals in the first column are expressed numerically and as a percentage of the national occupied population, (Total 11,187,564). Under the 'Salvation Army Officers' column, the totals are also expresssed numerically and as a percentage of the 506 strong sample.
[2] Class VI includes all children under five years of age.

Sources: Census of England and Wales. 1881. Vol II. Summary Table 4.
    The Appointments of Officers 1883.

occupations. A total of 506 officers comprising 314 men and 192 women were placed into their respective Classes, Orders and Sub-Orders. When comparing them in percentage terms, Class by Class, with the national pattern, it is clear that there is some variation between the two. For Classes I, II and III (Professional, Domestic and Commercial respectively), the previous occupations of Army officers closely reflects the national pattern although the percentage is slightly higher for the Army in Classes I and III. This is certainly not true for Class IV (Agriculture) which supplied only 1.4% of officers although occupying 12.3% of the employed population. Conversely, the Army recruited 64.8% of its officers from Class V (Industrial) against 57% of the employed population. The percentage pattern therefore supports the previous evidence that the Salvation Army found difficulty in establishing itself in the countryside but not in industrial areas.

In translating the percentages into numbers, it becomes apparent how small the Army sample is. However the detail given in Table 3.12 does allow a thorough survey for each Class. The 40 officers known to be from Class I represent a wide range of professions for the 24 men although few for the 16 women. The majority of officers came from I.3 1-8 (Persons Engaged in Professional Occupations). The largest two officer supplying Sub-Orders in this Class were Medical and Teachers, with nine and six people respectively. All but one of the fifteen were female and this perhaps reflects that these two professions occupied the largest numbers of women in Class I. Eight of the thirteen sub-Orders had large numbers of male employees relative to the remainder of the Class and all except 'Artists' contributed one or more officers. The actual largest number of male officers came from within I.3 1-8, namely, from the Clerical, Legal and Engineering professions. Each supplied four officers although Engineering had relatively few employees. Despite the fact that employees from I.3 1-8 were found across the country, as with the predominantly female Medical and Teaching professions, the Clerical, Legal and Engineering professions were more likely to be in large numbers in urban areas.

Class II was the only Class to have a female occupational numerical majority over men. The largest number of women were employed as Domestic Indoor Servants and the Salvation Army gained 65 of them as officers. This is the largest single identifiable officer group, male or female. Although these servants were ubiquitous, they would be most numerous in the densely packed towns and cities. This suggests that the Army gained considerable working-class female support from the urban areas.

Class III provided mainly male rather than female officers and this is in close proportion to the numbers of men over women employed. Most male officers came from III.6. 1-5 (Conveyance). The vast majority of men were employed upon railways, roads, canals and as messengers, all of which were mainly industrial/urban related activities. Thus this evidence suggests that the army gained strength from the male working-class in these areas.

Class IV was another primarily male activity yet few Army officers appear to have come from an agricultural background. This suggests that agriculture was unimportant in contributing to the early development of the Army.

Class V shows 224 male and 104 female Salvation Army officers coming from just over two-thirds of the Sub-Orders. The Army appears therefore to have attracted a wide range from the Industrial Class. However Table 3.12 shows that in several cases, only one person was attracted and that for men and particularly women, certain key occupations were important. For the male officers these were: V.10.1. Machines (fitters and stokers); V.II.1-3 Houses (including building, decorating and producing furniture); V.16.3. Food (grocers, bakers and millers); V.17.1-5. Textiles; V.18.1. Dress (drapers, tailors and bootmakers); V.21.1 and 8. Miners and Iron and Steel workers respectively; and the large V.22.1 and 2. General/Unspecified. Nationally all these occupations were the most substantial male employers. Although some of the occupations such as Food and Houses were found nationwide, they were all much more concentrated in the industrial areas and major conurbations where the Army had its greatest number of corps.

Just under three-quarters of the female officers came from two Orders which between them occupied approximately three-quarters of the women in Class V. These Orders were V.17 Textiles, and V.18. Dress. The greatest number from within 'Textiles' were employed in the Cotton industry. Those employed in Dress included milliners, dressmakers and staymakers. Both V.17. and V.18. were essentially urban based activities and in some counties, were the leading occupations. Women officers were rarely represented in the other Orders of Class V.

Table 3.12 has shown that as with the Christian Mission, the Salvation Army drew support from across the social classes, although it is evident that most support came from Class V, Industrial. When combined with Domestic Indoor Servant for the females and Conveyance of goods, messages and people for the males, it is clear that the Army thrived amongst the working-class in the towns and cities. This wide social range of support however did not appear to extend to many of the very poor, the category defined by General Booth as the 'submerged tenth'. This does not deny that a number of officer recruits were probably poverty-stricken through low wages, the poor living and working conditions ever present in the late nineteenth century industrial areas, and through drinking and gambling. Nevertheless, those from such backgrounds were relatively few. It must though be noted that many people did raise their status in real terms by becoming evangelists/officers and the Army was quick to point out those raised from iniquity and a life of 'evil'. At the higher end of the social scale, some officers and supporters were obviously of the middle-class. When they joined full-time as officers, without exception they quickly rose to achieve prominent rank in the Movement. This was also true for the very few officers who had held well-paid positions in local and national government employment, East India and Colonial Service, the law or were merchants (Table 3.12).

One noticeable factor amongst officer entries was the high number with some form of previous religious affiliation. This may well not have been an affiliation current at the time of their entry to the Salvation Army but there are strong indications that many Methodists favoured William Booth's approach to religion either in preference to their own or as a distinct reminder of something they had once known. Just as the Army was a product of the Home Mission Movement, it was also a product of William Booth's religious background. He attended Broad Street Wesleyan Chapel in Nottingham. Although he later preached for the Reformers and the New Connexion, his early teenage impressions were important to him and there is much recognisable as similar to Methodism and especially Wesleyanism about the early-day Salvation Army, albeit in the freer less ritualistic environment of the Home Mission tradition. This was one reason why, although Booth stated that the Army

"... openly avows its objection to accept as members any who belong to any of the churches, preferring the uncared for,"[74]

many Wesleyans, Primitives and other Home Mission evangelists joined the Army.[75] Another equally important reason was that the Army provided opportunities for Methodists who disliked the increasingly common feeling found to varying degrees in many of the chapels, of being at home in the world.[76]

The answer to the question of why officers left the Christian Mission and the Salvation Army indicates both the pressures on the officers and the type of people who remained. The official reasons given for the resignations were desertion, domestic reasons, marriage, illness and expulsion. The first was merely officers not telling Headquaters that they wanted to leave; domestic reasons tended to be leaving to nurse a sick relative; and marriage was finding a non-officer partner. Illness and expulsion accounted for more than half of the male and female resignations and came from the respective high intake age groups, that is, the very youthful officers. Expulsion from the officer ranks, sometimes after a 'Court Martial,' took place for a number of reasons. In December 1879

> "FOUR OFFICERS were reduced to the ranks in December.
> 2 for light and frivolous conduct and conversation.
> 1 for contracting a matrimonial engagement immediately after appointment and without the consent of Headquarters.
> 1 for misbehaviour in the presence of the enemy."[77]

Reasons would also include a return to drink and a refusal to obey orders or organise the corps according to Booth's instructions. These reasons probably also apply to the 'reason unknown' category.

Evidence on explusion because of breaking rules or the appearance of doing so is scarce but an incident in Hanley in 1882 appears typical of both the strictness and authority of the Booths. Upon his farewell from the corps, Captain Gipsy Smith, later an evangelist of international reputation but then the Army officer in charge, received a gold watch on behalf of the Free Churches in recognition of his services. This gift

> ". . . came from people who were outside the Salvation Army. The soldiers of the Army had some intention of making us a gift, but we stopped that movement, as we knew that the General did not approve of such presentation."[78]

The Army showed its displeasure and despite several entreaties and apologies by the Free Churches, Gipsy Smith was dismissed.

Such control was only a part of the immense pressure on the mainly single youthful officers. Other pressures included their being sent far from home,[79] presumably to stop the temptation of frequent return visits. They were required to make many moves from town to town, seven towns in eighteen months being known.[80] A close check was kept by Headquarters with marks being put into their service records to denote progress. Officers were

> ". . . expected to conduct from 19 to 25 meetings weekly, extending over 30 to 35 hours; (and) to spend 18 hours in visiting from house to house."[81]

This was in addition to form-filling and fund-raising.[82] The control emanated from Booth whose aim from the early days was to get evangelists trained in the Army's ways and without 'outside notions'.[83] Two other pressures were Booth's order ". . . that everything is to be paid before salary."[84] This was later modified to stop officers going hungry.[85] The other was the physical abuse and often violent attacks coming from the persecution of the Army. In Honiton the Captain's wife was kicked[86] and the junior officer beaten up.[87] He resigned seven months later and died at the end of the year.[88] His successor came in as Commanding Officer in March 1883.[89] Physical attacks and vilification continued and Captain Fairless resigned, leaving the corps with no officer.[90]

No resignation was ever acknowledged in the *War Cry* but previously unpublished manuscript and letter material gives further evidence on reasons for resignations. Henry Edmonds, the General's first A.D.C. and a territorial commander, wrote:

> "If an independent history of the Salvation Army should ever be written, part should be devoted to resignations and their causes.
>
> Without doubt, the General was responsible for bringing a great host of people out of obscurity, and making them useful spiritually and socially; but the Army system and his administration of it drove many to leave . . . (The Army) is also strikingly singular for the numbers of those who, after gaining considerable experience, and having built up a position of wide usefulness, have finally retired, mostly under unhappy circumstances, not to go back into the world, but usually to continue Christian work on lines where they could be free and happy, without the harrassing and vexatious conditions which led to their leaving the Army."[91]

In making further notes on the subject, he discusses the advantages of having an arbitration body especially as

> "Resignations are nearly always due to disagreements with the General or Headquarters on some question of administration affecting the persons concerned or their friends, and such disagreements are often difficult to adjust amicably . . . (especially as) . . . the General will not change his mind once an impression is set or an order given."[92]

Clearly no criticism of the Army or the General and his family was allowed and the

> ". . . extent to which, at a certain period, the General and Headquarters carried their *spying* and persecuting propaganda against those whom they suspect of seeking reforms in the Army system, or criticising any department of the Army, or any member of the Booth family, or their administration of their responsibilities, would be incredible but for the knowledge and experience of those who have suffered it."[93]

Above all, the Booth family were unquestionably in charge and orders had to be obeyed to the letter. This was maintained throughout the rank structure. Always the senior officer's word was true unless that officer were anti-Booth or was otherwise discredited in the eyes of the Booths. The spying which Colonel Edmonds writes of was partly the mass of detailed paperwork and reports to be regularly attended to. This took the form of reports on new candidates for soldiership and officership, regular Monday morning reports, and reports upon entering or leaving a corps, (Appendix 6). In addition to this there was the day-to-day paperwork involved in the running of a corps. This included letters, arranging for the arrival and distribution of the *War Cry* and other Army papers, preparing sermons and meetings, advertising talks, visiting, and general accounts.[94]

The second part actively involved reports being presented, sometimes verbally, to the Booth family. Senior officers were expected to visit and closely question junior field officers and their reports were sent to London.[95] Staff officers were similarly afraid of eavesdroppers at Headquarters and elsewhere. Sometimes they were watched as to their private actions.[96]

> "Distrust and suspicion are the leading characteristics of its interior dealings, and a system of espionage and an elaborate secret service are at the disposal of its chiefs . . . Headquarters directly encourages this. It takes each officer into its interior confidence as regards his fellows, and on the other hand confides in every one of his comrades in reference to the officer himself. The officer is eagerly listened to in reference to his chief, and the chief examined in reference to the officer . . . The intelligence office at Headquarters is ever busy and though authorities are never given and accuser and accused never brought face to face, yet reports are acted upon and people often-times disciplined . . . This espionage obtains throughout the whole affair (and internationally), and from highest to lowest all are more or less subject to its workings, indeed those that are not and cannot be affected are only the General himself and his immediate entourage."[97]

Officers clearly felt under threat. They dare not offend the Army which was personified in William Booth and his family. Such a family control bred nepotism as was seen in the 1881 appointment of the General's eldest son, Bramwell Booth, as Chief of the Staff. This was done over the heads of many senior men and led many officers of all ranks to resign.[98] According to Edmonds, several of these went as preachers and workers in other churches.[99] This predominance of the Booths was a point of issue with many officers. All the family had prominent rank and the married daughters kept

> ". . . the illustrious name before that of their husband's, who themselves also adopt it."[100]

The apparent difficulty of receiving a fair hearing against rumours and the Booths' dynastic power resulted in the resignation of many officers or, more rarely, their being ignored. Colonel Edmonds fell into the latter category. He was, after a period of rest in 1889, held responsible for the reforming spirit increasingly prevalent in the Army in the late 1880s. Because of this and a disagreement with the Booths over how he was spending his wealth (having his own private income and marrying the daughter of a wealthy merchant) he was not reappointed to his staff position. Although never actually resigning or being expelled, Colonel and Mrs. Edmonds were generally ignored.[101]

Two of the General's own sons, both senior territorial commanders, resigned over the question of obyeying his orders and both left the work and set up their own Christian organisations. Previously unpublished letter evidence suggests that even Bramwell had been occasionally reticent about obeying his father's orders.[102] Perhaps more than age, previous denomination or occupation, the ability to fit into William Booth's system was the main determinant of who remained.

Conclusion

The growth and development of the Salvation Army rested on a combination of supply and demand. General Booth supplied a vibrant form of religion which had a forceful but simple message at its core. His determination to ". . . go out to them"[103] forced people to listen to a novel form of religion. The people's interest, aided by the 1859 Religious Revival and possibly by the later persecution of the Salvationists, allowed the Army to rise out of the Home Mission Movement as a large and successful independent force. Its excitement and bonhomie was a viable alternative to the established religious denominations and the music-halls or public-houses. It was in effect a combination of religion and entertainment.

The Movement could not have become an established or accepted part of religious life unless there was a demand for it. The conditions conducive to its growth were caused by one, or more usually a combination, of industrial, socio-economic, and religious factors. As the Lancashire and Cheshire analysis has demonstrated, the most fertile areas for Salvation Army development were those based on industrial diversity, decay or a single industry, each with their attendant density of population and, in most cases, high wages. Possibly there was little other church or chapel activity in the area but where one or more denominations were active, they were usually dependent on already established congregations, seeing the new and growing communities as 'mission grounds'.

When the Salvation Army was dependent on one particular industry, if that industry was adversely affected for any length of time and if there was no alternative employment, the Salvation Army corps would close. This is particularly noticeable within the mining communities. Many mines were shut down in the 1880s and 1890s as coal reserves were finished, thus there were losses of corps in the coal-mining areas (Table 3.3). Conversely, many communities moved to fresh seams and as hamlets grew, so new Army corps were established. The Army's readiness to move to new areas could explain the large growth up to 1905 in the same coal-mining areas as the losses (Table 3.3).

The growth of the Salvation Army was therefore heavily reliant on industrial activity and its novel methods of preaching the Gospel. It is clear that General Booth made a considerable impact on the English countryside by his judicious use of resources and good organisation. Such innovative organisation can be seen after 1883 with the introduction of circle corps to take the Gospel message to rural locations. Many of these locations eventually established corps in their own right and this explains why so many neighbouring villages in the north and east of England had Army corps by 1905. The Salvation Army had certainly become a strong religious and, to a certain extent, social force by the early twentieth century growing from 57 English and Welsh corps in 1878 to 1,116 in 1905. Although a third of this growth took place between 1878 and 1883, an increasing number of the working-class must have joined to enable William Booth to open and retain on average 31 corps a year after 1883 and until 1905.

The success of William Booth in attracting officers capable of gathering large audiences (and perhaps to some extent local corps followers who left at the change of officers) lay in his adoption of Methodist first principles, namely a determined effort to attract people's attention; a direct appeal and stress on an individual's choice to be 'saved' or damned, (hellfire preaching); and freedom in worship. The fact that so many of his officers between 1865 and 1896 appear to have had some previous religious affiliations does not mean that he had completely failed in his policy to reach the unsaved. Many men and women did achieve a better quality of life and status by becoming officers than they could otherwise have done. The Army also allowed and continued to allow women a place in the leadership although rarely in senior management.[104] This role was not something generally found elsewhere until after the turn of the century.

Little evidence is available concerning resignations but between the mid-1890s and 1905, 26 per cent or just over one quarter of the names disappeared. This indicates a lower number of resignations per annum than the one third from 1865 to 1883, but as the actual number of officers recruited rose, it is possible to suggest that a large number of people were still not fitting into the Army's (Booth's) system.

The majority of Christian Mission evangelists and Salvation Army officers appear to have come from the old and new industries, although a minority were from agricultural and the economically-mixed counties. While few were of the 'submerged tenth',[105] the whole were spread across the social classes with a strong emphasis on the working-class. It was a renewed determination by General Booth that the lowest stratum should be reached which led him to vigorously pursue the social remedies outlined in his *In Darkest England and the Way Out.*

CHAPTER FOUR

OPPOSITION TO THE SALVATION ARMY

I. THE CONTEXT

The limited historiography concerning Salvation Army persecution suggests that, throughout England, opposition frequently followed an initial Salvation Army 'attack'; that such opposition tended to follow Army geographical expansion; that it was only organised in some southern towns; and that despite the violence shown towards the Army, during the later Victorian period there was a clear absence of widespread social disorder compared with earlier periods.[1]

Large-scale riots as a means of social expression were on the decline by the 1850s as trade unions, social and friendly societies, political associations and effective policing increased. However the violence against the Salvation Army was one response in the centuries-old tradition of opposition to anything considered to deviate from the norm. Such reaction normally related to sexual deviance but also encompassed others such as swindlers, gypsies or those introducing and supporting new religious ideas.[2] For many years missionaries of any denomination might be 'attacked'. If the group survived, they were generally accepted or at least tolerated. If they failed, the social control exercised was vindicated. Methodism is an example of the former and the Coaklers of the latter.[3] The generic name for opposition such as this is 'rough-music' but local names varied. In Cambridgeshire it was variously described as 'tin kettling', 'tin panning' or, in the Fens, 'tinging'.[4] Elsewhere as 'rattling',[5] 'Skimmity',[6] 'Riding the Stang', or 'Cool Staffing'. Whatever the name given,

> "... these ancient traditions incorporated a variety of ridicule and abuse"[7]

and their hallmark was considerable, often terrifying, noise created by metal objects such as kettles, saucepans and horns.

II. SOCIAL CONTROL, THE LAW AND RELIGIOUS PERSECUTION

New or reaffirmed religious deviance often offended the social mores of a society and opposition sometimes quickly built up to a country-wide or national level.[8] The Society of Friends ('Quakers') experienced such opposition in the mid to late seventeenth century. Methodists similarly suffered a century later. The feeling against Methodists, Congregationalists and Baptists reached its zenith during the Revolutionary and Napoleonic Wars and was part of an intense reaction to the spectre of revolution. 'The mob' was encouraged in its ill-feeling towards Nonconformity by the twin pillars of the Establishment, the Church of England and the gentry. The Establishment feared Nonconformity inculcated a lack of respect by the people and thus contributed to the breakdown of the centuries-old tradition of dependency upon the parson/squire.

The national opposition took a variety of forms which depended on several factors, in particular geographical position, the power of the Established Church, whether local gentry were sympathetic or not, and the type and strength of message preached. Action taken shifted during its most strident years of the 1780s to 1830s from the economic, social and physical to openly legal and economic. The harassment, if not at first encouraged by the Magistrates' Bench, was certainly generally accepted by them. It included dismissal from jobs, eviction from homes, driving animals into open-air meetings and the use of 'the mob' who were

> ". . . functioning on behalf of a hostile local establishment . . . "Wherever a mob continues any time, all they do is to be imputed, not so much to the rabble, as the Justices." (Wesley). The fact remains however that the 'rabble' and the gentry were working together against what they perceived to be dissent from the established order."[9]

From the 1790s this 'established order' and in particular the Church began to decline in power as industrial activity increased. The Church and the working-class, elements in the latter frequently being referred to as 'the mob' or 'rabble', became more separated and the use of 'the mob' to voice Establishment disquiet decreased. In his study of religious and social change between 1740 and 1914, Dr. Gilbert suggests that

> ". . . the religious Establishment was forced to rely increasingly on overt legal and economic pressures to curb religious deviance."[10]

They were able to do this because as a reaction to their decrease in spiritual power, it became the vogue for clergymen to become J.P.'s; by the 1830s, over twenty-five per cent of J.P.'s were clerics. The

93

Church could therefore maintain an anti-deviancy pressure through the often still receptive Magistrates' Bench. There were increasingly frequent reports of widespread legal persecution and of cases of magistrates refusing to obey the Act of Toleration in giving protective licences to chapels.

The relevant section of the Gilbert study provides evidence that there is a correlation between the often severe opposition and the growth in membership of the three major Nonconformist denominations. Evidence suggesting that opposition to a religious movement increases growth and support for it is in fact quite strong.[11] However Gilbert's overall conclusion, that because Establishment and especially Church power at the grass-roots declines, the law instead of 'the mob' is invoked, is too simplistic. It does not give 'the mob' any credence as articulate thinking beings. What is more likely is that by the early 1800s, the Nonconformists, having withstood derision and opposition, were becoming an accepted part of society at the grass-roots and therefore mobbing declined. Gilbert's evidence is that there was little religious violence against denominations after the 1830s. Although it is true that there was a very definite upsurge in religious intolerance between the 1780s and the 1830s, (from which date the Church reluctantly began to allow reform), mob violence against religious denominations existed well before 1780 and continued after 1830.

Religious Missions were a particular focus of attention in many towns and villages and some inhabitants saw them as a 'legitimate' target of fun. 'The mob' could perhaps be incited and encouraged but much of the persecution was well within the 'rough-musicing' tradition. Although 'rough-musicing' was usually spontaneous, it became a marked aspect of annual festivals in some towns and villages.[12] Hiding behind often elaborate costumes and masks, mobs used festivals such as 5 November to

> ". . . (pay) off old scores. . . It was not safe to venture out after dark, and not only was the person in danger, but property also."[13]

'The mob' would sometimes stone and cudgel hapless victims but more usually merely make life difficult by smashing windows, keeping victims awake and shouting rude slogans.

Such mobs often adopted names. The annual November rioters in Guildford were called 'The Guys'. The name commonly associated with such anti-Army violence was 'Skeleton Army' but it could vary; it was the 'Unconverted Salvation Army' in Whitechapel, the 'Red(-Nose) Army' in Guildford, and 'The Society for the Suppression of Street Parading' in Salisbury.[14] Several of these Skeleton Armies were financed and encouraged by powerful local opposition groups and often received support from the local authorities. Such organisation however only took place in conservative southern towns of mainly between 3,000 and 20,000 inhabitants. The Establishment ties were still strong in these well-defined and generally small towns. Elements in these towns merely offered support, albeit often tenacious, to the 'rough-musicing' that occurred to varying degrees of intensity throughout the country. As earlier in the century with the three major Nonconformist denominations, 'the mob' were not unthinking inarticulate beings but were encouraged and directed by the Establishment which was sometimes represented by the Church, but in this case more usually by businessmen, especially those involved in the drink interest. At the same time as the Army were being harassed, mobs were also turning against other obvious elements in society such as the Irish and, in efforts to vindicate certain local grievances, against the Establishment and authority figures as well. [15]

III. THE CHRISTIAN MISSION: 1865–1878

In June 1865, the month before Booth took over the Mission in the tent near the Mile End Road, there had been reports in *The Revival* of apparently concerted interference by police. Booth himself soon suffered a variety of acts of persecution from the East End 'roughs' and others. They ranged from cutting the tent ropes while a meeting was in progress (late 1865), to a missioner's imprisonment (Easter 1868), and to severe physical assault by men, women and children (February 1869). This latter incident occurred despite him having a bodyguard. Other than for sermonising on the tricks of the Devil, little capital was made out of these difficulties. While they were abhorred in local newspapers, they were an accepted part of a preacher's life if he was to 'reach the masses'[16] or at least 'go public'.

William Booth clearly aimed to upset the publicans by having children sing in their vicinity against the evils of drink. This led to the first 'organised' anti-Booth action when, in 1869, several licensees launched a concerted effort of complaint and the police arrested a number of missioners. The magistrates heard the publican witnesses and bound the missioners over. Booth suggested that his people were in the wrong by not complying with police requests to move and, while claiming more police protection, suggested moving if requested. This ensured police defence of their work and showed a conciliatory nature that Booth, in establishing his rights and in an attempt to create publicity, lost over the next decade.

Persecution grew as Booth's Mission became more widespread but it was perhaps no more than the expected ratio of amount of 'rough-musicing' to the number of new towns visited. In September 1874, violent opposition by the police, publicans and 'the mob' did seem very strong and was clearly encouraged by the public-houses where

> ". . . drunken men are instigated, and bribed with liquor to annoy, and, if possible, break up the meetings."[17]

Strood, Hastings, Harrogate and the East End were all affected during this year although there is no indication of anything other than opportunist reaction. In Harrogate, the tin-kettles were brought out in force as preachers were subjected to 'rough-musicing'. In October 1875 at Cardiff, the imprisonment of a Christian Missioner caused such a storm from local churches and newspapers that he was immediately released and missioners henceforth protected. Even the final meeting of the War Congress in 1878, which announced the name change and ratified control of the Movement in the hands of General Booth, was disrupted by

> ". . . a company of butchers (who) commenced a hullabaloo with blowing a horn, rattling of cans, and other articles so as to keep up a ceaseless din. . . (Then). . . the enemy had a new device. By burning something placed near open ventilators and in the stove-pipe, which passed through that wall, they filled the air through the building with an effluvium which set everyone coughing."[18]

IV. THE SALVATION ARMY: 1878–1900

Given the continuing 'rough-musicing' reaction, the focus for persecution in home affairs from 1878 became the now easily identifiable Salvation Army. The Army grew with tremendous rapidity and corresponding to this was the increase in numbers of incidents of not unexpected opposition. Perhaps more so than the surviving new denominations of the previous two centuries, this Movement was strikingly and quite publicly at deviance with much accepted social behaviour. For three main reasons it appeared a very powerful physical force at a time when people were aware of military might as the British Army and Navy were considered invincible and omnipotent. These reasons quickly became known and, reinforced by rumours, encouraged an intense degree of opposition. First, when the Christian Mission transformed itself into the Salvation Army in 1878, it adopted a centralised system of autocratic control as well as full military titles, uniform, troop-movements and 'colours'. Its strident declarations of warfare and battle-like terminology, while possibly befitting the age of imperialistic feeling evident especially during the Russo-Turkish War, were startlingly new ways of treating the hitherto respectable subject of religion; for over a decade after 1878 this must have seemed very frightening to some while attracting others. Second, William Booth was a supposedly despotic and omnipotent leader who controlled every aspect of his soldiers' lives. Third, the Movement was strange in its degree of religious fervour in a period of restrained Victorian codes of behaviour; the charismatic flavour of meetings was not always appealing to onlookers. The drink interest in particular must have feared this

> "... body with effective national coordination, despatching, replacing and rearing disciplined cadres who spoke directly to the poor, who were unamenable to the local patterns of social discipline."[19]

Between 1878 and 1900 there were three years of intense opposition, 1882, 1885 and 1890, the first being extremely physical and the latter two more literary. Throughout this period however, legal battles concerning the Salvation Army but of considerable national importance were being fought. Although a considerable amount of physical violence was carried out against the Army in England, mainly between 1878 and the mid-1880s, its highpoint was in 1882. The evidence comes from a variety of sources but most specifically from the *War Cry*. This was the Army's highly prominent organ for promoting the Salvation War. When, in the same pattern as 'attacks' on the missioners, a publican had Salvationists summonsed in Boston in December 1879, this organ heaped ridicule on the plaintiff and the law. The level of opposition varies from shouting and howling (Wednesbury), to the equally common pelting with tin-cans, stones, rotten fruit and mud (Notting Hill and Cheltenham), to more rarely seen actual bloody fighting (Liverpool), and to magisterial action against the Salvationists for obstruction (Blackburn). Conversely, in other areas such as Whitehaven

> "... we are allowed to stand on any street on the Sabbath, and the POLICE follow us around the streets to see that no one molests us."[20]

Table 4.1 summarises the number of physical attacks at two yearly intervals between 1880 and 1888 as reported in the *War Cry*. At best this is only a rough indicator of persecution because noisy and verbal abuse usually went unreported to the *War Cry*. The number of reports included were limited by space (despite the introduction of a twice weekly *War Cry* from September 1882) and even physical persecutions were not always reported to and certainly not included in the paper. The official Army figures for 1882 state that 669 soldiers were 'brutally assaulted', 251 of whom were women and 23 were children.[21] While not showing this number, the Table does suggest that 1882 witnessed the extremity of violence and that the intensity was felt primarily in southern and western England. Table 4.1 does not

TABLE 4.1

Physical Assaults on Members of the Salvation Army: 1880–1888

Regions	1880	1882	1884	1886	1888
London and Home Counties . . .	22	22	7	6	5
Southwest	5	15	5	4	14[1]
Rural Southeast	5	23	6	7	11
South Wales	1	1	—	—	—
Rural Wales and Herefordshire . .	—	1	—	1	—
Midlands	—	6	1	2	5
Lincs., Rutland, E. and N. Ridings . .	5	8	3	3	3
Lancs., Cheshire and the W. Riding .	5	10	2	2	5
Cumberland and Westmorland . . .	—	—	—	—	—
Northumberland and Durham . . .	—	—	—	—	—
Totals	43	86	24	25	43

[1] This high number is mainly due to a large number of reported clashes in Torquay.
Source: War Cry 1880, 1882, 1884, 1886 and 1888.

support Victor Bailey's findings that violence followed geographically in the wake of Army expansion. Rather, it suggests that in the first four or five years after the Salvation Army was established, (late 1878 to 1882/1883), there was an increasingly strong 'rough-musicing' reaction nationally. This reached its zenith in 1882 and was evidently strongest in the south of England. That there were relatively fewer cases of anti-Army violence in the Midlands and north of England compared with the south suggests perhaps that 'rough-music' was dying out in the industrial towns and villages. Possibly new ideas and activities were arising from the mixed backgrounds of the population now settled and still settling in these areas. Despite much townward migration involving moving to stay with, or at least be near, relatives or friends already in the town, and thus towns becoming

"... studded with little districts sharing common rural origins, (and) perpetuating a shared cultural tradition,"[22]

much interaction must have gone on and therefore new ideas on behaviour and respectability develop.

Increasingly from late 1879, the Army broadcast any opposition to it and took a stand against the accusation that by being so public in a town, they caused opposition. Such opinions were expressed not only by members of the public but also by members of various local authorities such as a Honiton magistrate and the Mayor of Salisbury.[23] However the Movement thrived on this opposition as William Booth well realised.[24] The *War Cry* even asked "Are You Persecuted

Enough?"[25] The organisation was novel, militant and increasingly well-organised, although many of the older missioners had left in protest at the autocratic-militaristic changes. In its papers, books and articles as well as from the platform, the Army glorified its soldiers, especially those who were facing any physical opposition. The *War Cry* was the mainstay here in presenting not only highly ambiguous report headings and terminology regarding death being imminent (all dying sometime), people in peril (because of sin), and the fights and battles being hard (spiritually), but also giving carefully orchestrated accounts of opposition to the Movement. These included details of court cases; stories of Salvationists' life in gaol and the large demonstrations organised to greet them on their release; pictures of rioters and pictures of ex-prisoners in full prison uniform at meetings throughout the country. Such meetings were always graphically described and freely publicised and the pictures ensured a striking visual portrayal of the stories.

The *War Cry* was also used to issue orders, comment on national and international news and refute rumours. In addition, it served to highlight the Army's strange aspects. Contemporary evidence suggests the Movement to have been charismatic with shouting, lying prostrate on the ground, and leaping in the air being reported in 1882.[26] Also practised was "Revelling on the floor in the Glory," "Jumping for Jesus,"[27] and

> "On Sunday morning we had a remarkable baptism of glory. One sister almost let her baby fall through the power falling on her. After a sister had taken the child, she stood in one posture shouting glory for nearly twenty minutes."[28]

One description of a Holiness Meeting[29] in 1878 contained several of these elements.

> "Big men, as well as women, fell to the ground, lay there for some time as if dead, overwhelmed with the power from on high. . . some, they laughed as well as cried for joy, and some of the younger evangelists might have been seen like lads at play, locked in one another's arms, and rolling each other over on the floor."[30]

However the Army's official position on charismatic meetings remained ambiguous although such activity was probably even more widespread than reported. The sight of perhaps dozens of people in trance-like state leaping or dancing around in the open-air or in their halls cannot have enhanced the Army's reputation. Added to this were ribald and militaristic-sounding brightly-coloured posters; strange outbursts of behaviour such as a woman officer riding a carriage through a town and playing the fiddle while a soldier banged a drum from the top; periodic allegations of immorality; and extensive reporting of faith-healing. Throughout the 1880s, the *War Cry* and other Salvation Army publications detail remarkable cases of faith-healing from cures of consumption and a stammering tongue, to restoring sight.[31] All of this together with its constant requests for money, its anti-drink stance, its physical reality as an Army and, from January 1884, the Salvationist's habit of kneeling and praying for two minutes every day at 12.30 no matter where they were, encouraged much scare-mongering about the Army and possible future consequences on any area it 'invaded'.

Rumours about the Salvation Army were inevitably a part of the organisation's novelty and during the height of opposition in 1882, allegations of immorality became particularly strong. The question was not the propriety of putting single male and female officers together as happened on numerous occasions in 1878 and 1879 but what happened during and after 'All-Night of Prayer' sessions. *The Hackney and Kingsland Gazette* (July 1882) commented on single pregnant women

> ". . . that the social evil had been greatly promoted by means of the Salvationist system, and that numbers of the young women who had joined it were in the Union Infirmary expiating their shame."[32]

In August 1882 the Army issued a warm denial of this charge but with sessions of 'groping for Jesus' where the lights were turned very low and the soldiers went on hands and knees to simulate being 'lost in sin', the allegations persisted. At the Church of England Mildmay Conference in 1882, the Reverend E. Bickersteth's name was linked with the allegation

> ". . . that after the physical excitement of an All-Night Meeting, the grossest immoralities took place."[33]

The fast-growing and now international organisation[34] easily overrode this one aspect of the many that formed opposition. While there is little evidence that any immorality took place, much of this over-exuberant behaviour did cause legitimate opposition. At times the Army became an obvious nuisance such as on the march in Birkenhead (May 1882)

> ". . . we go twelve a-breast, sweeping all before us."[35]

This was clearly liable to cause complaint as was the action in Shipley when

> "A rather heavy charge was made for admission to the meeting."[36]

Such a policy was however commonplace throughout the Army for any 'special' meeting. Another cause of complaint was the Army marching past places of worship playing instruments. This latter problem caused Booth to issue a General Order

"... not to procession past any place of worship in service time if you can help it, and if you cannot help going past, to march past in perfect silence."[37]

The Army was clearly in the wrong in many instances and over-zealous officers with an eye on novelty could cause legitimate disagreements with the authorities and public. However the Movement admitted its mistakes as rarely as it did its failures and instead used every opportunity to turn any opposition into a quest for support. It was increasingly powerful enough to send aid to 'battle weary' soldiers and so overcome minor local difficulties. Harder to overcome were organised groups of opposition.

V. ORGANISED OPPOSITION: THE SKELETON ARMY, DRINK AND THE LAW

Popular Opposition

The earliest reference to an organised opposition to the Army was in August 1880 in Whitechapel. 'The Unconverted Salvation Army', with its flag and motto of "Be just and fear not" paraded the streets in parody of the Salvation Army. In 1881 Skeleton Armies were organised in Exeter and Weston-super-Mare and the name was quickly taken up elsewhere as "organised rowdyism" was reported.[38] The term Skeleton Army was however generic and freely used so therefore must be treated with caution, especially in Army reports. The origins of the Skeletons appears to be based in the groups that in some towns and villages annually 'rough-musiced' festivals such as Guy Fawkes Night. Organised anti-Salvation Army mobs were however a phenomenon purely of southern England; no records exist of Skeleton Armies north of London. Their make-up was essentially working-class. Victor Bailey's work suggests that the Skeletons were drawn from the lower to middle working-class. His evidence comes from only a small number of court cases. A close examination of the *War Cry* and additional court cases reveals a wider spread of involvement across the working-class.

The tactics adopted by the Skeletons in the south were a mixture of ridicule by noise; flags; anti-Army broadsheets and newspapers; insults and violence. *Prima facie* this was merely more organised persecution than those conflicts seen elsewhere such as in Sheffield in January 1882 when an apparently unorganised mob of working-men fell on Salvationists causing considerable injury. However the organisation went deeper and became so effective that Skeleton Armies could supply mutual support between towns in Devon by late 1882 and along the Sussex Coast by 1884. At no time does there appear more than an inter-town collaboration but there were four common features of Skeletons in much of the south which made them different from those forces which created sometimes violent opposition towards the Army elsewhere. These features were backing by the brewery trade; occasionally very strong magisterial support; the conservative attitude of the towns; and their relative smallness. Few south-western or rural south-eastern towns had more than 20,000 inhabitants and all were marked by the conservative establishment still being strong in the form of the Church and 'squire-like' leading citizens who were usually engaged in business, often the drink trade. However the words 'organised' and 'organisation' must not be allowed to create an impression of an immense structure. No major anti-Army opposition was formed other than Skeletons from nearby towns lending occasional support. Usually the only 'outside' support came from the knowledge of Skeleton Armies in other localities using similar methods to curb the 'religious deviants'.

The Brewers

The Army's continuous attack on the evils of drink, conscientiously pursued in the written and spoken word, provoked publicans into bribing groups of 'roughs' into attacking the Salvation Army. As drinking places abounded so freely in Victorian England and were the major places for relaxation, their use as organisational bases is not so surprising. A search of extant local and national brewery records reveals no evidence of the larger brewing organisations directing publicans to support the Skeletons but they were suspected as a memorandum from William Booth to the Home Secretary demonstrates:

> ". . . in nearly every town where there has been any opposition we have been able to trace it more or less, to the direct instigation, and often open leadership of either Brewers or Publicans, or their EMPLOYEES.
> The plan adopted is by treating and otherwise inciting gangs of roughs . . . to hustle and pelt, and mob the people."[39]

Much evidence from the case-studies supports the view that brewers and publicans were frequently responsible for the violence, although most of the evidence comes from Salvation Army sources. The main exceptions are 1882 Honiton Court Records which show publicans employing (paying) men from the surrounding areas and Home Department (Office) correspondence between themselves and mayors

The Skeleton Army stoning the Worthing Salvation Army Barracks in 1884.

Brighton Congress Hall after being attacked in 1884.

and magistrates who were noted brewers. The most notable example of this was correspondence to the brewer-Mayor of Basingstoke in 1881 and 1882. On one occasion he organised a dinner in the Corn Exchange for those who had attacked the Salvation Army.[40] On two occasions speeches stressed the connection between the opposition and the brewery trade. The Chairman of the Wesleyan Methodist Bristol District believed that

> "The brutal opposition of an organised rowdyism, (is) encouraged, sometimes, by magistrates who make large profits out of sin, (and is) connived at by police in some places;" (April 1882).[41]

In a speech in the House of Lords, Lord Mount Temple stated that unless the publicans were taught to moderate their reaction to the Army, the country would have no security against their power (16 May 1882).[42]

The last known reference to a Skeleton Army occurred in 1893 in Egham, Surrey,[43] but little mention of them is found from the late 1880s onwards. Their growth and decline was matched by support for them by magistrates and publicans. When the former came under increasing Home Office pressure to protect the Army and the latter realised that the effect of the Army in practice was not as great as feared, the level of opposition dwindled to very sporadic, geographically widespread and definitely not organised assaults.

The Magistrates

More threatening to the Salvationists than 'the mob' or their 'organisers', the publicans, were the persecutor's protectors and supporters, the magistrates. This was especially true where the drink interest was strongly represented in local politics, particularly on the Magistrates' Bench. Although in reality only a small percentage actively worked against the Army (and not necessarily illegally), the legal actions resulting from their judgements had a radical effect on English law. The *War Cry* complained bitterly of magistrates and police acting against the Army as at Basingstoke in 1881, and refusing protection as at Poole in the same year. It was quick to point out where else this was happening around the world such as the very strong Scottish opposition (1881) and later in Scandinavia.[44] A frequent complaint, as in the earlier part of the century by the three major Nonconformist denominations, was that of magistrates going against the evidence and dismissing violent anti-Salvationists. The most blatant example was at Whitchurch in 1882. Some parallels were drawn in the *War Cry* with the arrival of the new denominations many decades before.

Although publicly denounced, several magistrates continued the policy of positive discrimination. The harsh words of M.P.'s failed to alter outcomes.

> "... these outrages of brutalisation are ... in many places ... connived at, if not permitted by the authorities who ought to be responsible for the peace and order of the community."[45]

This speech in March 1882 was prompted by the increasing number of Salvationists being jailed. Magistrates' cases and subsequent appeals concerning Weston-super-Mare and Whitchurch were to create legal history and force the more determined opponents onto a different legal tack but these two cases in 1882 were part of a number of cases including the Home Office, Parliament and the Law Courts.

In February 1881, the Secretary of State for the Home Department (Home Secretary), Sir William Harcourt, was telegraphed by Lieutenant-Colonel Pepper regarding

> "... the lawlessness and shameful proceedings that are nightly enacted in our streets (of Salisbury)."[46]

This marked the start of Home Office and Parliamentary involvement with the Salvation Army; such a well-connected military officer, although retired and a Salvationist, could not be ignored. An immediate Home Office inquiry was launched. The Mayor of Salisbury responded that it would have been too costly to employ sufficient policemen to protect such a small section of the community who should have the public good sense to confine themselves to their hall. He also noted the start of "The Society for the Suppression of Street Parading" aimed at stopping the Salvation Army.[47] After a meeting between the Mayor and the Home Secretary, it was decided that if the Chief of Police were to swear to J.P.'s that trouble would ensue from Salvation Army processions they could be banned. If the marches continued, first special constables and then the military could be used. This was based on advisory letters sent by two previous Home Secretaries when faced with possible serious rioting in the 1860s.[48] In putting his thoughts into writing, however, a close inspection of Sir William Harcourt's original papers shows that he was careful to cross out the word 'Salvationist' from the various drafts prepared by his aides and instead, put the general term processionists. This was presumably to avoid any charge of persecution. Processions did cease in Salisbury for a short time.[49]

The Home Secretary's correspondence makes it clear that he supported the stopping of processions if trouble were likely. This is particularly apparent in his letters to the Mayor of Basingstoke, the scene of some severe rioting.[50] The processioning continued here and further requests for protection were made to the Home Secretary but his advice remained — desist from marching because of the local ban for fear of trouble. However by October 1881, new magistrates had joined the Bench and the Salvationists gained more support. By a majority of five to two, the magistrates wrote to the Home Secretary advising him that once the Army's work hit the drink trade, this trade employed 'disorderly persons' to create disturbances. At their root lay the now ex-Mayor who, despite being the largest brewer in the town, should have acted with energy and fairness. They continued that the ban on processions was not wanted; now that the Mayor had left office, the encouraged 'rough-musicing' would perhaps cease with police arrests.[51] In fact it took until April 1882 for this to happen as the Watch Committee, dominated by the ex-Mayor, continually countermanded the magistrates' orders to the police for the protection of the Salvationists.

Although Sir William loudly proclaimed in correspondence[52] and in the House of Commons[53] that he could not direct but only advise and that such advice regarding processions was based on the actions of previous Home Secretaries, his words were regarded as an important guide. This was demonstrated in October 1881 when the Stamford magistrates wrote concerning an imminent Salvation Army 'invasion'. The Home Secretary's reply reiterated his advice to the Basingstoke magistracy; he stated that while

> ". . . Salvation Army processions, not being illegal in themselves . . . cannot be legally prevented,"

if police and magistrates felt such processions were going to endanger the peace of the town, they could be prevented.[54] This letter became public and a leader in *The Times* was severely critical of it[55] as was the *Solicitors' Journal* which stated:

> "*Prima facie,* a breach of the peace calls for repression and punishment of those guilty of it, and protection of those assaulted or threatened, not an interruption of the liberty of those against whom the violence is practised."[56]

In March 1882, the Home Secretary defended his letters in the House of Commons and also, by implication, the use by the Mayor of Basingstoke of a battery of artillery in the previous year to quell an Army 'riot'. Despite Salvation Army mythology to the contrary,[57] they were not needed and the military commander reported the mob to be in good temper.[58] The Army used such stories as this to show that the brewers would go to any lengths to stop them.

During early 1882 severe violence again broke out in Basingstoke as well as in Crediton, Weston-super-Mare, Chester, Oldham and

Whitchurch. It was matched in ferocity only by the anti-Irish feeling apparent in many parts of the country. Further anti-Army violence occurred in Guildford, Exeter and Gravesend. In addition magistrates at Poole and Eastbourne verbally abused the soldiers and General Booth while the Worthing magistrates refused to summons known Skeleton Army members. Of all these cases, the most important were at Weston-super-Mare and Whitchurch. This was because both were forced into the higher law courts.

The Queen's Bench Judgements

Although by sworn deposition Captain Beatty and two soldiers were walking at the head of a procession in Weston-super-Mare (March 1882) in silence, they were summonsed for, and found guilty of,

> "... unlawfully and tumultuously assembling to the disturbance of public peace."

Each was given three months imprisonment. Immediately a letter was despatched to the Home Secretary asking, on behalf of the Army, for an investigation.[59] The Home Secretary ascertained that the Salvationists were in breach of a local ban on processions but refused to comment on the decision in which he had indirectly advised. The case was brought before Mr. Justice Field and Mr. Justice Cave of the Queen's Bench (Beatty v. Gillbanks) on 13 June 1882.

A month earlier in the House of Lords, another member of the Queen's Bench, Lord Chief Justice Coleridge, declared during a debate on the Salvation Army

> "... that every Englishman had an absolute and unqualified right to go about his business and perform legal acts with the protection of the law; and he apprehended that walking through the streets in order and in procession, even if accompanied by music and the singing of hymns, was an absolutely lawful act, an act in the doing of which every subject had a right to be protected."[60]

The prosecution evidence in the Weston-super-Mare case was based on the fact that the Salvation Army had disregarded a notice issued by the magistrates not to march and had therefore given rise to the feared riot: *Ipso Facto* the Army were the guilty party.[61] Of this, and possibly remembering his colleague's speech in the House of Lords before a very receptive audience, Mr. Justice Cave remarked

> "So that other men's violence deprives men of their rights and renders what is peaceable unlawful."[62]

After a five-day hearing, the Bench found for the Army on 17 June 1882. The judgement appeared to state that the Army had the right to process in the streets and have full protection especially as it was their opponents who attacked first.[63]

The Weston-super-Mare case had taken three months to be dealt with because the magistrates had delayed by refusing to answer the case. At Whitchurch a similar delaying tactic was used. On 23 April 1882, the Captain, Lieutenant and two soldiers were arrested and later sentenced to one month's hard labour for attempting to start a march. They were led away handcuffed and although there were only 2,000 inhabitants in Whitchurch, none of the rioters were apprehended. Both these latter facts incited extreme criticism from many quarters nationally. The Whitchurch magistrates declined to provide their case upon the Army's appeal but in ordering them to do so, Lord Chief Justice Coleridge stated

> "To inflict the ignominious punishment of hard labour on men simply because they are religious enthusiasts is a thing not to be tolerated."[64]

While the case was awaiting appeal, the Home Secretary ordered that

> ". . . the prisoners should be treated with the greatest possible leniency during their confinement"[65]

Following the earlier decision regarding Weston-super-Mare, the Queen's Court quashed the conviction and gave costs against the magistrates.

The Law Officers' Opinion to the Home Secretary on these judgements was that his advice regarding Salvation Army processions needed amending.[66] He appears to have acted on this although most subsequent correspondence was destroyed. He did certainly act decisively against Honiton's only two magistrates, the Mayor and ex-Mayor, in December 1882. The latter magistrate had publicly and then in practice refused to convict anti-Army rioters. The Mayor later agreed with the Home Secretary that this was unjust but this agreement did not stop the Mayor being found partly to blame because he had sat on the same Bench listening. The Home Secretary discussed the matter with the Lord Chancellor who felt that both magistrates

> ". . . practically encouraged and afforded impunity to these disturbances."

The Lord Chancellor went further and wished to call for the resignation of the ex-Mayor from the Magistrates' Bench but, as both the ex-Mayor and the Mayor were Borough Justices *ex officio* by Act of Parliament, the Lord Chancellor did not have the necessary power or authority.[67]

Four further cases were brought before the Queen's Bench before 1891 on variants of the Beatty v. Gillbanks case. In the first two at Truro and Hastings during the latter part of 1883, Army officers were charged with disturbing the peace by playing musical instruments. In early 1884, both cases were found for the Army and in the latter instance, Lord Chief Justice Coleridge strongly reiterated the Beatty judgement and made a statement, well quoted at the time, that

"... it might as well be said Wesley had 'created a disturbance' when he was mobbed by Oxford undergraduates." [68]

The third appeal to the Court of the Queen's Bench came because of the arrest of the officer at Croydon for playing a musical instrument on a Sunday. Under a local byelaw only the military had permission to do this. The case was heard twelve months after the previous two. Again the appeal judgement, delivered on 3 May 1885, was for the Army and raised an important legal question concerning the reasonableness of a byelaw. Mr. Justice Hawkins remarked during judgement:

"The question therefore was whether the byelaw was or was not *ultra vires,* and he could only say that he had never known anything more unreasonable ... (for the appellant) ... had not caused any nuisance whatever." [69]

After 1878 a considerable number of Salvationists had been imprisoned, the figure for 1884 alone being in excess of 600. Despite the five Queen's Bench cases by 1885, imprisonment continued to be used as Salvationists generally refused to pay the fines imposed. Over a hundred places recorded prosecutions between 1886 and 1895 and it was not until a final unequivocal decision by the Queen's Bench in 1890 that such prosecutions died out.

The Queen's Bench case of 1 July 1890 was of public interest as it again involved Whitchurch, the scene of some considerable rioting and a Queen's Bench appeal eight years previously. In this village of under 2,000 inhabitants, 90 convictions of Salvationists had taken place over a twelve-month period based on the evidence of only three witnesses. *The Times* and other newspapers commented on the possible injustice here and on the apparent harshness of the sentences, especially in October 1889 when local 'persecution' was at its height. [70] The fact that the prisoners were generally handcuffed was also criticised. In addition it became apparent that many Salvationists in Whitchurch were employed by the magistrates who appear to have dismissed them from their jobs purely on religious grounds. Salvation Army leaders from London organised a grand procession of 2,500 people through the village as a protest against the persecution and the seeming inaction of the Home Secretary who had in fact sent letters reminding the magistrates of their impartiality.[71] Several senior Salvation Army leaders (and the bandmasters of the twelve bands 'on duty') were summonsed and found guilty of obstruction and riot during the procession. An appeal was lodged in the Queen's Bench. On 1 July 1890, Lord Chief Justice Coleridge again found for the Army, and categorically stated that the Army had a right to parade the Queen's highways providing they were not intentionally causing an obstruction.

Anti-Army Clauses in Local Acts

It is clear that a historical parallel had developed in the late 1880s with the actions by elements of the Establishment eighty years before. Then, 'the mob' had often been encouraged by the Establishment against religious deviancy and supported by many magistrates using Common Law. When mob use declined because of loosening social ties and the acceptance of the denominations by the local populations, new legal remedies were sought to destroy the deviants. This was helped by clerics becoming J.P.'s. Now the same was happening. As the Home Office was forcing local authorities to protect the Salvationists from 'the mob' who were perhaps losing interest in a not-so-new phenomenum, the Common Law could not be invoked, those authorities looked for new ways legally to prevent the Army from going onto the streets. Evidence suggests that it was not so much the clerics that were causing opposition but drink interest J.P.'s.

The new form of legal persecution came in the use of discretionary powers to Watch Committees and Local Boards afforded by Borough byelaws and provisions in Local Acts. Although the first Queen's Bench revisions were taken by the Army as a clear order for the protection of Salvationists, Professor Harry Street believes the Bench did not make it clear if a general rule of freedom to march in the streets was being laid down.[72] This only came with successive judgements, especially the Whitchurch decision of 1890. Some authorities as in Guildford used the 'loop-hole' and publicly warned the Salvationists about the risks in marching. The former had to be reminded of their legal duties by a Home Office memorandum which itself was put in the form of a public notice, (September 1882). Other authorities petitioned the Home Secretary for a general discretionary power for use against the Army but it was never granted.

The use of byelaws and Local Acts continually appeared between 1882 and 1891 and was the equivalent of the refusal to obey the Act of Toleration and the legal persecution of 70 and 80 years before. Ignoring the earlier remarks concerning byelaws, made by Mr. Justice Hawkins in the Queen's Court, at least two authorities produced

Local Acts containing clauses deliberately aimed at hindering the Salvation Army.[73] This new direction in legal 'persecution' led to protracted wrangling in the law courts and Parliament. The 38th Section of the Torquay Harbour and District Act, 1886, stated

> "No procession shall take place on Sunday in any street or public place in the borough, accompanied by any instrumental music, fireworks, discharging of cannon, firearms, or other disturbing noise, provided that the foregoing prohibition shall not apply to any of Her Majesty's Navy, Military or volunteer forces."

This law was freely broken by many societies and bands but only the Salvation Army suffered heavy fines. This continued for two years before a petition of allegedly over a quarter of a million people and including many leading Nonconformists, led the pro-Army Henry Fowler M.P. to bring in a Bill to repeal the clause (4 June 1888). The Bill was successful and with little opposition, the clause was repealed on 8 August. Bath Town Council was at the time considering adding such a byelaw but because of the controversy surrounding Torquay, it was unanimously dropped.

Although it was not widely known at the time outside Eastbourne, Clause 169 of their Town Improvement Act, 1885, was aimed expressly at

> ". . . preventing the Salvation Army from conducting its usual musical processions should it extend its operations to Eastbourne."[74]

This was later admitted in a letter to *The Times* by Councillor Chambers who helped draft the original bill.[75] The Eastbourne Corps was actually opened on 9 January 1890 but the first conflict did not take place until 8 September of that year when the officer and some soldiers were summonsed for singing in the street. The *Brighton Argus* was able to report that due to good legal representation, the Council was '. . . ignominiously defeated.' By June 1891, up to 30 soldiers at a time were being convicted of breaking the Act and many were fined £5 or a month's imprisonment. The latter was always accepted in what had become traditional Army policy. Bloody violence involving mobs of up to 7,000 people; anti-Army papers such as *The Eastbourne Scorpion*; police baton charges; increasing numbers of imprisonments (making the 'welcome home' rallies a well-practised routine); and columns of newspaper reports, especially those in *The Times*,[76] provoked questions in the House of Commons on 8 June 1891. Over the next few weeks, Mr. J. Stuart M.P. (Shoreditch, Hoxton), pursued the fact that as Clause 169 was identical to the now-repealed Torquay Clause 38, it in turn should be repealed. A number of M.P.'s seem to have taken a lively interest in this question. Not only did they hear about Clause 169 through the House of Commons, but many received affidavits and letters to testify to the persecution. Some members had even become involved through the process of the law. On 23 July 1891, Herbert H. Asquith, Q.C., M.P., acted for the defence of Salvationists in Eastbourne. Occasionally appeals followed certain of the convictions and consistently the High Court of the Queen's Bench found for the Salvation Army, reinforcing the Whitchurch and earlier decisions. The Parliamentary debates lasted until 10 March 1892 when Salvationists desisted from marching in the town because of a favourable second reading to a repeal Bill. The Act became law on 1 September 1892. Its importance was in proving that this new form of legal opposition was not tenable in a democratic society. The Parliamentary Committee who discussed the repeal felt that the anti-Army Mayor and Town Clerk had deliberately prepared a legal 'trap'for the Army by this Clause. The Committee stated that the Clause had to be revoked by a repeal bill because an Englishman's basic right to have ". . . liberty of speech and liberty of procession" was unassailable. *The Times* however suggested that the repeal came about not for such noble motives but because a General Election was imminent and the Eastbourne votes of Army sympathisers were important to the ruling Conservative party.[77]

Apart from the constant rebuffs given to both the invocation of Common Law and the insertion of anti-Army clauses in Local Acts by 1892, two other factors were equally important in the decline of reaction against the Salvation Army. The concerted opposition, orchestrated by the popular press and the *War Cry,* appears to have developed from a genuine fear of the effectiveness of the Army. The drink trade inspired some of the mob reaction and much of the legal opposition. Possibly because the effectiveness of the Army in slowing the drink trade was not as great as feared by them, this pressure relaxed. The second factor was that while on the widest social level the Army disturbed the life of a town to varying degrees and challenged social and legal influence in such a public manner that town councils and magistrates courts openly disagreed, the Salvation Army was becoming accepted as a religious denomination.

The severest 'rough-musicing' came in southern England and therefore it is not surprising that the cases brought before the Queen's Bench were from these areas. In the north, the little real violence that greeted the Army was mainly found in the large towns. Although occasionally severe, such as in January 1882 in Sheffield, the police quickly broke up the unorganised mobs. Possibly the quite considerable townward mobility in northern England led to new generally accepted ideas on behaviour and thus a decline in 'rough-musicing'. Certainly the northern drink trade was not in a powerful position within the local authorities as its members vied with industrialists and others for such positions as Justices of the Peace. In addition the Army may not have been as effective against the public houses in the bigger cities. In the generally smaller southern and western towns the reverse was true. The mobs were encouraged by several local authorities upon which sat many brewers and publicans whose trade was severely threatened by the Army. The conservative ties and homogeneous traditions allowed these local authorities to sustain grass-roots 'rough-musicing' which, when it did begin to fade, also allowed more legal anti-Army actions to be attempted.

VI. WRITTEN OPPOSITION

Union with the Church of England?

A considerable amount of written material was generated in 1882 by the distinct possibility of union between the Church of England and the Salvation Army. The background to this was the interest all religious groups had shown in the origin and development of the Army. From 1878 the *War Cry* carried reports of other denominations supporting General Booth. Those most active in this support were the Nonconformists, mainly the Methodists and especially the Wesleyans. In 1880 Booth was invited to address the latter's Annual Conference and found considerable sympathy for his work. One Wesleyan however wrote a pamphlet attacking the Movement on the basis that there was no real religion in them.

> "Their services are frequently a travesty of music-hall entertainment."[78]

The Baptists generally supported the Army and both senior men in England, Charles Haddon Spurgeon and John Clifford, allowed Salvationists the use of Baptist pulpits.[79] Members of the Church of England were only occasionally mentioned as either for or against but generally they seemed to reserve public comment. Several prominent Church leaders did however lend support to the Army as exemplified by the Bishop of Carlisle in October 1880 in a public statement.[80] A number of clergymen also invited the Army into their churches for joint services although newspapers often felt the Army's style could be less 'enthusiastic'. One example was when the Nottingham Salvation Army Corps went to St. Mary's Church on 21 November 1881. The *Nottingham Express* noted how the hymn

> ". . . 'How sweet the name of Jesus sounds' was sung to the tune 'Auld Lang Syne' conducted by the Salvation Army captain standing on a seat and keeping time with his arms."[81]

Church of England opinion on the Salvation Army appears to have been generally ambiguous although in local and national newspapers, both pro- and anti-Army feelings were strongly represented through to the late 1870s and entire 1880s. In the early 1880s there was a growing belief among Churchmen that the Salvation Army was not only an apparently effective socio-religious force in its own right but one that could be harnessed by the Established Church to make up for its deficiencies. This desire for union was led by Archbishop William Thomson, 'the People's Archbishop',[82] who wrote to William Booth on 18 April 1882 requesting informal discussions. In this he was encouraged by the Archbishop of Canterbury (from 1868 to 1882), Campbell Tait. The latter's religious and political belief lay midway between the Anglo-Catholics and the Evangelicals. This made him the ideal leader of the Broad Church Party who stood for a national church encompassing all denominations.[83]

Archbishop Thomson's open pro-Army stance caused a representative of the Lower House of the Convocation of Canterbury to present to the Upper House a *gravamen et reformandum* concerning the Salvation Army (10 May 1882). This requested their Lordships to

> ". . . ascertain the tenets and practices of this society. . . consider how far it is possible to attach it to the Church. .. (and). . .generally to advise the clergy as to their duty in reference to it."[84]

On 12 May the Upper House of the Convocation considered the requests and resolved to appoint a committee to discuss union with General Booth. Dr. Benson was appointed to open the discussions. Four days later, during a debate in the House of Lords on the Salvation Army, the Archbishop of Canterbury declared his full support for the aims of the Army and hoped that the Movement might do a great deal of good among 'uncultivated minds.'[85]

It is clear from Dr. Benson's diaries that both he and Dr. Tait were keen for a union to take place.[86] General Booth seriously considered the question for the Established Church was offering very advantageous terms in the level of autonomy and financial assistance. The difficulty on Booth's side was that the Army was rapidly becoming international and the reaction to any degree of union to the Established English Protestant Church might prejudice his efforts. On the Church's side, the prominence of women preachers in a position equal to that of men and the non-use of the Sacraments brought heavy criticism, not least from the *Church Times*. In 1883 at the Convocation of Canterbury, Dr. Benson (now himself the Archbishop of Canterbury), reported that, despite some discussions with General Booth taking place, the committee *per se* had not met. The conflicting nature of reports about the Army's teachings, the disdain of many churchmen for the Army's 'novel methods', and suggestions of immorality led to the discharge of the committee by nine votes to four on 10 April.[87]

Although General Booth had come to believe that union with the Church of England was impractical, he wanted to justify the Salvation Army in the eyes of the Church. Booth was therefore disappointed in the widely reported statements made during the Upper House's discussion. On 11 April he wrote

> "Our earnest desire to maintain friendly relationships with the Authorities of the Church has not in the least degree changed. . . what I regret and would fain avert, if not too late, is. . . that the scandalous reports circulated against (us), find ready credence with the Authorities in the Church."

To appease the concern expressed in the Upper House about the Army's teachings, methods and supposed encouragement in immorality, General Booth sent a considerable amount of literature to Dr. Benson, explained at length the Army's phraseology and techniques, and instructed Bramwell Booth to hold an immediate official inquiry into the Bishop of Oxford's statements on immorality within the Army. Bramwell as Chief of the Staff, sent a form entitled "The Salvation Army and Charges of Immorality" accompanied by a letter of instruction to all corps officers within the United Kingdom. The letter ordered the officers to

> ". . . put down as many cases as you really know of in which it might reasonably be thought that the birth of an illegitimate child was due to the attendance of the Parents at our meetings."[88]

The returned forms showed 449 stations questioned with 28 cases of illegitimate children within the Movement's history. At the next Convocation of Canterbury, in July 1883, these figures were presented and discussed. The Bishop of Oxford felt that the number of cases were conservatively estimated.[89]

The breakdown of Church-Salvation Army discussions did not deter the Church from officially forming its own Church Army. Several localised initiatives imitating the Salvation Army were being attempted by Christmas 1882. At Christmas 1880 a Church Gospel Army commenced at Richmond in Surrey under the leadership of the Reverend Evan Hopkins. In mid-1882 Wilson Carlile established a Church Army at Walworth in south-east London. The Church Army imitated the Salvation Army in its uniform, songs, terminology and open-air meetings.[90] At Christmas 1882 another organisation, the Church Salvation Army, was being formed in Berkshire under the leadership of 'General' Swift. A Church Mission Army had also been established in Bristol by this time. Wilson Carlile's organisation proved the strongest of the four and gradually received support from the Church authorities. Like its counterpart, the Church Army's open-air activities were often the subject of physical and verbal abuse and they were the butt of much amusement for the working-class.[91] As well as this imitation, and increasingly in and from the 1880s, the Salvation Army continued to receive generally sympathetic treatment from the Church and Chapels.

The theology of the Salvation Army, in particular its position on the Sacraments and the role of women, was highlighted during the discussions on union. Booth's theological views created considerable interest throughout the 1880s and 1890s. In the Christian Mission the question of infant baptism was generally ignored while adult baptism was considered to be signified by a spiritual regeneration with no use of ceremony or water. The Lord's Supper was given a dignified place in the services when it was used but, by mid-1882, barely two dozen stations continued it. Those that did gave it no consecration but

> ". . . break bread and pass it around with a cup of currant jelly-water in Remembrance."[92]

General Booth enjoyed the mysticism of the latter ceremony and wished to retain it. He was however persuaded by his wife and several of his closest advisers such as Railton, who had grown up without experiencing the Sacraments, that rather than baptism with water a baby could be 'dedicated' to God's service and safe-keeping while for anyone over the age of six or seven, there was only the baptism of the Holy Spirit. This meant conversion from a sinful life and a move towards Entire Sanctification of the soul, that is, an attempt at Holy living, not the radical idea of a person being able to reach a state of grace in God's sight such that whatever he did thereafter, he could not sin. As far as the Lord's Supper was concerned, Booth became convinced that Christ should be remembered before every meal and not just a ceremonial one; that as the churches disagreed over the nature of both Sacraments it would be best not to have any; and that as the only preconditions of conversion were repentance and faith, no Sacrament was necessary. In this last idea, William Booth was expressing a belief already held by the Society of Friends, (Quakers).

General Booth's views on the Sacraments only became crystallized during 1881 and 1882 but the position regarding women was clear from 1865. After the Movement became uniformed and women were sent to open stations without male escorts, the question of female ministry became of considerable public interest. Undoubtedly Catherine Booth convinced her husband of the equality of women in God's sight.[93] However many churches and others felt women should ". . . be of a retiring nature (taking) no *prominent* part"[94] and certainly a number of theological arguments could be put up against the use of women leaders. Whatever these arguments, Josephine Butler realised that without this enthusiastic and usually young "surplus woman-hood", the Army would not have spread so rapidly.[95]

1885: Maiden Tribute of Modern Babylon

Against the background of still continuing violence and legal struggles, the Army almost accidentally became involved in one of the great social questions of the 1880s, prostitution. In 1881 'rescue rooms' were established and in 1884, a house was rented in Whitechapel as a 'refuge'. The consistent failure of the Bill to raise the age of consent and thus help to alleviate child prostitution, combined with the Army's own evidence, caused them to investigate fully the extent of the problem in London. Their findings and a visit from W. T. Stead, the Editor of the *Pall Mall Gazette,* decided Booth, with the help of Mrs. Josephine Butler and the Chamberlain of the City of London, to authorise the buying of a young girl from her mother and her removal from the country.

Although such precautions as informing the Archbishop of Canterbury and Cardinal Manning had been taken, the *Pall Mall Gazette*'s revelations of 6 July 1885 caused a social and political storm. Under the title 'Maiden Tribute to Modern Babylon', Stead detailed, among other "explicit sexual revelations", the actions taken.[96] The paper caused an immediate furore with Booth opening International Headquarters as a distribution point and thus circumventing W. H. Smith's and other station bookstalls which refused *en masse* to take the publication; copies reaching half a crown each; George Bernard Shaw publicly offering to carry copies and peddle them in the streets; arrests of newsellers for selling obscene literature; and a large crowd besieging the newspaper's offices.

The quickly-organised and widely-reported trial of Bramwell Booth, W. T. Stead and others, rested on taking away the child without her father's consent. This was proven although Stead later proved that the girl was illegitimate and the man claiming to be her father was an imposter. Booth was acquitted but sentences of one to six months were imposed on the others. The resulting publicity from the 'revelations' forced the government to resurrect the Bill and on 14 August 1885, the Criminal Law Amendment Act raised the age of consent to 16. Such publicity also helped draw further attention to the Salvation Army but as well as gaining more supporters, there must have been many who questioned the strange activities of the Movement if such unusual actions as 'kidnapping' were a part of it, no matter how laudable the motive.

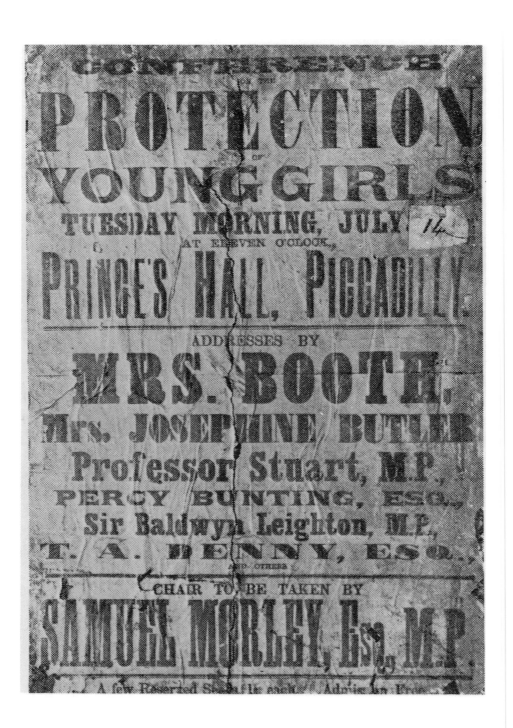

The reaction to the prostitution question gave fresh impetus to the numerous experiments in social work, many of them the creation of Commissioner Frank Smith (later an M.P.).[97] On 20 October 1890 William Booth published his *In Darkest England and the Way Out*. This was a radical series of social ideas, worked out between W. T. Stead who actually wrote the book, Smith and Booth. It was however widely greeted by both friendly and unfriendly observers with the suggestion that the Army was becoming a social organisation.

> ". . . in an attempt to minister to the social groups which neither the churches nor the Army itself had so far much influenced."[98]

Some felt that the Army had to develop social schemes because

> "The campaign of purely emotional religion in the East of London was a failure."[99]

Others contended that the scheme was genuinely motivated by Booth because he

> ". . . became convinced that poverty itself was a grave impediment."[100]

Ex-Commissioner Nicol wrote that in the latter 1880s, the cessation of persecution had left the Army without a theme for exciting public sympathy and mainly for this reason, attendance was down. Other evidence for a decline in membership is the decrease in sales of the *War Cry* from 350,000 in 1883 to under 290,000 in 1890.[101] In 1887 corps were warned to move to cultivate the ground they were in rather than 'attack' new ground.[102] Most critical of all was the *British Weekly* which, when analysing its census of religion in 1887, expressed strong disappointment at the low number of Salvationists (53,591) attending corps in London. Although the *British Weekly* failed to realise it, the figures submitted by the Army were in fact vastly inflated. Dr. Hugh McLeod has recalculated and found only 42,205 Salvationists attending.[103] Similar evidence of stagnation at this time in the provinces has been collected by K. Inglis.

The highly-detailed social scheme and remedy to the British Salvation Army's malaise set out plans for city, farm and overseas colonies, labour bureaux, refuse collections, marriage bureaux and aspects covering all spheres of life.[104] For twelve months the book excited considerable interest. In it Booth stated that he required £100,000 to commence this million-pound scheme and within three months this money had been subscribed. There were many influential supporters. The Queen, *The Times*, and several leading church, social and political figures favoured it. Cardinal Manning, a number of

The Headquarters of the city colony, 20 and 22 (formerly
272) Whitechapel Road, London.

Some of the dormitories at the 3,200-acre Hadleigh Farm Colony, Essex.

Church of England Bishops and numerous Nonconformists openly supported the scheme while others such as the Marquis of Queensberry also strongly approved. Conversely there was considerable opposition in the form of pamphlets,[105] the Charity Organisation Society (hereafter C.O.S.) who attacked William Booth's continual indiscriminate charity, and from T. H. Huxley who, like the C.O.S., detested the Army. Huxley, in a protracted correspondence to *The Times* in opposition to their generally pro-Booth leading articles, condemned Booth's religion as ". . . Corybantic Christianity"[106] and considered the 'In Darkest England Scheme' ". . . socialism in disguise."[107] *The Methodist Times* also thought that the General was embracing socialism because he had realised.

> ". . . that Christianity must save society as well as the individual. (He has therefore) accepted Social Christianity."[108]

There was a considerable degree of truth in this, for five articles concerning 'Sociology' appeared in succession in the *War Cry* during late 1890. The basic tenet was that it was the social duty of those with money to share their wealth to ensure fairer treatment for the lower classes. However these articles were penned by Commissioner Frank Smith who had given Booth in literary and practical form most of the ideas for *In Darkest England and the Way Out*. Once he resigned from the Army, the radical neo-political ideology gave way to the more immediately practical implementation of some of the less radical ideas such as a Farm Colony.

Ultimately the scheme foundered on lack of money and organisation. A large number of potential subscribers had doubtless been discouraged by public opposition. Smith's resignation and his subsequent bitter arguments with the Army, conducted mainly through *The Times*, made many doubt the Army's firm footing as perhaps did the bitter Eastbourne controversy of 1891 when the continuing imprisonments must have seemed a serious blow to the Army. Commissioner Smith resigned ostensibly because he was not given the promised control over the Social Reform Wing and therefore the implementation of the 'Darkest England' schemes. In fact, the autocratic Booth probably felt uncomfortable with this radical socialist. A clash of wills was inevitable so Smith was replaced by the very pro-Booth Commissioner Elijah Cadman who knew little if anything about social work.[109]

Newspapers, Journals and Pamphlets

Inevitably the entry of the Salvation Army into a town was reported in the local newspapers. This was encouraged by William Booth and one section of his *Orders and Regulations* (1878) was entitled 'Use of Newspapers'.

> "Notices in newspapers of any kind are always of great service. A capable C.O. will therefore take care to be published in them as soon as possible ... even if they write violently against us, the result is increased attendance and benefit."[110]

This policy achieved considerable success for throughout the country, from 1878 to the late 1880s, local and national newspapers frequently devoted entire columns to the activities of the Army, especially where a degree of opposition occurred. Reports of meetings were usually submitted to the newspapers by the officers but frequently editors sent journalists to discover just what went on. A journalist for the *Sheffield Independent* commented on the strangeness of Army meetings but concluded

> "... it is not for me to ridicule their services or scoff at the novel means they use to bring sinners to repentance."[111]

Another, writing in the *Manchester Evening News*, reported that the conversion of a notable drunkard was attracting crowds to the meetings. When a particularly interesting incident or series of incidents occurred, such as the Home Secretary corresponding with the magistrates of Honiton, several columns of the major local paper were usually devoted to the background and details. There were very few instances where the local newspapers took an anti-Army stance and only in two cases possibly incited further rioting.[112] They were however only heightening local tensions and were not actually creating the problem. It is interesting to note that both newspapers were in the conservative south and it may be conjectured that the editors and/or owners were perhaps socially intimate with members of the drink trade.

Generally the editorials and reports of both local and national newspapers mixed criticism with praise. No strong regional or political bias is discernible either for or against the Army in the secular press. *The Times* gave several reports of the violence against the Salvation Army in various towns and considerably more coverage to the various legal trials. The *Daily Telegraph*, which always aimed at human interest stories, faithfully reproduced various pro- and anti-Army views. Among the former was the Bishop of Rochester who asked for prayers for the Army's work.[113] However, the most noted secular newspaper in relation to the Movement was the influential evening *Pall Mall Gazette*. W. T. Stead joined it in 1880 and, as a devoted admirer of Booth, continually published material on the Army's work. A decade later, as editor of the powerful *Review of Reviews*, he was able to obtain considerable space for the 'In Darkest England' Scheme.

The religious press also scrutinized the Army carefully. *The Methodist Times* considered the Movement

"... a rude repetition of the work of Wesley and Whitfield."[114]

In considering the increase in the numbers of Methodists between 1879 and 1881, the *Church Times* felt that the Army was entirely responsible.[115] In the early 1880s *The Christian* stridently called for the government to protect the Salvation Army,[116] and numerous other examples exist in all the Protestant religious newspapers. Even the Roman Catholic *The Tablet* gave some qualified support.[117] As in their secular counterparts, innumerable pro- and anti-Army letters and comments were published in the religious press but overall there is a balance of criticism and praise.

Two unofficial newspapers were printed, aimed directly against the Salvation Army. In Honiton, *The Skeleton* slandered Salvationists, their supporters, and their aims and actions. Priced one penny, its five or six known editions retold stories about the Salvation Army and generally parodied the *War Cry*. Although the venture was short-lived, copies did circulate in the south-west during the winter of 1882 to 1883. The second 'newspaper' came nearly a decade later, again in the south. *The Eastbourne Scorpion* was also priced at one penny and had the same aims as *The Skeleton* in slandering the Army in an attempt to make it appear ridiculous. There were very few issues and these probably did more good than harm by keeping the Salvation Army to the forefront of people's minds.

In addition to the newspapers, various journals took an interest in the Army, the main example being the *Contemporary Review*. At various points during the 1880s and 1890s it ran articles on the Salvation Army, written either by Salvationists such as William Booth or by those with some degree of religious or social interest in the Movement. These latter ranged from the Roman Catholic Cardinal Manning to the very pro-Army Francis Peek. Each writer's views on the Salvation Army differed considerably. Manning particularly objected to the 'irreverent' literature produced by the Army. He and another writer, R. T. Davidson, felt *The Little Soldier* was the worst of the publications as it encouraged children to react against their 'unsaved' parents and therefore break up homes. Conversely Peek praised the Movement for its authority and methods of revivalism.

The other means of communication that reached a considerable number of people, albeit generally those more interested in religious subjects, was pamphlets. Several of these were avowedly anti-Army and considered the services to degenerate "... into the mere exuberance of animal spirits."[118] Others considered William Booth to dance his officers and soldiers like "marionettes at the end of a string."[119] In the latter case, La Comtesse Agenor de Gasparin compared William Booth to Ignatius de Loyola for, she felt, they both saw military despotism, autocracy and subjugation as the keys to the saving of the world.[120]

NOW, MR. BOOTH, LET US KNOW WHAT YOU ARE GOING TO DO WITH ALL
THIS MONEY!

A typical cartoon from 1882. It was published in *The Entr'acte* and raises a question
which was very topical in the 1880s.

Another 1882 cartoon, this time published in *Vanity Fair*.

The reverse of these anti-Army pamphlets generally came from prominent supporters. Despite some grandiose claims that the Salvation Army could save England

"... from the anarchic condition that Ireland is in and France was,"[121]

Admiral Fishbourne's pamphlet was an attempt to explain the need for the Salvation Army. He felt that regardless of some of the emotional excesses of the Army, it had a far-reaching work of spiritual regeneration to do. Another pamphleteer was Major William Corbridge. He used graphic pictures and prose in an attempt to convince readers to take shares in *The Salvation Mine* or to travel the right train on *The Up Line to Heaven*.[122]

VII. CONCLUSION

When physical and verbal opposition to the Christian Mission and the more easily identifiable Salvation Army occurred it was mainly as a reaction to their dramatic entry into an area and their novel methods of preaching religion. In the south of England, the 'rough-musicing' tradition reacted almost as strongly as it did to the Methodists, Congregationalists and Baptists some eighty years previously. In some of the relatively small close-knit southern towns, the authorities encouraged this. When they found that it was having increasingly little effect on the Army, more legal remedies were attempted. In the north of England, interaction between geographically mobile individuals from various backgrounds gave rise and credence to new ideas on behaviour and respectability. The Army therefore apparently found a generally friendlier reception in the Midlands and the north compared with the south.

The acceptance of the Salvation Army was eased by the usually friendly reception of the church and chapels; the support of some prominent local and national businessmen and politicians; and the constant publicity engendered from 1878. The opposition and its exploitation by the Army through pamphlets, the *War Cry*, books and mass rallies attracted people to join the Movement although their allegiance was not always lengthy. As the membership figures declined after the mid-1880s, so Booth turned increasingly to social schemes such as the abolition of child prostitution in 1885 and the reforms of working conditions in the late 1880s. This initial growth and then decline needed a refining of ideas and these came with the crystallization of the Army's limited theology in 1881 and 1882 and, due to the increasing number of social 'crusades' embarked upon, the 'In Darkest England' Scheme of 1890.

William Booth acted as a catalyst, organiser and orator for the many ideas which came to him and he accepted. He was certainly the "... autocrat of all Salvationists," but the Salvation Army's development was as much other people's ideas as his own leadership. In ideology and theology, Mrs. Catherine Booth and George Scott Railton convinced the Founder of the value of non-Sacramental worship, while clearly Frank Smith and W. T. Stead were working hard to convince him to bring about their own Christian ideals. All three men had visions, Smith about better pay and conditions for the working-class, Stead about using the poor to increase Imperial Unity by founding colonies all over the world,[123] and Booth came to believe in using the latter two ideals to bring about the world's conversion. Both Smith and Stead broke off their above connections with the Movement, but they had seen it through its struggling formative years. Their social ideas, the support from sympathisers and law courts in general but the higher courts in particular, and the decline in 'rough-musicing' allowed the Army to become an accepted part of society.

CHAPTER FIVE

POPLAR, LONDON: A CASE-STUDY

I. BACKGROUND

Although Victorian Poplar was considered to be in London's East End, it was technically situated in the County of Middlesex. The Parish of All Saints, Poplar, consisted of Poplar, Orchard House, the Isle of Dogs, Millwall and Cubitt Town. For Poor Law and sanitary matters (Superintendent Registrar's District and District Board of Works) Poplar was united with the Parishes of Bow and Bromley. Unless otherwise specified, Poplar in this book refers to the Parish of All Saints. The Parish grew up around the main shipyards and docks built by the West India Dock Company in 1802 and the East India Company in 1806. Both companies merged in 1838 and the docks established Poplar's predominance as Victorian London's shipping centre. This was reinforced in 1868 when the Millwall Freehold Land and Dock Company opened 184 acres of docks on the Isle of Dogs.

In the nineteenth century the Parish population increased by 1,198% and the Registration District by 1,939% (Table 5.1). The increase was most marked from mid-century and was clearly greater than anywhere else in the East End. Its main causes were

> ". . . the coming of railways, the chemical industry and the building of the Millwall Dock."[1]

In 1861, direct and ancillary work generated by the increasingly large docks accounted for 38.62% of the occupations of the Registration District's total male population.[2] The chemical industry was an increasingly large employer as was the domestic and factory match and cigar work, the latter using an essentially female and child work-force. Poplar was in fact noted as a match-making centre, especially after Bryant and May established their factory in Fairfield Road, Poplar. Other industries becoming increasingly dominant within Poplar, apart from the docks, railways and chemicals, were building and clothing while the remainder of the work mirrored that found in the East End generally. Sweated trades with all the accompanying ills began to boom in Poplar as labour was available and the City was tightening up its health regulations. White lead factories, a mint, and manure from blood manufacturers were some of the 'new trades' in

TABLE 5.1

The Population of Poplar 1801–1901

Year	Parish Total	Registration District Total
1801	4,493	8,278
1811	7,708	13,548
1821	12,223	18,932
1831	16,849	25,066
1841	20,342	31,122
1851	28,384	47,162
1861	43,529	79,196
1871	48,611	116,277
1881	55,077	156,510
1891	56,383	166,748
1901	58,334	168,822

Sources: *Census of England and Wales. 1801–1901. Population.*
Respective Vol.I.'s.

this part of the East End alongside others such as sewing, match-making, tailoring, and boot and shoe manufacturing.[3]

Some industries though were very much on the wane. In the East End and particularly Poplar, silk-weaving had become well established during the eighteenth century. However, as with ship-building, both industries collapsed between 1830 and 1870 as neither could

"... surmount the technological threats posed by industrialisation."

Numbers employed in the silk-weaving industry fell from 50,000 in 1824 to 9,500 in 1860 and 3,300 in 1880. Those unemployed who remained in the area joined the casual labour market, usually at the dock gate.[4] A similar decline can be seen in Poplar's sugar-refining and engineering industries. Both of these "succumbed to provincial competition".[5] The ship-building collapse was more sudden and catastrophic. An unparalleled speculative boom during the early 1860s raised the number of shipbuilding employees in Poplar from 13,000 in 1861 to 27,000 in 1865. The foundations for such expansion were not secure; the increasing use of iron in ships, the maintenance of traditional working methods and high wages needed

"Only a slight push. . .to throw the industry headlong into a chronic depression."

The crash of the Overend and Gurney Bank in December 1866 provided this 'push' which immediately resulted in 30,000 destitute in

Poplar alone. Craftsmen and tradesmen became casual labourers and the industry never recovered in the area to any extent.[6]

The ever increasing population of Poplar suffered enormously in periods of 'abnormal distress'.

"The most spectacular example of such distress had occurred in East London in the period 1866-9, when a combination of industrial collapse and bad weather created a crisis of such intensity that contemporaries feared a breakdown of the poor law there".[7]

This crisis, which coincided with an outbreak of cholera, produced the utmost extremes of poverty. Reports of death through starvation occurred in the local newspapers[8] despite funds and appeals for food being set up. Early in 1867 the local and national authorities debated rises in the Poor Law Rate, centralising these rates with perhaps a ½d levy over the whole metropolis, or emigration schemes. The latter were organised in Poplar from June 1867 and among those leaving over the next two years, mainly for Canada, were members of the Christian Mission. This was not an effective solution for following a severe drought in 1868, the Poor Law Rate reached 1/10 in the £ by Christmas, the highest in the Metropolitan area. This rise was exacerbated by the people from central London moving into Poplar District as the City and the West End were redeveloped. This accordingly helped shape Poplar's and the East End's "hopeless poverty".[9] Exploitation by landlords packing large families into one room and charging extortionate rents of up to half a man's weekly wage fuelled the poverty. The District population leapt up because of migration, an excess of births over deaths totalling 22,082 between 1871 and 1881, and immigration from Ireland and Europe (particularly Jews). The latter quickly became involved in the sweated trades. Many immigrants were already established in Poplar by the 1870s, most notably negroes, mulattoes, Chinese and Indians.

Such was the severity of the "abnormal distress"[10] that not only were the working-class affected but also members of other classes. The workhouse in particular bore the brunt of this poverty but there was considerable disquiet amongst and about the London Poor Law Unions with regard to how to deal with the crisis of the late 1860s and how to reduce the outdoor relief. It was feared that

". . . the large and chaotic London workhouses were still too attractive to incorrigible loafers."[11]

Thus in March 1872, the Local Government Board issued

"an order under which the Poplar Union was to designate its workhouse as being for the reception of the able-bodied only."

An agreement was formulated, first with Stepney and then all over London, for Poplar workhouse to take able-bodied essentially in exchange for the sick and infirm.[12]

The Poplar workhouse experiment, with its severe labour test and harsh conditions, lasted for nearly twenty years. However, by the later 1880s, the regime was no longer administered in such a strict fashion, possibly because of the changing social attitudes that saw poverty and especially unemployment less as an individual failing and more as a social problem. In 1892, William Crooks, a former workhouse child inmate, and George Lansbury, one time junior soldier in the Salvation Army and later a leading Labour politician, were elected to the Poplar Board of Guardians. Together they set out to establish new principles for workhouse operations. Outdoor relief became 'more open-handed' and as a result,

> "Under the Crooks-Lansbury regime the Poplar Guardians became nationally famous for their generosity."[13]

Known as 'Poplarism', the word "became a term of admiration and abuse".[14] However it was dealt with, a large proportion of Poplar's inhabitants suffered to varying degrees, much due to the fact that many were unskilled and casual labourers. The labour was

> ". . . dependent on the docks, transport and haulage, railways and manufacturing industries such as clothing, food, jam-making, matches, etc. Even engineering, Poplar's most skilled, best paid industry was prone to irregularity."[15]

It was essentially the unskilled and casual labourer who always fell foul of the changeable economic conditions most notably (after the distress of 1866-9), that of the winter of 1879, the period 1884-7, and 1892-5.

Poplar's endemic poverty of the late 1860s forced the poor to seek any possible salvation. One avenue was trade unionism, although this was not a viable option for many until the return of economic prosperity. In a bid to protect themselves against a range of 'evils' from low pay to job insecurity, many waterfront workers became unionised in the successful strike action of the early 1870s. A similarly successful waterfront strike twenty years earlier had not resulted in unionisation.

> "This time, however (unions were) established on a large scale."[16]

Another possible avenue of assistance was religion but by the 1860s, religion in Poplar was for the very small minority. Before 1817, Poplar came under Stepney Parish but after a long struggle, separatism

TABLE 5.2

Religious Accommodation and Attendance in Poplar, 1851

Denominations	Number of Buildings	Sittings	Number Attending		
			M	A	E
Protestant Churches:					
Church of England	5	4852	2190	1290	617
Independents...............	3	2693	1586	—	1485
Baptists	2	820	550	—	547
Wesleyan Methodists.........	5	2537	958	—	930
Mixed and Undefined	2	629	375	169	489
Other Christian Churches:					
Roman Catholics............	2	408	1340	—	600
Latter Day Saints...........	1	50	25	50	25
Totals.....................	20	11989	7024	1509	4693

Note: 1. Population was 47,162.
2. Under 'Number Attending' are the figures for morning, afternoon and evening services attended.

Source: Census of Religious Worship 1851. Table H. p.cclxxviii.

was achieved and a parish church was consecrated on 3 July 1823. By the 1860s,

> "Since the erection of the parish church, however, the population has so rapidly increased that it has been found necessary to establish a number of district churches."

There were three in Poplar, two in Cubitt Town, and one in Millwall by 1870.

The Census of Religious Worship provides a variety of information for the area (Table 5.2). 43.46% of the seats in Poplar's churches and chapels were free (5,189 as opposed to 6,750 appropriated making a total of 11,939). Despite this total only 25.42% of the population could be accommodated and Poplar ranked tenth out of 615 Registration Districts for providing the least accommodation.[17] These figures were low even for this apparently religiously indifferent period. The Wesleyan Methodists had the same number of chapels as the Church of England had churches although both the accommodation and attendance totals were approximately twice as high for the latter. The overall evidence however suggests that Nonconformity was stronger than the Established Church, the accommodation figures being 14.16% and 10.28% of the total population respectively, (0.86% Roman Catholics).[18]

II. THE SALVATION ARMY

The Christian Mission. 1866–1878

After Whitechapel and Bethnal Green, Poplar was the third East London Christian Mission station to be opened. The work commenced on 31 October 1866 at the Union Temperance Hall, High Street, Poplar. A cholera epidemic, the collapsed London ship-building industry, and trade (therefore dockwork) fluctuations made Poplar, according to Mission observers,

> ". . . an equally crowded and perhaps more destitute neighbourhood than Whitechapel. Between the Temperance Hall and stable and pigsties is only a wooden partition. The stench which oozes through the cracks in this is enough to poison us all."[19]

A further station, the Mission's ninth, was opened at the Oriental Theatre (Mission Hall), Poplar, on 7 March 1867. It was given up three years later because it was draughty, dirty and costly.[20] Also at that time, a site for a purpose-built hall was under consideration. As elsewhere, William Booth's work was helped in these first years by philanthropic individuals[21] and organisations. One of the latter, the Evangelical Society, aided the work at the Oriental Theatre by a monthly grant of £17 in both March and April 1867. Booth was not however given the £112 per annum he requested from them for the purchase of a site to erect a hall in Poplar.

The Mission work continued in the area with local support. The growth of any religious group is eased by having supporters both among the populace and in authority. Thus the Mission attracted the attention of the former while being welcomed by the latter in the shape of a prominent local factory owner. In 1867 Mr. Owen of Messrs. Owen, Merton and Company heard Mrs. Collingridge speak. She was one of William Booth's staunchest supporters. He invited her to hold meetings in the chemical factory of which he was a partner, and subsequently assisted the work even more, becoming personally involved as secretary to the East London Christian Mission.

The workers in Poplar were attracted by open-air witness around the factory and dock gates plus relief work.

> "During last winter we had a soup kitchen at Poplar from which we supplied about 140 quarts of soup with bread daily; this work we hope to resume there almost immediately." (1867).

Alongside was the proposal to provide a new hall, ragged school, Bible depot and reading-room.[22] Much of this was of the traditional Home Mission character but where the East London Christian Mission differed was in its apparently successful appeal to the working-class. Certainly by late 1868 the Mission was attracting huge crowds.

> "The Temperance Hall is crowded to the door every night in the week."[23]

Tea meetings (often free) proved popular events and together with social relief and the ubiquitous open-air meetings sustained the momentum. It was common for there to be

> "... 600 in front of the East India Dock gates ... (and) ... many young converts."[24]

It was also the open-air meetings which attracted the opposition then faced by anyone who preached in the street. However it is clear that because of the direct style of their message, the East London Christian Mission immediately became a focus for attack. *The East London Advertiser* reported in October 1868 that brewers

> "... mobilised their lower-class 'rowdies' to silence a religion which challenged their profits and their prestige."[25]

Opposition continued and is identifiable from three social groups. On the most common level was the opportunist physical and verbal abuse, basically although not entirely from members of the working-class. However the second and third categories, the Irish and the brewers, probably proved the greatest threat in the East End, especially as they were normally allied. A typical Mission report was that of a a respectable land-owning shopkeeper who together with fellow 'Romanists' mustered violent opposition; he died of natural causes, however, shortly afterwards.

As opposition worsened all over the East End during 1869 and 1870, it came particularly but not solely from the Irish Roman Catholics.[26] This was possibly a form of retaliation for the hostility shown to these immigrants

> "... not so much because they were Irishmen, but because they were Roman Catholics."[27]

There were approximately 3,500 Irish immigrants in Poplar in 1881 but opposition to the Mission was reflected in all sectors of the community. Gangs of Irish, mechanics or others would come from the public-houses to 'beat the Mission', especially on Saturday nights. The musical instruments, first introduced at Poplar in 1867 to attract the people during William Booth's dinner hour services at the East India Dock Gate and elsewhere, certainly attracted opposition.

The East London Christian Mission deliberately placed its open-air meetings and where possible its meeting halls in the poorest areas;

TABLE 5.3

Number of Members and Stations in the United Kingdom 1871–1877

Year	No. of Members	Stations	No. of London Stations	No. of London Members	Poplar
1871	998	22	17	818	129
1872[1]	—	19	15	—	—
1873[2]	1112	27	17	901	272
1874	1750	31	17	1039	199
1875	1986	39	20	951	90
1876	2455	38	18	1238	88
1877	2696	31	13	934	32

[1] No conference as William Booth was ill.
[2] No figures given for Hastings.
Source: The Christian Mission Conference Minute Book 1871–1877.

for example Sunday morning open-airs in Chrisp Street Poplar, were common. The officer's quarters (home) was established there by 1878. The street was one of the major thoroughfares in Poplar and a place of drink-houses, prostitutes and a daily market where

> "The butchers are crying "Buy — buy — buy !" the poor half-starved women with black-eyes and bruised faces, and scarcely clothes enough to hide their nakedness, turning over the block-ornaments on the stalls in the street; the fruiterer . . . and the fishmonger . . .; the whole street filled with the lowest and worst characters in this part of London, and from almost every other part of the world. Great big navvies with their short pipes . . . the filth and debauch of the over-night stained on their slop."[28]

Even the theft of all the band instruments in mid–1869 did not deter the Mission from 'attacking the unconverted.'

Although the Oriental Theatre was given up in 1870, the Christian Mission was firmly established in Poplar by that date with an average attendance at week-night meetings of 250. The Circuit Preacher was James Dowdle, 'The Saved Railway Guard'.[29] Up to 1873 Poplar's membership continued to increase (Table 5.3). The reasons for this were twofold; from the station's commencement in 1866 the mixture of religious services and practical social relief attracted many, and the construction of a new hall gave the Mission a sense of permanence. The new hall's stone-laying ceremony took place on 28 October 1872 and was attended by many Mission supporters. £57 10 shillings was raised on the day. The event was also well supported by other churchmen, in particular the Primitive Methodists, Free Methodists and Wesleyans. George Scott Railton, one of the Mission's leading evangelists, first contacted the Mission at this event. The new hall was to hold 1,000 people, have all its seats free, incorporate a soup-kitchen, ragged school and reading-room, and cost £500 to build and £30 per annum to use. It was opened on 27 January 1873 by Mrs. Booth, with the aim of it becoming a religious home for the working-class. Clearly the Mission had some success for:

> "I went to the meeting because "I remembered having heard the 'Christian Mission' people say at one of their open-air services they invited people to attend their hall in working attire." "[30]

After 1873 a decline in membership occurred (Table 5.3) although the Mission remained in evidence as the major East End newspaper, *The East London Observer*, made clear. It printed a letter of complaint (1874) which stated that the good name of Missions was damaged

> ". . . by the misguided efforts of a few religious zealots . . . (who) . . . parade the district to the annoyance of pedestrians . . . (and) . . . the obstruction of traffic. Invariably, every Sunday afternoon is to be seen a troop of characters, consisting of males and females marching . . .in military fashion. Led by a gentleman who takes delight in flourishing an immense umbrella, they proceed, chanting a variety of hymns, until they reach their destination . . . The whole thing is treated with ridicule, sneers and jeers."[31]

During 1875 Poplar Mission Station continued to lose members and the year was "not without difficulties".[32] These difficulties were not explained. The following year reveals much about the Christian Mission as a Movement. According to *The Christian Mission Magazine* the work continued well in Poplar and elsewhere. Tables 5.3 to 5.6 appear to contradict this and previously unpublished correspondence between Railton and two other evangelists (Appendix 7) supports the tabular evidence. From the correspondence it is clear that the Albion Theatre was taken over for Sunday nights while the Mission Hall was repaired. It is not clear if the new hall had fallen into disrepair through cheap construction or had been vandalised. In the letters Railton also reveals that

> ". . . people don't seem to feel how awfully London has gone down . . . We have abandoned several small stations in order to use up all our strength on those we can make something of."
> "I cannot help seeing how the Mission is fallen . . . I have been sadly let in at Poplar. We have allowed the people for two years to learn a different religion from ours."

Tables 5.3 to 5.6 clearly indicate that there were decreasing numbers in attendance and membership at the Poplar Mission services when Railton took command in mid-1876 with orders to 'revive' the Station.

While some new converts were made, despite the constant physical attacks by roughs and police inactivity, Railton failed to any extent to rekindle the interest of the working people of Poplar in the Mission. Part of the reason may have been that he was at the same time busy on the administrative staff at the Whitechapel Headquarters.[33] The conversions, of which many are claimed in *The Christian Mission Magazine*, were not even enough to keep up the preceding year's figures after 1873.

The decline of the Poplar Mission Station continued into 1877 and 1878. The writings in *The Christian Mission Magazine* talk at length about conversions in Poplar and there is only one brief acknowledgement in October 1877 that ". . . many have left us to toil on." Even this phrase is ambiguous due to its positioning in the report. It is placed under sentences referring to converted sailors leaving for foreign shores (but presumably still retaining their membership). It also has the following sentence, contradicted by the trend shown in Table 5.3, that ". . . our numbers are still increasing."[34]

The detailed progress of Poplar Station can be charted via a series of Tables worked out mainly from *The Christian Mission Minute Book*. Table 5.3 records a nine station increase nationally between 1871 and 1877 and a national membership increase of 170%. Poplar increased in membership up to 1873 when it provided just under a third of London's total. However by 1877 Poplar only had a quarter of its 1871 total and provided well under a twentieth of London's membership. London as a whole lost four stations and its membership numbers remained almost static over the same period. The Table also reveals a particularly large loss of members in Poplar between June (the Conference month) 1876 and June 1877. It took some time to recover from this. Loss through 'backsliding' (returning to 'evil' ways) or going to other churches and conversely, constant replenishment and increase in members, generally marked the Mission's progress.

Table 5.4 shows that apart from 1877 where there is no detailed breakdown of figures, the main reason for Poplar's loss is 'discontinued'. This was part of a general pattern apparent from this Table. A comparison of Tables 5.3 and 5.4 shows that of 2,455 members in the Mission in 1876, 1,180 were recorded as 'died or lost'. (We can assume the latter for most). Yet in 1877 there were 2,696 members, not only an increase of 241 but an addition of 1,180 new members to cover the losses. Therefore, 1,421 converts had been gained nationally, a larger increase than is at first apparent and an explanation of the frequent *Christian Mission Magazine* reports of new converts. For London, the figures are 1,238 members in 1876, 588 lost yet 934 remaining in 1877. The loss left 650 members so an addition of 284 new members had been found during the year. In Poplar, the figures are 88 members in 1876 and 32 in 1877. 80 came under the heading 'died or lost' leaving 8, so 24 new converts were gained.

TABLE 5.4

Deaths, Removals and Discontinued 1871–1877

Total	National				London				Poplar			
	D	R	Dis	Total	D	R	Dis	Total	D	R	Dis	Total
1871	9	25	115	149	9	5	69	83	—	4	12	16
1872	n/a	—	—	—	—	—	—	—	—	—	—	—
1873	15	64	94	173	12	38	43	93	—	12	8	20
1874	15	165	143	323	14	73	113	200	1	15	45	61
1875	21	166	324	511	8	88	175	271	1	3	7	11
1876	35	238	325	597	9	88	149	246	1	4	—	5
1877	'Died or Lost'			1180	'Died or Lost'			588	'Died or Lost'			80

Key: D = Death; R = Removed from members list; Dis = Discontinued.
Source: The Christian Mission Conference Minute Book 1871–1877.

Table 5.5 is divided into indoor and outdoor meetings. Nationally and for London, the numbers were on the increase and in Poplar, the number of indoor meetings increased in 1877 from 4 to 7. The number of those attending decreased in Poplar from the high of 1873 to the low of 1877, 1,151 to 224 respectively. This decrease was reflected throughout the Mission thus suggesting either, more meetings but reduced numbers in each or, a massive decline in attendance and a desperate attempt by Booth to 'capture' more converts through more meetings. Poplar's outdoor meetings by 1877 dropped to under a third of their 1873 total, 28 to 9 respectively, while nationally they increased by 166%. Attendance figures were not recorded.

Table 5.6 shows a loss for London and loss for Poplar in the sale of magazines while the national figures increase. All the Tables therefore agree that while between 1871 and 1877 the Army was increasing in membership, including a high number of new recruits per annum, London as a whole was stagnating and Poplar in particular suffered greatly. This was despite a multitude of societies, camp-meetings and announcements of free teas, even "A Free Tea to 2,000 persons."[35]

Table 5.7 allows a more detailed examination of the Poplar Registration District and it is possible to determine the variable life-span of stations. Despite only two out of five stations remaining by 1878, this does not necessarily indicate a loss of evangelistic work. The Methodistic circuits were constantly being reorganised and the loss of a particular meeting-place (few being their own halls) may or may not be because of local influence. It may simply be because a new circuit took over an area and ran it as an outdoor ministry. For example, in 1871/2, Bow came under the newly-formed Limehouse

TABLE 5.5

Number of Services and Average Attendance

Year	Stations	No. of Services			Average No.'s Attending		
		Nat.	Lon.	Poplar	Nat.	Lon.	Poplar
INDOOR SERVICES							
1871	22	70	53	11	5380	4580	450
1872			NO CONFERENCE				
1873	27	84	58	22	9624	4857	1515
1874	31	109	65	19	8780	3810	1450
1875	39	138	65	4	19540	6880	1000
1876	38	167	90	4	22800	9640	550
1877	31	202	105	7	16653	5279	224
OUTDOOR SERVICES							
1871	22	49	38	10	6350	5350	1500
1872			NO CONFERENCE				
1873	27	84	57	28	12750	10460	2250
1874	31	98	60	21			
1875	39	166	78	4			
1876	38	213	120	7			
1877	31	224	109	9			

Key: Nat. = National; Lon. = London.

Note: 1. These figures do not include temperance or Band of Hope meetings.
2. The sample covers one week only.
3. Some stations failed to return their figures therefore many 'Totals' are higher than those recorded above.

Source: The Christian Mission Conference Minute Book 1871–1877.

TABLE 5.6

Number of Magazines Sold

Year						Total	London	Poplar
1871	.	.	.	.	.	1156	836	100
1872	.	.	.	.	.	n/a	n/a	n/a
1873[1]	.	.	.	.	.	1350	960	160
1874	.	.	.	.	.	2369	1369	300
1875	.	.	.	.	.	3549	1498	100
1876	.	.	.	.	.	4676	1740	80
1877	.	.	.	.	.	5526	1481	50

[1] No figures were given for Hastings.
Source: The Christian Mission Conference Minute Book. 1871–1877.

TABLE 5.7

Stations within the Poplar Registration District

Place	1868/9	1870	1871	1872	1873	1874	1875	1876	1877	1878
Bow	✔	✔	✔	✔						
Cubitt Town. . .				✔		✔	✔	✔	✔	
Milwall	✔	✔	✔	✔	✔	✔	✔	✔	✔	✔
Old Ford. . . .	✔	✔								
Poplar	✔	✔	✔	✔	✔	✔	✔	✔	✔	✔

Source: The indices of *The East London Evangelist.* 1868–1869.
The Christian Mission Magazine. 1870–1878.

Circuit who decided to spend the 'rent' money in other ways but still of use in the neighbourhood.[36] Conversely, Cubitt Town, started in July 1871, ceased almost immediately because of adverse trade and extreme poverty. As trade revived in 1873, so the Mission work was restarted there although no permanent hall was ever established.

The 'different religion' referred to in 1876 by G. S. Railton was perhaps one of four major causes for the post-1873 decline in Poplar and possibly in London generally. Reports in *The Christian Mission Magazine* suggest that Poplar Mission may have been bordering on the charismatic. This was not entirely in line with William Booth's ideas. Conversely the statement may merely contain the word 'religion' interchangeably with drink and gambling. The second cause was 'declension', as Booth called the loss of members, and it occurred because leaders appointed to take charge

> ". . . have lacked the power to guide and control the society. Discipline has been wanting."[37]

Third, trade and therefore employment was improving dramatically in the early to mid-1870s and there was increasingly less reliance on Mission social relief. Fourth, the Christian Mission was keen to have people join and sign the pledge without any sign other than saying so or kneeling in prayer. It was however the frequently displayed lack of will to remain different from one's peers which prompted William Booth to note that few stayed members and that although hundreds witness the Salvation Army's strange and unusual religious services, it is difficult to

> ". . . drag men and women out from among all their associates and associations to commence a new life and to maintain that life stead- fastly."[38]

William Booth frankly admitted in 1878 that all was not as it could be with the Mission in London.

> "Some of our friends, I know, are a little disappointed that we don't do more in London. They cannot be more so than we are." [39]

The Salvation Army was making rapid national and international advances for a decade after 1878. Although occasional new halls were built before this date for example Limehouse in 1878 and much magazine space was devoted to London, a large amount of building, purchase or renting was not done in the capital until after 1882. Even then the emphasis was in south and west London and the outlying suburbs.

The early 1880s were the Army's most important years for expansion in England and between 1882 and 1886 the Movement did grow in London both in numbers of new corps and converts. By the time of the *British Weekly* Religious Census of late 1887, it was clear that the Army had at least made an impact in London, although not as strongly as William Booth claimed. The editor of the *British Weekly* asked Booth if only 53,591 attenders in London was "not most disappointing"? [40] The figures were in fact far worse than those quoted as

> ". . . something had gone wrong with the Army's geography and the *British Weekly's* arithmetic."

Hugh McLeod has recalculated showing a deficit of 21.24% in the *British Weekly's* figures and therefore revealing the Army's extreme weakness in the capital. Some writers felt that the 'In Darkest England' Scheme was introduced by William Booth in 1890 not just as a logical extension of spiritual warfare, 'saving' people by improving their surroundings and their souls, but to arrest the decline in membership figures.

Poplar illustrates the above pattern with the work there in November 1878 being at "a low ebb". [41] Part of this was due to the lack of good leaders in London for Booth's best evangelists, many of them the products of the East London Stations, were sent to open new Stations nationally. Poplar though reveals other possible reasons. Reports in the secular press over the next few years regarding the Corps are rare and in the *War Cry*, only sporadic. They refer to Corps debts and "slow progress". [42] Clearly opposition increased and strong local evidence suggests that behind the "bloody scene", brewers were encouraging opposition. [43]

141

"The publicans not only treat the roughs to all kinds of drink, but also pay them well for upsetting our meetings."[44]

The local police were rarely in evidence, refused to act upon complaints, and legally demanded payment for protection. The soldiers were

". . . persecuted from all quarters, pelted with flour, rotten eggs, dead cats, stones, and all manner of things."[45]

These quotations are from a local Salvation Army writer for the *War Cry* and while perhaps being exaggerated in some of their claims, they are consistent with what emerged from the early 1880s as organised opposition.

The 'Unconverted Salvation Army' held open-air meetings and processions in imitation of the Salvation Army proper. They were based in Whitechapel but were in evidence throughout the East End. Opposition to the hundreds of preachers from various denominations who were found every Sunday in the East End was a favourite occupation by some groups. The attacks on the Christian Mission evangelists were no different at first from the attacks on other preachers and were certainly treated in the same way by the press and the police. However the reorganisation of the Movement into the Salvation Army in 1878 made it a more definable object of interest.

Organised violence and police inaction, starting in the East End but spreading and developing as the Army spread and developed, was vigorously protested about by William Booth in 1881 to the Chief of the Metropolitan Police. Even after Home Office directives in 1882, violence continued but it appears to have worked to earn the loyalty of existing members and to encourage others to join. Persecution produced strength and by mid-1883, Poplar was increasing in numbers ". . . despite the rowdyism"[46] and perhaps because they ". . . were in a 'cognitive minority'."[47] Increasingly vicious attacks were noted and this, plus large open-air meetings, led to packed halls. *War Cry* selling figures increased to 700 copies per week but the 'Unconverted Salvation Army' with

". . . their own flag with the skull and cross-bones on it and about twenty people in full uniform"

were continually in the area. In this particular case the police moved in and took their flag.[48] It was from this point in February 1883 that the police started taking stronger action, mainly because of Home Office pressure and legal rulings.

On 8 February 1883 Captain and Mrs. Redstone took command of Poplar Corps. He carried out a number of necessary repairs and alterations to the hall upon his arrival. In his first holiness meeting Redstone was surprised by the undisciplined behaviour of the soldiers

"But why wonder? Sometimes they would wear uniform, at other times they would not, their feathers flying. I was too straight for these sort of soldiers, and they took their flight, leaving about a dozen people belonging to the corps."[49]

Low numbers and fierce opposition forced the temporary abandonment of open-air work except for that carried out from a raised platform or bench in the grounds of the hall. Open-air work on the public highway evidently restarted soon after Redstone 'farewelled' (moved to another corps) in June. However the opposition was clearly determined despite police pressure and severe violence continued up to late 1888.

"Driving storms of persecution and hate threaten to submerge our noble bands fighting on this battle-ground."[50]

Even the by now common open-air meetings in front of the dock-gates were still attacked in 1887 and early 1888 and the Salvationists

". . . driven away from the gates (and forced) to run like sheep. Cats, dogs, reochre and filth used to fly about."[51]

By the end of 1889 the situation had changed in Poplar, for two reasons. Partly it came about with the national decline in opposition to the Army but mainly because of the Great Dock Strike of that year. The Strike was called by Ben Tillet and Tom McCarthy on 15 August 1889 from the Union Headquarters at the Wade Arms, Jeremiah Street, Poplar. Although it was mainly brought about by the demand for 'the docker's tanner' and was conducted and won in "an atmosphere of carnival,"[52] extreme hardship was faced by the dockers and their families. Over 100,000 men came out and only official pickets received any pay (1 shilling per day.) The Salvation Army actively sought out the wives and children of real strikers and handed them food tickets. Most of the people were clean and decent but had pawned everthing except the clothes they were wearing. Food provided by the Army was approaching 100,000 meals per day according to *The Times* and was served mainly from a depot in the West India Dock Road. The paper believed that

"The Salvation Army are continuing to do a vast amount of good . . . and it is the opinion of the leaders of the strike that had it not been for this place of help the distress would have been much greater."[53]

Other Army food depots were also in operation. The annual 'Self-Denial' week devoted part of the money gained to the dockers' food

Early struggles in Poplar.

With our Comrades at the Food Depot,
West India Dock Road.

aid and a collection of clothes and furniture was made to help the dockers after the strike. Due to Booth's help, a contemporary commentator wrote

> "General Booth's been the backbone of this movement . . . (because) . . . he's helped to feed the men, and that's kept off riots."[54]

The Army was severely criticised for their aid, mainly by the Charity Organisation Society (hereafter C.O.S.). This was the second time that the two organisations had disagreed. The first was twenty-two years earlier. In February 1867 all charitable work in East London was being centralised under the C.O.S. but Booth preferred independence. When in 1889 the Army again refused to act on C.O.S. advice, this time in cutting down its relief, the Army was accused of indiscriminate charity. The C.O.S. believed the relief being given to the dockers was throwing money to the undeserving poor.

The Salvation Army's decision to continue its direct aid kept up the close worker-Army contact established through the food depots. As in the late 1860s, when the Mission became known as a place of social relief, so again during the Strike the Army became prominent. As twenty years before, the membership figures were increasing. The difference between the Mission and the Army now was that the latter was clearly identifying itself with the workers. It sided with them against injustices on the questions of pay, hours and conditions, although the Army's campaign was not political but one of food-aid and in the case of other occupations, leading by example. This work among the working-class in 1888 and 1889 earned the Army increased respect and encouraged William Booth to proceed with his social schemes. These schemes, formalised in 1890, were aimed at providing employment and respect for the masses and by inference raising their social status.

The process of the Army's awareness of the real social issues affecting many working-people reached a watershed in 1889–1890, not only with the Army's active involvement in issues or the 'Darkest England' Scheme, but with writers in the *War Cry* addressing themselves to the social evils of the day. This was most marked in a free supplement to the Christmas edition of the 1889 *War Cry* entitled *Salvation Socialism*. Its basic argument was not political or asking for an equal distribution of wealth but for fair treatment for the lower classes. This involved correcting the 'injustices' of irregular employment, poor wages, bad conditions and long hours. The supplement served two aims. First it demonstrated that (according to the writer, Major Frank Smith) the Army was in a

> ". . . better position than could be hoped a decade before."[55]

145

Second, it publicly triggered off a major extension of the Army's work, a campaign for workers' rights. By 1890 Booth felt convinced that many thousands of workers were being unjustly neglected by the churches and ignored by their employers. He noted with satisfaction the welcome accorded to the Salvation Army by the workers for their stand in the Dock Strike and during the previous year's Match Girls' Strike. No longer was there any serious disrespect other than the occasional outburts of ridicule. Physical aggression was replaced by a widespread acceptance of the Movement in the East End of London.

Typical of this new mood was an incident that took place at the height of the Dock Strike when, just before one mass meeting, the Army marched through 80,000 men. Where previously

> "... the little band of Salvationists would have been torn to pieces out of SHEER DEVILMENT, now, the mighty host just opened like a well."[56]

This concentration on social justice continued in 1890 when *In Darkest England and the Way Out* was published. The book was the work of William Booth, mainly based on the ideas of Frank Smith and rewritten by W. T. Stead. This forward-looking and in places quite radical volume demanded and showed the way to extensive social reforms. It stated that unemployment was the cause of most problems such as drunkenness and suggested a variety of farm, city and foreign colonies combined with industrial and social schemes, aimed at raising everyone's standard of living. Booth demanded, as the bare minimum, what he termed the Cab Horse's Charter, namely:

> "There are two points of the Cab Horse's Charter. When he is down he is helped up, and while he lives he has food, shelter and work."[57]

The Social Reform Wing of the Salvation Army then set out to demonstate that Booth's ideas were practical. Some experiments had already been attempted but nothing on the grand scale envisaged. These new experiments included a Farm Colony at Hadleigh, Essex, an experiment copied by the Poplar Board of Guardians soon after. In fact many of the cases cited in evidence for reforms came from the Army's Poplar experiences.

Many observers felt that the social work came about because of the declining impact of the Salvation Army and that the Movement needed to turn to social work in order to survive. It is probably true that it helped the Army's survival in the East End of London during the 1890s. Certainly non-Army contemporary and secondary commentators felt this to be the case. *The Methodist Times* stated "Here is General Booth turning socialist."[58] Others wrote:

"But for their social work and the great hall at Clapton, the Salvation Army would have been wiped out."[59]

"(The Army) has failed most conspicuously in the East End as a spiritual agency, but . . . (Booth thinks it might) . . . succeed as a social agency."[60]

Booth however abhorred the idea of giving relief in exchange for religion. While he may well have

". . . turned to social reform because he became convinced that poverty itself was a grave impediment to salvation,"[61]

he stated on the subject

"No compulsion will for a moment be allowed with respect to religion."

Booth's motivation was a genuine concern for the condition of the working-class. When giving free food and clothing, it was hoped to attract people to the religious services but not at the expense of

"Free teas, petticoats and blankets (making) hypocrites."[62]

His ideas though did seek a lasting answer to dealing with the problems (although not the causes) of unemployment and at first received considerable support.

Industry and the Salvation Army

Since its origins in 1865, the Army had concerned itself with some 'standard' mission social activities such as food provision, as well as certain highly publicised social issues such as child prostitution. William Booth's interest in a specific campaign on behalf of the working-class was kindled by the Match Girls' Strike in June 1888. Bryant and May's large match factory was situated in Poplar. When the Strike came, the Army gave financial support to it via the London Trades Council. General Booth also ordered investigations into the industry. Evidence was produced, not only of the appalling working conditions and low pay in this and connected trades, but also of dozens of cases of phosphorus necrosis or 'phossy jaw', a painful and often fatal disease attacking the teeth and jaw-bone.[63]

William Booth decided that eradication of the sweating system would become a major aim of the Salvation Army. He stated in his *In Darkest England and the Way Out*:

"The Labour Shops will enable us to work out our Anti-Sweating experiments. For instance we propose at once to commence manufacturing match-boxes, for which we will aim at giving nearly treble the

147

The Salvation Army's match factory, Lamprell Street, London, was opened in May 1891 and produced the 'Lights in Darkest England' brand matches.

amount at present paid to the poor starving creatures engaged in the work."[64]

The Army took over a factory at 55 Lamprell Street, Bow, on 3 March 1891 and probably only then decided to produce matches. The aims were to provide better working conditions and pay for the workers and safer matches for worker and purchasers alike.

The factory was opened on Monday 11 May 1891 after a conversion costing £2,000. It employed one hundred girls using only the safe red phosphorus. After the initial two years of boom, helped by considerable press support, sales began to fall off because the matches were more expensive than most other home and foreign produced brands. It was a constant struggle for sales over the next decade and despite continued interest and sales promotions, the Army's venture was a financial failure, although the social implications were considerable.

The Salvation Army proved by example to the very interested public that decent, safe conditions and good pay produced a high turn-out of a quality product. Their apparent influence on England's biggest match manufacturer, Bryant and May, to adopt the safety match and introduce factory reforms meant that their campaign could be brought to a close. The Army continued trading in matches until 1909 but on an ever-decreasing scale.

The Army also attempted other experiments in their Bow factory such as the safe preparation of disinfectants (August 1896). These were of little success although farming, furniture and musical instrument manufacturing were all built up successfully.

The Salvation Army, Trade Unionism and The Labour Movement

With the return of prosperity to the East End economy as elsewhere during the early 1870s, unionisation became a common topic, especially on the waterfront. By January 1872, Poplar stevedores probably had their own organisation and this became Branch Number 3 of The Labour Protection League. In April, Branch Number 4 was also opened in Poplar and Number 3 split into two sections

> "so as to be able to contain the flood of recruits. (This) . . . at last triggered off developments in other sectors of the port"

although not for another 17 years was a Docker's Union founded (1889).[65]

It was the Army's actions in helping to alleviate the considerable distress brought about by the Great Dock Strike of 1889 that "consolidated its position in the East End".[66] These actions were inspired not only by William Booth but also by Major Frank Smith. Only rare and unimportant mentions of him occur in Army sources but from other sources, such as his biography, it is clear that there was a strong link between Ben Tillett and Frank Smith. From the mid 1870s Smith had worked hard for the Christian Mission. He appeared to enjoy all aspects of his work, particularly preaching at Hyde Park Corner. In 1884 he was sent to the United States of America as Territorial Commander. While there he read Henry George's *Progress and Poverty* which apparently increased his already keen interest in labour relations and trade unionism. On his return, his preaching in London and elsewhere clearly showed this and he was warned by the General to keep unionism and politics out of religion. Throughout the 1880s however he

> ". . . was associating himself with many of the progressive men and women of the day"

and he was ever concerned about social evils.[67]

Smith resigned from the Army in the late 1880s because of the disagreement with William Booth over the former's political activities.

However he was encouraged back to develop the Movement's Social Reform Wing. For this he was made Commissioner and allowed to utilise his considerable knowledge of the needs of labour to introduce many of the social schemes he had developed and which were written into *In Darkest England and the Way Out*. In 1890 Smith's writings and ideas had become well known in *The Times* and other newspapers. It is certain that he had been the main instigator of efforts made by the Salvation Army on behalf of the Match Girls in 1888, the dockers in 1889, and the development of Salvation Army factories. Smith clearly kept up his contacts amongst those striving to improve workers' conditions. In August 1890 he invited Henry George to inspect the activities of the Social Reform Wing. George did so and was impressed by what he saw.

Frank Smith had many ideas about how the Army should proceed and one typical action in Poplar and the East End was to organise the sandwich-board men. In 1890 this successfully saved them

> ". . . from a cruel sweating system, and, by hiring them out himself, he was able almost to double their wages."[68]

Although William Booth accepted many of his ideas, Smith was upset at not being given the apparently once promised autonomous control of the Army's Social Reform Wing. In addition, he was concerned that not all the money given for 'In Darkest England' was finding its way to the schemes. Due to these two factors, he resigned from the Army in 1891.[69] This

> ". . . caused considerable discussion throughout the country, for very many had been watching developments with keen interest."[70]

The Times devoted much space to the resignation but Smith continued to champion the working-man by going into politics as a Labour M.P. He also strongly supported the second General, Bramwell Booth, in the Army's constitutional crisis of 1929.[71]

Numbers and Backgrounds of Members

The number of Christian Mission/Salvation Army members at Poplar reached a zenith in 1873 and a nadir between 1877 and early 1883 when only 32 and then 12 were present respectively. 1873 was the culmination of the Mission's hard work to relieve the social distress of the late 1860s and early 1870s. It is probable that there is a positive correlation between the stabilising of socio-economic conditions and therefore more employment (and less reliance on Mission relief) and a decline in attendance.

The *British Weekly* census conducted during the autumn of 1887 showed the number of attenders at one Sunday morning and evening service in Poplar Salvation Army Corps as 602. Allowing for 50% to be separate individuals at each service, that leaves 301 attenders. If a further 50% were non-Salvationists, that leaves approximately 150 members. The increase between 1877 and 1888 is 32 to 150, thus 368%. While this is fewer by 122 members than 1873, the Corps had clearly gained strength after its marked decline to 12 members in early 1883. The rise to 150 members by 1888 probably came about because of a mixture of severe persecution, a series of successful and liked officers,[72] the Movement's novelty, and the provision of a variety of activities for all ages. The figure of membership was sustained throughout much of the 1890s because of the Army's work for the working-class.

By the time of the *Daily News* Religious Census of 1903, attendance at Poplar Corps was 40% below the 1887 figure. There were 362 instead of 602 attenders. The District figures were equally as poor for the Army. 2.62% of the church-going population attended Army services, 0.44% of the total District population.[73] This decline can however partly be accounted for by the fact that the trend in lower attendances was not confined to the Army. The percentage of church-goers in Poplar District in 1903 was less than in late 1887 for all denominations, 17.13% of the population compared with 24.84% respectively.[74]

Although it appears that the Salvation Army suffered numerically, it must be remembered that no afternoon (therefore Sunday School and adult afternoon 'praise meetings') were recorded. Also regular nightly open-airs, visitation, classes and a variety of social work was being done by the Army, the consequences of which are difficult to estimate.

> "The counting of worshippers can at best be but a rough indication of the outward influences at work in any particular Church."[75]

It is not possible to establish the social background of the members of the Christian Mission at Poplar as no name lists are extant. Only 11 names and seven occupations can be identified from reports in *The Christian Mission Magazines* (Appendix 8). This sample is too small to draw conclusions from but it is not surprising that gipsies are represented amongst those converted for large numbers attended the Mission, mainly in the summer according to their nomadic tendencies. They lived

> "Not far from Barking Road Station on the Woolwich line . . . (on) . . . a range of marshy land, known to the inhabitants as Cherry Island."

Members attended Canning Town and Poplar, while those from the southern part of Epping Forest attended Stations nearer to their bases.

Gipsies were considered important to the Mission's evangelism as they carried the message of Salvationism with them across the country. When they left the area for the season, a large camp-meeting was held in their honour in 1870.[76] One of the Christian Mission and Salvation Army's leading evangelists, Gipsy Smith, joined the Mission on 25 June 1877 from a gipsy camp in East London.[77] There were clearly many such camps and these continued to exist into the twentieth century. In 1905 gipsies still

> ". . . perambulated the country in their covered vehicles, drawn by several small ponies."[78]

Occupationally little is known of the Salvationists. In 1887 the occupations of a neighbouring Corps (Limehouse) were given as

Biscuit makers;	Tinsmiths;	Coal merchants;	Housekeepers;
Sweet makers;	Boatmakers;	Painters;	Cooks;
Boiler makers;	Cork cutters;	Printers;	Housemaids;
Tank makers;	Dock men;	City porters;	General sevants;
Engineers;	Fishmongers;	Clerks;	Dress makers;
Machinists;	Shirt makers;[79]		

It is clear that the Salvationists came from a wide social range spread throughout the working-class. A list of bandsmen and their occupations at Poplar in 1905 reflects similar occupations. Therefore, while perhaps failing to reach large numbers of Booth's 'submerged tenth', the Army did continue to spread the Gospel amongst the entire working-class.

Conclusion

The impact of the Salvation Army in Poplar was greatest at times of extreme social problems. The "abnormal distress" of the late 1860s (much due to industrial collapse) and the strikes of the late 1880s marked the heights of local Army significance. The Movement's late 1880s practical social and industrial campaigns on behalf of the working-class identified it as being of and for that stratum. These campaigns brought a general respect for the Army from all levels of society but most importantly from the working-class themselves,[80] a respect that was ensured by its close contacts with the strikes of 1888 and particularly 1889.

The decline in membership, both after 1873 and 1890, was a result mainly of improving socio-economic conditions. In additon, during the 1890s, opposition had declined and there was apparently a continuing national decline in Church and Chapel attendance. Also the Movement was always very susceptible to a high turnover rate in membership, much due to its demand for a high level of commitment. The Army remained keen to experiment, not only with social schemes but also in ways to 'capture' converts. Thus, in 1903, it produced some of the first film shows for the people. This was seen as a radical and "... novel method of influencing the unsaved."[81] Despite such work, Poplar Corps failed to regain the strong numerical position it had held in 1873 to 1874 and in the late 1880s.

CHAPTER SIX

MANCHESTER, LANCASHIRE: A CASE-STUDY

I. BACKGROUND

The mid-nineteenth century cathedral city of Manchester lay at the heart of the industrialised north. Its contemporary nickname of 'Cottonopolis' reflected the city's key industry although increasingly in the nineteenth century, coal-mining and ironworks became important to the local economy. The Parish of Manchester had one of the largest numerical and concentrated working-class populations in England, (Table 6.1). It consisted of 30 townships and chapelries, the two most important being Manchester and Salford respectively. Between 1801 and 1851, the former's population rose by 165% while the latter's increased by 365%. Manchester's density fell thereafter while Salford's continued to rise until a peak in 1891. In particular, Salford grew by over 30,000 in the two decades before the Salvation Army 'opened fire' there in 1880. Table 6.1 shows that the overall Parish increase for the nineteenth century was 705%. Most of this

TABLE 6.1

The Population of Manchester 1801–1901

Year								Township Totals		Parish Total
								Manchester	Salford	
1801	.	.	.	.	.	.	.	70,409	13,611	112,300
1811	.	.	.	.	.	.	.	79,459	19,114	136,370
1821	.	.	.	.	.	.	.	108,016	25,772	187,031
1831	.	.	.	.	.	.	.	142,026	40,786	270,963
1841	.	.	.	.	.	.	.	163,856	53,200	353,390
1851	.	.	.	.	.	.	.	186,986	63,423	452,158
1861	.	.	.	.	.	.	.	185,410	71,002	530,126
1871	.	.	.	.	.	.	.	173,988	83,277	602,902
1881	.	.	.	.	.	.	.	148,794	101,584	720,481
1891	.	.	.	.	.	.	.	145,100	109,732	809,284
1901	.	.	.	.	.	.	.	132,316	105,732	905,000

Source: The Victoria History of the County of Lancaster. (London. 1908).
    Vol. 2. pp. 343, 344, 349.

increase was due to geographical mobility accompanying real or imagined social mobility.

Many of the people in the most densely crowded areas lived in squalid slums. The Manchester physician, James Phillips Kay, published in 1832 an account of *The Moral and Physical Condition of the Working Classes Employed in the Cotton Manufacture in Manchester.* In it he described the insanitary and poisonous condition of the working-class localities and the state of the houses. In one particular area near the River Medlock, the ground was so low

> ". . . that the chimneys of its houses, some of them three storeys high, are little above the level of the ground."

Factories surrounded the area, smoke hung heavily around and several families lived in one house or even in one room.[1] This area was Ancoats or 'Little Ireland' as it was known. It lay in the east of Manchester and was and remained solidly Irish Roman Catholic. One-fifth of the population of the city in 1840 were Irish and another sizeable group were foreign workers and foreign, mainly middle-class, merchants.

Edwin Chadwick 'discovered' many slum-dwellers in the 1840s living crowded into cellars of houses or in 'back-to-back' houses.[2] Other contemporary literature from Faucher, Carlyle, the mill-owning Engels, Dickens, Disraeli and, particularly relevant to Manchester's working-class, Mrs. Gaskell, clearly indicate a large economically poor and ethnically mixed bottom stratum of society. Slums continued to grow throughout the nineteenth century despite an easing of population density in Manchester itself. Even by the advent of the First World War, the ". . . immense poverty and wretchedness could still be observed."[3] Salford and the local areas of Bradford, Harpurhey and Deansgate were particularly noted for their slums.[4]

Manchester's most important industry, cotton, fluctuated according to the textile and more especially the cotton international market. In 1837, 50,000 local workpeople were unemployed or on short time and unemployment continued throughout most of the 'Hungry Forties'. Such depression in the textile industry fuelled periodic but persistent outbreaks of popular discontent during the first half of the nineteenth century. By 1851, trade had revived and well over 80,000 people were engaged in the cotton industry alone. The American Civil War produced a serious cotton crisis in the 1860s but the textile trade did show signs of recovery over the next decade.

By the time of the Christian Mission's arrival in Manchester in June 1878, the three staple industries of Lancashire were very depressed. Many pits and ironworks were closed as were textile mills. There was little national demand for iron and this affected the coal industry. In addition there was a low demand for round coal (domestic), common coal (shipping), slack (brickmaking), and engine classes (mills). The mills were shut because of a bitter ten week strike in the cotton trade caused by arguments over short-time and wage decreases. This had come about because of a trade depression in 1877 which worsened considerably in 1878. Riots broke out all over the cotton area and the military were called out on a number of occasions. Bitterness increased as more workers were locked out and Irish 'blacklegs' were brought in.[5]

Once work resumed, by 1881 11.32% of Manchester's total occupied population were engaged in the production of cotton and related articles. A further 21.13% were engaged in textile trades generally, making a total of 32.45%. This does not include such connected trades as carriers, messengers and porters. A certain amount of trade associated with any large town was also generated, particularly with the railway and in the 1890s, the building and running of the Manchester Ship Canal and Docks.

In many parts of Manchester but especially in the poorest areas, the publicans of the last quarter of the nineteenth century were amongst those occupying the premier positions in local working-class society. However they only rarely achieved places within the recognised local authority such as the magistracy. Unlike the smaller more conservative southern towns where businessmen of any sort frequently came to positions of official authority, in the northern conurbations, the brewers and publicans had to vie for such positions with generally more powerful industrialists. Brewers, publicans, shopkeepers and tradesmen were lower down the hierarchical structure and were generally considered to be working-class; in some cases, though, their offspring reached the lower middle-class in the shape of clerks or schoolteachers. Politically Manchester was becoming and remained increasingly Conservative after 1874. Prosperity for many, particularly in the shape of high wages, continued to take the sting out of the early and mid-nineteenth century radicalism.

Religion in nineteenth century Manchester had a considerable impact upon the city.

"There was more religious strife in Manchester or Bradford in the forties than in the Roman Empire under the rule of Augustus."

This view reflects the long recognised historical belief in there having been a mid-nineteenth century religious upheaval in the northwest of England.[6] When Manchester, with its long standing radical traditions, was expressing itself in the 1840s through the Anti-Corn Law league and the Chartists, it also

"... became thought of as the centre of Nonconformity as well as of League politics."[7]

Wesleyan Methodists, Congregationalists, Baptists and Unitarians were all strong denominations at the time of the *Census of Religious Worship 1851* (Table 6.2). In Manchester and Salford combined, the total accommodation amounted to 103,145 seats although more were appropriated than free, (60,670 as opposed to 41,675). Despite this seemingly large number of seats, only 22.28% of the Parish population could be accommodated. The county total was better with 40% (19.1% Church of England, 20.9% all others) but even this was a low figure compared to many other counties. Table 6.3 shows the accommodation breakdown for the two townships.

The evidence therefore suggests that Nonconformity was stronger than the Established Church in Manchester and Salford by 1851. The religious spectrum was clearly diverse and this reflected a similar pattern for the entire county.[8] Nonconformity continued to remain strong, particularly in local politics, throughout the second half of the nineteenth century. Religious influences on 'the masses' though remained at a low level. According to a Unitarian missionary in Manchester, the population could be divided into four groups,

"... the indifferent, non-professing Christians, members of various Christian denominations, and unbelievers. The latter two groups ... (are) ... small."[9]

II. THE SALVATION ARMY

Manchester II. Ancoats. Corps Number 90

The Christian Mission opened its first station in Manchester in Ancoats in June 1878.[10] It was apparent to the Mission leaders that the predominantly Roman Catholic Ancoats district, which had a reputation for having the greatest number of prostitutes, thieves and drunkards in the city, would have to be 'captured' first if any impression was to be made upon the masses. Brother William Pearson and Carrie and Miriam Smith hired the old Star Music Hall, Ancoats, for the opening Sunday. "It was the worst place of its kind in Manchester."[11] 250 people attended in the morning, 500 in the afternoon and 900 in the evening, thirty professed conversion. These, plus others converted in the first few weeks, established the Mission despite some opposition.

It appears that the Star Music Hall was immediately threatened with the loss of much of its regular trade and, fearing reprisals, the proprietor barred the Mission. However, the Mission felt "pledged

TABLE 6.2

Religious Buildings, Sittings and Attendances in Salford and Manchester, 1851

| | SALFORD | | | | | MANCHESTER | | | | |
| | Places of Worship | Sittings | Number Attending | | | Places of Worship | Sittings | Number Attending | | |
Denominations			M	A	E			M	A	E
PROTESTANT CHURCHES:										
Church of England	13	10,786	6,767	1,582	5,083	29	33,216	15,265	4,862	6,569
Church of Scotland	1	800	195	—	140	1	1,000	200	100	—
United Presby. Church	—	—	—	—	—	2	1,000	820	—	950
Presby. Church in England	—	—	—	—	—	2	1,570	770	—	600
Independents	6	4,712	2,494	—	1,851	12	6,734	3,287	210	2,555
Baptists	2	500	390	300	330	5	2,770	1,229	215	1,391
Society of Friends	1	110	45	—	—	1	1,330	453	202	—
Unitarians	—	—	—	—	—	4	2,350	1,060	160	450
Wesleyan Methodists	7	6,085	2,404	70	2,202	18	10,043	4,547	533	3,877
Methodist New Connect.	1	225	215	—	120	5	2,018	1,083	57	421
Primitive Methodists	2	1,004	390	—	510	2	553	423	105	280
Bible Christians	—	—	—	—	—	1	450	157	177	—
Wesleyan Associates	3	1,126	473	—	483	11	4,893	2,190	140	1,439
Welsh Calvin. Methodists	1	500	130	—	127	1	300	—	150	146
New Church	1	450	306	—	160	2	950	462	—	262
Brethren	—	—	—	—	—	1	250	20	—	26
OTHER CHRISTIAN CHURCHES										
Roman Catholics	1	1,030	2,500	—	1,100	6	5,876	17,642	950	3,179
Greek Church (Orthod.)	—	—	—	—	—	1	86	60	—	—
Latter Day Saints	1	70	—	75	46	—	—	—	—	—
JEWS	—	—	—	—	—	2	428	150	80	110
TOTALS	40	27,398	16,309	2,027	12,152	106	75,797	49,818	7,941	22,255

Note: Population of the Registration Districts of Salford and Manchester was 87,523 and 228,443 respectively.

Sources: *Census of Religious Worship. 1851.* Table F. p.cclxii. Division VIII. p. 95.

158

TABLE 6.3

Accommodation Pattern

Denomination	Salford	Manchester
Church of England	12.7%	14.5%
Protestant.	17.7%	15.9%
Roman Catholic	1.2%	2.6%
Total	31.7%	33.2%

Source: Census of Religious Worship. 1851. Table H. p.ccxc.

to Ancoats" but had to endure seven weeks of only open-air meetings, often in the rain, before managing to move to a 'Salvation Room' in Tutbury Street, Ancoats. Here they occupied the upper part of five houses.[12]

Reports in *The Christian Mission Magazine* of August and December 1878 describe many conversions and note occupations represented as stone-mason, shoemaker and collier. Clearly some Roman Catholics were becoming Mission members. The locally powerful Roman Catholic Church in this 'Little Ireland' community would have resented this intrusion. The Irish were always strongly sectarian and a very distinct group within the working-class. Anti-Catholicism was also noticeable in the press and this reinforced their sense of isolation. Any united local backing of publicans and church could have produced serious public disorder. "The roughs now and then disturb us a little" but there were few reports of major opposition and even in these, the police were usually in attendance to take action.

The Missioners (Salvationists) quickly recognised that a place in a public thoroughfare was needed to make access easier. In December 1878, despite a very trying financial position owing to bad trade conditions and consequent poverty (therefore poor collections), the Corps moved to Boundary Street while the officers lived in Whitby Street off the Bradford Road. In June 1879, the 'Salvation Room', Boundary Road, had 700 people of different types and classes present. The corps then decided to move to another new building in the Oldham Road.

Although it was the first Corps in Manchester, its number was 90, Manchester II. This was perhaps because of the temporary nature of the buildings and when the numbering was first done at the end of 1879, a new larger Corps with a more permanent building had been established (March 1879) and was given the priority number 46, Manchester I. There is no evidence that Manchester II temporarily

159

closed between December 1878 and June 1879 although if it had, Manchester I would have claimed a longer continuous period up to numbering. However there were no published reports from Ancoats during this period and in addition, a clear gap in the list of officers stationed there between September 1878 and August 1880. This is not conclusive evidence as reports were frequently pooled with Manchester I.

The *War Cry* throughout 1880 and 1881 reported that the 'Salvation Rooms' were still in use despite orders from the owners to quit them. The work was clearly difficult with reports mentioning "... plenty of mud and glory."[13] One officer, Captain J. T. Wilkins — 'The Cornish Fisherman', left in December for a rest home. His health had broken after three months of making little impression, (August to November 1880). Despite this, Ancoats Salvationists spread the attack into neighbouring areas particularly Bradford (in Manchester) and Beswick. They worked with typical flamboyant militarism with open-air meetings and the help of such preachers as the 'Hallelujah Milkman' who "... now uses kind words and not the whip on his pony."[14] Attacks by ruffians were prevented mainly by "... the kind weekly protection of the officers of C. Division."[15] Publicans undoubtedly lost trade and some had to find alternative employment. Revenge appears to have been almost entirely on an opportunist and personal level such as pushing a perambulator off the pavement as it passed the public house because the father did not spend money there anymore.

A new flag was presented to the Corps on 14 July 1882, Manchester II being one of the first corps nationally to receive the new style flag. Large numbers of people continued to profess conversion despite the opposing social influences. The fact that the *War Cry* was being sold to publicans and in public houses in the district by February 1883 suggests that the level of opposition in Ancoats was very small.

The first mention of a brass band and 'Big Ben' the drum, in the *War Cry* of 7 March 1883, noted how people were attracted by the band. Forty musicians were in the band by April and by June, a tambourine band had been added. In the December brass instruments were given to the band "... by Culcheth Temperance brass bandsmen, they having got new ones.[16]

In mid March 1883, the first person to 'farewell' (leave the Corps) expressly for the Training Home in London, left Ancoats. Having been made a Lieutenant, she revisited Manchester II from Wisbech in September 1883. Despite the stormy weather, between 300 and 400 people marched in the streets and 400 or 500 had a ham tea afterwards.

A little tardiness in attending meetings was occasionally suggested, despite the typically Lancashire and North Country practice of 'Knocking-up' for work, which was also extended to early morning

'Knee-drill' (prayer meeting). Two hours knocking-up resulted in forty soldiers. The officers did what they could to dress as the people, even wearing clogs. Some were indeed local people or from nearby towns. Money was continually being raised for the Corps and wider work. One gold offering raised £7 0s 6d in June 1884.

The first Salvation Army funeral in the area during June 1884 had thousands lining the streets to watch and 2,000 around the grave. The band, flags and singing on that occasion were of great interest. The corps had clearly made an impression on the neighbourhood by the end of 1884. The first rhyming report to appear in the *War Cry* came from the Barracks at Every Street, Ancoats. In it, the 'Round Barracks' were mentioned for the second time, the first time being in the *War Cry* of 16 July 1884.

Marches took place several times a week, especially in Forty Row or Long Lane. This

> ". . . used to be the worst place in Manchester, but it is not now so bad as it was; there is no doubt the influence of the Salvation Army has caused a change."[17]

Torchlight processions helped attract attention and continue a momentum of interest in early 1885. This was fuelled by an upsurge in faith-healing. In April 1885, the previous Commanding Officer, Captain Frank Sinclair, married Local Sergeant Rushton and the Army style wedding created further interest.

Corps anniversaries were celebrated regularly as were the major Christian festivals. Attendance figures by late 1885 were not as high as at some corps. This was perhaps because of the proximity in the area of thirteen other corps, (Tables 6.4 and 6.5). The comparative decrease in the number of published reports (Appendix 9) gives further evidence of Manchester II's declining influence. Conversely, periodic miniature revivals, often by new officers, helped the Corps and reports suggest a continual flow of people being attracted to the meetings, frequently by the band. Presumably the Corps also lost large numbers of people to other churches, corps or to their old ways, for the flow of converts over the Corps' ten-year history should have run into several hundreds had they all remained Salvationists of Manchester II. The Corps did keep up sufficient numbers and finances to keep running and in 1889 they had the third highest sales of the *War Cry* in Manchester (Table 6.6). This situation continued into the 1890s and occasional *War Cry* reports show the Corps functioning but never seeming to make a great impact, even in relation to, or perhaps because of, nearby or more popular corps. Manchester II survived into the twentieth century.

TABLE 6.4

Manchester and Salford Corps Opening Dates

No.	Name	Date	War Cry	No.
I	(M/C) Temple	March 1879	CMM May p. 123	46
II	Ancoats.	June 1878	CMM July p. 178	90
III	Lower Openshaw. . . .	7 August 1879	Jubilee Brochure 1930 p. 3	146
IV	Elm-Street.	4.12.80	11.12.80 p. 3	176
V	Bradford Road.	6. 4.82	4. 5.82 p. 3	254
VI	Newton Heath.	10. 2.83	17. 2.83 p. 3	393
VII	Gorton (1883)	21. 3.83	28. 3.83 p. 4	416 A
	Rusholme (1884)			(1477)
VIII	Harpurhey.	30. 5.83	6. 6.83 p. 2	419
IX	Deansgate	23. 9.85	30. 9.85 p. 2	655
X	Hulme.	23.12.85	23. 1.86 p. 2	685
XI	Moss Side	23.12.85	6. 3.86 p. 11	1633
XII	Longsight	18. 8.86	25. 9.86 p. 13	839
XIII	Greenheys.	4. 8.86	11. 8.88 p. 11	1646
XIV	Collyhurst.	May 1903	May 1903	1725 B
XV	Higher Openshaw . . .	May 1903	May 1903	1726 C
SI	Cross Lane, St Stephens St.	Dec 1880	27. 1.81 p. 3	170 D
SII	Liverpool St., Lower Broughton . .	17. 8.82	24. 8.82 p. 2	310
SIII		2. 6.88	9. 6.88 p. 13	
	Droylsden	24. 1.83	10. 2.83 p. 3	
	Denton	23. 6.83	30. 6.83 p. 2	474

Notes
1. All reports allow a one week lapse from time of report to date of opening;
2. Manchester Corps VII, XI and XIII were renumbered at an unknown date.
A. This district was run by Manchester III from late 1884.
B. An approximate date only, worked out by the corps' close numbering to Manchester XV.
C. *Manchester XV Corps History Book.* May 4th 1942.
D. The fourth anniversary service was held in December 1884. (*War Cry.* December 6th 1884 p. 2) S. indicates Salford.

Sources: The Christian Mission Magazine 1878. The Salvationist 1879.
        War Cry 1879–1903.

Manchester I. Chorlton-on-Medlock. The Temple. Corps Number 46

On 23 March 1879, a 'Hallelujah Brass Band' with Salvation soldiers marched into Chorlton-on-Medlock and by April, the 'Salvation Temple', Grosvenor Street, was opened. The work was specifically aimed at the operative and artisan classes. The Temple was designed to seat 1,800 but regularly had over 2,000 in it. General William Booth's second son, Ballington Booth, was in command. This gave

TABLE 6.5

The Number of Corps Opening Per Year

Year	Manchester No.	Total
1878	II	1
1879	I, III	2
1880	IV	1
1881	SI	1
1882	V, SII	2
1883	VI, VII, VIII, Droylsden Denton	5
1884		1
1885	IX, X, XI	3
1886	XII	1
1887		
1888	XIII, SIII	2
1889		
1890s		
1900s	XIV, XV	

Sources: *The Christian Mission Magazine 1878. The Salvationist 1879. War Cry 1880–1903*

William a special interest in the Corps. His son's command and the fact that Manchester was considered fertile ground for the Mission, led the General to say

> "Perhaps there is no building in the country after Headquarters itself, that we have come to look upon with more interest than this Temple."[18]

The opposition was fierce and the 'roughs' of this seemingly more respectable district than Ancoats broke seats, smashed windows and gas-pipes. Meetings and marches with other corps such as Manchester II helped meet this but eggshells, cabbage-stalks, mud and stones were still thrown. This continued although crowds inside averaged 1,650 per week-night. On Sundays thirteen or fourteen policemen kept the door clear with the help of several Salvationists. The extraordinary posters and continual open-air work kept up the momentum and several conversions of 'roughs' were recorded. In July 1879, Ballington Booth was sent to Belle Vue Prison for twenty-four hours on a charge of obstruction. However a later obstruction case was dismissed and both the police and the magistracy acted impartially from the time of the Army's arrival.

Army tactics ensured the most effective ground cover for example by splitting the 125 soldiers in an open-air meeting into three groups and marching into different districts before joining up again. Although

TABLE 6.6

War Cry Sales Chart Manchester 1886–1889

	1886				1887				1888				1889			
	1	2	3	4	1	2	3	4	1	2	3	4	1	2	3	4
Manchester I		520	598	520	559	702	689	533	572	715	507	559	*754*	754	806	806
Manchester II		312	390	364	390	572	650	702	637	754	494	546	*663*	611	559	559
Manchester III			390	403	481	507	611	767	819	819	494	494	*728*	806	845	871
Manchester IV		468	338	338	390	442	624	572	455	455	351	481	*546*	566	559	559
Manchester V																
Manchester VI													*364*	468	390	390
Manchester VII																
Manchester VIII		312	312	221				325	325	338	260	286	*416*	351	351	
Manchester IX																
Manchester X					325	325	312					260	*377*	429	455	455
Manchester XI							312									
Manchester XII				208			312	325	403	403	338	338	*429*	429	403	403
Manchester XIII																
Droylsden		208											*325*	325	325	364
Denton		208														
Salford I									312	312			*312*	338	338	
Salford II			234						377					312		
Salford III								364								

1. Only sales over 200 were recorded on the official published list.
2. Some districts, usually without corps in their own right, were worked by corps from other districts.
3. *Italic* figures indicate the corps received a special mention for the number of *War Cry* and *Young Soldiers* sold over Christmas 1888.

Source: War Cry 1886–1889.

some opposition was to be expected and was perhaps encouraged by the publicans, not everyone outside the Army agreed with physical opposition as a *War Cry* report notes. A milkman tried to obstruct the march but

".... many of the bystanders disagreed with the milkman's actions."[19]

Despite the marches and the attacks, the police remained supportive to the Army and were always

".... kind and attentive. The Superintendent testifies that his men are much better through attending the meetings and he himself is in full sympathy with the Army."[20]

The Army corps worked closely with each other and there were five within Manchester by March 1881. Manchester I received its 'Salvation Drum' in early June 1881 to attract more people.

"The Converted Drummer felt the glory and hit the drum so hard he broke it."[21]

Music by drum, triangle, cymbals, tambourines, three fiddles and a banjo plus gipsy and other costumes brought people into the Temple. Over 3,000 were crammed into the building by these means on one June evening. The meetings appear to have the hallmarks of revivalist meetings with

".... bitter weeping and people literally throwing themselves on the penitent-form and almost screaming for mercy."[22]

In addition, people gave up 'little idols' such as gold studs, earrings, Albert chains and pipes. It was suggested that the Army sell these but the policy was to stop them being used again. To this end they were rendered unserviceable and the old gold sold.

As this Corps was not in a solidly working-class or sectarian area, it is not surprising that people from different classes attended the meetings, some being converted. Attendance remained high and three years after its founding, people were sometimes literally fighting to get in. 'Overflow' meetings were held in the 'Hallelujah Dive', the Temple Cellar. Grand marches and processions were a way of maintaining the momentum. Numbers ranging from a few hundred to over 1,500 took part, usually with thousands lining the streets. Corps flags, chariots, music and 'Hallelujah Miriams' (factory lasses) with bare arms, clogs and playing timbrels all combined to make an attraction. The occasion varied from going to a joint church service to the first of many visits by the General. During the latter in August 1882, General Booth was the first officer to use other officers on their

TABLE 6.7

**Donations received for the Corps Debt Extinction Fund
July 1885 Manchester**

	£	s	d
Manchester I	17	5	6
Manchester II	5	11	5
Manchester III	4	12	½
Manchester IV	3	9	9½
Manchester V		18	10
Manchester VII	3	11	3½
Denton	3	16	7
Droylsden		10	8½
Salford I	5	6	2½
Salford II	4	1	11½

Source: War Cry. July 1885.

way to India to attract the crowds by costumes and later by their stories.

By October 1882, a debt of £65 had been incurred on the Temple. An eight-day campaign was launched to raise the money. Open-air and indoor meetings were arranged. The Sunday offerings alone reached £65 and this is indicative of the Army's support. Rich and poor alike mixed although the Army always claimed their particular preference was for "the poorest, lowest and worst". Attendance remained for many years that

> ". . . of a class of men and women who cannot be found in every congregation."[23]

The fact that "God saves the rich as well as the poor"[24] provided the Army with good financial support. Evidence of this was the £17 5s 6d raised by Manchester I in mid-1885 as their contribution to the Army's national attempt at eradicating all corps debts. This sum was the highest figure of any Manchester corps by nearly £12 (Table 6.7).

Ham teas, sometimes free, and soldiers in drill order continued to attract attention. Small marches took place to and from almost daily open-airs and there were some afternoon and frequent evening meetings. All Army meetings proved popular but most especially the Saturday evening 'Free and Easy'.[25] This was the Army's equivalent to the public house 'sing-song' although sometimes with testimonies in addition. The work of spreading Salvation grew with sergeants and soldiers holding open-air and indoor meetings in neighbouring districts. In the village of Birch, the Archdeacon lent the Army a room or meetings. Soldiers from the Corps, some of whom worked for the

Manchester Carriage Company, also 'worked' (conducted services and sold *War Crys*) in Rusholme. Any violence here or elsewhere, such as a soldier being ". . . knocked insensible by one of the devil's agents", was investigated thoroughly by the police.[26] The police kept up a particularly high profile at major Army events.

> "Here, there and everywhere in the crowd was to be seen the crested helmet of an officer of the Police. God bless them! Would that all others follow the example of the police of Manchester."[27]

The Army felt that there was little real serious opposition because the citizens realised that the Salvationists were trying to help them in whatever way they could.

The first recorded people from the Temple to depart for the Training Home were two female soldiers. They left in October 1883. One of the first converts was 'promoted to glory' (died) the next month. His funeral was witnessed by thousands including some who had originally thrown stones. In July 1884, Sergeant Starbuck, the writer of many of the reports and a staunch supporter of the Army died in an accident. The band, flag and singing at his burial created more interest.

In late 1884, faith-healing reports became widespread in Manchester and elsewhere. The *War Cry* reports gave details ranging from cures for brain fever and rheumatism to restoration of full eyesight. Even the most prominent of Manchester's newspapers, the Liberal *Manchester Guardian,* gave descriptions. Faith-healing meetings continued into the following year.

During the remainder of the nineteenth century, the Corps remained in a well sited geographic position, attracting good financial support from the surrounding mix of social classes. It also loudly proclaimed its fight against drink and Manchester's 5,000 prostitutes. There were comparatively fewer reports published for Manchester I in 1886 and 1887 although in all other years of that decade it had the most (Appendix 9). This suggests that the Corps experienced some difficulties although the figures are comparative with its earlier and later years and the Corps was always in a powerful and respected position. Table 6.6 shows an ever-increasing number of *War Cry* sales from 1886, evidence of a stable and growing Corps.

Towards the end of 1887 more converts were being made and more people regularly attended the meetings. A Junior Soldiers' Corps (young people) within the main corps framework was opened in April 1888 and Captain Marston was appointed in-charge. Both corps increased in size and strength. In July 1889, £600 of renovations and alterations were carried out to the meeting-place. This work included raising the floor, removing the pews and erecting the gallery. The Corps were fortunate in receiving financial support from Mr. F. W. Crossley J.P. The gas-strike during the winter of 1889–1890 did not prevent any service as candlelight was used. Manchester I continued services throughout the 1890s, maintaining a high level of support, and the Corps was in good order in 1905.

The Impact of the Salvation Army

The need to maintain the momentum of what was, after only a few weeks, a local spiritual revival, was not a problem because of the natural zeal of the Salvationists. This zeal came out in the activities making up the daily lives of the soldiers and tended to pervade their daily lives. Any and every occasion was used by the Army to 'reach the masses' and the activities demonstrated by Manchester I and II became commonplace throughout neighbouring corps. Marches were held, sometimes several times weekly, to serve the dual purpose of being seen as a happy, singing, unified body as well as serving to increase members' sense of identity. Salford I held drill-classes so that their precision marching and tactics of march — stop briefly to proclaim the Gospel, and march again — would be effective against the many "devil bound" people who gave only a limited response. The use of planned tactics became a feature of the Army's 'attack' on Manchester. Many of these tactics were highly successful, for example, the splitting up of available soldiers to march into different districts before meeting up again.

Various brigades for specific works were formed in the early 1880s and were common within all corps. Manchester III, Lower Openshaw, had brigades to sell *War Cry*, visit the ill and shop for the old. Droylsden's *War Cry* Brigade spaced themselves at 50 yard intervals along the main pavements in an often successful attempt to sell hundreds of papers within a few hours. The *War Cry* itself praised such attempts and published a regular league chart indicating those corps doing well or badly (Table 6.6). On important occasions such as Wakes (Holiday) Week, all the corps in the area attended rallies and held marches wherever large numbers of the public appeared.

Funerals of Salvationist Mancunians became large events with crowds of over two thousand attending and thousands of others lining the streets to watch. Each funeral was conducted with a "grand march"[28] and clearly followed the Founder's belief that

> ". . . wearing black clothing heavily trimmed with sombre crape as a sign of mourning (is) opposed to the teaching of Christ. . . (and that every funeral should be used for). . . urging the unsaved to seek and find salvation."[29]

To accompany the marches, be they funerals or the several held during the week, bands were formed as soon as membership and finances would allow. The first of Manchester's many Army bands was formed by March 1879, nine months before General Booth officially allowed their establishment. People were clearly attracted by bands and drums. The band of Manchester II had 40 musicians in it by April 1883. The first bands were often made up of a variety of instruments ranging from fifes, to a 'concertina and timbrel band' and, in Manchester VI's case, just 'a cornet and fiddle.'

On many occasions throughout the year soldiers and bands would support neighbouring corps. Manchester VI was opened on 10 February 1883. The 'Converted Greengrocer' wrote

"On Sunday morning Captain Mother Shepherd opened fire at this station. The band of Manchester IV roused the town in good time. A strong detachment of 'Blood and Fire' soldiers poured in the red-hot shot. The devil kicked at the truth. The Holy Ghost came down, and at night there was a mighty conviction, and we had nine souls in the fountain."[30]

Manchester VII had frequent visits of support from the bands of Manchester I and III, both bands being much in evidence in many parts of the city. Visiting speakers from other corps proved popular, particularly 'Busting Billy' from Manchester III and Billy McLeod of Manchester V.

Billy McLeod was one of the most famous 'captures' made by the Army in the nineteenth century. He was a champion pugilist, with a considerable national reputation, and became a member of the Salvation Army in December 1882 at Manchester V. *The Sporting Chronicle*

"... expressed the hope that if the rumour that Billy McLeod had joined the Salvation Army were true, he would be as zealous in his undertaking as in the old, and that he would make a 'Famous champion for the Army.' "[31]

Several other conversions were notable locally, one being Nancy Dickybird (Mrs. Cunningham). She was Manchester's most notorious alcoholic and served 173 terms of imprisonment. A Salvationist policeman who was often one of the three or four it took to arrest her, found her one evening asleep in an outside toilet.

"He gave her a hot drink and told her what God had done for him. He then invited her to the Army."[32]

She went to a meeting after accidentally coming across an open-air meeting. After her conversion, many people attended meetings just to hear her sing. She became so well known that the Army used her on one of their turn of the century 'before and after conversion' postcards.

To encourage people to enter Army halls, a number of unusual sights were advertised, often by prominent and brightly coloured

Nancy Dickybird, once the terror of the Manchester Police, served 173 terms of imprisonment, now a modern miracle, AS SHE IS.

General Booth during one of his "Two Days With God" campaigns. He is seen here at the Exeter Hall, London, on 17 November 1890.

posters. One of the most popular events proved to be visits and talks by officers on their way to India. General Booth first used this in Manchester in August 1882. Other corps then had 'Indian Durbar and Missionary Demonstrations', and talks by officers in their Indian clothing. Another popular event were teas for soldiers or children or the poor and unemployed. Meetings were sometimes followed by "Hallelujah (apple-dumpling and pudding) suppers."[33] Some of the teas would be free such as that given for 500 poor children by the corps of Manchester V in July 1885. Many of these children.

> "... were both hatless and shoeless ... (their families) ... are almost destitute of the common necessities of life. Yet it is a singular fact that there are scores of drinkshops in the neighbourhood, and each of them do a thriving business in the very midst of literal starvation."[34]

Sometimes the teas would be charged for with the profits going to various funds. This was the case with the Good Friday Tea at Droylsden where the £9 16s profit went to the new Barrack Fund.

A number of other activities as well as the style of many of the meetings kept up the interest in the Army and continued the revival in the city. The Junior Soldiers' Corps belonging to Manchester I grew strongly in the latter 1880s although the strongest children's Corps was at Manchester III in May 1884. There were 237 'Little Soldiers' who, modelled on the senior Corps, held meetings and marches. Soldiers leaving for the Training Homes in London were always given large 'farewell-meetings' and large crowds also attended the releases from prison of the very few Salvationists charged and found guilty, usually of obstruction. The most notable cases occurred in July 1879, when Ballington Booth was sent to Belle Vue Prison, and in September and October 1888. In the latter case, three charges of obstruction were brought against the officers of Manchester IV. The first (8 September), against Lieutenant Courtney, was dismissed; the second (22 September), against Captain Daymond, was proven and he was sent to Strangeways prison on his refusal to pay the fine imposed; the third (6 October) came about because Captain Daymond and Lieutenant Fowel held a celebratory procession on the former's release. Both were arrested, placed "before the beaks", and found guilty. The fine was 2s 6d plus costs or three days. The prisoners took the latter.[35]

Two of the most unusual aspects of the Army in Manchester in the 1880s were the style of its meetings and the faith-healing practised in many corps. The Salvation Army had an unashamedly charismatic approach to many of its meetings. Jumping, singing and prayer were often reported to have taken place in meetings. At Salford I in August 1885, it was reported that

"We are having remarkable manifestations of the outpourings of God's Holy Spirit . . . many sob and cry (especially in the open-air meetings). Hallelujah."[36]

The faith-healing was most evident in late 1884 and throughout 1885. The healing was widely reported in the religious and secular press.

The enthusiasm of the Salvationists to promote their religious beliefs gave the impetus for the rapid local expansion of the Army. Small groups of soldiers evangelised in neighbouring districts and, often with the help of other nearby corps, fledgling corps were established. One such was Denton, first mentioned as an 'outpost' or fledgling Corps, worked by Droylsden in June 1883. It was described as a "promising infant".[37] Although numbers were small at first with only 39 on a march to the Corporation Hall in July, the work did slowly progress. No proper rooms had been found for meetings by February 1884. The Barracks could be had only one night a week and so cottage meetings were held. On Thursday nights and all day Sunday, the Barracks (the Corporation Hall holding 400) was well used.

In early March 1884, Denton became a Corps in its own right. A flag was presented and 76 soldiers were present at the night meeting. It had a Little Soldiers group and in late August 1884, opened an outpost at Houghton Green. In July 1885 the Corps donated the comparatively high sum of £3 16s 7d to the Corps Debt Extinction Fund (Table 6.7). This indicates a well established Corps which later reports tend to confirm. Denton was therefore one of the best examples of the 'springboard' policy of growth, first initiated in the early 1870s by William Booth.

Opposition

Although the early Manchester and Salford corps did suffer some bloody opposition, there is no evidence to suggest it was organised or widespread. In considering the question of opposition to the Salvation Army, Victor Bailey wrote that

"... there was a rough correspondence in time between the direction of Salvation Army expansion and the riots."[38]

However at the time of the Army's first appearance and subsequent rapid development in north-west England between 1878 and 1882, there was only brief rioting, the worst being in Sheffield (Yorkshire) in 1881 and Birkenhead (Cheshire) in 1882. With so little opposition in Manchester, one of the most powerful cities in the heartland of the industrial north and therefore a place of major importance to the Salvation Army, Bailey's view cannot stand. The mere arrival of the Army was in itself not enough to cause widespread disorder. There were other causes, most notably elements of the local authority utilising the twin vehicles of repression: tradition and the law. These elements represented interests likely to be affected by the Army, either via trades benefiting from riot damage or more probably via the drink trade which at least at first feared the Army. Elements in the local authority could firstly organise the 'rough-musicing' tradition where possible and secondly encourage it by using the police and magistrates' courts to fine or imprison the Army and be lenient on 'the mob'. This appears to have only happened though in the conservative south where centuries old social ties remained stong. In Manchester many old social ties had broken down due to massive migrations of workers from various communities.

There was little 'rough-musicing' in Manchester and the legal authority did not persecute the Army. In fact they encouraged it with conscientious police action being backed up by the magistrates, particularly magistrate sympathisers such as Mr. Crossley. The local newspapers had no doubt that the increase in religion had benefited the city. The *Manchester Examiner* of 6 January 1881 reported the Recorder as congratulating the Grand Jury on the lightness of the calendar. This, he suggested, was probably due to the "... increase in morals in the city in recent months."[39] The anti-Army violence was generally opportunist and attracted little support. Any action, such as the publican of the Church Inn, Ashton Old Road, dousing some soldiers of Manchester III with water, could cause considerable debate in the newspapers. Whether the opposition was opportunist, due to the sectarianism in 'Little Ireland', or to 'rough-musicing', it did not find sympathy with the Law.

Support

The Army's expansion in Manchester was aided by the generosity and public support of a number of prominent local citizens. Foremost amongst these was Mr. F. W. Crossley, a leading local businessman and the inventor of the internal combustion engine. He contacted William Booth in the mid-1880s, 'found Salvation', and thereafter remained staunchly pro-Army. At one point in the late 1880s, when a Salvation Army lass was on a charge of obstruction, he left his place on the Magistrates' Bench and stood beside her. Such an action encouraged the already strong police determination to protect the Army. Crossley became probably the Army's most liberal helper and was unofficially known for a period as 'The Paymaster', giving well over £100,000. To facilitate further the Army's work in Manchester, the Crossley family bought the Star Music Hall at a cost of £20,000. It was their intention to convert it into a large corps complex or demolish it and put a purpose built hall on the site. It was then to have been given to General Booth. They opted for the latter scheme but decided to run the mission hall themselves. It was however willed to the Army who took charge on 24 October 1918. The building replaced the old Temple and became Manchester I, Star Hall. By 1920, as Manchester II, Every Street and Manchester V, Bradford Road, were in close proximity to Manchester I in Pollard Street, they amalgamated.

Another prominent supporter in Manchester was Thomas Renshaw Esq. He took a particular interest in Manchester III, Lower Openshaw, but financially and publicly helped the Movement generally. This help included gifts of money and attendance at meetings. In Higher Openshaw, the factory-owning and Salvationist Hallard family requested the establishment of a corps near their factory. They guaranteed its finances and in May 1903, Manchester XV opened. Within a few months it had 170 soldiers and the Corps continued to have high attendances for many years.

The churches appear to have had a friendly attitude towards the Salvation Army and joint services with the Wesleyans and other denominations took place on a number of occasions. During the Army's expansion to the villages, various churches lent rooms for services. Where the Army had few friends at first, the inter-corps support proved invaluable. Additional support came from the visits of senior officers, particularly General Booth. He visited Manchester nine times between 1880 and 1889. The Free Trade Hall in Peter Street was usually used as, although the cost was high, it could seat 3,236 people. On one occasion St. James' Hall was engaged as this could hold as many. Mrs. Booth and one or two of their children accompanied the General (except in 1889) as did senior staff officers. Each visit was marked by a procession through the streets with banners, flags, pennants, bands, mounted officers and chariots. Their usual route would take them to The Temple and then to the Free Trade Hall. *The Times* wrote of the 'Council of War' in 1882

> "The proceedings throughout were of an enthusiastic but orderly character."[40]

By 1888 regular "Two Days With God" were being conducted by the General in all major cities in the United Kingdom. The first of that year was held in Manchester and was followed by Bristol (February), Plymouth (February), Leeds and Glasgow (March), Norwich (April), and others as the year progressed. In January 1889 the cycle started again. Such 'rallies', all of which were packed and a great success, were used to disseminate news about the Army, remind the soldiers and friends what the Army was fighting for, give the General's views on matters such as faith-healing and evangelism, and for senior staff to meet corps officers. Hundreds of people came in from the surrounding towns and villages, often by trains put on at the Army's special request. In January 1888, six railway companies cooperated to cover some 250 stations from as far away as North Wales, in order to bring Salvationists to Manchester.

Membership and Finance

There are only a few extant references to numbers and occupations of members of the Salvation Army in Manchester. The majority of these references refer to a wide social range spread predominantly, although not always, through the working-class. Reports of hundreds of people being converted in Manchester during the late 1870s and early 1880s would suggest large corps by 1885. Certainly there were such corps, for example the successful Manchester I. Other corps, particularly those in the poorest areas such as Manchester XI, Moss Side, suffered from a lack of members despite "a desperate hand-to-hand conflict".

A previous commanding officer of Manchester IV, Captain Agnes Peck, returned for a visit to the Corps in late 1885. During her eight month stay between 1881 and 1882, 1,800 people professed conversion. Referring to these people during her visit she said some were still there, others were at newer corps nearer their homes, some were at other churches, some had moved, some were officers, some were dead, and some had left. She made no mention of the numbers in each category. It is therefore not possible to give even approximate numbers of soldiers in Manchester although the figure would have been in excess of 2,000 with a larger actual attendance.[41]

As elsewhere in the Army's sphere of operations, the Manchester corps had to finance themselves. Money making ideas, in addition to the collections at meetings, became common. Gold offerings and teas were often used as were direct appeals to help clear debts. A general appeal in 1885, to clear debts incurred by the building and running of corps, revealed which Manchester corps were wealthy and which were poor (Table 6.7). Many of the soldiers, particularly those from Manchester III, contributed very small amounts, thus suggesting a large number of very poor soldiers.

The Officers

The first Divisional Commander (hereafter D.C.) of the Lancashire Division, as it was originally known, was Major Pearson. The District Officer in charge of the Manchester area was Major (and Mrs.) Taylor. His A.D.C. in February 1883 was Captain Brain. The Captain had been in command of Manchester I, the Temple, from 13 August 1882 until he took up this appointment on 21 December 1882. The junior staff officers did not change at the same time as the senior officers in an attempt to keep some continuity, especially in knowledge of the area and its officers.

The importance of Manchester to the nation's economy led to its obvious choice as a command centre for the Salvation Army's operations in that area. The rapid extension of the Army in the north of England meant that smaller Divisions were created so as to be able to cope with the increasing amount of work. In August 1886, the Lancashire Division thus became the Liverpool and Manchester Division. In May 1888 it was further split and was called the Manchester and Bolton Division. Three months later it was being referred to as the Manchester Division. The Divisional Headquarters in 1884 were in Ardwick Green which neighboured Ancoats. The Divisional (Supplies) Depot was at number 3 and the Lancashire Finance Brigade was at number 8. The Brigade raised money, especially by having people promise 5s or 2/6 twice a year. By July, the Divisional Headquarters was in Swan Street. The cashier was Captain Cadman. All the Divisional Staff worked hard in visiting corps and would frequently conduct weekends or meetings. Their aim was to encourage as well as see for themselves that all was progressing. Other officers from outside the Division would visit the city; for example Captain Bullock of the Women's Training Home visited the Temple in August 1883.

The movement of officers was also frequent (Table 6.8). This was a national policy to maintain momentum. Sometimes the officers moved to other corps in the area; for example Captain Webly of Salford II moved to Manchester II in January 1887. Occasionally they moved to Divisional positions as with Captain Brain. Officer training was very quick with candidates first being assigned to officers. They then went to the Training Home at Clapton and after an individually varying period of classroom and corps training in the vicinity, were commissioned as either Captain or Lieutenant depending on their progress. As increasing numbers joined the officer corps, by 1886 the standard practice became to be commissioned Lieutenant. This early training generally took only a few weeks.

The officers would frequently use nicknames, sometimes to indicate their place of origin as with Captain 'Blackburn' Smith of Manchester VIII, or to suggest a special aspect of their ministry. An example of the latter might be Captain Perkins, the 'Cornish Fisher Lad', of Salford II. This name is both geographic and suggestive as fishing may have been his previous livelihood. More likely it is used in the spiritual sense of

> "... moving around the congregation in a prayer meeting, trying to help those who seem to be concerned about their souls' welfare and

TABLE 6.8

Average Stay of Officers per Corps

	1880s		1890s	
Corps	Months	Days	Months	Days
Manchester I	5	—	—	—
Manchester II.	6	—	11	—
Manchester III	6	—	7	—
Manchester IV	8	7	—	—
Manchester V	5	19	—	—
Manchester VI	5	16	—	—
Manchester VII	5	7	—	—
Manchester VIII	6	15	12	—
Manchester IX	7	—	—	—
Manchester X	6	—	—	—
Manchester XI★	3	—	—	—
Manchester XII	5	12	—	—
Manchester XIII.	6	—	—	—
Salford I	5	12	—	—
Salford II.	6	—	—	—
Salford III	6	—	—	—
Droylsden.	6	—	—	—
Denton	4	20	—	—

Notes:
1. The average stay of officers in Manchester during the 1880s was 5 months 21 days. Some officers were at their corps for such a short time that their names have not survived.
2. This Table is based on the Commanding Officer. In some cases the second in command, usually a Lieutenant, remained to provide a continuity.

★ This corps had only two recorded officers in approximately 6 months.

Sources: War Cry 1880–1900.
    Corps History Books. Manchester I, VIII, IX, Star Hall.

appear to be almost persuaded to kneel at the Penitent-Form and pray that God will forgive sins."[42]

'Fishing' is also conducted from the platform. Nicknames in the Army were in vogue from the earliest times and were publicly used by the General for all his children as they took on positions of responsibility. Their daughter Catherine, who became the pioneer of the Army's work in France, was known as 'The Maréchale' (The Marshal) in 1881.[43]

Corps Buildings

None of the early Manchester corps buildings remain today. The few extant pictures show the "usual Army style"[44] of a fortress-like building. Wherever the Army had its halls purpose-built, they resembled a miniature fortress complete with turrets and crenellation. Where they could only lease land (or in the villages for reasons of cost), they often erected Barracks of corrugated iron. As such constructions were cheap and easy to put up, they played an important part in the spread of the Salvation Army, the development of the Home Mission Movement,[45] and therefore religion in the nineteenth century.

In January 1884, the eight corps (Manchester I to VIII) buildings then established held 2,000, 600, 800, 1,200, 500, 1,500 and 600, respectively. Salford I held 600 and II, 1,000. Denton held 400 and Droylsden, 300.[46] The seating capacity was therefore 10,100, approximately 1.36% of Manchester Parish's population. Little is known of the interior of the buildings, but the impression is of simply furnished rooms with benches, a raised platform and no decoration. The Army willingly used any accommodation such as a local Co-operative Hall. There are many descriptions of apparently unsuitable rooms being used for a long period of time. The siting of such places was important and the Army preferred halls on or near public thoroughfares for ease of access. In accordance with General Booth's policy of having non-Church like names for the Army's buildings, a number of corps adopted such titles as the Salvation Shed or Poor Man's Palace (Manchester III), Old Glory Shop (Manchester VI), and Salvation Army Tabernacle (Salford I).

Corps Openings and Closures

Between 1878 and 1883 inclusive, the Army opened twelve corps within Manchester Parish, five of these in 1883 itself (Table 6.5). This growth corresponds with the fastest period of Army growth nationally. Manchester had the largest concentration of corps in any city throughout the Army's history. The first Manchester Corps was in a poverty-stricken area, the second in a middle to upper working-class area. Over the next two decades the Army established a further 18 corps all over the Parish. The majority of them were in the lower working-class areas. Some of the corps such as Manchester V and VIII found it hard to survive, probably mainly due to lack of finances as both districts were extremely impoverished. The *War Cry,* although occasionally reporting 'difficulties', never announced the closure of a corps. To identify closures, Appendix 9 (monthly reports), Table 6.4 (opening dates), Table 6.6 (*War Cry* sales), Table 6.7 (donations), and evidence of corps renumbering are invaluable. It is possible to see where the Army 'attack' faltered or collapsed and taken together, the evidence provides an accurate picture. The closures of Manchester VII, IX and XI, all corps originally opened by December 1885, are

The Poor Man's Palace was opened in Dyer Street, Openshaw (Manchester III), on 29 August 1885. It was designed by Commissioner Sherwood and could hold 2,000 persons. The total cost to build and equip was £1,800.

clearly demonstrated from the Tables and Appendix, thus, Manchester XI had no reports after June 1886 in Appendix 9, no *War Cry* sales (Table 6.6), and an obvious later renumbering (Table 6.4).

All but one of Manchester's 20 corps were in existence in 1905.[47] The Movement's success was mainly due to its initial novelty and the obvious sincerity of officers and soldiers in helping people. This in itself does not entirely explain why the Army thrived not only in areas of considerable deprivation, often worsened by trade fluctuations, but also in areas of socially mixed groups of workers and working middle-classes. Why did it appeal to the different strata? Much of the answer may well relate to the mobility, both social and geographical, experienced by tens of thousands of people. The high wages of many Mancunians contrasted with the plight of thousands of others, especially textile workers on low wages, who lived in impoverished conditions. Thousands of people were therefore upwardly and downwardly mobile depending on their occupation, the condition of trade, and, to a certain degree, age, health and marriage. The period roughly bounded by 1850 to 1875 was also one of continued population rise

(Table 6.1) mainly due to further rapid urbanisation. In cases of social and more particularly geographical mobility, it is possible that the increasingly ubiquitous Army acted as E. P. Thompson suggests Methodism did a century earlier, that is as a "kind of community" replacing older, displaced community patterns. Certainly the Army, with its daily meetings and frequent marches, demanded a total commitment which included attempting to convert workmates and those you came into daily contact with. E. T. Davies suggests something similar to Thompson to explain

> ". . . the great growth of Nonconformity in industrial south Wales . . . He suggests that the chapels were especially attractive to immigrants from the countryside, seeking some tenuous link with home."[48]

Certainly John Kent sees the success of the Army in these terms for it stirred up, particularly in its 'holiness meeting',

> ". . . a strong surviving urban nostalgia for the methods and excitements of earlier Methodism, not least in its Primitive Methodist form."[49]

Conclusion

The tactics adopted by the Salvation Army in their 'invasion' of Manchester were clearly successful. Nationally once a corps moved into an area, its aim was to consolidate and reproduce. This 'springboard' policy, used town to town by the Christian Mission, not only continued to be used by the Salvation Army, but was refined for 'attacking' district to district. Upon establishment, movements such as Droylsden Corps holding meetings in Denton, which in itself became a Corps holding meetings at Houghton Green, were commonplace. Different corps 'attacked' different areas and sometimes, as in Deansgate, the same area.

Once a number of corps were established within an immediate area, mutual aid played a very important part in maintaining momentum. Great encouragement must have been derived by soldiers and bands from one corps visiting another, visits from staff-officers, officers on their way to India, and the numerous activities taking place within the corps. All such factors contributed to keep the Army to the forefront of local life. In addition the discipline of the officers and soldiers ensured persistence. This persistence came in not stopping open-air meetings because of the weather and, once out, marching and spreading the Gospel with well-drilled efficiency. Such drill included stopping every few minutes when on the march to allow soldiers to enter side streets to sing a song (hymn) or 'fire a volley' (shout Gospel verses).

Within the corps structure, the organisation of sergeants and brigades ensured the best use of manpower as well as people having a job and being active within the Movement. The Army also made effective use of its time, especially during Wakes Week when the Salvation Army bands and soldiers would be out in force.[50] This again kept the Army to the fore as did a consistent attitude to the selling of *War Cry*. It was sold not only to the public but also to the soldiers. The paper was optimistic, encouraging and moralistic and easily conveyed the General's messages. Much of the evangelical militaristic jargon was only understood by the soldiers and this, plus seeing corps reports and corps names in official lists such as *War Cry* sales, must have increased their sense of identity as people as well as their dedication to the organisation.

As all the Manchester corps other than Salford III were in operation in 1905, the city had indeed proved fertile ground for the Army. Manchester was the Army's great success. The policy of attempting to integrate and identify with the people be they in the socially-mixed or poor working-class areas, worked well. The possible early setback of the first Manchester Corps, Manchester II, situated in the poverty of 'Little Ireland', was relieved by the opening of Manchester I and III in the nearby socially mixed Chorlton-on-Medlock and mixed working-class Lower Openshaw. When the numbers and positions of corps opening are considered alongside the support of local Army patrons such as Crossley and Renshaw, the local authorities and, although rarely mentioned, the various churches and especially Wesleyan Chapels, it is clear that the Army received often considerable support from across the social classes.

CHAPTER SEVEN

GUILDFORD, SURREY: A CASE-STUDY

I. BACKGROUND

The Victorian town of Guildford lay thirty miles from London in the south-west quarter of the county of Surrey. During the first four decades of the nineteenth century, the town's population increased only slowly. After 1841 this growth became more rapid and the overall increase for the century was 758% (327% for the Registration District, Table 8.1).

> "Most of this was by immigration, the birth-rate of the town being consistently below the national average."[1]

Many of these immigrants settled into the ever more crowded working-class Parishes of St. Nicholas and Friary. The latter was the poorest part of Guildford and contained the bulk of the town's slums in an area bounded by the High Street in the south, the river in the west, Chertsey Street to the east and the better type of artisan dwellings of

TABLE 7.1

The Population of Guildford 1801-1901

Year	Town Total	Registration District Total
1801	2,634	14,548
1811	2,974	15,854
1821	3,161	18,421
1831	3,916	21,045
1841	4,074	23,081
1851	6,740	25,072
1861	9,643	29,330
1871	11,113	35,667
1881	14,738	42,696
1891	19,448	51,676
1901	22,616	62,122

Sources: Census of England and Wales. 1801-1901. Population Respective Vol. I.'s.

Markenfield Road to the north. The neighbouring 'new' housing estate of Charlotteville, started in 1862 to cope with the influx of people into the town, had very few lower working-class citizens.

Generally untouched by the better-built housing being erected from the 1860s, many of the lower working-class clearly suffered extreme hardship in accommodation. Guildford's Medical Officer, in a letter dated December 1879 and addressed to the Editor of the main area newspaper, wrote:

> ". . . such is the demand for cottages in this town that they are easily let with all drawbacks . . . Many new cottages of a pretentious appearance are not a whit better than the old ones (being) too thin a structure."

He suggested both that new laws be passed and enforced to ensure that speculative builders and owners built and kept houses that were habitable and not a health hazard, and that new housing of a better standard and cheaper rent was needed.[2] Clearly little immediate notice was taken for in the following year the old Militia Barracks were sold for conversion to accommodation. Within two years the rooms were amongst the poorest in the town.

> "The Medical Officer reported that the houses were in a deplorable condition with up to eleven families per house."[3]

The majority of Guildford's population was employed in brewing, printing, the hostelry trade, the iron foundry, farming or retail work. A few were employed by the railway companies.[4] Guildford was essentially a rural market town which thrived on its cattle, trade with the surrounding British Army camps, and its extensive retail trade based in the High Street. This trade

> ". . . was rarely subject to adverse fluctuations deriving material support from the great thoroughfare position of the town."[5]

As a religious centre, Guildford had for many centuries maintained a relatively important position and, by the time of the *Census of Religious Worship, 1851,* a wide range of denominations had been established (Table 7.2). By national standards the town was religiously well served, being able to accommodate 54.62% of the Registration District's population. This was better than the county figure of 49%. The Church of England was in a dominant position in the town as it was in Surrey generally. The Established Church had approximately three times as much accommodation as all the other denominations combined, mainly due to the spate of church-building evident in the preceding decade. This does not mean that the majority of people attended church or chapel despite the fact that over half the seats in Guildford's religious buildings were free, (4,898 as opposed to 4,022

TABLE 7.2

Religious Accommodation and Attendance in Guildford, 1851

Denominations	Number of Buildings	Sittings	Number Attending		
			M	A	E
Protestant Churches:					
Church of England	25	9,670	5,641	4,666	566
Independents.	7	1,487	920	106	837
Baptists	4	570	237	198	260
Society of Friends	2	350	27	10	—
Wesleyan Methodists	1	384	250	—	250
Undefined	3	310	40	118	60
Other Christian Churches:					
Roman Catholic	1	120	60	24	—
Catholic and Apostolic Church	1	50	30	—	30
Totals.	44	12,941	7,205	5,122	2,003

Notes:
1. Population was 25,072.
2. Four places of worship failed to complete their returns as to sittings. The enumerators therefore estimated that an additional 754 seats were available bringing the total to 13,695.

Source: Census of Religious Worship. 1851. Table H. p. cclxxix.

appropriated).[6] Adding together the highest attendance figures for each denomination produces a total of 29.14%. Although this is well under a third of the population, it does indicate that attendance at a religious service was of some importance. There is evidence to suggest that this did not apply throughout the social classes and it appears that the majority of those absenting themselves were the lower working-class and the very poor.[7] Possibly the geographical positioning of all, including the newest buildings of the Established Church, reflected its unpopularity with the working-class. It was the Nonconformist places of worship that were grouped and continued to establish themselves[8] within the poorer and slum area of the town centering around the Friary. Several of these though had 'pew-rents' and this, plus their image of respectability, apparently left the bulk of the working-class unaffected.

II. THE SALVATION ARMY

It is possible that Salvationists visited Guildford in 1878. The Corps number is 117 and numbers around that particular one were allocated to corps commencing in late 1879.[9] Further evidence comes from the *War Cry* of 10 January 1880 when Guildford was mentioned as having had this paper sold in the town at the rate of 280 and 250 copies on the previous Thursday and Saturday respectively.[10] There is no other mention of the Army in Guildford in any extant source until December 1881.[11] Thus, either an attempt to establish a corps here failed or more likely, late 1879 and early 1880 was a reconnaissance period.

As in other areas such as Poplar[12] and Honiton, the Salvation Army was invited into Guildford. The invitation was issued by the Reverend Francis Paynter, one of the local leading Church of England men, rector of Stoke-next-Guildford, and prominent Blue Ribbon (temperance) campaigner.[13] Mrs. Booth had been invited to preach in Guildford in mid-1881. Her subject was the development of immorality and sin in the country which necessitated an organisation such as the Salvation Army being established.[14] Exactly when this took place and how it was received are not known but it is possible that the Reverend Paynter attended and then wrote to William Booth asking him "to send someone down to Guildford."[15]

In the by now typical Salvation Army fashion, the Movement ensured that its arrival on Sunday 19 December 1881 was well-heralded. Coloured posters were put up in advance and 'Hallelujah Lasses' ringing a hand-bell announced their arrival on the Saturday night. The first Sunday morning meeting was attended by about 300 people who came principally to see and hear this "Church Militant". In the afternoon meeting between 500 and 600 met but on the preceding march

> "... nearly the whole town offered some slight opposition in the way of counter-singing, shouting and so on."

However although many of these verbal opposers were

> "... habitués of places of worship far different from churches and chapels,"

there were some pro-Army supporters

> "including many well-known Guildfordian faces and several ladies."

Mr. Law, the Police Superintendent, attended the evening meeting in case of trouble. He had to intervene once from the platform to prevent a breach of the peace. He reminded the 'worshippers' that they were in a Chapel (although originally it was the armoury of the Militia Barracks). In reporting the above, *The Surrey Advertiser* accorded a warm welcome to the Salvation Army.[16]

The Army's reception in the town was cleary mixed. The *War Cry* maintained a buoyantly optimistic approach with reports of many converts in the first three months.[17] It was also reported though that ". . . the devil and his host were let loose on us" and people complained that Sundays were no longer quiet days because of the noise engendered by the Army and their opposers during processions.[18] The initial anti-Army disturbances rapidly became more serious. On 7 January 1882 Salvation Army indoor services were interrupted despite the presence of police officers. Although there was a large body of worshippers inside each time, a mob became intent on breaking up the meetings. Five people were summonsed for riotous and indecent behaviour in a place duly certified for public worship. The defence and prosecution amicably agreed that one guilty plea should be lodged and in a packed court room, a fine of £1 was imposed as ". . . a lesson to other persons not to behave in a like manner."[19]

Newspaper advertisements, handbills and posters were made use of by the Army in an attempt to maintain a high profile and turn people's minds to religion. This charismatic, and to many, enigmatic Movement certainly drew attention to itself and succeeded in triggering off the 'rough-musicing' which, up until the mid-1860s, had been common in Guildford. As marches were a daily occurrence, the 'roughs' had plenty of opportunity to indulge in anti-Army actions. Several of the attackers were summonsed by the police on charges of nuisance and/or obstruction. Contrary to the expression of disapproval in the previous and first magistrates' case involving the Guildford Corps (where however only one defendant had been fined), here most of the defendants were released and the Army blamed for causing the violence. The magistrates considered that the Movement was by its very nature stirring-up passion and, being so public about it, could expect opposition.[20]

In early March Captain Knight was severely injured in a bloody and "cowardly assault". At the same time the atmosphere was hardening against the Army as typified by Councillor Bullen. He requested the Town Council to stop the disturbances caused by the Salvation Army by banning them from marching. The Mayor, William Triggs, replied that action would be taken. He then, as presiding magistrate, dismissed the charges brought against those believed to have attacked the Captain. The Mayor wrote to the Army:

> "My brother magistrates and myself trust that these processions will cease as their tendency is to create a riot."

Before and despite this, Mr. Law ordered police protection against the continuing violence and made it clear that the Salvation Army must and would be given protection, at least in their own meeting-house.[21]

186

Captain Knight being kicked and beaten in a Guildford street.

Correspondence in the local press during March and April suggests that opinion was very divided about the Army in Guildford. From newspaper reports though, it is clear that financial and moral support was being given to the Movement by the Onslow family, Denzil Onslow being the town's Liberal M.P.[22] In addition, many members of the religious community welcomed the Army. The Reverend Paynter offered schoolrooms in the neighbouring parish of Stoke for the Army's use. He and other churchmen held a Church of England–Salvation Army service on Good Friday 1882 which was well attended. The following month, a pro-Army sermon at Holy Trinity, the bastion of Anglicanism in Guildford, was well received.[23] During the anniversary services of the Primitive Methodists in Guildford, verbal support was given to both the Salvation Army and the Blue Ribbon Army. The objects of the latter Movement were similar to those of the Army in converting people and having them become total abstainers.[24]

The Army heeded the Mayor and abandoned its processions during much of March.[25] However in April, Captain and Mrs. Bryan took command of the Corps, Captain Knight and Lieutenant Griffiths moving to new appointments.[26] The Bryans attempted to restart the processions led by Guildford's twenty strong band. The first march ended with the Captain being ". . . struck in the face and receiv(ing) a dreadful cut on his face." General Booth therefore again ordered the processions to cease,[27] which they did apparently from mid-May to early August.[28]

During this period the indoor meetings continued, as did considerable literary support. In mid-May *The Surrey Advertiser* reported that Mr. Law had reissued instructions to his men to protect the Salvationists. At the same time, church support for the Army was clearly stated in an open letter to the paper. Eight clergymen and ministers, led by the Reverend Paynter but from a range of denominations, defended the Army's legal right to go unmolested. They also attacked the Local Authority's dilatoriness in protecting the Movement. A second letter from the Reverend Paynter pointed out that the National Convocation of the Church of England and the Salvation Army leaders were soon meeting to discuss the possibility of unification. The following week an editorial condemned the Government for not facing the issues involved in national violence against the Army and also defended the Army's right to protection.

With the processions temporarily halted the physical violence lessened but interruptions within the Barracks continued as did attempts at defamation of the Army. A story appeared in *The Surrey Advertiser* that a fifteen-year old girl had disappeared after coming into contact with the Army. Mr. Law investigated the case and found the young lady was not detained by members of the Movement but had in fact arranged to run away from home.[29] One point to emerge from this was that the officers had no quarters of their own and were living with the respected Guildford photographer, Mr. Bassett of Stoke Road. During the following month quarters were found at 12 Hill Place, Sydenham Road.[30]

At the end of July General Booth issued a general order that processions and open-air meetings were to be carefully conducted. Church services were not to be disturbed nor were umbrellas or sticks to be used to conduct bands or singing as this might be seen as a threatening gesture. At the start of August processions in Guildford resumed. About the same time a detachment of Guildford Corps soldiers marched to 'attack' the nearby village of East Clandon and Captain George Milliner took charge there.[31]

The restarted processions provoked fresh physical assaults. In East Clandon Captain Milliner was found guilty of assaulting Mr. Earwaker, a worker who had in earlier months physically attacked the Army.[32] In Guildford itself, the Army wrote to the Watch Committee seeking protection.

"A letter from the Salvation Army accompanying the Report was also read asking that the Police should afford protection to the Army in their processions through the town when it was resolved that the Police be instructed to prevent as far as possible any breach of the peace being committed and to give every assistance in their power on prosecutions being instituted by the members of the Army in identifying and securing the punishment of any persons who have committed an assault."[33]

Conversely a request was made to the magistrates that the Army be banned from processing in the streets. According to *The Surrey Advertiser* however, this request was made by an "unrepresentative" 150 townspeople.[34]

Throughout early and mid-1882 the assaults on the Army nationally were creating intense feeling and had provoked Government and Home Office action. On 17 June 1882 the Queen's Bench decided that the Army had the right to process in the streets and have full protection. The Home Secretary therefore directed local authorities to take up the Court's ruling as a general principle.

In early September

> "Guildford's Mayor told 'Captain Bryan . . . that the bench had decided to give no police protection' adding that he knew the Salvation Army had a legal right to procession in the streets, which they could exercise if they liked, but if they did so it would be on their own risk and responsibility."[35]

Such statements encouraged a mob to set upon the Guildford Corps building

> ". . . with the determination to destroy it. Every window in the place was broken, and for a time the lives of the audience appeared to be in jeopardy. Yet no one was apprehended. . . This spirit of antagonism showed itself the next night also, when fireworks were freely thrown amongst us and the Captain's wife thrown to the ground."[36]

The Vicar of Holy Trinity and William Booth corresponded with the Home Secretary and the Mayor of Guildford concerning this violence. An opposite reaction was seen through the public meetings, petitions and letters censuring the rectors of Holy Trinity, St. Mary's and Stoke for encouraging the Army. However a 'reminder' concerning the Army's rights was dispatched by the Home Secretary to Guildford's Mayor and magistrates.[37] This was then put into the form of a public proclamation. The Mayor clearly ignored the Home Secretary and personally appeared in the Market Place on Tuesday 27 September, publicly berating the soldiers who were selling *War Cry* to those attending Market. This further encouraged

> "The enemy, in the shape of brewers and publicans, (who) mustered in opposition . . .(plus). . . opposition of high and low opponents."

In an attempt to highlight this, the *War Cry* praised the efforts of Guildford Salvationists in words and pictures. Under the front page headline 'Heroic "War Cry" Selling at Guildford', they stated the Mayor's anti-Army position.[38] Clearly the Mayor was supporting the stand by other local authorities, such as Basingstoke, in their open opposition to the Salvation Army.

Mr. Law appears to have attempted to follow the magistrates' directions while adopting a judicial approach to the Army. He had undoubtedly read the newspaper reports of the Beatty v. Gillbanks pro-Army findings in June which were widely reported at the time. As Superintendent of Police he would also have been aware of the Watch Committee's directive in August and the Home Office 'reminder' in September. During the latter part of September and early October, the police did not prosecute Army assailants, probably because the magistrates had continually dismissed the earlier cases. However by late October Mr. Law had decided to take positive preventative action to stop the violence on the streets. In particular he enrolled 100 special constables for the 'farewell' meeting of Captain and Mrs. Bryan. As a result only a little verbal opposition took place. Among those attending the meeting was the minister of the Congregational Church. After reading the lesson, he praised the Army's work and complained of the laxity of some of the other ministers in Guildford.[39]

During the first six months of 1883 a range of physical, verbal and defamatory attacks continued. Several cases of assault and obstruction were brought by both pro- and anti-Army supporters. In February a Salvationist was fined for obstruction. He followed standard Army practice and went to gaol for refusing to pay. Various townsfolk were fined relatively small amounts for assault on the Army. A seventeen year old girl was convicted of assault on her mother and the police. Her parents gave evidence that they had lost control of her eleven months previously after she became connected with the Salvation Army.[40] Despite the opposition, on Monday 25 June the Corps celebrated the opening of its new Barracks by Mrs. Booth. These were situated in Onslow Street, well within the slums of Friary Parish. The Barracks had seating for 1,800 people, cost £1,826 and were built in typical Army fortress style.

The fact that a considerable number of cases on both 'sides' were being brought before the magistrates shows not only the amount of antagonism remaining towards the soldiers but also the persistence of the police. These men had amassed 361 extra man-hours "in connection with the Salvation Army disturbances". The Town Council were asked to pay the bill of £9 0s 6d, the pay being at the rate of 6d per hour. The Watch Committee made a point of

> ". . . it being distinctly understood that such payment is not to be taken as a precedent."[41]

The pressure of the police actions controlled the level of opposition which thus by late 1883 became intermittent. Possibly also the 'rough-musicing' was naturally dying away as the Army became more accepted. That there remained quite considerable interest in the Movement is apparent from the wide coverage in the press to anything connected with them. One example came in October 1883 when two local Salvationists were jailed for assault over accusations of wife-stealing.

Apart from verbal abuse, there was little opposition over the winter of 1883/1884. However in April a violent clash involving Salvationists, the police and 'roughs' took place when the Barracks was attacked. After a quiet summer, the landlord of The Horse and Groom Public House in neighbouring Merrow was summonsed and dismissed for twice riding his horse and cart at the Army.[42] Conversely *The Surrey Advertiser* reflects the continued support for the Army by the clergy and across the social classes. It is also clear that a large influx of navvies into the area during the latter half of the year helped the Army. Over 1,000 were involved in building a new railway line and many of them attended the Army meetings, mainly in their working clothes, being "sympathetic" to its work.[43]

During 1885 a similar picture of intermittent violence and opposition appeared. In February, two Salvationists were found guilty of obstruction and opted to go to gaol. This was on the disputed evidence of P.C. Wakefield. Councillor Colebrook, who with his wife had supported the Army from the beginning, stated in a Council meeting that he regretted that

> ". . . two very respectable young men — apparently very intelligent young men — had been sent to prison."

Further he had heard that P.C. Wakefield had been bribed. Council and press uproar followed,[44] enlivened by the revelation that crime was down 50% since the Army arrived.[45] Although the officer had been officially cautioned two years earlier for excessive use of violence against the Army, the Watch Committee, meeting immediately after the allegation, could find no evidence to substantiate it.[46]

As mob use was clearly not deterring the Army, some councillors attempted to control the Movement with a clause stopping processions on Sundays incorporated into a new Corporation Bill. This was presented by Guildford's Urban Sanitary Authority but was eventually defeated.[47] Not until 1901 was a bye-law passed forbidding people to

> ". . . play any musical or noisy instrument, or sing in any street within 50 yards of any dwelling-house, after being requested to desist by any inmate."[48]

This did not interfere with the Army processions. From 1886 the instances of verbal and physical abuse became increasingly rare. The

191

worst case of the remainder of the century was a gun-powder attack in March 1889.[49] All the magistrates from the late 1880s took a much harsher attitude to anti-Army violence than their immediate predecessors.

Causes of Opposition

The first eighteen months after the arrival of the Salvation Army in Guildford were thus marked by a considerable degree of 'rough-musicing', apparently much encouraged by brewers and magistrates. A number of sources carry references to 'rough-musicing'[50] and violent groups in Guildford's history. One group who was always expected to 'rough-music' festivals was known as the 'Guys'. Boxing Day, Shrove Tuesday and 5 November were all dates on which they could be expected to appear.[51] Accounts of their activities up to the early 1860s show the difficulty the Police Superintendent and his ten men had in keeping the peace when the Guys, dressed in their fantastic costumes, roamed the streets lighting huge bonfires and destroying property.[52]

November was the time of the municipal elections and 5 November was always the worst of the occasions Guildford surrendered itself to "Mob Rule".[53] The riots were not overtly political but clearly threatened all social levels, particularly with the damage to property. In November 1863 a new Police Superintendent, Mr. Law, and a new strict Mayor, sought to end the violence, particularly after a police officer was thrown on to a lighted bonfire for being bumptious. Infantry, cavalry and 300 special constables ensured the town was quiet that year. It then took another two years and some bloody street-fighting which resulted in four Guys being charged with attempted murder (1864) before the Guys were finally stopped.[54]

Although this most blatant form of "Mob Rule" was crushed in Guildford by 1865, 'rough-musicing' did remain alive for at least another twenty years or so.[55] Echoes of the 'Guys' clearly reappear in the anti-Army groups which generally became known as Skeletons although the local name often varied in different towns. In Guildford they were termed Red-Nose or Red Ribbon Army[56] because of their habit of carrying a red flag or wearing red ribbons. It was also a play on the title Blue Ribbon Army, another organisation 'the mob' disliked but, as the latter rarely appeared on the streets, they tended to be ignored.

The Red-Nose Army of 1882 were led by a brewer's son on a white horse.[57] His followers were made up of ". . . lewd fellows of the baser sort" who appear to have enjoyed the support of many of Guildford's most important townfolk.[58] These latter included brewers and publicans whose persistent presence within the Local Authority reflected the importance of the 'drink interest' in the town's life.

> "Victorian and Edwardian Guildford was very much a beer-drinking as well as a beer-producing town. Throughout most of the last century there were over thirty pubs in the High Street alone."[59]

A small but significant percentage of aldermen, town councillors and magistrates were intimately connected with the drink trade throughout the 1870s and 1880s.[60] Typical of these decades was 1882 when one of the four aldermen, two of the twelve town councillors and one of the eight magistrates were brewers.[61] These people might well have been worried by the possible loss of revenue and jobs if the apparently growing temperance movement[62] achieved any lasting success. The Salvation Army, being the most vociferous of the temperance movements, therefore found a number of opponents in the Local Authority. This opposition was probably quite broad as the 'drink interest' could combine with those such as Councillor Bullen and apparently the Mayor, who found the Army's exuberant militancy distasteful. Its main weapon was to encourage the 'rough-musicing' and such encouragement would help explain the opposition's viciousness and longevity.

Support and Membership

The Salvation Army in Guildford would have suffered far worse had not Mr. Law pursued an impartial role. He ensured that the police were equally just and persistently brought those disturbing the peace to court. Although there is no extant evidence to suggest his personal views, his actions allowed the Army and its supporters to continue work. Of those openly supporting the Army, the Liberal Onslow family financially and morally helped counter the essentially anti-Army Local Authority, especially in 1882. Not all the Local Authority members were opposed to the Movement, for example Councillor and Mrs. Colebrook believed in the Army's work. In addition, the Reverend Paynter provided invaluable help and through him, the Church of England and most other denominations openly supported the Army in joint services and words.

The town's reaction to the Army was therefore split but the *War Cry* considered the anti-Army reaction here more determined than in any other town of its size.[63] As elsewhere the persecution probably strengthened the determination of the members and encouraged others to join. The membership itself did not reflect a particular class bias. From reports in *The Surrey Advertiser* and the *War Cry*, thirty-three names of Salvationists are identifiable (Appendix 10). By using Guildford directories and the *1881 Census of England and Wales* several addresses, ages and occupations have been matched to the names. The Appendix Table shows a diverse soldiership in terms of age and occupations, the latter ranging from lower working-class to middle-class, general labourer to shopkeeper. The housing shown also suggests a range of incomes. Nothing else is known about membership of Guildford Corps other than in 1905 it had 122 soldiers and recruits.[64]

Conclusion

Immediately upon its arrival in Guildford, the Salvation Army suffered a degree of 'rough-musicing' which was quickly exacerbated by elements in local business and authority. Clearly the anti-Army stance of the Mayor was important and in turn, his influence on the magistrates of which he was one. It was perhaps unfortunate for the Army that Guildford had the same Mayor elected in 1881 and 1882. There is no extant evidence associating him with the drink trade but the Salvation Army's reputation, combined with the seemingly growing support for teetotalism, perhaps worried the trade sufficiently to put pressure on the Mayor through the 'drink interest' in the Local Authority. The persistent dropping of cases by the Mayor/magistrate plus his statements regarding the Army could certainly be explained in this way.

The Army survived because of a considerable number of factors, namely, its high street profile keeping it to the fore of local discussions; the increasingly respected variety of socio-religious activities centred on its Barracks in the poorest area of Guildford; the frequent changes in Commanding Officer repeatedly bringing in fresh zeal;[65] the opposition strengthening the resolve of members; the support of some tradesmen,[66] councillors, the police and the Onslow family;[67] and perhaps also because of its failure to prove as great a threat to the drink trade as first appeared.[68] This latter fact and more liberal minded Mayors from the mid-1880s ensured that the anti-Army violence became increasingly sporadic. The Salvation Army was an accepted part of Victorian Guildford's Nonconformity by the late 1890s and remained so into the twentieth century.

CHAPTER EIGHT

HONITON, DEVON: A CASE-STUDY

I. BACKGROUND

The parish, ancient borough and market town of Honiton lay in the south-east of the Victorian County of Devonshire and to the south of the River Otter. It was sixteen miles E.N.E. of Exeter and the same E.S.E. of Tiverton. The town's *raison d'être* was its strategic position where the London–Exeter road emerged out of the surrounding hills.

Table 8.1 shows that between 1801 and 1841, the parish of Honiton's population increased by 63.86% but thereafter a decline set in. The overall nineteenth century increase was 37.61%. The Registration District total mirrored this with a high in the 1840s. Between 1801 and 1841, the increase was 71.81% and 41.71% overall. The 1840s peak and subsequent decline was common in nineteenth century Devonshire inland towns, although Honiton's loss was less drastic than most, mainly due to its geographic position. Many of those who

TABLE 8.1

The Population of Honiton 1801–1901

Year	Parish Total	Registration District Total
1801	2,377	13,906
1811	2,735	18,012
1821	3,296	20,893
1831	3,509	22,330
1841	3,895	23,892
1851	3,427	23,824
1861	3,301	22,729
1871	3,464	22,291
1881	3,358	21,132
1891	3,216	20,522
1901	3,271	19,707

Sources: Census of England and Wales. 1801–1901. Population.
Respective Vol. I.'s.

moved probably went to Exeter or to the north of England. With a declining population, Honiton physically grew very little.

From the 1240s Honiton was an important centre of the Devonshire cloth trade. In the early sixteenth century the town manufactured and gave its name to a new type of lace. When the lace industry declined in Honiton after 1816, tourism took its place. This development was aided by the establishment of the railway in 1860. Pottery was the other major industry from the seventeenth century onwards. A large new pottery was established in 1881. In addition to tourism, pottery and a little lace manufacturing, the townsfolk in 1880 worked either in tanneries, breweries, corn mills, the iron foundry or malting. Agriculture was also an extensive employer and the cattle and provisions market held every Saturday was large.

Honiton's Corporation consisted of a mayor, six aldermen and eighteen councilmen. The corporation acted as the urban sanitary authority. The Mayor and ex-Mayor were the magistrates for the borough. The Mayor from November 1881 was W. Hook; from November 1882, John Murch Jnr.; and from November 1883 to August 1884, Henry Fowler who died in office. Within the town were a number of libraries, a reading room, a police station and magistrates' hall, a dispensary run on the provident system, alms-houses, a hospital, a Union Workhouse, two Army Volunteer Companies, and a market complex. A new water system had been laid in 1879 and the town was considered to be healthy and clean. Poverty did exist but little reference is made to it. Although unemployment appears to have been minimal, earnings for the lowest paid averaged 8/6 per week in 1893.

In religious terms, Devon was well-served with churches and chapels in the mid-nineteenth century. They could provide accommodation for 69.08% of the population. The Registration District was above the county average with accommodation for 75.7%. Table 8.2 shows a pattern typical of many old rural market towns relatively unaffected by industrialisation. The Church of England was strongest in terms of churches and numbers attending. After came various Nonconformist denominations, namely Congregationalists, Wesleyan Methodists, Baptists, Unitarians and a few Brethren respectively. Taking the highest attendance figures for each of the six groups from Table 8.2, 33.55% of the population attended a religious service of some kind in the District. The evidence therefore suggests that religion was an important part of life in Honiton.

Although Protestantism in Devon grew strongly after 1549, Methodism did not gain a foothold until after 1850. The upsurge in Protestantism after this latter time could probably be accounted for by changes of allegiance from the Church of England rather than by reaching the masses. By 1884, the five major denominations in Honiton

TABLE 8.2

Religious Accommodation and Attendance in Honiton, 1851

Denominations	Number of Buildings	Sittings	Number Attending		
			M	A	E
Protestant Churches:					
Church of England	32	9,152	5,516	5,184	1,300
Independents.	12	2,517	1,036	1,215	1,008
Baptists	4	760	233	355	281
Unitarians.	2	391	72	56	—
Wesleyan Methodists	8	1,455	462	710	790
Brethren.	1	—	45	—	40
Totals.	59	14,275	7,364	7,520	3,419

Note: Population was 23,824.

Source: Census of Religious Worship. 1851. Table H., p. cclxxxv.

were the Church of England, Bible Christians, Congregationalists, Wesleyans and Baptists.

II. THE SALVATION ARMY

As frequently happened because of the publicity the Army was generating, particularly in 1882, the year of its greatest advances, William Booth was invited to send officers to Honiton.[1] The invitation came from Richard Thorne, a local shoemaker, who read about the Army in a *War Cry*. An officer arrived in mid-September 1882 and a tent was provided by Thorne. Seventy or eighty recruits were made in the first few weeks but within days of the Army's arrival, the town reacted against the intrusion. On Sunday 8 October a mob attacked the residence of Mr. George Wood. He was a farmer and toll collector who had invited the Army to hold an afternoon meeting at his home. This violence, perhaps directed not only at the Army and Wood as a sympathiser but also at his position as toll collector, resulted in five cases of assault and damage being brought before the magistrates. Three labourers had minor financial penalties imposed but two tradesmen, one a fellow butcher with the magistrate/mayor, had their cases dismissed. The defence for one of these latter cases, which were heard a month after the attack,

> ". . . characterised the Salvation Army as a "perfect pest" in Honiton, so much so that the clergymen of the parish had been obliged to lecture on the subject of their proceedings."

197

The Bench warned of heavier penalties for further offences by anyone.[2]

The warning was ignored by the mob who were perhaps encouraged by the smallness of the fines and the clergymen's reactions. The official opening of Honiton Corps, number 338, was on Tuesday 7 November 1882.[3] The hall was a publican's malthouse in Hind Street, bought and converted for Salvation Army use by Richard Thorne. The opening meetings, at which some Salvationists from Exeter attended, and the following Sunday afternoon open-air meeting at the usual stand at the top of the High Street, were attacked with flour, mud, red powder, and a violence apparently far exceeding that of the larger towns.

On Friday 17 November Honiton's new Commanding Officers, Captain and Mrs. John Lomas, arrived. On the Sunday, the events of the previous week were repeated. During the afternoon march the band and soldiers were pelted with red powder in bags, mud and other missiles. Clearly a Skeleton Army had been organised. The two Armies met in New Street where the Skeletons,

> ". . . headed by a red banner bearing the inscription "down with fanatics","

physically assaulted the processionists. Although the latter sought sanctuary in the grounds of the Baptist Chapel,

> "Several of the musical instruments of the Army were smashed and kicked about the streets."

The police eventually rendered assistance when asked.[4]

The disruption of the Army's outdoor evangelism had by mid-November become a popular local activity. Trouble often started when Exeter or other corps officers and soldiers arrived by train to 'reinforce' Honiton. On such occasions a mob usually assembled to act as 'escort' from the railway station. Interest in the Army was also heightened by newspaper reports in the last quarter of 1882 when lengthy articles concerning local and national Army actions appeared. The Sunday afternoon battles in particular were a focal point for popular amusement. 'Rough-musicing', although of increasing rarity in the late nineteenth century, was still something to be witnessed with interest and enjoyed by some. *The Devon Weekly Times* reported that the disturbances of Sunday 19 November had been expected

> ". . . and, as a consequence, hundreds of people flocked into the town from surrounding towns and villages."[5]

Captain Lomas was badly injured in this disturbance involving over 1,000 people. The violence continued the next day when he had a man apprehended. The mob pelted the Captain as he returned from the police station to a Salvationist's house where he had lodgings. Every window in that house was smashed as were those of the High Street shop belonging to Richard Thorne. Forty extra police were called in on the Tuesday to guard the homes of Salvationists against arson (for fear of setting the town alight). It was hoped that these police would discourage further disturbances. That evening the Salvationists did not meet.[6]

Captain Lomas asserted that the Skeletons had been primed with drink. They were undoubtedly well-organised within a very few weeks. It is probable that their organised and orchestrated 'rough-musicing' was helped by the already established and nearby Skeleton Army at Exeter. Organised opposition first occurred in Whitechapel in the summer of 1880. Previously the name Skeleton Army was thought to have been first used in Weston-super-Mare (Somerset) at the end of 1881. However the name was probably in use in Exeter in April 1881, at least six months earlier. The Honiton Skeletons had their own newspapers, sellers and collectors going round inciting the people. These papers (Appendix 11) were well produced, quickly countered all reports made about them in the *War Cry,* and freely commented upon the 'invasion' and fanaticism. The organisation behind this anti-Army movement came from local leading tradesmen who also encouraged the Skeletons to be mutually supportive between towns. In the same way as Salvation Army corps were mutually supportive within and between towns, Skeleton inter-town forces attacked not only Honiton but also Exeter (established 11 April 1881) and Newton Abbot (established June 1882).

Lack of police protection for the Army appears to have encouraged the Skeletons throughout Devon and Somerset. Clearly the police in Honiton received no support from the two magistrates as all cases brought about by the riots of Sunday 26 November were dismissed after Mr. Hook, the ex-Mayor, consistently argued with the policemen and the Police Superintendent over evidence. A case against Samuel Stone, brought by police for assaulting a woman Salvationist, was clearly proved yet he was dismissed with a caution. Captain Lomas refused to respect the Bench as he believed Mr. Hook

". . . is not a fit and proper person to sit in judgement on the cases."

This widely-reported statement was precipitated by the latter stating to the Captain that no protection would be afforded the Army as they were at fault for disturbing the peace.[7] It is clear that the ex-Mayor reflected the consensus of opinion amongst the Council for at a Council meeting on Wednesday 22 November, councillors debated having 'their Skeletons' put the Army drummer inside his drum, cover the processionists with red ruddle, and keep them from their Barracks.

Honiton's magistrates and councillors had gone far beyond the unofficial backing given to the Skeletons in many other towns. The debate of 22 November and the magistrate/ex-Mayor's declaration three days later, (no protection), had made policework concerning the Army impotent. In England, only the Exeter Mayor at this time had come out so openly in favour of the Skeletons. However magistrates and mayors in some other southern towns had also been vehement in their opposition to the Army during the previous months. Such opposition had been resolved either by the intervention of the Home Secretary or via the Law Courts. Further 'attacks' then tended to become legal attempts at removing the Army from the streets.

In late 1882 Honiton's magistrates must have felt encouraged by the Exeter Mayor's open anti-Army stance. The local Skeletons certainly felt encouraged by the moral and physical support of Skeletons from Exeter, Ottery St. Mary and other nearby towns. Thus the "Reign of Terror at Honiton" continued into December. As Captain Lomas was injured, Lieutenant Edward Arch arrived to help. The Army though remained ". . . entirely at the mercy of the roughs".[8] Salvation Army soldiers had their house windows smashed and few people attended the meetings for fear of beatings. Despite continued help from Exeter Salvationists and four deputations to the Home Office, the violence continued. Soldiers were beaten even when trying to take refuge in the Police Station. Some lost their jobs and a plot to blow up the Barracks was discovered. Mrs. Captain Lomas was kicked by a publican.

On the evening of Thursday 21 December, Exeter officers and soldiers found Honiton in uproar and in the hands of the mob. Yet again the daily meeting was under attack. Pistols were fired and the Barracks taken over. The few police were powerless to make arrests in the mob of over 2,000. They did eventually manage to clear the Barracks after a London barrister made a formal application for police protection. On 22 December, the Honiton magistrates refused General Booth's application to ban the Skeleton Army from assembling and so Booth ordered a temporary halt to the marches. The Chief Constable visited Honiton that evening to witness the violence but Booth's orders were executed immediately and thus no trouble ensued.[9]

The first six weeks of 1883 were crucial to the Salvation Army in Honiton. At the start of January *The Western Times* reported that

> ". . . no place within the four corners of this tight little island has opposed the Salvation Army with more violence."

The report made public Mr. Hook's statement that the Army would receive no protection and then detailed seven cases brought by the

Army and heard at the end of December. These provide evidence that several 'respected citizens' were involved in physical attacks on Salvationists and also that some councillors were publicans. Three cases, one against the Postmaster for leading roughs and two against town councillors (one being the publican of the Fountain Inn), were dismissed. Four other cases were proven and fines imposed.[10]

The January editions of the *War Cry* carried reports of some "good services" at Honiton. It was also reported that at the Devon Quarter Sessions, Mr. Neumann, a county magistrate and resident at Honiton, stated that the very expensive riots costing between £200 and £300, could have been quelled earlier with less expense had not people enjoyed them and profits been made. He continued that it had been well known in which house the missiles were kept. The Police Committee ordered an investigation into the truth of these statements. That such accusations concerning the Honiton magistracy and public disorder were considered of national importance is clear from the concern of *The Times*. On 13 January this newspaper reported that

> "The Home Secretary has called to account the Honiton magistrates, who are only two in number, the Mayor and ex-Mayor, for their proceedings in relation to the Salvation Army."[11]

Reinforced perhaps by this report, while on a visit to Exeter shortly afterwards, William Booth publicly proclaimed his support for Captain Lomas. Futher local newspaper reports now appeared on the subject of correspondence between the Mayor, the Home Secretary and the Chief Constable of Devon. The debate on the future protection of the Salvation Army in Honiton became very public with the magistrates openly denying that they had refused protection and claiming misrepresentation, while the Town Council refuted Mr. Neumann's statements at the Quarter Sessions.

The Salvation Army held no processions throughout most of January and the violence was minimal. The hall was repaired for £15 and new instruments bought. The Army then gave notice of processions restarting on the weekend of Friday 26 January. The Skeletons expected a march on the Saturday but as the Salvation Army did not have one, they had their own. The Sunday afternoon Army march did take place and was violently opposed with the Skeletons carrying coffins and placards. The Mayor again clearly refused the Army protection. Due to this and the mob's ferocity, on the Monday's march Honiton's five-man police force refused to leave the police station while the Army procession was stoned and the barracks damaged to £50 value. These circumstances caused the Mayor to request the Chief Constable for more men.

The Home Secretary had been notified of the magistrates' statements and actions and the condition of Honiton by mid-November 1882 but

> ". . . the closing of Parliament and the opening of the new law Courts occupied the attention of the Home Secretary, and the officials to whom we reported the state of things saw no reason to interfere."[12]

Repeated deputations to the Home Office in December and newspaper reports of the magistrates' conduct led to the Home Secretary discussing the matter with the Lord Chancellor. Both agreed on 28 December

> ". . . that the proceedings appear to have been most disgraceful and that . . . the Superintendent of Police appears to have been much to blame, and the Mayor, as well as the ex-Mayor, is charged with having practically encouraged and afforded impunity to these disturbances."

A letter to this effect was dispatched to the Mayor.[13] "The complete table of correspondence gives the date and content of all relevant communications:

15.12.82	The Home Secretary demanded an explanation of Honiton magistrates' actions and statements.
17.12.82	The Honiton Mayor replied admitting some statements.
11. 1.83	The Home Secretary deplored the "Highly reprehensible behaviour" of the magistrates.
19. 1.83	The Mayor stated that part of the evidence to the Home Secretary was misrepresented.
30. 1.83	The Mayor wrote to the Chief Constable requesting more men following the disturbances of the previous two days.
31. 1.83	The Chief Constable stated that the cost was already high and advised the Mayor to swear in special constables.

The heated council discussion of 2 February which considered these letters and the violence associated with the renewed Army marches the previous Sunday demonstrated the clear anti-Army stance still taken by the majority of councillors. It was ultimately decided that the request to the Chief Constable was to be reiterated.

The editorial in *The Western Times* reporting the council meeting believed that money and men from neighbouring towns and villages continued to help in the organisation and running of Honiton's Skeleton Army. Even those limited fines imposed were taken care of along the lines of the Fenian Brotherhood for Skeleton members and sympathisers made regular contributions to a central fund. The editorial laid much of the blame for the disturbances upon the magistrates, especially Mr. Hook, the prosperous butcher of Honiton. It was also noted that as well as the Salvation Army, the Blue Ribbon Army suffered violence (perhaps because it too attacked the drink trade). Directly after the council meeting the two magistrates heard four cases, two of assault by the Commanding Officer and two of assault upon Salvationists. The C.O. was found guilty on both counts and fined 10 shillings plus costs.[14] The others were also found guilty and fined 5 shillings plus costs.[14]

The legal, governmental, police and newspaper pressure brought to bear on the magistrates was extensive. Broader opinion was asserting itself over local and gradually harsher penalties were inflicted by the magistrates in the ensuing months. There were more cases of assaults upon Salvationists than by them and because of the harsher fines, up to £5 plus costs in one case in February 1883, there was a marked decrease in lawlessness. Possibly the magistrates had taken heed of the Home Secretary's feelings but more likely the harsher penalties were imposed because a County Magistrate sat on the Bench for much of the year. He sat only on Salvation Army cases and his adjudication ensured that everyone had a fair hearing.[15]

Throughout the violence which had taken place since the Army's arrival, the Movement had continued to grow in numbers. Members came in from several miles around and included a 'converted Skeleton Army coffin carrier'. Clearly the Army was having some effect for the trade of Honiton's twenty-four publicans was decreasing. The police were giving the marchers good protection in accordance with the June 1882 High Court Judgement, in 'Beatty v. Gillbanks'. Outbreaks of violence clearly did not stop immediately but shouting and jeering quickly took the place of physical agitation. Letters to the press still indicted the ". . . respectable young tradesmen of the town" for being Skeletons and the latter still parodied the Army in the streets but, mainly because of the County Magistrate, violence was only rarely used.

The *War Cry* continued to record several conversions, increases in numbers of 'the right sort' and good marches and meetings in 1883. Throughout Devon the books of the magistrates' clerks showed a decline in the number of cases of drunkenness and disorder in the same year. The Salvation Army made the obvious claim that their campaign was having some effect. That Honiton's Army Corps had achieved extensive public notoriety is seen in the fact that *The Times* recorded the new Commanding Officer (from 20 March 1883) as being charged with cruelty to a horse. A mixture of criticism and support for the Army in news items and editorials as well as letters were recorded in the Devonshire newspapers. Sporadic throwing of eggs and 'offensive liquids' continued in Honiton[16] as did upsets caused by the visit of important Salvationists such as the Divisional Commander, Major Davey, but serious violence appeared to have ended. Major Speid, the County Magistrate, left the Bench in

November 1883 when Mr. Murch retired from the Mayor's office and therefore Mr. Hook retired as the ex-Mayor magistrate. Captain Fairless left in October 1883 and no new officers arrived, but under Richard Thorne and Henry Denner, the Corps continued and new band uniforms were purchased in November.

There were no recorded disturbances involving Salvationists at Honiton during December 1883 and January 1884 although the Army's south-east Devon lawyer was kept busy, especially as the Exeter magistrates and cross-sections of the press still persecuted the Army to varying degrees. A Salvationist was physically assaulted in early February in Honiton and an upsurge in local government and newspaper discussion on the Army is again obvious.[17] Much of this may have been due to the arrival of new officers in the previous month. In March vicious attacks on Salvationists in the town restarted. These were probably prompted by the presentation of new colours to the Corps at the end of February. The afternoon march on Sunday 17 March was ambushed with considerable precision. Many people were covered in 'sickening filth' and some injuries received. Uproar continued in the meeting at the Barracks. A similar occurrence took place on Monday 21 April when a Salvationist was badly hurt and

"For a long time there was great excitement and the police had some difficulty in dispersing the mob."[18]

Salvationists and others were variously summonsed in Honiton for obstruction or assault in these troubles and occasionally later in the year. All cases were dealt with on the evidence provided and both Armies received similar fines on a par with those for offences not involving the Salvation Army.

In May 1884 Honiton Corps contributed £3 2s 3d to the Salvation Army Relief Fund. This was a good average figure in the Division. In June 1885 however, only £1 15s 11d was raised for the Corps Debt Extinction Fund (National), placing Honiton 40th out of the 42 corps in the Devon and West Somerset Divison. Although Captain King declared in August 1885 "Our marches and open-airs are better than ever,"[19] in March of the following year a report stated "Lately it has seemed very hard here."[20]

The typical Army expansionism is evident in visits made to neighbouring villages such as Beckin (June 1886). Special meetings still attracted large crowds in Honiton and in September 1886, the Commanding Officer was jailed for seven days for obstruction, despite the support of the local Baptists. By the Fourth Anniversary meetings in December 1886, it was reported that

"The only hindrance we have ... (now is to our open-air work. This). . . is caused by certain of the authorities, who will seldom allow us to stand a few minutes anywhere to preach Salvation to the people."[21]

In 1887 and 1888, there were only three different mentions of Honiton Corps in all the secular and religious newspapers. The second, in October 1887 stated

"Hard and severe has been the nature of the fighting for a long while past."[22]

The final one reported that the Sixth Anniversary meetings were celebrated with the help of the neighbouring corps, (December 1888). As no directory mentions the Salvation Army and as no further reports were printed anywhere, it must be assumed that the Army in Honiton closed in 1889.

Conclusion

The Army's 'attack' on Honiton came about from an invitation. The Movement had strong supporters in the town and was well organised. A band was quickly formed and a tent and Barracks respectively bought by a townsman. The violence that greeted it was vicious for six months, (September 1882 to February 1883), and then sporadic for the next fourteen. The apparatus for the anti-Army outbursts was well organised. As in the history of other Nonconformist sects, certain local dignitaries encouraged the 'rough-musicing' tradition still prevalent in the south. This together with the initial leniency of fines and church support for anti-Army ideas prompted some of the rougher elements of the town to acts of extreme violence.

The Honiton court cases provide the clearest evidence of local council/respectable citizens/publican links, magistrates' persecution, and bias in favour of anti-Army tradesmen. Most of the town councillors, who all owned businesses in the town, encouraged and led the Skeletons from Honiton and the surrounding areas. Their motivation was to protect the brewery trade; to profit by competitors' (Salvationists and sympathisers) property being destroyed and by repairs; and perhaps a genuine fear of an apparently disciplined force which changed its officers on average every six and three-quarter months and could call upon the support of large numbers of 'soldiers' (members).

The fact that the Home Secretary had to have direct involvement here as well as in Guildford made it clear to the Government that certain local authorities were flagrantly violating Home Office instructions issued after the Beatty v. Gillbanks ruling on the Salvation Army's right to process.[23] The Home Secretary and the Lord Chancellor laid the blame for the excessive violence on the Mayor and ex-Mayor who, they said, deliberately failed in their duty. Likewise the Chief Constable blamed them for not swearing in special constables. As neither of the magistrates could be removed by the Home Secretary owing to their being popularly elected, this raises the question of

205

accountability in nineteenth-century English law. The majority of magistrates in the smaller (therefore conservative and mainly southern) towns were still popularly elected in the last quarter of the nineteenth century whereas in the larger (and mainly northern) towns, a different process had to be undergone. In the latter, candidates who desired to become magistates not only had to previously prove their worth as members of the community but once elected, were accountable to the Home Office. However Honiton's magistrates were *de facto* the foremost civil and legal authority in the town and acting as such, they were protecting their power-base and businesses while openly reflecting what appeared to have been the views of the majority of businessmen and leading citizens.

The Honiton case-study confirms the view that the organised and worst riots occurred in the small- and medium-sized towns of southern England, where the conservative social ties sustained local rather than national loyalties,that is to the successors of the town squire; that the Skeleton Army was directed at the Salvation Army and its supporters within towns by important tradesmen with connections on the council; and that the Army was often considered to be the initial perpetrators of the violence by actually being there.

In Honiton then the violence can be argued to have been a form of social control, used deliberately by the supreme local authorities as the only available means of direct opposition to the Government's toleration of the Salvation Army. The Army had theoretically won the national right to march but local opposition in many southern towns had still to be overcome. In an attempt to do this, the Army often brought cases against individuals on matters arising out of its persistence to exercise its rights. It also adopted the ploy of not paying fines. Gaol was what the Army wanted and received.[24] The publicity and 'victory celebrations' on a prisoner's release were enormous. Had the opposition not been so fierce, thus keeping the Movement to the forefront of local consideration (and perhaps encouraging members), the Army in Honiton might have died out in less than the seven years that it took. The eventual local acceptance of the Movement and the considerable degree of commitment required for open-air and indoor meeting attendance, led to apathy and rejection by its members, who no longer had the psychological unity that comes from being a persecuted minority. After the Army's initial impact of some seventy converts in the first few weeks, numbers of this magnitude were never again recorded. In Honiton many of these 'converts' were part of what W. G. Hoskins has identified as a post-1850 move among Protestants away from the Established Church in Devon and towards various denominations. The Army, merely by its arrival in Devon, increased the pace of this move and many of those dissatisfied flirted with the Movement before very quickly moving towards a more established denomination such as the Bible Christians.

The Salvation Army initially grew in Honiton as part of the people's experimentation with various denominations, its novelty, and because of the very bitter persecution. In order to become permanent though the Army perhaps needed to find a degree of social and geographical mobility affecting potential recruits. There was some decay in the traditional crafts but as these declined, other spheres of work such as pottery and tourism replaced the lost jobs and people tended to remain in their traditional social positions. Also, far from increasing in population, the town was actually declining in numbers (Table 8.1). Honiton's lack of social and geographical mobility on the level of the larger towns where the Army had sustained growth, the lessening of enthusiasm for a high degree of commitment, and a decline in persecution, resulted in the Movement's local collapse.

CHAPTER NINE

WALES: A CASE-STUDY

During the last quarter of the nineteenth century, Wales experienced a dramatic religious revival that changed the lives of thousands of inhabitants. The entire spectrum of society gave a warm and sometimes ecstatic welcome to a flamboyant, vociferous yet obviously sincere movement, the Salvation Army. Between 1878 and the end of 1899, one hundred and twenty major centres of Army work were established across Wales and each centre sent its members to evangelise neighbouring villages and towns. Even the remotest dwellings did not escape the attention of the Movement and few people had not seen a uniformed member by the turn of the century. This being so, it is necessary to establish both why and how the Army grew.

Between 1861 and 1865, William and Catherine Booth toured Great Britain, evangelising wherever the opportunity arose. In 1863 the prominent Welsh ship and colliery owners John and Richard Cory invited the Booths to Cardiff and the latter led a highly successful campaign. The Corys remained lifelong friends of William and Catherine Booth as did another leading Welsh family, the Billups. The head of this family was J. E. Billups, principal contractor in the 1870s and 1880s for the Taff Railway Company and the Dowlais Ironworks at East Moors.[1]

The Spread of the Army in Wales

The first eight Welsh Mission stations/corps were opened in Cardiff (1874), Merthyr Tydfil, Dowlais, Aberdare, Mountain Ash, Tredegar, Newport and Ebbw Vale (all 1878).[2] However not until October 1881 did the Movement venture to the north commencing with an 'attack' on Wrexham. Between 1878 and 1883 the Army in England was finding its most receptive welcome in areas of concentrated population ranging from large urban conurbations to small mining communities. It is therefore of little surprise that the coalfields of southern Wales attracted the Mission's attention in the same period. Typical of the contemporary thought at International Headquarters was a passage written by George Scott Railton:

> "The great mining centre [of Aberdare] around which 40,000 people cluster and thrive or starve as times change has long attracted our attention."[3]

A selection of case-studies across Wales will help to identify the basic factors responsible for the Salvation Army's tremendous growth and impact in Wales. Cardiff, populated by approximately 60,000 people in the early 1870s, was the first of Booth's centres in Wales and it commenced operation on Sunday 15 November 1874. John Allen, 'The Converted Navvy', was in charge of the Gospel Hall at 280 Bute Street. The hall had previously attempted to cater specifically for the working-class and its trustees lent it free of charge to the Mission. It was shortly afterwards bought by Mr. John Cory and given to the Christian Mission to continue and build up their work. Within a few weeks sixty people were converted.[4] Around four hundred people could sit in the building and by early 1875 it was regularly full. John Allen not only preached in the hall, he also took the Gospel into the streets and on board the ships. As the work was aimed specifically at the working-class, another hall was lent to the Mission in 1874 in the newer working-class neighbourhood of Canton. This was part of the soon established pattern that once a station (corps) was established, its members (soldiers) enthusiastically attempted to spread the Gospel in other geographic locations.

By the end of March 1875

"... the number of public speakers in the Cardiff area was nine, the number of outdoor services held there was ten per week, the number of indoor meetings seven, and contributions to the work £60."[5]

As the work was flourishing, a new meeting place was sought and thus the 1,200 seat Stuart Hall was taken. The work continued in the form of indoor and open-air services but little is recorded of it apart from the fact that the members continued to minister to the poorest classes. The recently formed Salvation Army held a Welsh 'Council of War' at the Stuart Hall on 1 March 1879 and hundreds of Salvationists from Cardiff and the surrounding areas heard Mrs. Catherine Booth address them on 'Aggressive Christianity'.[6] In addition she presented flags to various corps as the stations were now known.

The Mission's appearances on the street were not without opposition, but when this happened public opinion was frequently motivated by the Mission to protect its right to preach wherever it chose. Often however the public reaction to opposition was spontaneous. Thus in October 1875 when John Allen was charged with obstruction, there was a tremendous outcry from other ministers of religion and the press. Such was the public pressure that the Watch Committee sought an explanation from the police who, it was decided by the Committee, had to protect and not hinder the open-air services.[7] As an indentifiable uniformed Army, the opposition attracted occasionally became physical:

"There was an attack by the mob and soldiers were wounded. The Hallelujah Trumpeter brought thousands, and the enemy followed the march throwing large flint stones, hitting the soldiers both male and female. However, the Police were protecting them."[8]

"On Saturday night we were much encouraged to see a great big landlord at the door ringing a bell to annoy us. We hope he tries it again as it attracts crowds."[9]

Any opposition was welcomed by the Army who always saw it as a hallmark of success in stirring up the Devil and as an aid to growth.[10] In 1878 two other Salvation Army corps were opened in Cardiff, namely Roath and a new permanent hall at Canton. The latter Barracks were situated in Wellington Street near the Duke of York public house. Such growth of corps within a close proximity could only serve to reinforce the Movement's activities by mutual support. Not only the Cardiff corps helped each other but corps from the neighbouring communities gave mutual aid. This was particularly true of the bands:

"A grand demonstration was led by the Ebbw Vale Brass Band, who could play anything, any amount of times without stopping."[11]

Alongside the spiritual work there was a constant desire to do physical good, putting into practice the Christianity preached. During the 1880s the Army put its social welfare policies on a more organised footing. Amongst its work in Cardiff was a rescue home for prostitutes which had been helping girls for several years before a report of it appeared in 1888.[12] Nine years later a new rescue home was opened at 38 Charles Street. By 1896 the amount of spiritual and temperal work had increased enormously and food and work was being found on a considerable scale. This ranged from subsistence diets and rehabilitation of prisoners to the setting up of a labour exchange and an Army laundry.[13] As the Army increased its works the number of corps grew. Cardiff IV (Grangetown) and Cardiff V (Cathays) were opened in 1885 and 1887 respectively. Three more followed to make a total of eight corps by 1905.[14] Clearly the Army's style of worship and practical Christianity was a considerable success in this major conurbation.

Some Mining Towns

The Army's early corps in South Wales spread rapidly within the coalfield communities touching as it went the nearby iron-working centres such as Dowlais. In early 1878 Merthyr Tydfil was 'attacked'. Kate Watts and Harriet Parkin received an enthusiastic if sometimes bemused welcome from the local people and ministers. The latter

"... are really grand. They pray for us in their Chapels. On Saturday nights several come to the Prayer Meeting, and they do pray."[15]

Mrs. Sayers and Miss Smith took over the Corps and were in turn succeeded a few months later by Captain John Roberts. He arrived late on Friday 8 August 1879. Despite the hour,

"... a hundred of our own people were awaiting me at the station, (all reclaimed sinners). Some were black, some were white, some wore a good coat, some were collarless. One had a wooden leg and another no fingers."

Within a year or so Mr. Israel Price (Senior) formed a band using instruments mainly acquired from the local pawnshops. The Corps initially met in the Old Theatre and then in Glebeland Street. After several more moves, the present Citadel was opened in the same street in 1937.[16] Throughout the Corps' long history they followed William Booth's belief that Salvationists should preach and do Christian works in the neighbouring towns and villages. In 1878 the work soon spread to Dowlais, Aberdare and Mountain Ash. These stations or corps worked closely together, even on an 'All night of Prayer' held in Merthyr Tydfil in late 1878 attended by three hundred people.[17]

From Merthyr Tydfil the Army 'attacked' nearby Dowlais:

"This town is about two and a half miles from Merthyr, and contains about 25,000 inhabitants, chiefly sustained by its large iron works and some neighbouring collieries. From the first a goodly number of people attended our meetings in Merthyr, and several got converted and very soon these and others who could not walk so far began to plead that our Evangelists would go and hold some meetings in Dowlais. The Temperance Hall, which we believe holds over 1,200, was found and could be had for a reasonable sum, and as an experiment it was taken for a Sabbath afternoon. Sister Watts preached there, while Sister Parkin conducted the service in the Drill Hall in Merthyr. The place was crowded, and the interest deepened, and we were urged to make arrangements for establishing a branch of our work there."[18]

During a 'Campaign' visit to Dowlais on 1 March 1879 the Odd-fellows Hall was used for a 'Council of War'. At this meeting Mrs. Booth presented a Salvation Army flag to the Corps. She took the opportunity to explain that the colours of the flag had special significance: yellow for the fire of the Holy Spirit, red for the blood of Christ, and blue for the sanctifying power of Christ. The motto 'Blood and Fire', she said, was synonymous with the red and yellow. After the 'Councils', General and Mrs. Booth marched at the head of several hundred people to Merthyr Tydfil for another 'Council of War'.

After Dowlais came the two major mining communities that lay between Merthyr and the Rhondda, Aberdare and Mountain Ash. As

'Hallelujah Lassies' were proving their worth in attracting people to listen to preachers, William Booth sent a Welshwoman to evangelise in Aberdare. Mrs. Pamela Shepherd (née Morgan, of Talywain, Gwent) was converted by James Dowdle, 'The Saved Railway Guard', in the London East End district of Poplar in 1867.[19] Despite being deserted by her husband and with four daughters to bring up, she threw herself into the work of the Christian Mission. William Booth made her cook and housekeeper at the Mission Headquarters. Sending her to evangelise in Wales was a masterstroke and typical of Booth's inventive flair in finding new methods of reaching the masses. Despite Mrs. Shepherd's initial surprise and reluctance, she agreed to open the Mission's work in Aberdare.[20] Thus it was that at the age of forty-two Mrs. Shepherd and three of her daughters began preaching in Aberdare's Market Square one Saturday night in September 1878. She began in English telling of what the Lord had done in her life, but the local inhabitants taunted this strange 'English Woman'. As a mob surged around her

> "She erupted into a scalding torrent of Welsh: 'GWRANDEWCH!! (LISTEN!). CHWARAE TEG!! (Let's have fair play). I'm a Welshwoman — born in Talywain — I'm in my own country — I have a right to be heard. IF YOU ARE MEN, STAND BACK! YOU'LL CRUSH MY CHILDREN!"[21]

She quickly began that mixture of preaching and practical Christianity that was so much a part of William Booth's work. Word spread rapidly amongst the 70,000 inhabitants of Aberdare and the Mission received tremendous support, even from the police who ". . . are on our side. They have told us we can preach in any part of the town."[22] Operations were centred upon a large mill, nicknamed 'The Old Saw Mill', situated in Gloucester Road, Aberdare. The sincere and direct preaching of Mrs. Shepherd ignited a flame of religious fire that swept the town. They were so successful that they had to visit the Rhondda and Aberaman in response to calls made upon them.[23]

Under William Booth's orders, Mrs. Shepherd sought to fill the obvious demand, and thus the work spread rapidly into the requested areas. Mrs. Shepherd's eldest daughter, eighteen year old Kate, commenced corps in both Aberaman and Pentre in early 1879.[24] Before she went to Aberaman Kate was told by General Booth not to reveal her age for although she was full of the Holy Spirit, she was but young in years. Once there her powerful prayers convinced hundreds and a large number of new converts were registered by the Army and the chapels within a few weeks. She then moved onto Pentre and Sister J. Elliott took over. The work continued apace in Aberaman and Mr. Richard Cory had a new iron building erected for them. He asked only that the Army pay the interest on its cost and at its opening in early November 1881 he preached three sermons during the day.[25]

As was usual with the Army, the work was spread by the Salvationists either cycling or walking to neighbouring communities such as Cwmbach and Cwmaman where Army cottage meetings became a regular activity.

In Pentre, the appeal of Kate Shepherd's message could fill the large Shiloh Chapel to overflowing.[26] The *South Wales Daily News* of Saturday 15 March 1879 noted that after being in Pentre a month, five hundred converts had been made. The 'Hallelujah Lassies'

> ". . . have been the means of drawing hundreds of the lowest classes of people to hear the Gospel preached, people who are undoubtedly beyond the reach of our ministers."[27]

Within six weeks of entering Pentre, 2,300 people from the town and surrounding area had become members of various religious denominations. Thousands packed the largest halls available to listen to Salvationists. Small prayer meetings were held in dozens of cottages in the locality, although not always with the expected results.

> "Sudden termination of a Cottage Prayer Meeting
> AN ALARMING OCCURRENCE
> On Sunday evening, a startling accident happened at Treherbert. A Cottage prayer meeting, arranged by the Salvation Army was being held in the house of James Evans, collier, Bute Street, when suddenly the flooring of the sitting room which was tightly packed with people, gave way. The people, together with the furniture in the room, were thrown down and many persons were badly bruised, but none seriously injured."[28]

Undoubtedly the spirit of revival was spreading rapidly in 1879 and Kate's next appointment, to Brynmawr, helped the process.

Upon her move, Pentre was taken over by Captain Louisa Locke. While addressing a congregation of 3,000 people in the Noddfa Chapel, Treorchy, William Booth stated that the likes of the present religious awakening had not been seen in living memory and he praised the sincere work of Miss Shepherd. It is interesting to see what this work involved. A contemporary wrote of it:

> "If the masses are to be evangelised it is folly to think of reaching them by the same methods as are suitable to people of culture, or even to ordinary congregations and if existing denominations are not prepared to adopt such methods, then it is not for them to look down with scorn upon those servants of the Lord Jesus, who are prepared for anything and everything so that souls are saved. Miss Shepherd attempted no lengthy services as is the case with all Christian Mission services. The hymns sung are lively, the prayers offered are short and any remarks made are few and to the point."[29]

The message was taken to the people and Kate even ventured to visit the workers in the pits.[30] This could only reinforce the men's respect for this young girl and the Movement which wanted to help them. Kate was not the only young girl to venture down the mines and into the ironworks. Another was Rosina Davies, 'The Little Welsh Girl', who was converted at Treherbert in early 1879. She went on to help open corps in several communities commencing later the same year with Maesteg.[31] The message preached there and by other Salvationists was simple, understandable and unavoidable, and always accompanied by good works. The female officers were treated with great respect and their male counterparts were equally welcomed; for example, the ebullient John Lawley who was in charge of the rather impoverished mining community of Mountain Ash. Although no scholar, he appealed to the people because of his love, enthusiasm and song.[32] The effect of the revival was felt everywhere:

> "All over the mining areas the public houses were empty, the Chapels gradually opened their doors, and there was less swearing in the mines and on the streets. The horses were better treated under ground. During the dinner hour men and boys gathered together and held prayer meetings to the joy of the older Christian miners."[33]

From the Rhondda the revival swept into the whole of Wales. The Army spread rapidly along the coalfields, often borrowing chapels or, if nothing else was available, preaching continually in the open-air. Large towns were always an obvious 'target'; thus soldiers 'invaded' Aberystwyth from the earliest days of the Army. From the local headquarters in Cardiff, Major Coombs and his ADC, Jonah Evans, opened a corps in Aberystwyth in 1882. Two 'Hallelujah Lassies' were then placed in command. The Army was successful with every strata of society in the town, mainly because of its music, obvious sincerity and enthusiasm. From rare contemporary records we know that amongst the first converts were two railwaymen, two railway firemen, two stonemasons, two tailoresses and one milliner. Singing was conducted in both English and Welsh although the official language of the Corps was English. A local schoolmistress, Miss Sarah Owen, entered the Salvation Army's London Training Home from Aberystwyth in 1884. She then took charge of Pembroke Dock before being sent as an officer to Canada.[34]

North Wales

In 1881 the Army commenced its attack upon North Wales, 'Hallelujah Lassies opening fire' in the major mining town of Wrexham on 23 October. Within two months three hundred members from all social classes had joined.[35] There was some opposition from the 'Jolly Army'[36] but it soon died out as the majority of people supported the Salvation Army's work if not always its methods. A correspondent to the local newspaper, writing under the nom de plume 'No Play', asked what right women had to preach and who ordained the officers. The following week an answer from 'Fair Play' noted that many famous women had been inspired by God and that as long as they could save souls, no one was worried. He (or she) also noted that several famous revivalists had not been ordained.[37]

A brass band was formed in 1883, replacing the fiddle and tin-whistle used in the early days. The local Council refused it permission to play in the streets on Sundays[38] and this remained in force for many years. However, despite this, the Mayor of Wrexham gave an unofficial welcome to General Booth when he visited the town. Booth was received with great fervour:

"There was a large crowd of persons at the Great Western Railway Station on Saturday afternoon to witness the arrival of General Booth and his reception by the Wrexham 'Praying Boys', the Caergwrle Songsters, and the Cefn Warriors, who assembled to do honour to the Founder and commander-in-chief of the Salvation Army."[39]

The Army remained in high profile and in March 1885 a slum brigade was formed. This brigade was responsible for visiting, washing, cleaning, nursing and shopping for the ill, infirm and poor. The Army also helped the workers in times of great distress such as the 1893 colliers' strike and generally spread the Gospel in any way possible. As usual, the Movement expanded into neighbouring communities and Wrexham Salvationists regularly held open-air meetings at nearby Caergwrle, Cefn Mawr and Holt (where permanant corps were established, the first two in 1883 and the latter in 1888). However Mold was the next Corps to be established in the north and this was in 1882.

The Army quickly spread throughout North Wales and few communities remained untouched by 1890. A number of corps held two meetings per night, one in Welsh and other in English, to cater for the linguistic duality of the communities. Rhyl was opened in November 1885 and maintained this two language system for some years. So successful was the Corps that they took over the large St. George's Hall as their Barracks.[40] Amongst the many other corps reporting a specific dual language scheme were Oswestry (opened 8 November 1885) and Welshpool (opened 1886). Another town 'attacked' in 1886 was Caernarfon. This was at the request of a local solicitor.

"At Regent Hall London on the 9th January 1886, God saved a solicitor of the town, and knowing what the Salvation Army had done for him, he wanted it in his town. On his return he at once set to work, and was enabled to overcome what objection there was to the Army on the part of those who had suitable premises to let, and the result is that good barracks are secured in a central situation and the Army commenced Sunday by a good knee-drill [early morning prayer meeting] of one hundred and seventy five. At 10 o'clock an open-air was held in the poorest part of the town, and hope came into many of the weary hopeless lives, and tears flowed freely from the hearers and speakers too."[41]

The Turf Square Presbyterian Chapel became the Salvation Army Barracks and two 'Hallelujah Lassies' took command. These 'lassies' were Captain Clara Winfield and Captain Louisa Christmas, the latter a fluent Welsh speaker. As there was considerable local demand not merely for meetings in Welsh but for a Welsh speaking corps, two separate yet mutually supportive centres were established. The Welsh speaking Corps became known as Welsh Corps Number I. Within a few weeks *The Carnarvon and Denbigh Herald* reported that the latter corps

"... has increased to close upon five hundred members ... [The officers' efforts] have been crowned with such success that the barracks have become too small.

It was estimated by the newspaper that approximately 1,600 persons in total attended both the English and Welsh corps.

The same newspaper carried a report from the English Calvinistic Methodist Conference meeting at Llandudno. One speaker praised the Army for its work and the fact that its soldiers were "not afraid of what they were and in that fact lay some of their strength." Another report mentioned a Wesleyan Methodist who, at a local quarterly meeting, talked upon similar lines:

"The quarterly meeting desire hereby to congratulate your Corps upon the effectiveness of its work in reclaiming so many precious souls from evil courses since the advent of the Army to Caernarfon, to acknowledge the consideration shown by your Corps for the sacred sensitiveness of the Churches, and to wish you God speed in your excellent work throughout the Principality."[42]

With the approbation of the chapels, the work of the Salvation Army expanded rapidly but the sterling service given was seen almost as soon as they had entered the town. A cholera outbreak hit the town in late 1886 claiming many lives, especially in the poorest areas. The Army officers in charge noted that there was more and worse poverty in some parts of Caernarfon than the Salvation Army had met with in any part of London, thus the outbreak was dramatic.[43] The 'Hallelujah Lassies' worked hard amongst the local inhabitants to bring relief to their suffering — another example of their practical Christianity. In recognition of their valuable services, Mrs. Catherine Booth presented a flag to the Corps in early 1887. A few months later the General himself visited Caernarfon and four thousand people gathered in the Pavilion to hear his address. Caernarfon became the centre for annual rallies in Wales and the first, over Whit weekend 1889, saw thousands of soldiers attending mass open-air and indoor meetings. On Whit Monday the first Salvation Army wedding in Welsh took place. General William Booth again visited the town on 21 May 1891. He had been touring Ireland and had held meetings at Holyhead before moving on to Caernarfon. The General preached to a densely packed congregation about his recently published *In Darkest England and the Way Out*.[44] This outstanding social scheme, comprising farm, city and foreign colonies and containing all the ramifications of social and religious regeneration, had been receiving widespread attention. The assembled soldiers gave General Booth their whole-hearted support for the project.[45]

The idea of numbering Welsh speaking corps as at Caernarfon, independent of the English numbering system, soon caught on. Blaenau Ffestiniog was opened on the last Saturday in January 1887 as Welsh Corps Number 2 and others followed. The Army used the Rhiw Chapel and within a few days had enrolled twenty-two converts. Towards the end of February the Salvationists worked closely with the Congregationalists who, inspired by the Movement, had a week-long revival meeting at Brynbowydd conducted by the Revd. D. M. Jenkins. This was highly successful and typified the new spirit within the town, the Vale of Conway, and indeed the whole of Wales. The *War Cry* contains many reports of similar events. One such was over the weekend of 12/13 March when hundreds gathered under Staff-Captain Evans and Louisa Christmas and a charismatic outpouring of the Holy Spirit took place.[46]

In 1891 a building appeal was launched and a grand demonstration later held on the newly acquired building ground. This was near Duffys Station. Invitations went out for people to come and contribute towards the fifty pounds needed to commence building. All those who contributed had their names inscribed on a flag which was hoisted over the building plot. In March 1893 the Salvation Army Barracks opened in the centre of the town.

In Blaenau Ffestiniog soldiers took the Gospel message into the surrounding villages, establishing an 'outpost' at Penrhyndeudraeth Assembly Rooms in May 1888.[47] Unfortunately the small village was too poor to maintain the rent and the cost of having officers (each corps being responsible for the payment of their officers' wages). The 'outpost' closed in 1890. This was however only a temporary setback. In 1893 a Salvationist couple newly arrived from Blaenau Ffestiniog began using their small cottage as a meeting place and, typical of many small communities throughout Wales, a regular series of meetings was maintained there for many years.

The Salvation Army began its campaigns in the largest industrial communities in Wales and spread rapidly along the coal-seams. The Army was not only an alternative to the religious life of the chapels as it picked up those not seen in them, it also encouraged others to join existing bodies. The Movement was quickly perceived as being a genuine attempt at spiritually and physically helping all those in need. However the question remains: what elements made up the Salvation Army's appeal?

Undoubtedly the use of women was a major factor. Since 1859 Mrs. Catherine Booth had argued for the idea of female ministry. In 1860 she had written her own thirty-two page pamphlet on the subject.[48] Although William Booth was at first reluctant to send young girls to establish and run the work in towns, he did experiment with it in early 1878. Any doubt remaining in his mind about their effectiveness was removed by the work of Mrs. Shepherd and her daughter Kate in spreading revivalism throughout the Rhondda. The Welsh respected these women but the novelty of female preachers is not enough to explain the lasting success of the Movement. The willingness of the Army to adopt the native language was another crucial element. A number of Welsh speaking corps were founded and the vast majority of corps were at least bilingual. Frequent appeals were made for Welsh speaking officers and certainly their availability helped establish the work within Wales. On 9 April 1887 the first Welsh version of the Salvation Army's paper, the *War Cry,* was published. This was under the guidance of Staff-Captain Jonah Evans who had been converted at Aberdare by Mrs. Shepherd in November 1879. *Y Gad Lef* was edited from Caernarfon where Captain Evans and his wife controlled the Army's work in North Wales, their headquarters being at 29 Marcus Street. Although initially published as a fortnightly publication, such was the demand for *Y Gad Lef* that after the third issue, a weekly edition was printed. By May 1889 the paper sold ten thousand copies per week. However it was deemed by Headquarters in London to be uneconomic and thus it ceased publication on 19 November 1892. By 1888 copies of books by William and Catherine Booth were translated into Welsh and a Welsh version of the Army's song book, entitled *The Military Hymnal,* was published in May of that year.[49]

Women and language were indeed important factors in the Army's Welsh success but the Movement also relied on aid not just at corps level but from several influential people. Each corps had to support its officers and, if this proved impossible, the corps closed. Machynlleth was one such corp. The Army 'opened fire' here in 1889 but because the ten shillings per week rent was not easy to find, the corps did not remain open for very long. The vast majority of corps did survive

218

The *Iole*, whose visits to the fishing fleets gave much encouragement to trawler captains to fly the Army flag. She sank, without loss of life, after hitting a sandbank whilst entering the Humber on 19th June 1886.

well into the twentieth century and this shows the willingness of the people to contribute what little they had. However the work of certain highly influential people must be acknowledged, for example, the Cory brothers gave financial and other gifts which were of incalculable value to the spread of the Movement. One of several examples was at Aberaman where Messrs Richard and John Cory had mining interests. The Army building there was built by Richard and the brothers were present at this and many other corps openings. To enable easier transmission of the Gospel, the brothers also presented the Army with a large horse-drawn van. This saw sterling service across Wales and visited dozens of small, isolated hamlets. In addition the Corys gave the Army a mansion at Ystrad in South Wales to be used as a convalescent home for sick 'battle-weary' officers. In June 1885

> ". . . the General was given a steam yacht [the *Iole*] by John Cory. . . [This centre piece] of the Salvation Army navy was to do for those who went to sea what the Army did for those attending no place of worship on land."[50]

Also the brothers gave part of the profits from one of their ocean-going colliers, *The William Booth*, to the Army's work and allowed young Kate Shepherd and others to hold meetings down their pits.[51] Apart from the obvious generosity so freely given, the signs of support from these well-known and respected ship and colliery owners lent the Movement an aura of respectability.

Having respectable support from important persons and the chapels, for example at Porth the Baptists joined the Army in the open-air meetings,[52] reinforced the female and linguistic elements of the Movement to create an overall appeal to the population, but that was not all. The Army was a highly centralised broad-based movement. Its appeal involved uniforms, flags, bands, songs and a simple broad-based theological message couched in easily understandable working-class rhetoric.

The Army certainly reached many people and wherever possible, made full use of any local difficulty to attract a very genuine sympathy. In England the organised 'opposition' armies, commencing with the 'Unconverted Salvation Army' in Whitechapel in 1880, were used by Booth to attract support. He published numerous instances of their brutality. Although there were few instances of physical violence against Salvationists in Wales, there was actually little need to attempt to manufacture sympathy to retain the Movement's momentum. On the odd occasion when something felt to be unlawful took place, the public reaction in defence of the Salvationists was intense and therefore serves as an indicator of the Army's standing in the community. This took place even when the police summonsed Salvationists. One example was the imprisonment of Captain Louisa Locke and four male soldiers of the Pentre Corps. These Salvationists were charged with obstruction but, as was usual in the Army as a way of stating their right to pray anywhere and as a way of publicising the case, the members chose gaol.

> "The news that an officer of the Salvation Army had been imprisoned, shook Pentre. After the conviction on Monday last, the defendants refused to pay their fines and were marched from the hall to the Taff Vale station, accompanied by an immense mass of people, singing the whole of the way. Several offers were made to pay the fine but Captain Locke refused. The public were not aware that the arrest would be made on Saturday afternoon as it was contemplated to lay the pits idle for the occasion. Sunday School teachers and ministers held a mass meeting in sympathy. . . .[53]

A similar happening took place in Trealaw in 1883. Here four soldiers were sent to Cardiff gaol. Upon arrival at Cardiff a brass band met them and escorted them to prison. At their release a large meeting was held in their honour at the Cardiff Stuart Hall.[54]

Alongside attracting attention, Booth's workers had to prove that they were one with the people. The devotion to this end by the Shepherd family rapidly became known but each Salvation soldier was required to minister to everyone. This was not just in open-air services but included a door-to-door visitation and actively seeking out the bereaved, ill and poor. By this the Army was seen as an organisation of the working-class. The Army identified with the local inhabitants, especially in times of disasters and strikes. In Trealaw in late 1880 a mining disaster killed eighty-eight men. The Army comforted relatives and survivors, offering what spiritual and practical aid they could.[55] The coal-mining strikes of 1893 and 1898, and the quarrymen's strike of 1896 , showed the continued commitment of the Army to the people and conversely, the people's respect. The great coal-strike of 1893 originated in the Ogmore valley and for many weeks miners across Wales went without work and therefore pay.[56] The poverty in communities such as Nantymoel in the south and Wrexham in the north was at least partially alleviated by food distribution by the Army corps. In fact,

> "The coal strike of 1893 having entered upon its sixteenth week during November, without any definite hope of an immediate settlement, the General instituted a 'Sufferers Saturday' on the 18th to help alleviate the hunger horrors, and in connection with what became the General Food Fund."[57]

The quarrymen's strike of 1896 hit Bethesda particularly hard but again the local Salvationists organised soup-kitchens and food distribution. Finally, when the 1898 miners' strike swept Wales, food and clothing were found. At Porth, for example, a well organised relief committee gave two meals a day to children.[58] Similar reports appeared about Trealaw[59] and Abertillery. In the latter community the Salvation Army

> ". . . Barracks were used as a soup kitchen and food was supplied by the townspeople. Many of the shops have stopped giving trust and this means that those affected are dependent on relief."[60]

By 1900, then, the Salvation Army had proved itself as a lasting and effective working-class movement in Wales. It had quickly become accepted because of Booth's use of women preachers, the Movement's broad-based appeal, its use of local people and the Welsh language, and above all its willingness to help the poor no matter what their circumstances were. The revivalism engendered by the Army was shared by the churches and chapels, all of whom accorded the Movement a warm welcome. In addition, the Army was given an added degree of respectability by the backing of the Corys and others. These factors clearly enabled it to increase and maintain its momentum well into the twentieth century.

CHAPTER TEN

OVERVIEW AND CONCLUSION

The 1859 evangelical awakening within England gave a new credence to the revivalistic tools of evangelism. Coming after the shock figures of Horace Mann's report[1] and spurred on by the increasing number of revelations concerning the conditions of deprivation within industrialising towns, evangelism became the touchstone of taking religion to the masses in the 1860s.[2] The Home Mission Movement attempted such work but it was rarely forced on the people in the manner of the later Salvation Army. The majority of missions were viewed by the masses with suspicion for their apparently condescending attitudes; they were not always readily identifiable as being of the people. The most successful denomination was the Primitive Methodists although they generally operated only in certain geographical areas. The Primitives unashamedly 'attacked' the poor through the techniques of revivalism: open-air meetings, mourners' benches,[3] utilisation of barns and sheds for meetings, hell and damnation preaching, charismata, freely moving ministers from area to area, and the proclamation of their persecuted state.[4] However many Methodists in general and the Wesleyan Methodists in particular tended to regard such revivalism with distrust. The latter effectively blocked any revival in 1862.[5] Yet it was through his connection with the Methodists that Booth came to understand the use of such methods to supplement his innate belief in taking the Gospel to the people.

William Booth was converted through the Wesleyans, dallied with the Wesleyan Reformers, Congregationalists, and returned to the Wesleyan Reformers before spending seven years in the Methodist New Connexion. The latter appealed so strongly to him that he became ordained in it. Its key attraction was the omnipotence of conference which

> ". . . aimed at strong government as the only way of directing Methodist expansion."[6]

Ultimately a disagreement with conference over Booth's desire for itinerant evangelist status led him to resign, despite his considerable success as a minister. Between 1861 and 1865, across the nation the Booths expounded and improved upon Methodist methods. He also

222

initiated the first Hallelujah Band, and such enthusiasm for reaching the masses, when combined with the intellectual and teetotal spirit of his preacher-wife, created a forceful team. Their creed was to preach directly to the poor. When therefore the East London Special Services Committee offered Booth the temporary charge of its Whitechapel tent, he readily seized the opportunity.

Although it appears that Booth's mission developed along traditional Home Mission lines with ragged schools, a variety of buildings and some food relief in times of socio-economic stress, there were certain methodological differences from other missions. Booth's control, narrow aim, the equality of women and his constant probing for new centres of work, combined with his fiery oratory to produce solid if initially slow gains. Expansion outside East London took place after 1869, first to the south and then to the north-east. Invitations often came to open a station and once established, William Booth used it as a 'springboard' to nearby areas. The crucial factor in Booth's favour was his tight control. He was in practical control before and during the period of the Council and Conferences. He was the Christian Mission, as evidenced by there being no Conference when he was ill in 1872. From the June 1877 Conference he was also theoretically omnipotent. He had gradually tightened his legal control, believing that a central authority was vital for progress. The Wesleyan Reform Movement had suffered for want of such leadership and the Methodist New Connexion's Conference decisions were weakened by lay local government. Booth realised that lessons about effective leadership must be learnt, even at the cost of losing a number of followers.

The Christian Mission adopted the name Salvation Army in May 1878 and between that date and late 1883, the Movement experienced its most rapid growth. Its 519 centres in England and Wales by the end of 1883 were widepread but the majority were concentrated in four main areas. The emphasis lay in areas of concentrated population ranging from large urban conurbations to small mining communities (Map 3.1). The Army was essentially an urban movement for although the corps-population density was lower in agricultural areas, the fact of the population being so widely spread proved a hindrance only combatted in the early 1880s by the introduction of circle-corps.

General Booth's 'springboard' policy combined with the use of women, judicious local assimilation with clothes and language, the militarism (most notably bands, flags, uniforms and songs), and detailed autocratic control, made a novel, direct and unavoidable impression on the working-class. His largely working-class staff took the message to the people in a rigorous high-profile campaign using tactics that sometimes scandalised[7] and frequently amused Victorian society.[8] The persecution which the Movement inspired in some mainly southern areas apparently served to heighten its appeal. Booth's success in supplying a phenomenon would however have foundered quickly if there had not been a demand for it. This demand side of the equation existed through a combination of factors concerned with occupations, socio-economic climate, and paucity of religious provision.

Nineteenth century industrial occupations needed concentrations of labour. In the maelstrom of Victorian economics, industries were decaying, geographically shifting, or growing, often resulting in social mobility and certainly in large scale geographical mobility. In densely-packed communities, particularly the northern industrial conurbations where the Army had many of its early and lasting successes, the Movement perhaps offered a sense of community as well as a way to Salvation. Occupations have a direct relationship to the socio-economic health of an area. The 1870s and 1880s were times of considerable trade fluctuations and changes in working-practices. The declining numbers of textile workers, the relocation of iron and the decline of the steel industries, increases in coal production and rapid geographical shifts to new seams produced chronologically, geographically and sometimes within a community internally varying socio-economic climates. Decay in some occupations, reminiscent of that over preceding decades in many south-western counties, paralleled a boom in others. Economic vagaries therefore precipitated distress or a steady rise but were less predictable than the more natural barriers to work of age and health. Thus the socio-economic climate depended on the work being available. When work ceased in one or more occupations and no immediate geographical or occupational move was possible in the long or short term, huge numbers of workers and their families joined the base stratum of those daily struggling to survive. Providing however that the Army had some source of local finance, a corps could survive and indeed, would often find itself with increasing numbers of soldiers.

The paucity of religious accommodation and the psychological, financial and time barriers to attending places of worship meant that any organisation appealing to the working-class had at least an initial impact. When combined with the directness and novelty of the Army, this appeal often proved quite strong.

Two crucial factors in the Army's success were its officers and the public reaction. From his earlier experiences with the Methodist New Connexion and as an itinerant preacher William Booth realised the value of utilising members of the working-class to 'attack' the working-class. By aiming to make the people listen and by using converts to attempt immediately to 'save' others, he gained an effective grass-roots support. The majority of his Christian Mission evangelists were working-class. Some were Methodists, mainly Primitives, whose kindred experiences with Booth's proved invaluable in quickly grasping his aims and methods. Although the loss of workers and members was about one-third and one-half per annum respectively, mainly due to disagreements with Booth's innovations and demands, new members joined in greater numbers than hitherto realised.

Once the Movement became identifiable, the numbers of officers and members increased, thus enabling the Army to expand further. Of those officers with previous religious experience, two-thirds were Methodists of Wesleyan or Primitive ideology. A small but growing number of Anglican women were joining and in late 1878/1879 there was a marked influx of women. By 1880 numbers of men and women joining were approximately equal. Doubtless women found the Army's ideology appealing. Equality was stressed although it was not practised in the middle to upper echelons of power, in pay or in conjugal rights of corps commanders. This led to some dissatisfaction although the key causes which resulted in the continuance of up to one-third resignations annually were those imposed by the Boothite system: the rapid geographic mobility, frequent loneliness, the need to pay the corps' way, paperwork, omnipotence of the Booth family, opposition and the degree of unquestioning obedience. The majority of officers in the 1880s were also very young and a later desire to marry non-officers or those outside the Army led to other resignations. The peak age for new women officers at this time was 17 to 21 although some as young as 14 were recorded. The largest number came from London and the Home Counties. The majority of male officers joined between the ages of 20 to 23 with Lancashire supplying the highest number and the majority coming from the north in general. Few came from the predominantly agricultural counties and of those that did, their homes tended to be not in farming but in the industrially-decaying areas.

By the 1890s offices came from a wider geographical area and were slightly older when 'joining-up'. More women Methodists and Anglicans were becoming officers, for the Army still offered a greater degree of equality than available elsewhere in religious societies. As in the preceding years the majority of officers continued to be recruited from a wide social range across the working-class. However, again as previously, few actually came from the 'submerged tenth'. Resignations had decreased in proportion to about one-quarter per annum but with the large numbers of officers joining in the late 1880s and 1890s, the actual figure was still quite high. Many of those who did resign went to other churches or charitable works.

Corresponding to the early years of the Methodists, Baptists and Congregationalists, the Salvation Army faced an extremely hostile opposition in some geographical areas. The Army triggered off the 'rough-musicing' tradition which in a few cases was supported and organised by important members of the local establishment who feared that the arrival of the Army would disrupt the brewery trade or cause violence. Such reaction occurred mainly in the conservative southern and western counties with their small and close-knit traditional communities. The Skeleton Armies were the initial focus of organised anti-Army activity while the Army glorified in the struggle. Booth's soldiers used it as a bench-mark of their success as well as to excite some very real public sympathy. The Movement's apparently strange activities and charismatic meetings, aimed at spiritual regeneration (partly achieved by closing down drinking-houses), intensified the grass-roots reaction directed at anyone disturbing the *status quo*. What was more problematical to the Army than mere tradition was the establishment support of the opposition.

1882 was the most violent anti-Army year marked by numerous cases of magistrates gaoling Salvationists who refused on principle to pay the fines. The Home Secretary, Sir William Harcourt, at first pursued a course apparently in support of such magistrates. He, like they, felt that the Army was at fault for parading the street in a manner likely to cause a breach of the peace. Sir William therefore suggested banning such marches if opposition was expected. Subsequent High Court judgements, starting with the June 1882 Beatty v. Gillbanks case, forced him to revise his suggestions and order protection for the Army. Further High Court judgements reinforced the initial decision that Salvationists had the right to parade the streets. The Army then had to contend with various local authorities introducing bye-laws against non-military processions but by this time (1886 to 1891) and despite sporadic violence such as at Whitchurch (1890) and Eastbourne (1891), the Movement was well-established nationally and internationally.

With the absence of persecution, the Army needed to continue to catch the public's imagination as well as retain old and make new members. It needed a cause fresher than mere novelty. Some of its officers therefore turned to the vexed questions of moral issues and labour relations. The Criminal Law Amendment Act of 1885, raising the age of consent to 16, was the culmination of a successful anti-child prostitution campaign waged by the Army and certain of its sympathisers. It was though only one of several issues in which William Booth sometimes reluctantly became involved. He increasingly visualised the millennium and in an article of that title in 1890 saw such ultimate visions as Hyde Park being roofed in to become "The World's Great Grand Central Temple."[9] Many of the ideas came from Commissioner Frank Smith and W. T. Stead but Booth was the catalyst. Unfortunately for the Army, the launch of his grand social schemes through *In Darkest England and the Way Out* (1890) was marred not only by personal tragedy with the death of Catherine Booth but also by the resignation of Commissioner Smith over the very question of his autonomy of control over the Army's social policy. Smith had however steered the Army into helping and organising various labour movements such as the match-girls and the sandwich-board men. Most importantly the Army had shown the way by practical example for factory-health care and higher wages amongst some of the country's sweated trades.

The five case-studies in this book, chosen for their varying geographical position and socio-economic climate, give detailed backing to the conclusions expressed above. In Poplar, the Christian Mission/Salvation Army benefited most in terms of membership when the social problems of the densely crowded district were exacerbated by poor trade conditions or strikes. The Army's programme of social reforms and social aid gained it respect but only after several years did the reforms become an accepted part of the community. Its social work and factory reform gained the Movement a rapport with the working-class and an identity as an organisation of and for them. Whether William Booth at first intended this identification through the social work is doubtful but as it was effective and allowed the preaching of Salvation, Booth was prepared to encompass it as long as he retained control.

The Manchester case-study highlighted the effectiveness of Booth's 'springboard' policy both community to community and within a large conurbation. It showed the value of inter-corps aid, a variety of successful methods of taking the Gospel to the people, and the importance of using people easily assimilated into the local community. Three important facts to emerge from this study point to or confirm reasons for the Salvation Army's success. First, the Army operated best in and from areas of mixed working-class communities and not in the poorest quarters such as Bradford, Harpurhey and Deansgate. This was because money was needed for corps expenses and the very poorest areas could rarely support even a small corps for long. Second, the Army provided a very real sense of community to many of those socially and geographically mobile. Third, local sympathisers, such as Frank Crossley J.P., the 'Army's Paymaster', and Thomas Renshaw, were invaluable in lending moral, physical and financial support.

The Guildford and Honiton case-studies demonstrated that the further south and west the Army penetrated, the harsher the 'rough-musicing'. This tradition was all but dead in the jumbled background communities making up Manchester, weak in Poplar, and strongest in the conservative south and west. Clearly the actions of local magistrates encouraged the tradition to sometimes quite bloody heights. A decline in 'rough-musicing', church and chapel support (particularly in Guildford), a change of local magistracy, and Home Office intervention brought an end to such opposition and a slowing down in Army growth in England. The Salvation Army became accepted and increasingly respectable . In Honiton the Army died out due to public apathy.

The study of Wales showed the Army as both an alternative and a complement to the existing religious bodies. Its use of female officers, willingness to adopt the native language, support from influential friends, and eagerness to go to the people (particularly in times of crisis), ensured the Movement's spread and explains its ability to open on average one new corps every six and a half weeks throughout the 1880s.

The Salvation Army then was the ideological creation of an inspiring couple who built on the physical work of a growing but often changing number of officers and soldiers. Once emerged from the Home Mission tradition as an identifiably distinct unit, the Army expanded and metamorphosed to meet varying internal demands and national issues. Its distinctness, leadership and narrowness of aim combined to create success. William Booth's aim was to convert 'the masses' while avoiding all contentious questions, particularly those concerning doctrine.[10] This narrowness of aim in itself attracted considerable early support as both onlookers and members could seemingly identify a noble cause within the much vaunted and persecuted Movement.

A decline in novelty value and the eradication of opposition created a growing public lethargy towards the Army by the late 1880s and forced the Movement to experiment with Booth's millennial idealism. It was Booth who decided the pace of such experiments. Due to this he lost the only officers who could have made the 'In Darkest England' scheme successful in practice instead of it becoming a series of suggestive if often important examples. Alongside his millenarianism, Booth was compelled to develop and refine his ideas on such issues as sacraments and faith-healing, thus unavoidably pontificating upon contentious questions. By the turn of the century though, the Movement numbered approximately 100,000 soldiers in the United Kingdom[11] and was second only to the 200,000 strong Primitive Methodists as an organised working-class denomination.[12] This was an immense achievement in the 35 year period from 1865.

NOTES AND REFERENCES

Chapter 1. THE VICTORIAN RELIGIOUS AND SOCIAL ENVIRONMENT

1. *Census of England and Wales. 1851. Religious Worship in England and Wales. Parliamentary Papers 1852–1853.* Vol. LXXXIX. (Hereafter *Religious Census.*)
2. Gay, J. D., *The Geography of Religion in England* (London, 1971), 60.
3. Mayhew, H., *London Labour and London Poor* (London, 1851), Vol. I, 21. This suggestion is also borne out by McLeod, H., *Class and Religion in the Late Victorian City* (London, 1974), 24–5.
4. Kitson Clark, G., *The Making of Victorian England* (London, 1962), 163.
5. Currie, R., Gilbert, A. D. and Horsley, L., *Churches and Church Goers* (Oxford, 1977), 87.
6. Bullock, C., *The People's Archbishop* (London, 1891), 39.
7. Gay, J. D., *op. cit.,* 145.
8. So called after the publication, in 1849, of scurrilous pamphlets accusing prominent Wesleyan leaders of despotism and appealing for a more liberal form of government. From 1849 to 1855, the Wesleyans lost a third of their members and other Methodist churches reported declines. Chadwick, O., *The Victorian Church*, Part 1 (London, 1966), Ch. 6.
9. Inglis, K. S., *The Churches and the Working Classes in Victorian England* (London, 1963), 18.
10. McLeod, H., *Religion and the Working Class in Nineteenth-Century Britain* (London, 1984), 26.
11. Gay, J. D., *op. cit.* Also Horridge, G. K., *The Growth and Development of a Family Firm, Chivers of Histon, 1873–1939* (Cambridge, 1983). The Chivers family, all Baptists, were the only major employers in Cambridgeshire.
12. Gay, J. D., *op. cit.*, 141. Also Brown, K. D., *A Social History of the Nonconformist Ministry in England and Wales 1800–1930* (Oxford, 1988), 24.
13. Kitson Clark, G., *op. cit.*, 185.
14. Gilbert, A. D., *Religion and Society in Industrial England* (London, 1976), 40–1.
15. *Ibid.*, 40. Also Isichei, E., *Victorian Quakers* (Oxford, 1970).
16. Inglis, K. S., *op. cit.*, 130.
17. Orr, J. E., *The Second Evangelical Awakening* (London, 1949).
18. Gilbert, A. D., *op. cit.*, 44.
19. The Coaklers were a religious sect not previously investigated. They were active in the second half of the nineteenth century, mainly in the south of England.
20. Begbie, H., *William Booth. Founder of The Salvation Army* (London, 1920), Vol. I, 311–2.
21. For example the London City Mission founded in 1835. See Heasman, K., *Evangelicals in Action* (London, 1962), 35–6. Also Weylland, J. M., *These Fifty Years. Jubilee Volume* (London, 1885).
22. Kent, J., *Holding the Fort. Studies in Victorian Revivalism* (London, 1978), 106–7, 113.
23. Ward, J. T., 'Britain c. 1830–1850: The Background', in Ward, J. T. (Ed.), *Popular Movements* (London, 1970), 5.
24. Stedman Jones, G., *Outcast London* (Oxford, 1971), 22–3.
25. Midwinter, E. C., *Victorian Social Reforms* (London, 1968), Ch. 2.
26. No relation to William Booth.
27. A phrase current in all nineteenth century church and chapel phraseology, including that of the Salvation Army.

229

28. Briggs, A., *Victorian People: a reassessment of persons and themes, 1851–1867* (London, 1965), 13. Also Stevenson, J., *Popular Disturbances in England 1700–1870* (London, 1979), Ch. 13.

29. The idea of social conditions being revealed was very prominent in contemporary newspapers, pamphlets and books. Notable authors were George, H., *Progress and Poverty* (London, 1881); Mearns, A., *The Bitter Cry of Outcast London* (London, 1883); Stead, W. T., in his newspaper *The Pall Mall Gazette*; Sims, G. R., with articles in Pictorial World in the early 1880s and *How the Poor Live in Horrible London* (London, 1889); Booth, W., *In Darkest England and The Way Out* (London, 1890); plus a number of surveys by researchers such as Charles Booth and Seebohm Rowntree.

Chapter 2. THE CHRISTIAN MISSION

1. Ervine, St. J., *God's Soldier. General William Booth* (London, 1934). The eldest boy, Henry, died on 6 January 1828. Samuel Booth had earlier lost his first wife and only child. Vol. I, 10.

2. Stead, W. T., *General Booth. A Biographical Sketch* (London, 1891), 25.

3. The paper was *The Pall Mall Gazette*.

4. Begbie, H., *William Booth. Founder of The Salvation Army* (London, 1920), Vol. I, 61–2.

5. *Ibid.*, 71.

6. Irvine, St. J., *op. cit.*, 69–70. Also Begbie, H., *op. cit.*, Vol. I, 144. Also Sandall, R., *The History of The Salvation Army* (London, 1947), Vol. I, 6.

7. Railton, G. S., *Twenty-One Years Salvation Army* (London, 1886), 40.

8. Sandall, R., *op. cit.*, Vol. I, 37.

9. *Revival*, 17 August 1865.

10. The Christian Revival Association; The East London Christian Revival Union; East London Christian Revival Society; The East London Christian Mission; The Christian Mission; The Salvation Army.

11. *Revival*, 3 September 1865.

12. Railton, G. S., *op. cit.*, 39.

13. Collier, R., *The General Next To God* (London, 1965), 41.

14. Booth, W., 'How We Began', in Railton, G. S., *op. cit.*, 22–3.

15. Stead, W. T., *op. cit.*, 64.

16. *Ibid.* Also Booth, W., 'How We Began', in Railton, G. S., *op. cit.*, 22.

17. *Revival*, 6 February 1868.

18. *Christian Mission Report. 1867*, 40–1.

19. *The Christian Mission Magazine*, September 1870, 142. There is only a very limited amount of material relating to the finances of the Christian Mission extant.

20. *The East London Evangelist*, May 1869, 127.

21. *Ibid.*, August 1869, 172.

22. *The Christian Mission Magazine*, December 1870, 182.

23. *Ibid.*, January 1871, 15.

24. *The Christian Mission Magazine*, May 1873, 79.

    "Brother Ireson, one of our members at Croydon, removed, some time ago, to Wellingboro' and, through his representations, several friends requested us to visit the place."

25. Railton, G. S., *Heathen England* (London, 1883, fifth edition), 26.

26. Begbie, H., *op. cit.*, Vol. I, 79.

27. One point that was not based on John Wesley concerned the question of Holiness (Article 6). Although this received little attention from the Booths in the 1860s, it assumed considerable importance for them from 1870. See Kent, J., *Holding the Fort. Studies in Victorian Revivalism* (London, 1978), Ch. 8.3.

28. Watts, A. W., *Lion Hearts. Memoirs of the Christian Mission afterwards known as the Salvation Army* (London, n.d.), 30.
29 *The Christian Mission Conference Minute Book* (hereafter *Minute Book*), 1870, Section XII, 13.
30 The Society of Friends (Quakers) would have been familiar with the idea of full equality but even amongst them it "... was more more apparent than real." Isichei, E., *Victorian Quakers* (Oxford, 1970), 107–9. Certainly Methodist women never achieved full equality although some branches, at least initially, allowed them preaching rights. McLeod, H., *Religion and the Working Class in Nineteenth-Century Britain* (London, 1984), 27–30, 46.
31. *Minute Book*, 1870, Section III, 2.
32. *Ibid.*, 1870, Section XXXIII, 22.
33. Coutts, F., *No Discharge In This War* (London, 1974), 23.
34. Sandall, R., *op. cit.*, Vol. I, 178.
35. Nicol, A. M., *General Booth and The Salvation Army* (London, n.d., *circa* 1910), 72.
36. *Minute Book*, 1870, 32.
37. Nicol, A. M., *op. cit.*, 79.
38. *The Christian Mission Magazine*, June 1872, 89.
39. *Ibid.*, February 1871, 30.
40. Ervine, St. J., *op. cit.*, Vol. II, 324.
41. *Minute Book*, Minutes for 1873.
42. *The Christian Mission Magazine*, July 1875, 176.
43. *Foundation Deed Poll*, 4–5.
44. *Ibid.*, 11, Rule 11.
45. *Ibid.*, 13, Rule 14.
46. Begbie, H., *op. cit.*, Vol. I, 416.
47. *The Christian Mission Magazine*, July 1877, 177.
48. Sandall, R., *op. cit.*, Vol. I, 186–7.
49. Railton, G. S., *Twenty-One Years Salvation Army* (London, 1886), 42, 45.
50. Watts, A., *op. cit.*, 22.
51. Sandall, R., *op. cit.*, Vol. I, 198.
52. Railton, G. S., *op. cit.*, 63.
53. Lunn, B., *Salvation Dynasty* (London, 1936), 72.
54. Railton, G. S., *op. cit.*, 65.
55. Sandall, R., *op. cit.*, Vol. I, 198.
56. *The Christian Mission Magazine*, July 1877, 177–8. (The *italic* passage was in italics in the original.)
57. *Minute Book*, 1877.
58. *The Christian Mission Magazine*, July 1877, 168.
59. Ervine, St. J., *op. cit.*, Vol. I, 433.
60. Nicol, A. M., *op. cit.*, 73.
61. Begbie, H., *op. cit.*, Vol. I, 425.
62. Railton, G. S., *Heathen England* (S.A. 1883, fifth edition), 29. (Early May, 1878.)
63. *Minute Book*, 1878.
64. *The Christian Mission Magazine*, September 1878, 250.
65. *Deed of Constitution. Close Roll (Chancery)*, 7 August 1878, Part 72, m. 28, 3.
66. *The Christian Mission Magazine*, September 1878, 250–2.
67. Watts, A. W., *op. cit.*, 9–10.
68. Nicol, A. M., *op. cit.*, 87–8.
69. Ervine, St. J., *op. cit.*, Vol. I, 423.

Chapter 3. THE GROWTH AND ORGANISATION OF THE SALVATION ARMY

1. *The Salvation Soldier's Pocket Book For 1884* (London, December 1883). Hereafter *Pocket Book 1884*.
2. *The Christian Mission Magazine*, March 1878, 67.
3. *The Salvationist*, June 1879, 147–8.
4. *Pocket Book 1884*.
5. 'Captive' because the communities were small and therefore there were few places where the Salvation Army could not penetrate and be heard.
6. Hayle. St. Ives and Falmouth.
7. These figures were calculated by comparing the number of Corps listed in the *Pocket Book 1884* with the population recorded in the *Census of England and Wales. 1881. Population.*
8. Edmonds, H., *My Adventures with General William Booth* (Manuscript, 1933), 92. The reconnaissance of areas was a standard Army policy. Booth, W., *Orders and Regulations for the Salvation Army* (London, 1878), 14–40. Any such reconnaissance was usually carried out by a staff-officer such as Henry Edmonds who was conducting a number of them by the age of 18.
9. Chadwick, O., *The Victorian Church* (London, 1970), Part II, 232.
10. Mews, S., 'The General and the Bishops: Alternative Responses to Dechristianisation', in Gourvish, T. R. and O'Day, A., *Later Victorian Britain, 1867–1900* (Basingstoke, 1988). Also Shiman, L. L., *The Crusade Against Drink in Victorian England* New York, 1988).
11. Anderson, O., 'The Growth of Christian Militarism in Mid-Victorian Britain', in *English Historical Review*, Vol. 86, January 1971. (Sankey and Moody are two of the most well known examples.)
12. Cunningham, H., 'Jingoism in 1877–8', in *Victorian Studies*, Vol. XIV, No. 4, 1971.
13. Anderson, O., *op. cit.*, 44; Cunningham, H., *op. cit.*, 71.
14. Sandall, R., *The History of The Salvation Army* (London, 1950), Vol. II, 39.
15. The sun was changed to a star signifying The Holy Ghost. This occurred in 1882 when officers were being sent to India, probably because the sun was very important to one of the major religious groups. Sandall, R., *ibid.*, Vol. II, 39–40.
16. Railton, G. S., *Heathen England* (London, 1883, fifth edition), 31.
17. *The Salvationist*, August 1878, 224.
18. Sandall, R., *op. cit.*, Vol. II, 113.
19. Early band music was sometimes written out or printed with symbols beside the tunes to identify them and so avoid the problem of illiteracy. For example South Shields Corps' band music had a picture of a boat at the start of the tune 'Out on the Ocean Sailing'. Similarly 'Oh to be over Yonder' showed an armchair with a weary man fumbling his way towards it.
20. *The East London Evangelist*, 1 November 1868, 30. Above the hymn there was a portion of scripture followed by the six verses to be sung to the tune 'The Voice of Free Grace'.
21. *The Christian Mission Magazine*, September 1877, 233.
22. Booth, W., *All About the Salvation Army* (London, 1882), 9.
23. *Ibid.*, 8.
24. Collier, R., *The General Next to God. The Story of General William Booth and the Salvation Army* (London, 1965), 65.
25. Bramwell-Booth, C., *Catherine Booth* (London, 1970), 267.
26. Booth, W., *op. cit.*, 18–9.
27. Bramwell-Booth, C., *op. cit.*, 267.
28. Sandall, R., *op. cit.*, Vol. II, 11.

29. *The Christian Mission Magazine*, July 1877, 182–3.
30. Stead, W. T., *General Booth* (London, 1891), 51.
31. *The Christian Mission Magazine*, July 1877, 183.
32. *Ibid.*, March 1877, 67.
33. Sandall, R., *op. cit.*, Vol. II, 51.
34. Booth, W., *Orders and Regulations for the Salvation Army* (London, 1878), 5, 9.
35. Gasparin, La Comtesse A. De, *Read and Judge the (So Called) Salvation Army* (Paris, n.d., English translation London, 1883), 34.
36. Begbie, H., *William Booth. Founder of the Salvation Army* (London, 1920), Vol. II, 158.
37. *War Cry*, 14 November 1891.
38. Previously unpublished letter, General Booth to Bramwell Booth, Chief of the Staff, 1 January 1896. Salvation Army Archive Unit, London.
39. Booth, W., *Orders and Regulations for Salvation Soldiers* (London, 1891), Ch. VIII, Sections 2–4.
40. *The Christian Mission Magazine*, July 1877, 179.
41. *An Outline of Salvation Army History* (London, 1932), 31.
42. Booth, W., *Orders and Regulations for the Salvation Army* (London, 1878), Ch. IV, Section 8, 103.
43. *The Salvationist*, May 1879, 128.
44. Hunt, E. H., *Regional Wage Variations In Britain 1850–1914* (Oxford, 1973), 129.
45. Gray, R. Q., *The Aristocracy of Labour in Nineteenth Century Britain c. 1850–1914* (London, 1981), 15.
46. Moorhouse, H. F., 'The Marxist theory of the Labour aristocracy', in *Social History*, Vol. 3, No. 1, January 1978; Reid, A., 'Politics and economics in the formation of the British working class: A response to H. F. Moorhouse', in *Social History*, Vol. 3, No. 3, October 1978; Moorhouse, H. F., 'History, sociology and the quiescence of the British working class: a reply to Reid', in *Social History*, Vol. 4, No. 3, October 1979; Reid, A., 'Response', in *Social History*, Vol. 4, No. 3, October 1979. For further reference to the 'Aristocracy of Labour' debate see Crossick, G., *An Artisan Elite in Victorian Society: Kentish London 1840–1880* (London, 1978). Also Morris, R. J., *Class and Class Consciousness in the Industrial Revolution, 1780–1850* (London, 1982). The acceptance of the difficulty in identifying clear-cut cultural divisions within the working class (and therefore an 'Aristocracy of Labour') has led those historians who retain the phrase (such as F. M. L. Thompson) to treat it with caution while others (such as R. Harrison) have abandoned it entirely. See Thompson, F. M. L., *The Rise of Respectable Society. A Social History of Victorian Britain, 1830–1900* (London, 1988), 199. Also Harrison, R., 'Introduction', in Harrison R. and Zeitlin, J. (Eds.), *Divisions of Labour* (Brighton, 1985), 6.
47. McLeod, H., *Religion and the Working Class in Nineteenth-Century Britain* (London, 1984), 30.
48. Fraser, D., *The Evolution of the British Welfare State* (London, 1973), 124.
49. Coppock, J. T., 'The Changing Face of England 1850 — circa 1900', in Darby, H. C. (Ed.), *A New Historical Geography of England* (Cambridge, 1973), 641.
50. Mitchell, B. R. and Deane, P., 'Abstract of British Historical Statistics' (Cambridge, 1962), 60. Quoted in Coppock, J. T., *ibid.*, 641.
51. Smales, B. J., *Economic History* (London, 1975), 78, 79.
52. Coppock, J. T., *op. cit.*, 628.
53. Court, W. H. B., *British Economic History* (Cambridge, 1965), 103.
54. The fourth 'region' London, has been considered in detail in Ward, C., *The Social Sources of the Salvation Army* (M.Phil. thesis, University of London, 1970), 113–131.
55. Six of the original 13 corps of 1883 had been closed by 1905 but six others had been opened (Table 3.3).

56. Author's manuscript analysis of *Census. 1881. Occupations*, 53–4.
57. Hughes, W., *A New County Atlas of Great Britain and Ireland* (London, 1873), 31–4.
58. Taylor, J. P., *Fighting and Conquering in Lancashire and Cheshire* (Manchester, 1884).
59. *Census of Religious Worship 1851*, Table H, cclxxvii.
60. McLeod, H., *op. cit.*, 17–8, 30–3. There is a fuller discussion of this question in the pages cited.
61. This of course does not allow for cottage or open-air meetings which may have taken place. Also, lack of religious provision does not indicate lack of religious belief. McLeod, H., *ibid.*, 9.
62. Lax, W. H., *LAX, HIS BOOK. The Autobiography of Lax of Poplar* (London, 1937), 50–4, 99–100. This corps at Ince was opened in 1884 apparently only a few years after ". . . the advent of the Methodies" there. The corps remained in existence until at least 1905. *Index. 1905*, 34.
63. McLeod, H., *op. cit.*, 26.
64. *Ibid.*, 15. Also Obelkevich, J., *Religion and Rural Society: South Lindsey, 1825–75* (Oxford, 1976), 317.
65. Ervine, St. J., *God's Soldier. General William Booth* (London, 1934), Vol. I, 38–9.
66. Sandall, R., *op. cit.*, Vol. I, 217.
67. Booth, W., *How to Reach the Masses with The Gospel* (London, 1872), 76–7.
68. Booth, W., *Orders and Regulations for the Salvation Army* (London, 1878), 13.
69. Brook, D., *Foundations of Methodism* (London, 1927). Also, Orr, J. E., *The Second Evangelical Awakening* (London, 1949).
70. Earning a high wage did not always mean having a high standard of living. Much money was spent in the drink houses, in the music halls, and on gambling. High rents also took a large portion in some cases. The word 'dissolute' is a relative term meaning at worst debauchery and at best the occasional drink — all of which to the Booths was evil.
71. An analysis of the age-ranges and other related factors is given in graph form in my doctoral thesis, presented to Birkbeck College, University of London in April 1990.
72. From 1878 until the mid-1880s the Army did not consider it worthwhile to train married women as officers in their own right. Wives had the option of accompanying their husbands into the Training Home or remaining at home. In either case, the Army demanded to know how the husband would financially support his wife. Redstone, J. J. R., *An Ex-Captain's Experience of The Salvation Army* (London, 1888, second edition), 8–9.
73. *Ibid.*, 15. Also Booth, W., 'The Salvation Army', in *Contemporary Review*, August 1882, 181.
74. *All About the Salvation Army*, 1882, 23.
75. There are many examples of this in Army literature, for example, Tracy, R., *Marianne Pawson. The Zulu Queen* (London, 1944).
76. McLeod, H., *op. cit.*, 33.
77. *War Cry*, 29 December 1879, 4.
78. Smith, G., *Gipsy Smith, His Life and Work. By Himself* (London, 1903), 133.
79. *The Appointments of Officers 1883*. The majority of new officers were sent virtually to the other end of the country.
80. *Ibid.*, 9. Various case-studies have revealed the following information regarding the frequency of moves made by officers (1880s): Poplar, 4 months, 16 days; Manchester, 5 months, 21 days; Guildford, 5 months, 7 days; and Honiton, 6 months, 21 days. The different branches of Methodism at this time had varying possible periods of stay in any one circuit, the usual being a maximum of three years. All the men, with or without families, were moved regularly, sometimes

234

from one end of the country to another. The strains imposed by this system of itinerancy were such that it was an important factor in the high resignation rate sustained by the Methodists. Brown, K. D., *A Social History of the Nonconformist Ministry in England and Wales 1800–1830* (Oxford, 1988), 136–140.
81. Booth, W., 'The Salvation Army', in *Contemporary Review*, August, 1882, 181.
82. Booth, W., *Orders and Regulations for the Salvation Army* (London, 1878).
83. Sandall, R., *op. cit.*, Vol. I, 216.
84. *Ibid.*, Vol. I, 215. Also Redstone, J. J. R., *op. cit.*, 54.
85. Booth, W., *Orders and Regulations for Field Officers* (London, 1885), 39.
86. *War Cry*, 21 December 1882, 1.
87. *Ibid.*, 30 January 1883, 4.
88. *The Appointments of Officers 1883*, 4.
89. *The Times*, 17 October 1883, 10.
90. *War Cry*, 15 December 1883, 2. Also *The Appointments of Officers 1883*, 41.
91. Edmonds, H. *op. cit.*, 441–2.
92. *Ibid.*, 442.
93. *Ibid.*, 443. (Henry Edmonds underlined the word 'spying'.)
94. Redstone, J. J. R., *op. cit.*, 15.
95. Redstone, J. J. R., *ibid.*, 64, 75.
96. Geikie, C., 'Introduction', x–xi, in Redstone, J. J. R., *op. cit.*
97. Ex-Staff Officer, *The New Papacy. Behind the Scenes in the Salvation Army* (Toronto, 1889).
98. Edmonds, H., *op. cit.*, 433ff gives the details of two such resignations.
99. *Ibid.*, 403, 441–2.
100. Geikie, C., *op. cit.*, ix.
101. Edmonds, H., *op. cit.*, Ch. XXXIV.
102. Letter from George Scott Railton to Mrs. Booth, 6 November 1877.
103. Booth, W., *How to Reach the Masses with The Gospel* (London, 1872), 8.
104. The first woman General of the Salvation Army was not elected until 11 November 1934. General Evangeline Cory Booth was the Army's fourth General. Troutt, M., *The General was a Lady* (Nashville, 1980). The twelfth and current General, Eva Burrows, was elected in May 1986 and is only the second woman to hold this office.
105. Booth, W., *In Darkest England and the Way Out* (London, 1890), 136.

Chapter 4. OPPOSITION TO THE SALVATION ARMY

1. Bailey, V., 'Salvation Army Riots, the 'Skeleton Army' and Legal Authority in the Provincial Town', in Donajgrodzki, A. P. (Ed.), *Social Control in Nineteenth Century Britain* (London, 1977), Ch. 9. Also Sandall, R., *The History of the Salvation Army*, Vol. I (London, 1947); Vol. II (London, 1950).
2. Pearson, G., *HOOLIGAN. A History of Respectable Fears* (London, 1983), 197–202.
3. Previously unpublished material on this religious sect is held in the Surrey Local Studies Library, Guildford. The Coaklers attempted to establish themselves in southern England during the latter part of the nineteenth century.
4. Porter, E., *Cambridgeshire Customs and Folklore* (London, 1963), 8.
5. Longmate, N., *The Workhouse* (London, n.d.), 132. Andover.
6. Hardy, T., *The Mayor of Casterbridge* (London, 1974 edition), 302.
7. Pearson, G.,*op. cit.*, 197.
8. Gilbert, A. D., *Religion and Society in Industrial England* (London, 1976), Chs. 3–4.
9. *Ibid.*, 78–9, 82. Also McLeod, H., *Religion and the Working Class in Nineteenth-Century Britain* (London, 1984), 28.

10. Gilbert, A. D., *op. cit.*, 79.
11. Bailey, V., *op. cit.*, 233. Also Kent, J., *Holding the Fort. Studies in Victorian Revivalism* (London, 1978), 332. Also General Booth clearly realised the value of physical and literary opposition in attracting recruits.
12. Thompson, F. M. L., *The Rise of Respectable Society. A Social History of Victorian Britain, 1830–1900* (London, 1988), 277. Professor Thompson notes that from the late eighteenth century, this type of behaviour at annual festivals in particular but in society at large was meeting increasing opposition as were many "traditional popular pleasures".
13. *The Keep* (Guildford), January 1913, 2.
14. P.R.O. HO45/9605/A1775/4.
15. Royle, E., *Radical Politics 1790–1900. Religion and Unbelief* (London, 1971), 7–8. Also Bailey, V., *op. cit.*, 242.
16. *How to Reach the Masses with The Gospel* was the title of a small book published by William Booth in 1870.
17. *The Christian Mission Magazine*, October 1874, 275.
18. *Ibid.*, September 1878, 251.
19. Bailey, V., *op. cit.*, 247.
20. *War Cry*, 17 July 1880, 1; 28 August 1880, 4 (Nottingham); 16 June 1881, 3 (Cheltenham).
21. *The Salvation War. 1882* (London, 1883), 6. No author.
22. Thompson, F. M. L., *op. cit.*, 178.
23. The same opinion was expressed by Captain Drummond, the Chief Constable of West Sussex and by at least two of the Worthing magistrates. Briggs, A., *Salvation Army Riots: 1884* (unpublished paper), 15–7, 25.
24. Peek, F., 'The Salvationists', in *Contemporary Review*, No. 49, January 1886, 60.
25. *War Cry*, 11 April 1883, 3.
26. *Ibid.*, 11 May 1882, 3.
27. *Ibid.*, 27 November 1880, 3. Also *The Christian Mission Magazine*, October 1878, 274.
28. *Ibid.*, 20 March 1886, 15.
29. The Holiness Meeting was usually held on a Sunday morning, although occasionally also on weeknights.
30. *The Christian Mission Magazine*, September 1878, 252.
31. *War Cry*, 16 October 1888, 11. Not until 1902 did General Booth discuss the subject in any detail. Booth, W., *Faith-Healing. A Memorandum* (London, 1902).
32. *War Cry*, 27 July 1882, 2.
33. *Ibid.*, 10 August 1882, 1.
34. By the end of 1882, the U.S.A., Australia, France, Canada and India had all been 'attacked'. *The Salvation War. 1882* (London, 1883), Chs. 7–9.
35. *War Cry*, 18 May 1882, 3.
36. *Ibid.*, 10 August 1882, 1.
37. *Ibid.*, 29 June 1882, 4.
38. Sandall, R., *op. cit.*, Vol. II, 194–5. Also *War Cry*, 13 April 1882, 2.
39. PRO HO45/9607/A2886/13.
40. (LOO 690). PRO HO45/9613/A9275/16 and 17. Also Begbie, H., *William Booth. Founder of the Salvation Army* (London, 1920), Vol. II, 7; Ervine, St. J., *God's Soldier. General William Booth* (London, 1934), Vol. I, 536.
41. *War Cry*, 13 April 1882, 4.
42. *Hansard*, Third Series, Vol. 269, 16 May 1882, 822–3.
43. *The Surrey Advertiser and County Times*, 23 September 1893, 1ff.
44. *War Cry*, 5 June 1886, 9. Also France and the U.S.A. from the early 1880s. *Ibid.*, 28 April 1881, 4.
45. *Ibid.*, 6 April 1882, 2. Sir William Lawson was addressing a political rally in London. He also stated that a number of M.P.s supported the Salvation Army.

46. PRO HO45/9605/A1775/1.
47. PRO HO45/9605/A1775/4.
48. (LOO 690). PRO HO45/9613/A9275/17/1 and 2.
49. PRO HO45/9605/A1775/5 and 6.
50. (LOO 690). PRO HO45/9613/A9275/17 ff.
51. (LOO 690). PRO HO45/9613/A9275/16.
52. (LOO 690). PRO HO45/9613/A9275/17 and 18.
53. *Hansard*, Third Series, Vol. 267, 16 March 1882, 990.
54. (LOO 690). PRO HO45/9613/A9275/17 and 21.
55. *The Times*, 11 October 1881, 6, Col. 6.
56. Sandall, R., *op. cit.*, Vol. II, 176.
57. *Ibid.*, 175.
58. Bailey, V., *op. cit.*, 245.
59. *War Cry*, 6 April 1882, 2.
60. *Hansard*, Third Series, Vol. 269, 16 May 1882, 821-2.
61. Street, H., *Freedom, Individual and The Law* (London, 1977, fourth edition), 53. Also Bailey, V., *op. cit.*, 244.
62. Sandall, R., *op. cit.*, Vol. II, 187, 327.
63. Williams, D. G. T., 'The Principle of Beatty v. Gillbanks: A Reappraisal', in Doob, A. N. and Greenspan, E. L. (Eds.), *Perspectives in Criminal Law* (Ontario, 1985), 108-13.
64. *War Cry*, 11 May 1882, 2.
65. *Hansard*, Third Series, Vol. 268, 2 May 1882, 1941.
66. (LOO 690). PRO HO45/9613/A9275/17 and 19.
67. PRO HO45/9629/A22415/8.
68. Sandall, R., *op. cit.*, Vol. II, 187-8.
69. *Ibid.*, 189-90.
70. *The Times*, 7 October 1889, 6; 15 October 1889, 11; 25 October 1889, 10.
71. PRO HO45/9967/X34164 A.
72. Street, H., *op. cit.*, 53.
73. The two authorities were Torquay in 1888 and Eastbourne in 1891.
74. Wiggins, A., *The History of the Salvation Army* (London, 1964), Vol. IV, 264, 269.
75. *The Times*, 14 September 1891, 9.
76. *Ibid.*, 58 columns of reports appeared between 1 July and 31 December 1891.
77. Wiggins, A., *op. cit.*, 270, 277, 279.
78. Newton, B. W., *Address Respecting the Methods of the Salvation Army* (London, 1882), 6-7.
79. Booth, B., *Echoes and Memories* (London, 1925), 35, 40.
80. *War Cry*, 16 October 1880, 1-2.
81. *Nottingham Express*, 22 November 1881, 3.
82. Bullock, C., *The People's Archbishop* (London, 1891).
83. Marsh, P. T., 'The Primate and the Prime Minister. Archbishop Tait, Gladstone, and the National Church', in *Victorian Studies*, December 1965.
84. *The Chronicle of Convocation 1882*, Lower House, Session XXXVIII, 9-10 May 1882, 169, 178-9.
85. *Hansard*, Third Series, Vol. 269, 16 May 1882, 823.
86. Davidson, R. T. and Benham, W., *Life of Archbishop Campbell Tait. Archbishop of Canterbury* (London, 1891), 510-2.
87. *The Chronicle of Convocation 1883*, Upper House, Session XLVII, 10 April 1883, 10-21.
88. Previously unpublished letters and papers, copies in the author's possession.
89. *The Chronicle of Convocation 1883*, Upper House, Session LI, 3 July 1883, 126.
90. *War Cry*, 21 September 1882, 1.

91. Heasman, K., *Army of the Church* (London, 1968), 18. Also Cornish, F. W., *The English Church in the Nineteenth Century* (London, 1910), Vol. II, 134.
92. Benson, E. W., *Diaries* (1882), 145.
93. Inglis, K., *Churches and the Working-Classes in Victorian England* (London, 1963), 191. Also Murdoch, N., 'Female Ministry in the Thought and Work of Catherine Booth', in *Church History*, Vol. 53, 1984, 355.
94. O.W.L.A., *Some Reasons why I do not Sympathize with the Salvation Army* (London, 1882), Section 2.
95. Butler, J., 'Catherine Booth', in *Contemporary Review* (1890), 649–50.
96. *Pall Mall Gazette*, 6 July 1885.
97. Champness, E. I., *Frank Smith, M.P. Pioneer and Modern Mystic* (London, n.d.).
98. Inglis, K. S., *op. cit.*, 196.
99. Woods, R. A., *English Social Movements* (New York, 1895, revised edition), 170.
100. Inglis, K. S., *op. cit.*, 195.
101. *War Cry*, 17 May 1890, 4.
102. *Ibid.*, 2 July 1887, 5.
103. McLeod, H., *Class and Religion in the Late Victorian City* (London, 1974), 38.
104. Booth, W., *In Darkest England and the Way Out* (London, 1890).
105. Boudier, J. H., *A Sequel to "Darkest England"* (London, December 1890). Also Foote, G. W., *Salvation Syrup or Light on Darkest England. A Reply to General William Booth* (London, 1891).
106. Nicol, A. M., *General Booth and the Salvation Army* (London, n.d.), 280, 327. Also the Corybantes were ancient fanatics who clashed cymbals in honour of the goddess Cybele. Coutts, J., previously unpublished notes under the title *William Booth and the Salvation Army*, 28.
107. Coutts, F., *No Discharge in this War* (London, 1974), 115.
108. *The Methodist Times*, 18 September 1890, 956.
109. Wallis, H., *The Happy Warrior. The Life-Story of Commissioner Elijah Cadman* (London, 1928), 121.
110. Booth, W., *Orders and Regulations for the Salvation Army* (London, 1878), Part 1, Ch. 3, Section 8, 69, 90.
111. *Sheffield Independent*, 13 August 1879, 5.
112. Bailey, V., *op. cit.*, 242. Also Briggs, A., *op. cit.*, 9, 16–7.
113. *Daily Telegraph*, 1 July 1881, 1.
114. *The Methodist Times*, 2 June 1881, 2.
115. *Church Times*, 18 November 1881, 4.
116. *The Christian*, 30 March 1882, 4.
117. Sandall, R., *op. cit.*, Vol. II, 143.
118. O.W.L.A., *op. cit.*, Section 3.
119. Gasparin, La Comtesse Agenor de, *Read and Judge the (So Called) Salvation Army* (Paris, n.d., English translation London, 1883), 6.
120. *Ibid.*, 34. Also Luff, G. R., *Edward Street Literature*, No. 2 (Brighton, November 1890), 6–9.
121. Fishbourne, Admiral, *A Calm Plea for the Enlargement of Salvation Army Work* (London, 1883), 15.
122. Corbridge, W., *The Up Line to Heaven and the Down Line to Hell* (London, 1883).
123. Whyte, F., *The Life of W. T. Stead* (London, 1925), Vol. II, 13.

Chapter 5. POPLAR, LONDON: A CASE-STUDY

1. Ryan, P. A, 'Politics and relief: East London unions in the late nineteenth and early twentieth centuries', in Rose, M. E., *The poor and the city: the English poor law in its urban context, 1834–1914* (Leicester, 1985), 136, 9.
2. *Census of England and Wales. 1861*, Occupations, Table 13, 22–3.

3. Weightman, G. and Humphries, S., *The Making of Modern London, 1815–1914* (London, 1983), 89–90.
4. Stedman Jones, G., *Outcast London* (London, 1971), 100-2.
5. Ryan, P. A., *op. cit.*, 138.
6. Stedman Jones, G., *op. cit.*, 102. Also Weightman, G. and Humphries, S., *op. cit.*, 87.
7. Ryan, P. A., *op. cit.*, 135.
8. *The East London Observer*, 2 February 1869, 3. This is a report of a 46-year-old rigger dying from hunger at Poplar.
9. Stedman Jones, G., *op. cit.*, 99–104.
10. Ryan, P. A., *op. cit.*, 135.
11. Crowther, M. A., *The Workhouse System, 1834–1929* (London, 1981), 74.
12. Ryan, P.A., *op. cit.*, 143.
13. McLeod, H., *Class and Religion in the Late Victorian Town* (London, 1974), 118.
14. Crowther, M. A., *op. cit.*, 78. Also Lansbury, G., *My Life* (London, 1928), 1.
15. Ryan, P. A., ' 'Poplarism' 1894-1930', in Thane, P. (Ed.), *The Origins of British Social Policy* (London, 1978), 57.
16. Lovell, J., *Stevedores and Dockers* (London, 1969), 59–60.
17. *Census of Religious Worship. 1851*, Table I, ccxcvi.
18. *Ibid.*, Table H, cclxxviii.
19. Sandall, R., *The History of the Salvation Army* (London, 1947), Vol. I, 73–4.
20. Booth, W., *How to Reach the Masses with The Gospel* (London, 1870), 52.
21. The amounts given varied but a typical example was of an old gentleman giving 5 shillings at Poplar on Saturday 10 June 1869, *The East London Evangelist*, August 1869, 170. Also Sandall, R., *op. cit.*, Vol. I, Appendix E.
22. *Report of the East London Christian Mission*, 1867, 31-3.
23. *The East London Evangelist*, October 1868, 14.
24. *Ibid.*, November 1868, 27-8.
25. *The East London Advertiser*, 28 October 1868, 14.
26. Booth, W., *op. cit.*, 8-14. Also Redstone, J. J. R., *An Ex-Captain's Experience of the Salvation Army* (London, 1888, second edition), 26.
27. Harrington, B. W., *The London Irish: A Study in Political Activism, 1870–1910* (Ph.D. thesis, Princeton University, U.S.A., 1976), 100.
28. *The Christian Mission Magazine*, September 1874, 249-50.
29. Railton, G. S., *Commissioner Dowdle* (London, 1912, second edition), 9.
30. *The Christian Mission Magazine*, July 1873, 106-7.
31. *The East London Observer*, 13 May 1874, 6.
32. *The Christian Mission Magazine*, September 1875, 237.
33. Douglas, E. and Duff, M., *Commissioner Railton* (London, 1920), 47.
34. *The Christian Mission Magazine*, October 1877, 268.
35. *The East London Observer*, 28 March 1874, 4.
36. *The Christian Mission Conference Minute Book. 1871*, 4.
37. *The Christian Mission Magazine*, August 1871, 122.
38. Sandall, R., *op. cit.*, 154-5.
39. *The Christian Mission Magazine*, September 1878, 238.
40. McLeod, H., *op. cit.*, 89. Also *British Weekly*, 13 January 1888.
41. *The Christian Mission Magazine*, November 1878, 291.
42. *War Cry*, 31 March 1881, 3; 14 April 1881, 3.
43. *Ibid.*, 24 January 1880, 3.
44. *Ibid.*, 24 April 1880, 4.
45. *Ibid.*, 10 October 1880, 3.
46. *Ibid.*, 3 August 1882, 3.
47. McLeod, H., *op. cit.*, 69.
48. *War Cry*, 3 February 1883, 2.

49. Redstone, J. J. R., *op. cit.*, 25.
50. *War Cry*, 29 January 1887, 14.
51. *Salvation Socialism*, a special supplement to the *War Cry*, 25 December 1889.
52. Stedman Jones, G., *op. cit.*, 315.
53. *War Cry*, 14 September 1889, 7.
54. *Ibid.*, 21 September 1889, 2.
55. *Salvation Socialism*, supplement to the *War Cry*, 25 December 1889, 2.
56. *Ibid.*, 25 December 1889, 2–3.
57. Booth, W., *In Darkest England and the Way Out* (London, 1890), 20.
58. *The Methodist Times*, 18 September 1890, 956.
59. Alden, P., 'The Problem of East London', in Mudie-Smith, R., *The Religious Life of London* (London, 1904), 25–6.
60. Hancock, T., *Salvation by Mammon* (London, 1891), 3.
61. Inglis, K. S., *Churches and the Working-Classes in Victorian England* (London, 1963), 195.
62. Sandall, R., *op. cit.*, Vol. I, Appendix S, 293–4.
63. Mitchell, D. C., *The Darkest England Match Industry* (private printing, 1973), Part I, 7; Part II, 3.
64. Booth, W., *op. cit.*, 110.
65. Lovell, J., *op. cit.*, 63, 73.
66. Keating, P. J., 'Fact and Fiction in the East End', in Dyos, H. J. and Wolff, M. (Eds.), *The Victorian City* (London, 1973), Vol. II, 595.
67. Champness, E. I., *Frank Smith, M.P. Pioneer and Modern Mystic* (London, n.d.), 14. These progressives included Annie Besant, Cunningham Graham, and William Morris.
68. Woods, R. A., *English Social Movements* (New York, 1895, revised edition), 171–2.
69. From this date he attempted to form a 'Labour Army'. His aim was for men to co-operate under a military-style regime ". . . for the sake of their own advancement and in order to elevate their less favoured fellows." Woods, R. A., *op. cit.*, 172.
70. Champness, E. I., *op. cit.*, 15.
71. When General Bramwell Booth faced being deposed from office by a High Council of Officers, Smith championed his case in the Parliamentary Debate this internal crisis caused. It was discussed in Parliament because the Constitution of the Salvation Army was sanctioned, therefore guaranteed, by Parliament. See Mackenzie, F.A, *The Clash of Cymbals* (London, 1929) [anti-Booth]. Also Bramwell-Booth, C., *Bramwell Booth* (London, 1933); Smith, F., *The Betrayal of Bramwell Booth* (London, 1929); Ervine, St. J., *God's Soldier. General William Booth* (London, 1934), Vol. II, 815–1027 [all pro-Booth].
72. Captain Redstone, the Commanding Officer of Poplar Corps from February to June 1883, was unpopular with the majority of his soldiers because of his harsh stand on discipline. Many soldiers left the Corps during his time. Officers changed frequently between 1870 and 1900. Their average length of stay in Poplar during the 1870s and 1880s was 4 months, 16 days. In the 1890s it was 6 months, 17 days.
73. Alden, P., *op. cit.*, 47–8.
74. The percentages were worked out from Alden, P., *ibid.*, 47–8, and the *British Weekly* Religious Census results, 13–20 January 1888. An adjustment has been made by leaving out the afternoon attendance figure from the *British Weekly* as none were recorded in Alden's work.
75. Mann, H., 'Facts and Forces not Enumerated', in Mudie-Smith, R., *op. cit.*, 273.
76. Booth, W., *How to Reach the Masses with The Gospel* (London, 1872), 62–3.
77. Smith, R., *Gipsy Smith, His Life and Work. By Himself* (London, 1905), 87.
78. *Stepney Borough Engineer's Report*, 31 March 1905, 35.

79. *War Cry*, 10 September 1887, 382.
80. Fishman, W. J., *East End. 1888* (London, 1988), 260.
81. *The East London Advertiser*, 21 August 1964, 14. Attached in the *Poplar Corps History Book* under August 1964.

Chapter 6. MANCHESTER, LANCASHIRE: A CASE-STUDY

1. Kay, J. P., *The Moral and Physical Condition of the Working Classes Employed in the Cotton Manufacture in Manchester* (Manchester, 1832). Republished and edited by Cass, F. (London, 1968).
2. Hume, C. H., 'The Public Health Movement', in Ward, J. T. (Ed.), *Popular Movements c. 1830–1850* (London, 1978), 186.
3. Roberts, R., *The Classic Slum* (Manchester, 1971), 175.
4. *War Cry*, 17 July 1885, 2.
5. *Gorton, Openshaw and Bradford Reporter*, 18 May 1878, 3; 25 May 1878, 3.
6. Phillips, P. T., *The Sectarian Spirit: Sectarianism, Society and Politics in Victorian Cotton Towns* (Toronto, 1982), 3.
7. Briggs, A., *Victorian Cities* (London, 1963), 124.
8. *Census of Religious Worship. 1851*, Table C, ccix.
9. Royle, E., *Radical Politics 1790–1900. Religion and Unbelief* (London, 1970), 5. The idea of a 'non-professing Christian' was very common amongst the working-class, the majority of whom considered themselves in some ways innately Christian. See Chadwick, O., *The Victorian Church*, Part I (London, 1971 edition), 333.
10. *The Christian Mission Magazine*, July 1878, 178.
11. *Manchester Star Hall. Corps History Book*, 4.
12. *The Christian Mission Magazine*, July 1878, 178.
13. *War Cry*, 14 April 1881, 3.
14. *Ibid.*, 24 November 1881, 3.
15. *Ibid.*, 26 January 1882, 3.
16. *Ibid.*, 12 December 1883, 3.
17. *Ibid.*, 29 October 1884, 3.
18. *Ibid.*, 11 December 1880, 4.
19. *Ibid.*, 9 October 1880, 4.
20. *Ibid.*, 14 April 1881, 3.
21. *Ibid.*, 9 June 1881, 3.
22. *Ibid.*, 7 July 1881, 3.
23. *Ibid.*, 19 January 1884, 2.
24. *Ibid.*, 17 June 1885, 3.
25. *Ibid.*, 14 February 1883, 3.
26. *Ibid.*, 23 June 1883, 3.
27. *Ibid.*, 17 August 1882, 3.
28. *Ibid.*, 3 March 1883, 3.
29. Booth, W., *Orders and Regulations for Soldiers* (London, 1899), Ch. XII, Section V, 'No Black Mourning'.
30. *War Cry*, 17 February 1882, 3.
31. Williams, S., *Punching Pride of Ancoats* (London, 1957), 13.
32. *Manchester VIII Centenary Brochure*, 1983, 3.
33. *War Cry*, 16 November 1882, 3; 1 October 1887, 3.
34. *Ibid.*, 18 July 1885, 2.
35. *Ibid.*, 6 October 1888, 12. This refusal to pay fines was a common Army practice. The aim was to excite sympathy and attention. This was usually successful, especially as a 'celebration' march and feast frequently accompanied the release of prisoners and therefore created more interest.

241

36. *War Cry*, 8 August 1885, 2.

37. *Ibid.*, 30 June 1883, 2.

38. Bailey, V., 'Salvation Army Riots, the 'Skeleton Army' and Legal Authority in the Provincial Town', in Donajgrodzki, A. P. (Ed.), *Social Control in Nineteenth Century Britain* (London, 1977), 234.

39. *War Cry*, 6 January 1881, 3.

40. *The Times*, 1 February 1883, 4.

41. This figure is based on an estimate of 150 soldiers in each of the 15 corps established in Manchester by the end of 1885. A large number of *War Cry* reports speak of numerous corps activities requiring considerable manpower (such as *War Cry* brigades), thus the estimate of an average number of 150 soldiers per corps.

42. Barnes, C. J., *Any Questions* (London, 1981), 22.

43. Begbie, H., *William Booth. Founder of the Salvation Army* (London, 1920), Vol. I, 312.

44. *War Cry*, 10 August 1882, 1.

45. There were many examples of these corrugated constructions by the turn of the century, for example, South Hornsey Salvation Army Corps. Redstone, J. J. R., *An Ex-Captain's Experience of the Salvation Army* (London, 1888), 13.

46. *Pocket Book 1884*, 19–20, 24, 27.

47. Although Manchester VII, IX, XI, and Salford III had closed at some point in the late nineteenth century, the first three had reopened by 1905.

48. McLeod, H., *Religion and the Working Class in Nineteenth-Century Britain* (London, 1984), 23, 30.

49. Kent, J., *Holding the Fort. Studies in Victorian Revivalism* (London, 1978), 310.

50. *War Cry*, 1 October 1887, 3.

Chapter 7. GUILDFORD, SURREY: A CASE-STUDY

1. Chamberlain, E. R., *Guildford. A Biography* (London, 1970), 11, 16.

2. *The Surrey Advertiser and County Times,* 27 December 1879, 3. (Hereafter *The Surrey Advertiser.*)

3. *Ibid.*, 24 December 1881, 2.

4. Chamberlain, E. R., *op. cit.*, 14. Also Alexander, M., *Guildford. A Short History* (Godalming, 1986), 41–3.

5. *Guildford in the Queen's Reign. 1837–1897* (Guildford, 1897), 10.

6. *Census of Religious Worship. 1851*, Table C, ccxxiv; Table D, ccxlvii; Division II, Part 39, 10.

7. *The Surrey Advertiser* of the late 1860s and 1870s contains articles on the pleasures and pastimes of Sundays. These indicate considerable absence from religious worship amongst the 'labouring-classes'.

8. Between 1851 and 1881, the Unitarians and Primitive Methodists both built Chapels in the town. *Directory of Guildford for 1882* (Guildford, 1881).

9. *Corps Opening Date List*, Salvation Army International Heritage Centre, London. This is a handwritten document with many gaps and some errors.

10. *War Cry*, 10 January 1880.

11. *The Surrey Advertiser*, 24 December 1881, 2.

12. Railton, G. S., *Heathen England* (London, 1883, fifth edition), 23.

13. *War Cry*, 8 April 1882, 3.

14. *The Surrey Advertiser*, 24 December 1881, 2.

15. *Ibid.*, 6 December 1913. Cutting recording the annual Salvation Army Bazaar, in *Guildford Corps History Book*, Vol. I, December 1913.

16. *The Surrey Advertiser*, 24 December 1881, 2.

17. *War Cry*, 29 December 1881, 4; 12 January 1882, 3; 2 February 1882, 3; 9 February 1882, 3; 16 February 1882, 3; 2 March 1882, 2.
18. *Ibid.*, 10 March 1882, 3.
19. *The Surrey Advertiser*, 11 January 1882, 3.
20. *War Cry*, 27 February 1882, 3.
21. *Ibid.*, 6 March 1882, 3; 11 March 1882, 2; 18 March 1882, 2; 11 March 1882, 5; 13 March 1882, 3; 18 March 1882, 2. The latter three are examples of police protection.
22. This family of philanthropic Liberals, who had controlled much of the town and surrounding countryside since the seventeenth century, were also keen supporters of the temperance campaign and the Sunday closure of public houses. *War Cry*, 7 January 1882, 4; 30 January 1882, 3.
23. *War Cry*, 6 March 1882, 3; 8 April 1882, 3; 13 May 1882, 2.
24. The Blue Ribbon Army was also known as the Gospel Temperance Movement. Its greatest effects came in the early 1880s for example in Swansea where an upsurge in teetotalism caused the closure of three large breweries. Fryer, R., *Mrs Grundy. Studies in English Prudery* (London, 1963), 140, 303.
25. *The Salvation War*, 1882 (London, 1883), 17.
26. *War Cry*, 29 April 1882, 2. Nearly 100 years later *The Surrey Advertiser* stated that:

> "The first officers were kicked along the streets . . . and the situation grew worse and ended in tragedy when Captain Knight, a young married officer who came to Guildford to establish the corps, was killed."

The Surrey Advertiser, 4 December 1981. Captain Knight was neither married nor killed for she served in London for several years after leaving Guildford. It is possible that the story has become confused with that of the supposed murder of a woman officer in the town in 1902 while preaching in the High Street. *Souvenir Brochure for the Opening and Dedication of the New Suite of Buildings. Guildford Salvation Army*, 11 June 1977, 10. However even this story cannot be substantiated. The most likely explanation is that "Happy Mary", a woman Salvationist whose death in 1882 was attributed to the street clashes (*The Salvation War*, 1882, 17), has become confused with Captain Knight or later with the woman officer of 1902.
27. *The Salvation War*, 1882, 17.
28. These dates are worked out from the approximate date of the last recorded march (mid-May, taking about two weeks for the report to appear in the *War Cry*, of 1 June), and the *Minute Book of the Watch Committee of the Borough of Guildford* (hereafter *Minute Book*). An entry for 15 August 1882 records a letter requesting police protection for the Army's processions.
29. *The Surrey Advertiser*, 13 May 1882, 2, 5; 17 May 1882, 5; 20 May 1882, 5.
30. *The Guildford Almanac and Directory for 1882* (Guildford, 1881); *War Cry*, 6 July 1882, 3; *The Surrey Advertiser*, 19 June 1882, 3.
31. *War Cry*, 3 August 1882, 4; 10 August 1882, 2. There are no extant records of a corps being established at East Clandon and the *War Cry* reports cease after a few months.
32. *The Surrey Advertiser*, 28 August 1882, 3.
33. *Minute Book*, Vol. I, 15 August 1882.
34. *The Surrey Advertiser*, 2 September 1882, 5.
35. Bailey, V., 'Salvation Army Riots, the 'Skeleton Army' and Legal Authority in the Provincial Town', in Donajgrodzki, A. P. (Ed.), *Social Control in Nineteenth Century Britain* (London, 1977), 245.
36. *The Salvation War*, 1882, 17.
37. *The Surrey Advertiser*, 9 September 1882, 5; 16 September 1882, 2.
38. *War Cry*, 9 November 1882, 1.

39. *The Salvation War*, 1882, 20.
40. *The Surrey Advertiser*, 10 February 1883, 5; 23 April 1883, 3; 5 May 1883, 5.
41. *Minute Book*, Vol. I, 14 June 1883.
42. *The Surrey Advertiser*, 13 October 1883, 5; 6 October 1884, 3.
43. *War Cry*, 9 August 1884, 3.
44. *The Surrey Advertiser*, 4 February 1885, 3; 14 February 1885, 2. Also *The West Middlesex Herald*, 21 February 1885, 3.
45. *The Surrey Advertiser*, 14 February 1885, 2. Evidence from other towns suggests that a reduction in crime frequently followed the Army's arrival, for example, Haverfordwest. *War Cry*, 20 February 1886, 3.
46. *Minute Book*, Vol. I, 14 June 1883; 20 February 1885.
47. *The Surrey Advertiser*, 6 February 1885, 2.
48. Peak, H., *Diary*, Vol. N, 1181–2.
49. *The Surrey Advertiser*, 30 March 1889, 3.
50. Guildford Museum. Notes on 'rough musicing'.
51. Chamberlain, E. R., *op. cit.*, 176. Also private communication from Matthew Alexander, Curator, Guildford Museum. Another event was the Wedding Day of the Prince of Wales, 10 March 1863.
52. *The Keep. The Quarterly Magazine of the Guildford Institute*, October 1912; January 1913.
53. Peak, H., *op. cit.*, Vol. D, 273–80. Peak uses the words "Mob–Rule" in his description of the 'Guys'.
54. *The Keep, op. cit.*, October 1912, 3–4; January 1913, 2–4. Also Chamberlain, E. R., *op. cit.*, 178.
55. Guildford Museum. Notes on 'rough musicing'. One incident in the 1880s involved the local chemist, found one day ill-treating his wife. The police "turned a blind eye for some time" while crowds 'rough-musiced' him. No action was taken although property had been damaged and threats made.
56. *War Cry*, 9 November 1882, 1. *The Salvation War*, 1882, 18.
57. *Guildford Corps History Book*, Vol. II, October 1976. Memoirs of Mrs. E. A. Turner whose father was one of the first Salvationists in the town. These memoirs were written at an earlier date.
58. *The Salvation War*, 1882, 16.
59. Alexander, M., *op. cit.*, 43.
60. This has been ascertained from a search of *The Guildford Almanac and Directory* for each year from 1870 to 1890. On average, just under one-fifth of aldermen, town councillors and magistrates were brewers during this period.
61. *Ibid.*, 1882 (Guildford, December, 1882), Introduction. William Triggs, the Mayor, was not a brewer. He was, however, one of the four aldermen and eight magistrates.
62. *The Surrey Advertiser*, 1882. Throughout the year temperance activities were reported with increasing regularity.
63. *War Cry*, 16 February 1884, 2.
64. *Index of Salvation Army Corps. 1905* (London, 1905), 13.
65. I compiled a list of officers stationed at Guildford. Their average stay was 5 months, 1 week.
66. At least two of whom became Salvationists: W. G. Collins and G. Siggers (Appendix 10).
67. One factor missing here but important for many other corps was the mutual support of nearby Salvationists. Guildford was only the second corps in Surrey although, by 1885, Aldershot, Kingston, Reading and several others had been established. *War Cry* reports, 1882–1885.
68. Despite the temperance movements, there were still many people applying for licences to sell liquor. *War Cry*, 30 January 1882, 3.

Chapter 8. HONITON, DEVON: A CASE-STUDY

1. Railton, G. S., *Heathen England* (London, 1883, fifth edition), 23.
2. *The Devon Weekly Times*, 3 November 1882, 8.
3. *The Salvation Soldiers Pocket Book for 1884* (London, 1885), 41. Also *The Western Times*, 10 November 1882, 5.
4. *The Devon Weekly Times*, 24 November 1882, 7.
5. *Ibid.*, 1 December 1882, 6.
6. *The Salvation War. 1884* (London, 1883), 13–5.
7. *The Devon Weekly Times*, 1 December 1882, 8. *The Skeleton*, 2 December 1882, 2.
8. *War Cry*, 16 December 1882, 2; 21 December 1882, 1.
9. *The Devon Weekly Times*, 22 December 1882, 8; 29 December 1882, 3.
10. *The Western Times*, 2 January 1883, 3.
11. *The Times*, 13 January 1883, 5.
12. *The Salvation War. 1882* (London, 1883), 15.
13. PRO HO45/9629/A22415/8.
14. *The Western Times*, 2 February 1883, 5.
15. *Ibid.*, 7 February 1883, 4. This not only ensured fair hearings, it also helped alleviate the problem of delay in hearing cases. Delay was caused by the build-up in the number of cases concerning the Salvation Army and, because serious cases needed two magistrates, if one was away ill or on business, several weeks could elapse before the cases were heard. *Honiton Gazette*, 16 August 1884, 5.
16. *Ibid.*, 4 July 1883, 3; 18 July 1883, 3; 24 July 1883, 8.
17. *Ibid.*, 14 March 1884, 7.
18. *Ibid.*, 23 April 1884, 3.
19. *War Cry*, 29 August 1885, 3.
20. *Ibid.*, 6 March 1886, 13.
21. *Ibid.*, 11 December 1886, 10.
22. *Ibid.*, 22 October 1887, 12.
23. PRO HO/A9275/17.
24. *War Cry*, 25 September 1886, 7.

Chapter 9. WALES: A CASE-STUDY

1. Preece, C., *Woman of the Valleys. The Story of Mother Shepherd* (Port Talbot, 1988).
2. *The Christian Mission Magazine*, 1878.
3. *Ibid.*, August 1878.
4. Parry, W. D., *Gwaed a Than* (Caernarfon, 1986), 14.
5. *The Christian Mission Magazine*, March 1875.
6. Booth, C., *Aggressive Christianity* (London, 1881).
7. Sandall, R., *The History of the Salvation Army* (London, 1947), Vol. I, 163.
8. *War Cry*, 10 March 1880.
9. *Ibid.*, 17 June 1881.
10. Peek, F., 'The Salvationists', in *Contemporary Review*, No. 49, January 1886, 60.
11. *War Cry*, 17 August 1882.
12. *Ibid.*, 25 December 1888.
13. *Ibid.*, 23 May 1896.
14. *Index to Corps. 1905*, 45–6.
15. *The Christian Mission Magazine*, May 1878.
16. Jones, V., 'The Salvation Army', in *Merthyr Tydfil — A Valley Community* (Cambridge, 1981), 458.
17. *The Salvationist*, December 1878.
18. *The Christian Mission Magazine*, May 1878, 150.
19. Preece, C., *op. cit.*, 64.

20. *Ibid.*, 79–84.
21. *Ibid.*, 87. Also Parry, W. D., *op. cit.*, 15.
22. Preece, C., *op. cit.*, 82. *The Christian Mission Magazine*, October 1878.
23. Parry, W. D., *op. cit.*, 15.
24. The following corps were commenced, in order, in 1879: Cardiff 2 (Roath); Treherbert; Aberaman; Pentre; Porth; Maesteg; Brynmawr; Cardiff 3 (Canton); Blaina.
25. *Merthyr Express*, 5 November 1881.
26. Preece, C., *op. cit.*, Ch. 6.
27. *Ibid.*, 117.
28. *Ibid.*, 126.
29. *The Treasury*, 1879, 88.
30. Preece, C., *op. cit.*, 108.
31. Davies, R., *Rosina Davies, Evangelist. The Story of my Life* (Llandyssul, 1942), 30–3.
32. Carpenter, Mrs. Col., *Commissioner Lawley* (London, 1924), 71.
33. Davies, R., *op. cit.*, 28.
34. Parry, W. D., *op. cit.*, 25–9.
35. *Ibid.*, 19.
36. *Ibid.*, 19.
37. Parry, W. D., *op. cit.*, 18–19.
38. *The Wrexham Advertiser,* 1 September 1883.
39. *War Cry*, 19 July 1884.
40. Parry, W. D., *op. cit.*, 70.
41. *War Cry*, 18 December 1886.
42. *The Carnarvon and Denbigh Herald*, 22 October 1886.
43. Parry, W. D., *op. cit.*, 34.
44. Booth, W., *In Darkest England and the Way Out* (London, 1890).
45. Parry, W. D., *op. cit.*, 112–5.
46. *War Cry*, 26 March 1887.
47. *Y Gad Lef*, 28 May 1888.
48. Murdoch, N., 'Female Ministry in the Thought and Work of Catherine Booth', in *Church History*, Vol. 53, September 1984.
49. Parry, W. D., *op. cit.*, 71.
50. Sandall, R., *op. cit.*, Vol. II, 99.
51. Preece, C., *op. cit.*, 108–9.
52. *War Cry*, 19 June 1880.
53. *The South Wales Daily News*, 8 September 1879.
54. *War Cry*, 9 October 1881.
55. *Ibid.*, 7 December 1880.
56. *Ibid.*, 2 September 1893.
57. Wiggins, A., *The History of the Salvation Army*, Vol. IV, 392.
58. *War Cry*, 21 May 1898.
59. *Ibid.*, 14 May 1898.
60. *Ibid.*, 14 May 1898.

Chapter 10. OVERVIEW AND CONCLUSION

1. *Census of England and Wales. 1851*, Religious Worship, Report.
2. Chadwick, O., *The Victorian Church*, Part II (London, 1970), 286.
3. These were places in the front of the congregation where those seeking Salvation could 'wrestle with God'.
4. Chadwick, O., *op. cit.*, Part I, 376, 379, 387–8.
5. Stead, W. T., *General Booth* (London, 1891), 56.
6. Chadwick, O., *op. cit.*, Part I, 373.

7. For example female officers wearing nightgowns over their uniforms in the street to attract attention. Also the Eliza Armstrong child prostitution case.
8. The Army was considered a novel and inexpensive entertainment as well as a target for music-hall fun.
9. Booth, W., 'The Millennium; or, The Ultimate Triumph of the Salvation Army Principles', in *All the World*, II, August 1890, 337–43. Also see Booth, W., 'My Idea of the Millennium', *Review of Reviews*, Vol. II, July–December 1890, 130.
10. *The Chronicle of Convocation*, Session XXXVIII, Lower House, 10 May 1882, 178.
11. Manson, J., *The Salvation Army and the Public* (London, 1906), 367.
12. McLeod, H., *Religion and the Working Class in Nineteenth-Century Britain* (London, 1984), 25.

Abbreviations

LOO Law Officers' Opinion.
PRO Public Record Office.

247

APPENDIX 1

THE BOOTH FAMILY

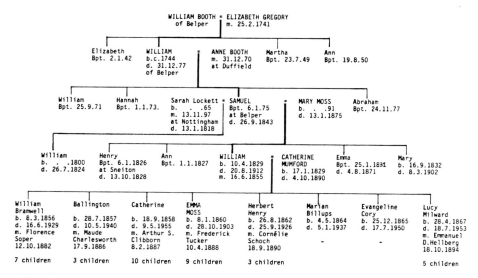

NOTES: Belper and Duffield are neighbouring parishes.
Bpt - Baptised.
b. - Born.
d. - Died.
m. - Married.
c. - Circa.

SOURCES: Registers of Births, Marriages and Deaths. Various biographies.

248

CHRISTIAN MISSION STATIONS, 1868–1878

1868/69	*1870*	*1871*
Bethnal Green	Bethnal Green	Bethnal Green
Bow Common	Bow Common	Bow Common
	Brighton	
	Bromley	Bromley
Canning Town	Canning Town	Canning Town
		Carshalton
Croydon	Croydon	Croydon
		Cubitt Town
Edinburgh	Edinburgh	Edinburgh
		Globe Road
Hackney Road	Hackney	Hackney
	Hastings	Hastings
		Isle of Man
Limehouse	Limehouse	Limehouse
Millwall	Millwall	Millwall
		Ninfield
Norwood		
Old Ford	Old Ford	
Poplar	Poplar	Poplar
Sclater Street		
Shoreditch	Shoreditch	Shoreditch
	Stoke Newington	Stoke Newington
Stratford	Stratford	Stratford
Three Colt Lane		
		Thomas Passage
	Tottenham	Tottenham
Whitechapel	Whitechapel	Whitechapel
Totals **16**	**18**	**22**

1872	1873	1874
Battle	Battle	
		Barking
Bethnal Green	Bethnal Green	Bethnal Green
Bow Common		
		Boreham
Bromley	Bromley	Bromley
		Buckland
Canning Town	Canning Town	Canning Town
	Chatham	Chatham
Croydon	Croydon	Croydon
	Cubitt Town	Cubitt Town
	Fieldgate	
Globe Road	Globe Road	
Hackney	Hackney	Hackney
		Hammersmith
Hastings	Hastings	Hastings
	Kettering	Kettering
Limehouse	Limehouse	Limehouse
Millwall	Millwall	Millwall
Ninfield	Ninfield	Ninfield
	North Woolwich	
		Penge
	Plaistow	Plaistow
Poplar	Poplar	Poplar
	Portsmouth	Portsmouth
		Rudmore
		Rye
Shoreditch	Shoreditch	Shoreditch
		Soho
	Southsea	Southsea
Stoke Newington	Stoke Newington	Stoke Newington
Stratford	Stratford	Stratford
Tottenham	Tottenham	Tottenham
Tunbridge Wells	Tunbridge Wells	
	Wellingborough	Wellingborough
Whitechapel	Whitechapel	Whitechapel
		Woolwich, North
Totals 19	27	31

1875	1876	1877
Barking	Barking	Barking
Bethnal Green	Bethnal Green	Bethnal Green
Boreham		
Bromley	Bromley	
		Bradford
Buckland		
Canning Town	Canning Town	Canning Town
Canton		
Cardiff	Cardiff	Cardif
Chatham	Chatham	Chatham
Croydon	Croydon	Croydon
Cubitt Town	Cubitt Town	
		East Hartlepool
Fulham		
Hackney	Hackney	Hackney
Hammersmith	Hammersmith	Hammersmith
Hastings	Hastings	Hastings
Kettering	Kettering	
	Leeds	Leeds
	Leicester	Leicester
Limehouse	Limehouse	Limehouse
	Lydd	
	Mayfield	
Middlesborough	Middlesborough	Middlesborough
Millwall	Millwall	Millwall
New Brompton	New Brompton	
New Romney	New Romney	
Ninfield	Ninfield	
	North Ormesby	North Ormesby
North Woolwich	North Woolwich	
Penge	Penge	
Plaistow	Plaistow	Plaistow
Poplar	Poplar	Poplar
Portsmouth	Portsmouth	Portsmouth
Rye	Rye	Rye
Shoreditch	Shoreditch	Shoreditch
Soho	Soho	Soho
Southsea		
St. Leonards	St. Leonards	St. Leonards
Stockton-On-Tees	Stockton-On-Tees	Stockton-On-Tees
Stoke Newington	Stoke Newington	Stoke Newington
Stratford	Stratford	Stratford
Strood		
Tottenham	Tottenham	Tottenham
Wellingborough	Wellingborough	Wellingborough
		West Hartlepool
Whitechapel	Whitechapel	Whitechapel
		Whitby

Totals	**39**	**38**	**31**

1878	1878 — *continued*
Aberdare	Manchester
Accrington	Merthyr
Acton	Mexborough
Attercliffe	Middlesborough
Barking	Millwall
Barnsley	North Ormesby
Bedlington	North Shields
Bethnal Green	Plaistow
Bishop Auckland	Plymouth
Blackburn	Poplar
Blaydon-On-Tyne	Portsmouth
Blyth	Rotherham
Bolton	Salisbury
Bradford	Seaham Harbour
Burnley	Sheffield
Canning Town	Shildon
Cardiff	South Shields
Chatham	South Stockton
Consett	Spennymoor
Coventry	St. Leonards
Dowlais	Stockton-On-Tees
East Hartlepool	Stoke Newington
Felling	Sunderland
Hammersmith	Tredegar
Hastings	Wellingborough
Jarrow	West Hartlepool
Leeds	Whitby
Leicester	Whitechapel
Limehouse	

57

Sources: *The East London Evangelist.* 1868–1869.
The Christian Mission Magazine. 1870–1878.

THE BELIEFS OF THE EAST LONDON CHRISTIAN REVIVAL SOCIETY

East London Christian Revival Society

"Fear none of these things which thou shalt suffer: behold, the devil shall cast *some* of you into prison, that ye may be tried; and ye shall have tribulation ten days: be then faithful unto death, and I will give thee a crown of life." Rev. ii.10

"All for Christ, and always for Christ."

ARTICLES OF FAITH

1. We believe that the Scriptures of the Old and New Testament were given by inspiration of God, and are the only rule of Christian faith and practice.

2. We believe that there is only one living and true God; the Father, the Son, and the Holy Ghost — three persons in one God — equal in power and glory; and the only proper object of religious worship.

3. We believe that in the person of Jesus Christ the Divine and human natures are united, so that He is truly and properly God, and truly and properly man.

4. We believe that all mankind, in consequence of the disobedience of Adam are sinners, destitute of holiness, and justly exposed to the penalty of the divine law.

5. We believe that the Lord Jesus Christ has, by His suffering and death made an atonement for the whole world, so that whosoever will may be saved.

6. We believe that repentance towards God, faith in our Lord Jesus Christ and regeneration by the Holy Spirit are necessary to salvation.

7. We believe in the immortality of the soul — in the resurrection of the body — in the general judgment at the end of the world — in the eternal happiness of the righteous — and in the endless punishment of the wicked.

BOND OF AGREEMENT

1st. We engage from henceforth to strive earnestly to depart from all iniquity, and to aim at the highest degree of personal devotedness to God.

2nd. We agree to set our hearts upon the salvation of souls, and to put forth constant personal effort to secure the conversion of sinners.

3rd. We engage, so far as we have the opportunity to attend the meetings held by the Society, both in-doors and in the open air, and to co-operate to the utmost of our ability, in every effort put forth by the Society to bring souls to Christ.

4th. We will strive to cultivate a spirit of brotherly affection towards the members of the Society, and to manifest this by seeking, so far as we have the opportunity, each other's temporal and spiritual welfare.

5th. We will contribute according to our weekly offerings to assist the Society in its operations.

Source: Salvation Army International Heritage Centre, London.

EXTRACTS FROM THE 1870 CONSTITUTION OF THE CHRISTIAN MISSION

The Rev. William Booth in the chair.

III — General Superintendent

1. The Mission shall be under the superintendence of the Rev. William Booth who is spoken hereafter as the General Superintendent.
2. The General Superintendent shall possess the power of confirming or setting aside the decisions and resolutions of any of the official society, or other meetings held throughout the mission, which in his judgement may be in any way prejudicial to the object for which the mission was first established.
3. The General Superintendent shall, when present, preside at all meetings throughout the mission, unless he desire otherwise; or in his absence he may, if he deem it necessary, depute some person to preside in his place.
4. In case the General Superintendent should resign or be, or in the unanimous opinion of the Conference become incapacitated to continue the general superintendence of the mission, then the duties, powers, and responsibilities of the office shall pass into the hands of the Conference.
5. The General Superintendent may, if he think proper, appoint a successor to his office, but in such a case the appointment shall be approved by least three-fourths of the Conference.

IV — Official Meetings

No person may hold office who is not a total abstainer from intoxicating liquors, tobacco and snuff except in cases of absolute sickness.
[Here followed very detailed regulations as there did for most sections.]

V — Members

[Paragraphs 1 to 7 stated that members should be cared for, lists kept of attendances, and that members were urged to abstain from intoxicating liquors and from smoking and all other offensive habits.]

8. No person shall be received or continue as a member who shall keep a public house or brewery, or be engaged in the demoralising traffic or sale of intoxicating drinks; or who shall frequent any public house or dram shop, except on business; or who shall sell obscene books or

pictures, fortune-telling books, or ballads, or any publication of irreli-
gious tendence or who shall exhibit bills for theatres, concerts, or balls
in their windows or premises.

9. Our members shall not read or sell the "London Journal" "Family
Herald" or any other publication of a similar character.

[Dress, hair, silly behaviour, backbiting and trespassing against each
other were all then dealt with. This Section concluded with:]

Members formally sanctioned by the elders of a mission have the right
to appeal to quarterly meetings. If this is not satisfactory to either side,
they may appeal to the General Superintendent who will give a final
decision.

XII — Female Preachers

As it is manifest from the Scripture of the Old and especially the New
Testament that God has sanctioned the labours of Godly women in his
Church; Godly women possessing the necessary gifts and qualifications, shall
be employed as preachers itinerant or otherwise and class leaders and as such
shall have appointments given to them on the preacher's plan; and they shall
be eligible for any office, and to speak and vote at all official meetings.

XV — Itinerant Preachers

4. Shall be abstainers from intoxicating drinks and shall neither smoke,
use tobacco, nor take snuff . . . and under no circumstances should they
contract any debt.

9. They shall not be members of any secret societies such as Odd Fellows.

10. They shall not take part in political meetings or parliamentary election.

XX — Quarterly Meeting

[Under this section many committees were established for example]

6. This meeting shall also appoint the committee for making the preacher's
plans and the arrangement for renewal of members' tickets or appoint
any committee required to carry out its decisions.

XXII — Annual Conference

1. A conference shall be held once in every year to review the progress
and working of the Mission during the past year and to frame such
measures as may be deemed necessary to promote its objects in the
future.

2. The Conference shall be composed of the General Superintendent, the
guardian representatives (when members of the Mission), the Super-
intendents of Circuits and two lay persons elected by each Circuit.

3. Members of the Mission may attend any of the meetings of the
Conference by showing the last quarters Society tickets except when
on any special occasion the Conference shall have declared its sittings
private.

4. The business of the Conference shall be to:
    1. Elect a secretary.
    2. Receive the certificates of members in order that they may be enrolled in the Conference Journal.
    3. Fill up by election any vacancies that may have occurred in the list of guardian representatives.
    4. Consider the general state of the Mission and what can be done to promote its extension and prosperity.
    5. Elect a committee of three lay persons to confer with the General Superintendent as to the stationing of the preachers for the ensuing year.
    6. Elect a committee which shall be called the Conference Committee to assist the General Superintendent in the management of the Mission during the ensuing year.
    7. Receive reports from the different Circuits as to their spiritual and financial condition.
5. All the elections of the Conference shall be by ballot.
6. The Conference shall meet on the second Monday in June at 11 o'clock.

XXIII — *The Conference Committee*

1. The Conference Committee shall consist of the General Superintendent, the Secretary of the Conference and five members of the Mission, appointed at each annual conference and to represent as far as possible the entire Mission.
2. The duty of the Committee shall be to take the oversight, promote the interests and conduct the general business of the Mission during the year.
3. The Committee shall meet every month or more frequently if desired.

Source: The Christian Mission Conference Minute Book 1870.

APPENDIX 5

RULES OF THE CHRISTIAN MISSION

(Under the General Superintendence of Rev. William Booth)

Established 1865

---

1. The object of the Christian Mission is to Preach the Gospel to the masses of the people who attend no place of worship, and to form its converts into societies for the purpose of training them in habits of holy living and useful labour.
2. The principal doctrines taught in the Mission are as follows:
    1. We believe that the Scriptures of the Old and New Testaments were given by inspiration of God, and that they only constitute the Divine rule of Christian faith and practice.
    2. We believe there is only one God, who is infinitely perfect, the Creator, Preserver, and Governor of all things.
    3. We believe that there are three persons in the Godhead — the Father, the Son, and the Holy Ghost, undivided in essence, co-equal in power and glory, and the only proper object of religious worship.
    4. We believe that in the person of Jesus Christ the Divine and human natures are united, so that He is truly and properly God, and truly and properly man.
    5. We believe that our first parents were created in a state of innocency, but by their disobedience they lost their purity and happiness: and that, in consequence of their fall, all men have become sinners, totally depraved, and as such are justly exposed to the wrath of God.
    6. We believe that the Lord Jesus Christ has, by His suffering and death, made an atonement for the whole world, so that whosoever will may be saved.
    7. We believe that repentance towards God, faith in our Lord Jesus Christ, and regeneration by the Holy Spirit, are necessary to salvation.
    8. We believe that we are justified by grace, through faith in our Lord Jesus Christ, and that he that believeth hath the witness in himself.

9. We believe that continuance in a state of salvation depends upon continued obedient faith in Christ.

10. We believe that it is the privilege of all believers to be "wholly sanctified," and that "their whole spirit and soul and body" may "be preserved blameless unto the coming of our Lord Jesus Christ." (1 Thess. v. 23.)

11. We believe in the immortality of the soul; in the resurrection of the body; in the general judgment at the end of the world; in the eternal happiness of the righteous; and in the endless punishment of the wicked.

3. The Members of the Mission are strongly urged to meet together in what is termed a "Believers' Meeting," where they may be counselled and encouraged with regard to the Salvation of their souls.

4. Members must not attend Theatres, Concert Halls, or any places of worldly amusements.

5. No member must read or sell any publications of an immoral tendency.

6. Members are recommended to keep out of debt, and on no account to incur liabilities without a good probability of being able to meet them.

7. Members are earnestly requested to abstain from the use of intoxicating liquors and tobacco, and to dress with christian simplicity, and not as the world dresses.

8. No Member may marry an unconverted person, and all are earnestly urged to select partners whose opinions and feelings are in perfect sympathy with earnest christianity.

9. The Members must contribute weekly according to their ability to sustain the work of the Mission in Seeking the Salvation of Souls.

10. Members must avoid bad company, and are entreated not to enter a Public-house unless duty absolutely requires it.

11. No Member must either receive evil reports or speak evil of others.

12. Members must carefully avoid any quarrel, and should any differences arise, they must endeavour as speedily and quietly as possible to arrange them according to the Rule laid down by the Saviour.

13. No Member may teach or discuss any doctrine in such a way as to cause division or unpleasantness in the Society.

14. Every Member should maintain the privilege of constant unbroken communion between God and his soul: to this end he must attend to private prayer, the reading of the Bible, and the use of all other available means of grace.

15. Members should strive to establish and maintain family prayer in whatever household they may be called to live.

16. Every Member is expected to take that part in the work of the Mission for which in the judgment of its officers he is best qualified.

17. When removing from one place to another, a member shall inform the Evangelist of his District, so that he may, if necessary, be recommended to the fellowship of some Christian Church.

18. When sick or confined to his house, a Member should send word to the Evangelist of his District, so that he may be visited.

19. No Member may be an officer of the Mission who does not abstain from intoxicating liquors and tobacco, and who is not thoroughly attached to the doctrines, rules, measures, and government of the Mission.

20. Any Member may appeal to the General Superintendent, 272, Whitechapel Road, London, E., with regard to any matter affecting himself or the work of the Mission.

Source: Salvation Army International Heritage Centre, London.

SALVATION ARMY REPORT FORMS

1. CANDIDATE'S ENTRY FORM FILLED IN BY THE CORPS OFFICER

1. Age last birthday? _____ Height? _____
2. Has the candidate got that sort of pluck, and go, and godliness that is likely to make an officer in the Salvation Army? _____
3. How many times a week does the candidate come to the open-air? _____
4. How often does the candidate attend the seven o'clock prayer meeting? _____
5. Can the candidate sing? _____
6. Can the candidate play any instrument, and what? _____
7. How long in present situation? _____
8. What wages does the candidate receive? _____
9. What is the occupation? _____
10. Ever had fits of any kind? _____
11. If so, what kind? _____
12. Has the candidate had any serious illness? _____
13. If so, what? _____
14. Is the candidate in debt? _____
15. If so, how much, and why? _____
16. When and where converted? _____
17. How long has the candidate been a member of the Army? _____
18. Can the candidate write _____ or read? _____
19. Can the candidate speak any other language besides English? _____
20. Has the candidate ever been in the Training Home as a cadet? _____
21. Has the candidate ever been in the Army as an officer? _____
22. Does anybody depend on the candidate for support? _____ If so, to what extent? _____
23. Is the candidate courting? _____
24. If so, who, and is the person a soldier? _____
25. Are the candidate's parents saved? _____
26. Do they belong to the Army? _____
27. Has the candidate obtained their consent to become an officer? _____
28. Is the candidate light, trifling, or giddy? _____
29. Is the candidate such a person as you would like as a lieutenant? _____
30. Do you consider the candidate strong enough for the work of an officer? _____
31. Has the candidate ever belonged to any other religious society? _____ If so, which? _____

32. Does the candidate sell *War Cry*s in the streets? _____
33. Is the candidate willing to sell *War Cry*s on Sundays? _____
34. Is the candidate to be relied upon? _____
35. Will the candidate pay travelling expenses to London, if we decide to receive _____ into the Training Home? _____
36. How much can the candidate pay for maintenance while in the Training Home? _____
37. How long notice will the candidate require? _____
38. Married or single? _____
39. How many children? _____
40. What are their ages? _____
41. Wife saved? _____
42. Does she take any part in meetings? _____
43. If so, what? _____
44. How long married? _____
45. Is she clean in her home and person? _____
46. Does she wish _____ to become an officer? _____
47. Or is she only willing that he should be one? _____
48. Send us the candidate's photo. _____

"Captain _____, Corps _____

"(Return enclosed letter.)"

2. COMMANDING OFFICER'S REPORT UPON LEAVING A CORPS

THE SALVATION ARMY

Farewell report of Captain _____ , commanding _____ Corps:

What is the average number of soldiers in the open-air week nights?
What is the average congregation inside on week nights?
What is the average attendance at 7 o'clock prayer meetings?
What is the average attendance at your Sunday morning holiness-meeting?
What is the average attendance at your Sunday afternoon meeting?
What is the average attendance at your Sunday night meeting?
What is the average number of soldiers in Sunday open-air meetings?
Are there any accounts owing by the corps? If so, give particulars.
What amount have you in hand (including money in Army bank, if any)?
To what date has your hall rent been paid up?
To what date has your officers' quarters' rent been paid up?
To what date has your gas been paid up?
What is the amount owing on book and uniform stock at present date?
What is the amount of your book and uniform stock at present date?
What is the amount of cash in hand for books and uniforms?
How many soldiers have you on roll-book?
How many of this number can be thoroughly depended upon?
Are your officers' quarters (if any) fully furnished?
How many *War Cry*s do you sell _____ Wednesdays _____ Saturdays?
How many *Little Soldier*s do you sell?

Have you any old *War Crys* or *Little Soldiers* on hand?
If you have, say how many.
What was the amount of last week's cartridge money?
Give any other information which you think would be useful to us when
   considering the appointment of your successor.

(Signed   _____, Captain.

                  _____, Lieutenant.

                  _____, Treasurer.

July 27th, 1884.   _____, Secretary.

3. OFFICER'S MONDAY REPORT

"The Salvation Army.

"Officer's Monday Report.

"Name and No. of Corps _____

"Monday _____

"Number of open-air services held last week.
"Number of hours spent last week in visiting.
"Number of families visited last week.
"Was your hall full on Sunday night?
"How many were present at principal week-night? —
"In-door meetings?
"*Members* present at beginning of largest week-night open-air meeting?
"Members present at close of same?
"Persons at Sunday morning 7 o'clock prayer meeting?
"Prisoners taken last week?
"Who spoke at the public Sunday night service?
"Number of Little Soldiers' meetings last week?
"How many children present at the largest?
"Amount of offerings yesterday? £. s. d.
"Total amount of income for the week, including Sunday?
"How many *War Crys* did you sell, Wednesdays?
"How many *War Crys* did you sell, Saturdays?
"How many *Little Soldiers* did you sell last week?
"What is the entire amount of liabilities for the week?
"Salary? How much salary did you draw?
"Is the station in debt? If so, how much?
"Have you any money in hand? If so, how much?
"In Army Bank? In hands of treasurer?

(Signed) Captain _____ Lieut. _____

Source: Redstone, J. J. R., *An Ex-Captain's Experience of the Salvation Army*
(London, 1888), 6, 7, 8, 20, 67, 68.

PREVIOUSLY UNPUBLISHED LETTERS FROM GEORGE SCOTT RAILTON TO TWO CHRISTIAN MISSION EVANGELISTS

(re. Cadman)

3rd August, 1876.

My dear Brother,

Thanks for yours. I am glad that you are really getting on solid foundation laid.

They have already got a class of 10 at Leicester, and seem to be doing something at all the country stations.

Alas for London....................was a poor lifeless do, and the worst of it is people don't seem to feel how awfully London has gone down. But thank God we are getting a real base laid at Poplar and gaining steadily every day. We are determined to have a real concern and shall get a big one in due time.

I never felt so much of the power and light of God as I have done the last few weeks. It is all right, victory is ours and when we have got a living society then we shall I hope be able to strengthen our brethren.

We have abandoned several small station in order to use up all our strength on those we can make something of. Poor Watts has had to go home ill. Mace has resigned and so we should have been awkwardly fixed but for having just got a man called Cadman from Rugy.

It is no use keeping up appearances. We must lay the axe to the tree roots and make a real living Mission all round. Kindest regard to Mrs. D. Broadbent (?)

Yours faithfully and affectionately,
G.S. RAILTON.

Mr. Dowdle.

P.S. Receipt to follow for cheque. They want to divide the amount between the two properly. How much for Mags? I also enclose postcards to save you trouble on Mondays in writing us to describe the week and the day before. Returns for August sent by book post.

7th Sept. 1876.

Dear Bro, Dowdle

Thanks for yours. Mr. Mrs. & Miss Booth are at the seaside now and are I think gaining strength though slowly.

I find I must never chaff you for fear of hurting your feelings which I would not do for the world. My brother Bramwell will perhaps be giving you a/call on his way South and will be able afresh to assure you how the very thought of you cheers my heart in this weary godless world with so few who really know the Father.

Don't ask me how the poor old mission is doing. Read the Magazine and be content with what it tells you. I sometimes try to hope it is because I keep getting up and making a higher standard myself that I look so sadly upon the state of things around. But I cannot help seeing how the Mission is fallen, in a number of cases falling.

I have been sadly let in at Poplar. We have allowed the people for 2 years to learn a different religion from ours and now to lead them to live for God and souls is almost hopeless because they will not. We had however got a nice company of folks together who were beginning to go in for God when Mr. Booth's illness and accompanying cir-cumstances cut me off for a fortnight. Poor B. is a very dear good chap, but young and utterly incapable of leading anything at present and on first tide is lost. Even now I cannot get there till the evening and B and all suffer sorely. Still I never felt so much of the power of God in all my life as I have done there and I hope now even with evenings only to rally them for another charge. Religion short of dwelling in God and God in us is no use and it is bitter indeed to reflect how few anywhere know anything of this.

But never mind I have come this first few weeks to give up setting my affections even on the work of God on the earth. I am content to live and witness for Him as long as He will let me whatever the result be or be not and then I will get into heaven and try and find out why He allowed the Devil to have it so much his own way here.

Love to Mrs. D and all your fellow labourers.

Yours affectionately,

G.S. RAILTON

Mr. J. Dowdle.

P.S. Dear old John Smith of Hastings is just off to heaven. He was speaking at Croydon most delightfully and then sat down and died. Praise God.

9th Sept. 1876.

A Russell

My dear Bro,

I have been very thankful to hear of the advance you
have been making in the great work and am still more so to
find that you have been making great strides forward within
your own ranks.

What we want above all in our Mission is the might of
God. We have a gigantic, humanly impossible task on hand
but in the strength of the Lord we can do it and make
Devils and angels wonder. But nothing short of the mighty
moving of the Holy Ghost within and through us can prodce
any serious effect upon the unbelieving world.

I bless God that ever I was stationed at Poplar for
the tempest of opposition and the mass of ungodliness have
driven me in upon my Support more than ever and I have felt
more than I ever did of the power of the Highest. The
illness of Mr. Mrs. and Miss Booth too has formed in me a
sense of dependance upon God and of utter submission to
him such as I never knew before. I look with very very
deep sadness I must confess upon the poor world and the
work of God and prospects of the cost in it; but I am
determined just to work and witness on till the end whatever
the result may or may not be and then for eternal weight
of glory.

Let us be more than ever out and out for God. It is
sad indeed to find so few who are so and the pure teachings

of the Holy Ghost are more and more unpopular as shallow
religion grows and spreads; but never mind, let us at least
be 'faithful unto death'.

Old John Smith of St. Leonards has been so. He died
at Croydon the other evening after service. We bury him
there on Saturday afternoon. If it be not too late to
manage I should much like you to be with us and I write
Bro L. to that effect. Then you might return with those
who will doubtless be there from Hastings and the south
where I suppose you would naturally like to spend your
holiday.

We understand that we cease to pay you after the 3rd
inst. That is well. We are not only perfectly willing
for you to remain in Leicester, but have reckoned upon it.
It is time .... dreadfully off in London; but
we must forever abandon the folly of squandered efforts
over a wide surface where little is or can be done and
must go in for furious concentrated assults where we can
produce a great result.

I am sorry that my clerk being ill and away today
I cannot enclose you a cheque or P.O. but I daresay if
coming up you can borrow from Bro L. and I will send in
a day or two.

Yours faithfully,

G.S. RAILTON.

Mr. A. Russell.

Source: Salvation Army International Heritage Centre, London.

NAMES AND OCCUPATIONS OF MEMBERS OF THE POPLAR CHRISTIAN MISSION STATION

Names	Occupations
Bro. Bob Clark	—
Sis. Clark	—
Bro. Davis	—
Sis. Davis	—
Bro. Owen	Factory owner
Sis. Rainsbury	Dock labourer's wife
Bro. Smith	Gipsy
Sis. Smith	Gipsy's wife
Bro. Stevens	—
Bro. Tidman	—
Bro. White	Stevedore
Several young women	
—	Policeman
—	Navvy aged 25

Sources: *The East London Evangelist.* 1868–1869.
The Christian Mission Magazine. 1870–1878.

PUBLISHED REPORTS FOR
MANCHESTER CORPS, 1880–1889

1878, Manchester I, 3 reports. 1879, Manchester I, 4 reports and Manchester II, 2.

1880	MONTHLY TOTALS	I	II	III	IV	V	VI	VII	VIII	IX	X	XI	XII	XIII	DEN	DROY	S.I	S.II	S.III
JAN	2			2															
FEB	1	1																	
MARCH	1	1																	
APRIL																			
MAY	1	1																	
JUNE	1	1																	
JULY	.																		
AUG	3	1	1	1															
SEPT																			
OCT	4	2	1	1															
NOV	4		2	2															
DEC	9	2	3	2	2														
GENERAL REPORTS	4																		
TOTALS	30	9	7	8	2														
1881																			
JAN	8	4	1	1	1												1		
FEB	7	2	3		2														
MARCH	5	2	2														1		
APRIL	4	2	1														1		
MAY	8	2	1	2	1												2		
JUNE	8	4		2	2														
JULY	8	3		3	2														
AUG	10	4		3	2												1		
SEPT	7	3		1	3														
OCT	13	4	2	2	4												1		
NOV	12	3	3	2	2												2		
DEC	11	3	1	3	2												2		
GENERAL REPORTS	4																		
TOTALS	105	36	14	19	21												11		
1882																			
JAN	9	3	2	2	1												1		
FEB	10	3	3	2	1												1		
MARCH	7	1		4													2		
APRIL	4	1															2		
MAY	2				1	1													
JUNE	6	2	1	1	1												1		
JULY	4		3														1		
AUG	13	4	3	3	1	1												1	
SEPT	9	2	1	1	2	1												2	
OCT	10	2	1		2	1											2	2	
NOV	29	5	3	6	4	4											3	4	
DEC	20	5	2	5	3	1											3	1	
GENERAL REPORTS	2																		
TOTALS	125	28	19	24	17	9											16	10	

1883	MONTHLY TOTALS	I	II	III	IV	V	VI	VII	VIII	IX	X	XI	XII	XIII	DEN	DROY	S.I	S.II	S.III
JAN	14	3	1	6	3												1		
FEB	14	3	1	1	2		1									1	3	2	
MARCH	17	4	4	3	1			1									1	3	
APRIL	12	2	2	1	2	2										1	2		
MAY	11	1	2	2	1	2											3		
JUNE	23	5	1	3	1	2	3	1	2						1	1	1	2	
JULY	18	4	2	1	1	1	1		1						3	3		1	
AUG	23	3	2	1	2	3	1	1	1						2	2	2	3	
SEPT	10	1	2		1		1	1	1						1	1	1		
OCT	19	2	1		3	2	1	3	1						2	2	1	1	
NOV	14	3	1		2	1	1		1						1	1		3	
DEC	10	1	3	1	3			1										1	
GENERAL REPORTS	4																		
TOTALS	189	32	22	19	22	13	9	8	7						10	12	15	16	

1884	MONTHLY TOTALS	I	II	III	IV	V	VI	VII	VIII	IX	X	XI	XII	XIII	DEN	DROY	S.I	S.II	S.III
JAN	18	3		2	2	1	2	3	1							2	2		
FEB	17	3	1	1	3	1		1							2	2	1	2	
MARCH	21	2	2	2	2	1	1	2	1						1	2	4	1	
APRIL	8	2	1		2	1		1									1		
MAY	16	1	1	2	3	2		2								1	4		
JUNE	11	1	2		1		2	1	1							1	1	1	
JULY	9	1			1	1		2								1	2	1	
AUG	14	3	1	1	1		2	1							1	1	1	2	
SEPT	10	3		1	2	1									2	1	1		
OCT	11	3	2	3	2											1			
NOV	17	3	2	3	2	1	1	1								1	1	2	
DEC	7		1	3	1		1									1		1	
GENERAL REPORTS	6																		
TOTALS	165	25	13	18	22	9	9	13	4						6	12	19	9	

1885	MONTHLY TOTALS	I	II	III	IV	V	VI	VII	VIII	IX	X	XI	XII	XIII	DEN	DROY	S.I	S.II	S.III
JAN	19	4	2	3	3	1		1								2	1	2	
FEB	15	2	3	3	2	2	1	1									1	1	
MARCH	4			2		1		1											
APRIL	7	3	1	2					~~~							1			
MAY	8	1			1	2	2		1									1	
JUNE	6	2				1	1	1								1			
JULY	19	2	1	1	2	3	2	2	1						1	1	2	1	
AUG	9	2	1				2	1	1								1	1	
SEPT	7			2			3			2									
OCT	7		1			1			3	1					1				
NOV	8		1	1	1	1	1		1							1		1	
DEC	6	1	1		1	1									1			1	
GENERAL REPORTS	2																		
TOTALS	117	17	11	14	10	13	12	6	7	3					3	6	5	8	

1886	MONTHLY TOTALS	I	II	III	IV	V	VI	VII	VIII	IX	X	XI	XII	XIII	DEN	DROY	S.I	S.II	S.III
JAN	7		2	1							1								
FEB	11	2		1			1		1		1					3	4		
MARCH	5			1								1			1	1	1		
APRIL	4	2		1								1				2			
MAY	4			1	1		1				1					1			
JUNE	3		1	2															
JULY	6			1	2	2									1				
AUGUST	2			1													1		
SEPT	4	1				2							1						
OCT	4			1		1				1					1				
NOV	6			2	1				1	1			1						
DEC	4	1		1							1		1						
GENERAL REPORTS	4																		
TOTALS	64	6	3	11	4	5	2	-	2	2	4	2	3		3	7	6	-	

1887	MONTHLY TOTALS	I	II	III	IV	V	VI	VII	VIII	IX	X	XI	XII	XIII	DEN	DROY	S.I	S.II	S.III
JAN	2			1							1								
FEB	3			1	1												1		
MARCH	2												1						
APRIL	4	1	1												2				
MAY	-																		
JUNE	1			1															
JULY	8	1		2	2	1	1										1		
AUGUST	7			1	1	1	2				1		1						
SEPT	16	2	2	1	2	1	1		1				1		1	1	2	1	
OCT	10	1	1	1	2	1	2				1		2						
NOV	8			1	1								2		1	1	1	1	
DEC	3			1	1												1		
GENERAL REPORTS	-																		
TOTALS	64	6	4	9	10	4	6	-	1	-	3	-	7		4	2	6	2	

1888	MONTHLY TOTALS	I	II	III	IV	V	VI	VII	VIII	IX	X	XI	XII	XIII	DEN	DROY	S.I	S.II	S.III
JAN	2			1	1														
FEB	5		1						1	2								1	
MARCH	5	1	1			1	1				1								
APRIL	6	2		1		1			1		1								
MAY	2			1	1														
JUNE	6	1			1					1					1		1		1
JULY	1				1														
AUGUST	10			1	1		2				1		1	2			1		1
SEPT	8	1	1		2	1			1					1					1
OCT	3	1			1													1	
NOV	16	2	1	2		2			1		2		1		2		2	1	
DEC	5	1	1	1						1	1								
GENERAL REPORTS	7																		
TOTALS	76	9	5	7	8	5	3	-	4	4	6	-	2	3	3	-	4	3	3

1889	MONTHLY TOTALS	I	II	III	IV	V	VI	VII	VIII	IX	X	XI	XII	XIII	DEN	DROY	S.I	S.II	S.III
JAN	14	2	1	2	1		1		1		1		1		1	1		1	1
FEB	4										1						1	2	
MARCH	1													1					
APRIL	10	1	1	1	1	1					1		1				1	1	1
MAY	1			1															
JUNE	–																		
JULY	1	1																	
AUGUST	–																		
SEPT	–																		
OCT	10	2		2	2		1						1	1					1
NOV	4		1											2				1	
DEC	6	1			1			1						1			1		1
GENERAL REPORTS	3																		
TOTALS	54	7	3	6	5	1	2	1	1	–	3	–	3	5	1	1	3	5	4

TOTALS:

		YEARS:	
MANCHESTER I	175	1880	– 30
MANCHESTER II	101	1881	–105
MANCHESTER III	135	1882	–125
MANCHESTER IV	121	1883	–189
MANCHESTER V	59	1884	–165
MANCHESTER VI	43	1885	–117
MANCHESTER VII	28	1886	– 64
MANCHESTER VIII	26	1887	– 64
MANCHESTER IX	9	1888	– 76
MANCHESTER X	16	1889	– 54
MANCHESTER XI	2		
MANCHESTER XII	15		
MANCHESTER XIII	8		
DENTON	30		
DROYLSDEN	40		
SALFORD I	85		
SALFORD II	53		
SALFORD III	7		

GENERAL REPORTS   36

DECADE TOTAL: 989

NOTES:
1. One reason why the total number of reports declined after 1884 although a number of Manchester corps remain important, (as in the case of Manchester I), is that because of the Army's rapid expansion, many more reports were filed than could possibly be included in the War Cry.
2. Reports often note help from other corps, for example War Cry 31 March 1881 p.4 talks about Manchester I but refers to help from Manchester III and IV.
3. The thick line at the start of a corps report indicates the opening month of that corps. ∿ indicates reopening of a corps.

SOURCE: The Christian Mission Magazine. 1878.
    The Salvationist. 1879.
    War Cry. 1880 – 1889.

APPENDIX 10

Census and Directory Information on the Age, Sex, Family and Occupation of Known Guildford Salvationists in the 1880s

Name and Address	Family	Age	Occupation
1. William G. Collins, 34 Markenfield Road	Wife, Son, Mother	26	Ironmonger's Shopkeeper
2. William Clarke & Family, 3 Quarry Street	Wife, Son, 2 Daughters	62	Tailor
3. William K. Capp, 9 Sydenham Road	Wife	24	Letter Carrier
4. Frederick James Short, 6 Millmead	Lodger (?)	—	Bricklayer
5. Arthur Notley, Rose Cottage, Denzil Road	Father, Mother, Sister, Stepsister, Lodger	18	Stonemason's Apprentice
6. William Courtney Snell, Denzil Road	Father, Mother, 3 Sisters, 3 Brothers	16	China Warehouse Assistant
7. Albert Giles			
8. William Henry Loveland, 8 Milk House Gate, High St.	Wife, 2 Sons, 1 Daughter	50	Engine Fitter at Foundry
9. William Groves		Young	Grocer's Assistant
10. Robert Lamb, Quarry Hill, Shalford			Labourer
11. James W. Parker, 5 Sparkes's Row, Park St.	Wife, Daughter, 2 Sons	62	Tailor
12. Rose Smith, Charlotteville			
13. A. Batchelor, 2 Chertsey Street			Hairdresser & Umbrella Maker
14. Fygins			
15. F. E. Fold, 6 Bury Fields	Lodger		
16. (Sister) Hall			
17. Homes			
18. William J. Larby, North Square	Wife, 2 Daughters, 1 Boarder	30	Timber Merchant, Carter
19. (Sister) Martin			
20. H. Pyle & Emily Pyle, 6 Babington Place, Sydenham Rd.	Son, 2 Daughters	42 + ?	Railway Guard
21. R. Ricketts, 4 Poplar Place, Drummond Rd.	Wife, Son	46	General Labourer
22. (Sister) Woodman			
23. Edward Young, Quarry Hill			
24. G. Siggers, 3/4 High Street	Wife, Sister	28	Ironmonger's Shop, employing 2 men + 2 boys
25. William Pollard, Shalford			Butcher/Labourer
26. Walter Hanson			
27. Mary Ann Pincott, Tuns Gate, High St.	Husband, Son, Lodger	44	
28. David Full			
29. Charles Knapp			
30. Thomas Williamson			
31. George Simpson			
32. Catherine Puttock			

Sources: Census of England and Wales. 1881. Population. R.G. 11/776–8.
Guildford Directories. 1882–1889.
The Surrey Advertiser and County Times. 1881–1889.
War Cry. 1881–1889.

THE SKELETON NEWSPAPERS

Property of S. Foster Adjt, Mizpah H. Marlboro R? Salisbury

THE "SKELETON."

HONITON, DECEMBER 2nd, 1882.   PRICE ONE PENNY.

HEAR WHAT THE GENERAL OF THE SKELETON ARMY HAS TO SAY!!

Head Quarters, Friday, Dec. 1, 1882.

THE GENERAL'S SPEECH—Officers and Men, I claim your attention for a time while I address a few words to you respecting the future. Since the recent engagements in which you have taken part, different rumours have spread abroad concerning the intentions of that inestimable army, known as the "Skeleton Army," to which you have sworn your entire allegiance. You have fought admirably well during the past, you have strictly, obeyed the orders of your Commander and consequently numerous promotions will be made. You know, as well as I know, that our original aim was, and still is, to crush fanaticism, and to uphold the dignity and purity of the borough of Honiton. That a few dancing strangers should come here to upset our equilibrium, without of ....ing and endeavouring to maintain our of privileges, is, I say, officers and fellow comrades unreasonable and certainly not to be tolerated by any Skeletonist. I wish it to go forth that our whole and sole object is to restore order in Honiton, and restore order, we will ! (Voices : "We will," which were immediately suppressed) I want no interruption but if you will simply follow my behests and commands, the Salvation Army will be rushed out of the town order will be restored, the Skeletonists will be dismissed to their homes, and no further fear or apprehension will exist. I must speak plainly and let you know once for all, that I most strongly object to glass breaking and otherwise damaging property. Indeed, were I to discover a "soldier," whether an officer or a subordinate, partaking of such wanton destruction I would order a Court Marshal at once and the utmost severity of the law would be enforced. Obey my order men and I will carry you through this painful ordeal safely (loud cheers). Recollect we must use sound judgment at this critical time and if there be no further need for our interference we must not interfere ; but on the other hand, if the so-called Captain of the celebrated "Intruders" appears on the battle field with drum and men we must, we will !—(voices "We will")—strain a nerve to restore peace.

Men, my last words to you are, and don't forget them, for no cause whatever do you attack property.—simply remember we want to stop the Salvation processions (tremendous cheering).

The men were then put through some slight exercises including throwing the turnip ; artistic decoration with red ochre ; and turf planting.

It was rumoured after the General's speech that prizes would be offered in the future for the best "red ochre shot."

"You're Hignorent" quoth Captn. Loomas, to a would be quiet Skeleton last sunday evening. To which the mild reply was "where ignorance is bliss it is folly to be wise."

Bones Woode last Sunday Afternoon in his Address stated that he had looked in his Dictionary for the meaning of the word *Skeleton* and found that it meant "to thin," What do you think?

Bloater wants to know if anyone can tell red "Ocher" is pisin.

Captn. Deanner says if it had not been for his whiskers and the Captn's coat he should have known them Sunday Afternoon.

It's strange but the War Cry dent have much to say about their progress in Honiton.

If any of our Skeletons go to quod this week we shall put them down "Gone on a Furlough."

I can see the Villian in your face, quoth a Salvation member to Skeleton, oh you can, can yer, well that's first time I new my face was a looking glass.

Mr, New St. Cheese had better be cautious of his language in the Market House otherwise you'll know dont you know "Bob."

The Skeleton's if all is well will enter their new Barracks on the 5th of next month.

"*War Cry* " Sir said a news boy Saturday to a Farmer, Dang the "War Cry" said he I wants a "Skeleton."

THIS SOUNDS HEALTHY.

A Gentleman from the North of England writing to us on the 28th ult. says my wife is ordered a change by our medical man, her spirits are low, and he says she must see some life can you secure me a house in Honiton, if so let it be as near the Salvation Army Barracks as possible.

THE SALVATION ARMY ROWS.

EXTRAORDINARY CONDUCT OF THE "CAPTAIN."

At the Police Court, (Wednesday), before J. Murch, Esq. (Mayor), and H. Hook, Esq. (ex-Mayor), the following cases in connection with the Salvation Army disturbances were called on —:

Samuel Stone, a young man, was summoned for disturbing the members of the Salvation Army by throwing a white material at them in the streets. The case was proved by Sergt. Jeffery and p. c. Merrifield, who said that they saw defendant, while the Army was marching through the streets, throw a white substance, which struck one of the members of the Army. Defendant admitted that he flung the material, but said that he did not aim at any particular individual. The Bench thought defendant had been guilty of indiscretion, but they decided to dismiss the case with a caution.

John Kerslake, labourer, pleaded guilty to being drunk and disorderly near the Salvation Hall, on the 20th Nov., and was fined 1s and costs.— *William Woodrow*, for a similar offence, at the same time and place, was also fined 1s and costs.

Thomas Harris, butcher, was summoned for unlawfully assaulting the Captain of the Salvation Army, on the 19th of Novem. Mr. Fryer, of Exeter, appeared for the defence. John Lomas, the "Captain," of the Honiton branch of the Salvation Army, who was the complainant in the case, was called upon to enter the witness box.

Upon being called upon to take the oath, he said—refuse to take the oath or make an affirmation, on the ground that Mr. Hook is not a fit and proper person to sit in ... on the ...

Mr. Fryer—What an insult to the bench!

Mr. Hook—I never heard such a thing in my life.

Mr. Fryer—In the course of my experience I never heard such an insult offered to a bench of Magistrates. (To complainant)—do you wish to support this case, or to withdraw the summons? You must do one or the other.

The Captain—I have stated my reason.

Mr. Fryer—I do not require your reason. Do you withdraw?

The Captain—I have stated my reason. I refuse to be sworn before the present bench.

Mr. Fryer—Then there is no case, and I ask for expenses on behalf of my client.

Mr. Hook—We will consult with the Town Clerk with reference to the application.

The next case was then called.

William Meads—Railway Bricklayer, was then called upon to answer a summons for interrupting the members of the Salvation Army. Mr. Fryer defended. The "Captain," was again the complainant.

On being placed in the box, he said—The same as in the last case. I decline to be sworn so long as the ex-Mayor sits on the Bench, and I wish you would allow me to state my reasons, so that they may be made public. On saturday last I had a conversation with the ex-Mayor, and he told me that if we carried on our processions we should have no protection. I have witnesses to prove that he has said that if he had 100 cases in connection with the services of the Army he would dismiss them all. A butcher in his employ is one of the defendants, and under those circumstances I wish to take the cases further.

Walter Harris was then called upon to answer a similar summons, being brought up in custody on remand, and was also defended by Mr. Fryer. Defendant pleaded not guilty. The "Captain," on being called on, said—I refuse to be sworn on the same grounds as I stated in the two previous cases.

The Town Clerk, (Mr. Tweed)—Then that concludes the business.

Mr. Fryer—I will tell the captain at once that this man having been taken in custody and imprisoned upon a false charge, I shall take an action against him for false imprisonment. (Applause in Court, which was instantly suppressed). More disgraceful conduct than that of complainant I never saw in any Court of Justice.

The Court then rose.

[With regard to the imputation made by the "captain" against Mr. Hook, the ex-Mayor, that he was "not a fit and proper person" to sit on the Bench, great indignation was expressed in the town, for during Mr. Hook's official career as Mayor—a position he has attained by a continual course of straightforward conduct—as well as during his long business connection in the neighbourhood, he has never done a single act to forfeit public confidence. The charge thus levelled against him by a perfect stranger has, therefore, naturally aroused much feeling, and Mr. Hook intends, we believe, to enter an action against the "captain" for slander.

SALVATION ARMY'S CREED.

Money, oh money, thy praises we sing ;
You art their Saviour, their God, and their King,
'Tis for that they preach, and for that they pray ;
They make a collection thrice, each Sabbath day.

'Tis their creed, they don't preach without it,
And heaven is closed against those who doubt it
This is the essence of all their religion,
Be regular to them and be plucked like a pigeon.

The poor in my parish that need some relief,
We preach for their poverty, we pray for their grief
We send our bags round morn, noon and night,
And hope they'll remember the poor widows' plight.

They gather their knowledge from wisdom's great tree,
All their religion is £ s. d.
Pounds, shillings and pence is all that they crave,
From the first step on earth, to the brink of their grave.

When they are dead and their body at rest;
Put a box in their coffin, is their last request,
That friends may all see, when they come for reflection,
They will be first on their legs to make a collection.

Their pay may be hundreds or thousands a year;
Double it, treble it, still they are here,
With their bags and their boxes collecting your brass
For we can't do as Jesus did, ride on an ass.

They must have drummers, fifers and all;
They are not going to foot it like Peter and Paul,
Neither like John live on locust and honey
So out with your purses and down with your money. ;

Some fools may ask what they do with their money,
They may just as well ask what bees do with honey,
They will answer you all with a wink or a nod
They keep three-thirds themselves and give praises to God.

In the cold silent earth they may soon be laid low
To sleep with the blest that has gone long ago,
They will slumber in peace till the great resurection
But the first on their legs to make the collection.

LIEUT. DOBSON,
1st Battery Turf Shiers.

[The following extracts are from a poor quality four-page copy of
The Skeleton *dated HONITON, DECEMBER 16TH, 1882.*
PRICE ONE PENNY]

[Page 1]

TO CORRESPONDENTS

Information intended for the columns of The Skeleton must be addressed to the Editor, Honiton. As the real object of this paper is to stamp out the fanaticism and blasphemy of the Salvation Army, which is doing so much to bring Christian religion into ridicule, it is hoped that our Correspondents will send all the information they can from different parts of the country

---

Agencies will be at once opened in every town invaded by the Salvation Army.

ROUND SHOT

"CAPT." BROAD-AM wishes it to be understood that buttons are not legal coin of the realm.

A PLYMOUTH contemporary is fond of throwing bricks. And he is also fond of nailing the off-shoots of other people's brains, especially if it runs down the "Skeletons." The result of these extraordinary efforts is the production of one of the most disjointed and ridiculous articles we have ever read. It may be as well for us to give a conversation we heard upon it between two farmers. "Look at yer, Bill. Even if thic chap has no brains of his own, why the dickens do 'er make so vree with other folks for? Strikes I, if the sale of thic paper is no greater out East than 'er be west, the best thing 'er'd better do 'ud be to turn his printin' office into a Salvation Army Barracks. 'Er'd find it pay better than printin, I'll bet a cow; that is, if what we hear about General Booth's collection be gospel. Darn me if I don't think I'll set up myself."

AND lo and behold! while the county magistrates were yet in the Guildhall, two Pharisees came unto them and craved their assistance, and they went back again weeping bitterly.

A HALF-STARVED, poor-looking devil called upon the General on Wednesday and asked if he was thin enough to join the Skeleton Army. The General dismissed him with a shilling — because he was too thin.

THE SKELETON

"A WOUNDED head and a disabled arm." Such was the heading of a paragraph which appeared in that blasphemous paper, the War Cry, a copy of which appears in another column, kindly sent us by a correspondent. If this is a specimen of the "religion" and of the "Captains" who furnish reports for the War Cry, save us from their intercession. What can respectable people think of a man of this type, who talks about "out-flanking the devil," "You're hall going to 'ell," and in the same breath mutters "Praise the Lord" or "Hallelujah" with an expression on his face that would lead one to suppose that "butter would not melt in his mouth?" What can we designate such proceedings other than rotten, stinking, hypocrisy? Then again, note how he (late a soldier in Her Majesty's army) draws attention to his wounded head and poor disabled left arm. Poor thing! How he must have suffered! And then, not to be found sticking-plaster? From the bottom of our very boots we pity him.

To judge from the "Captain's" address, and the manner in which he murders the English language — going to great pains by carefully taking out his "h's" and dropping them into words never intended by Lindley Murray — it causes us to suppose that he knows as much of the Bible as the Bible knows about him. And yet, on looking through the columns of the War Cry "novelty," the man who lately conducted the services here appears in comparison with many other Salvation Officers, a perfect gem, a pearl without price, an Archangel! We read of a Music Hall Clog-Dancer, who, having been "saved," got on the so-called "Penitent Form," and enlightened the wicked "unsaved" ones before him by saying that he used to clog-dance to such as them, but, in future, he'd Clog-Dance to Jesus!

We are afraid if our Redeemer were to descend now there would be a greater clearance than the occasion on which He cast out the Buyers and Sellers from the Temple.

A GATLING SHOT AT BOOTH, WELL AIMED
by the Mayor of Exeter

His Worship, the Mayor of Exeter, speaking at a public meeting there, referred, in the course of his remarks, to the Salvation Army in the following words — "Alluding specially to the Salvation Army, his worship characterised their action as a disgrace to civilisation. Standing before them as the Chief Magistrate of the City, he did not hesistate to say his feeling was shocked on finding the streets turned into a sort of pandemonium on Sunday by the action of the members of this Army, actions reminding one of the dancing dervishes of India, or of persons escaped from an asylum. (Hear, hear.) The conduct of a body of fanatics in creating disturbances such as we frequently see in the streets was a disgrace to any civilised community. The law said as long as these persons kept moving they could not be interfered with. But suppose any licensed victualler got up a band and procession to draw people to his place of business on a Sunday, what would people say? (Hear, hear.) He agreed that the Salvationists had a right to protection — within their own walls; but they had no right to disturb the peace of the public. He regarded the Salvation Army merely as a craze, and believed the last stage of many of the members would be a good deal worse than the first. He denied that there was any desire on the part of the trade to encourage drunkards — the

279

customers the licensed victuallers wanted were those who, in the words of Mrs. Gamp, 'takes it regular and takes it mild.' (Hear, hear)." — Western Times.

[Page 3]

QUARRELLING OVER THE SPOIL. A SNARL AMONG THE SAINTS

A dispute had taken place at Winsford, Cheshire, between the local branch of the Salvation Army and "General" Booth as to the proportions which the "General" can claim of the funds collected there. The "General" demands a much larger sum than the local contingent are prepared to yield to his control, and how the matter will terminate is at present exceedingly problematical. A split is contemplated.

"THE SALVATION ARMY PLAGUE." CAN IT BE CURED?

All Respectable Towns and Cities troubled with this pestilence should not fail to apply at once to the Lieut.-General Commanding Skeleton Troops, Honiton.

He guarantees that three doses from Company K, "Yellow Ochres," assisted by Companys G and F, "Red and White," will be a sure and radical cure.

Never known to fail,

No cure no pay.

The three companies, including the Band, will be let by the week on easy terms.

For full particulars, apply to LIEUT.-GENERAL Commanding Skeleton Army, Honiton.

CORRESPONDENT'S COLUMN

Head Quarters, December 10th, 1882.

SIR, — At 1.30 to-day the Skeletonian Garrison were thrown into an uproar through a report that the enemy intended to march. Great credit is due to Major W. H. Benzoline and Capt. Cuffy for the rapid manner in which they brought their men to the front by 2 p.m. Companies A, B, and L — red white, and yellow — took the left-wing. The 3.10 train brought K Battery Heavy Artillery from West Hill, Ottery St. Mary; this company was placed in position on the right. But unfortunately they were doomed to disappointment — the enemy didn't march. At 3.35 a shot or two was fired by the sharp-shooters, but without effect. The General in command had great difficulty in dismissing the different companies to their quarters. Every man seemed eager for the fray, more so because the enemy had been reinforced from the Exeter division by two Hallelujah Prize Fighters, whom the Skeletons have designated "Buckskin Bill" and "Red Dick, the Tiger of California." At 7 p.m. the Skeletons made for the enemy's forts. Stormed the place and routed the enemy. The

[page 4]

General, however, does not agree with certain actions on the part of the troops, namely, that of ten members of A Compy. attacking a defenceless "Hallelujah Lass," whom, to

280

use the General's own words, was as "good as wheat," and also of destroying a window of a poor defenceless widow. Although the men declare in both cases the outrages were committed by outsiders and not Skeletons, still from what I can hear, the General thinks otherwise. However, from remarks that I heard drop from our worthy commander, I have reason to believe that should there be a repetition of similar proceedings, it is the General's intention to resign his command of the troops. This, I am sure, would be a sad blow to the cause, and therefore I entreat every true Skeleton to keep in his place and obey orders. What the General says is correct to the minds of sensible men. Therefore let us obey orders.

I am, Sir, yours truly,

PRIVT. H. B. (OBEY ORDERS.)

ACROSTICS

Lanky looking lob-ster
Open not your gob-ster,
Make for another job-ster,
Away with your 30 bob-ster,
Skedaddle with your Mob-ster.

THE GENERAL'S REPLIES TO CORRESPONDENTS.

YEOVIL. — Arrange the men as I told you on Tuesday.

COLYTON. — If they do come Capt. F. F. will be with you to put you in style.

LYMINGTON. — See answer to "Ottery St. Mary."

SEATON. — I don't know, ask the Station Master.

EXETER. — "Why cert'nly," leave the other until I see Capt. W. H. Benzoline.

BRIDPORT. — It serves you right. What on earth is the use of my giving orders unless you obey them?

OTTERY ST. MARY. — Don't ask such foolish questions.

MUSBURY. — Many thanks, but the company is made up.

CREWKERNE. — We return the money with thanks. We don't want coin, but peace and respectability — Try General Booth.

YOUNG WARRIOR, Aged 3¾. — Try again next week.

ADVERTISEMENTS.

TO NEWS AGENTS. — WANTED, AGENTS in every Town in England for the sale of this paper. Liberal commission. Address, Editor, The Skeleton, Honiton.

MAY I ask the kind "Skeletonians" to deliver their "Hen-fruit" in Bulk, instead of presenting them singly. The donors are sometimes excited, and do not throw quite straight, and most of them landing on my person, makes it unpleasant, especially having regard to the "Gamey" flavor of some of the fruit. I am fond of eggs (fresh), but prefer their being delivered as above. My wife will provide a basket. It will save a lot of trouble, on both sides. BONES, Big Village, Honiton.

[We consider the above advertisement most impertinent, and were it not that a member of our own body had introduced the advertiser, we should not have inserted it. The advertiser has no more gratitude than a Cat. ED.]

Printed for and published by HERMON C. CLARKE, of Honiton, Devon, December 16th, 1882.

Source: Salvation Army International Heritage Centre, London.

SOURCES

ARCHIVES AND MANUSCRIPT COLLECTIONS
(Every item is in The British Library except where indicated)

Benson, E. W., *Diaries* (Trinity College, University of Cambridge).

Corps History Book, Droylsden, Vol. I. (Each Corps History Book is in the possession of the respective Commanding Officer.)

Corps History Book, Guildford, Vols. I and II.

Corps History Book, Manchester I, VIII, IX, XV and Star Hall. Respective Vols. I.

Corps History Book, Poplar, Vol. I.

Corps Opening Date List (Handwritten document, Salvation Army International Heritage Centre, London — hereafter S.A. Archives.)

Coutts, J., *William Booth and the Salvation Army,* typed notes (in author's possession).

Deed of Annulment. Close Roll (Chancery), 1878, Part 72, m. 27.

Deed of Constitution. Close Roll (Chancery), 1878, Part 72, m. 28.

Edmonds, H., *My Adventures with General William Booth,* Vols. I–III.

Edmonds, H., *My Home News Sheets. Twenty-five years of family life and work,* Vols. I–VIII (in author's possession).

Extracts from Army publications concerning Poplar Corps. (In the possession of the Commanding Officer of Poplar Corps.)

Foundation Deed. Christian Mission. Close Roll (Chancery), 1875, Part 64, m. 30.

National Register of Archives, Chancery Lane, London.

Joliffe, Lt.-Col., Letters (Cambridge University Library).

'Map of the British Isles' (London, *c.* 1880). Presented with *Beeton's Illustrated Encyclopedia.*

Peak, H., *Diary,* Vols. D. and N.

Public Record Office, Home Office Files, 1878–1890.

Railton, G. S., Letters 1876–1877 (S.A. Archives).

Report of the East London Christian Mission, 1867 (S.A. Archives).

Rough-musicing (notes at Guildford Museum).

Stepney Borough Engineer's Report, 31 March 1905 (The Local History Library, The Central Library, Bancroft Road, London E1).

Supplemental Deed of Constitution. (Chancery), 1904.

The Appointments of Officers 1883 (S.A. Archives).

The Christian Mission Conference Minute Book, 1871–1877 (S.A. Archives).

The Skeleton, 1882 (S.A. Archives).

ARTICLES

Anderson, O., 'The Growth of Christian Militarism in Mid-Victorian Britain', in *English Historical Review,* Vol. 86, January 1971.

Beales, H. L., 'The 'Great Depression' in Industry and Trade', in *Economic History Review,* Vol. 1, October 1934.

Booth, W., 'My Idea of the Millennium', in *Review of Reviews,* 1890.

Booth, W., 'The Millennium; or, The Ultimate Triumph of the Salvation Army Principles', in *All the World,* 1890.

Booth, W., 'The Salvation Army', in *Contemporary Review,* 1882.

Butler, J., 'Catherine Booth', in *Contemporary Review,* 1890.

Cobbe, F. P., 'The Last Revival', in *Contemporary Review,* 1882.

Cunningham, H., 'Jingoism in 1877–8', in *Victorian Studies,* Vol. XIV, No. 4, 1971.

Davidson, R. T., 'The Methods of the Salvation Army', in *Contemporary Review*, 1882.

Hartwell, R. M., and Hobsbawm, E. J., 'The Standard of Living Debate', in *Economic History Review*, Vol. 16, 1963.

Hobsbawm, E. J., 'Artisan or Labour Aristocrat?', in *The Economic History Review*, Second Series, Vol. XXXVII, No. 3, August 1984.

Manning, H. E., 'The Salvation Army', in *Contemporary Review*, 1882.

Marsh, P. T., 'The Primate and the Prime Minister. Archbishop Tait, Gladstone, and the National Church', in *Victorian Studies*, December 1965.

Moorhouse, H. F., 'The Marxist theory of the Labour aristocracy', in *Social History*, Vol. 3, No. 1, January 1978.

Moorhouse, H. F., 'History, sociology and the quiescence of the British working class: a reply to Reid', in *Social History*, Vol. 4, No. 3, October 1979.

Murdoch, N., 'Female Ministry in the Thought and Work of Catherine Booth', in *Church History*, Vol. 53, September 1984.

Murdoch, N., 'Wesleyan Influence on William and Catherine Booth', in *Wesleyan Theological Journal*, Vol. 20, Autumn 1985.

Murdoch, N., 'The Salvation Army and the Church of England, 1882–1883', in *Historical Magazine of the Protestant Episcopal Church*, Vol. 55, March 1986.

Peek, F., 'The Salvationists', in *Contemporary Review*, 1886.

Reid, A., 'Politics and economics in the formation of the British working class: A response to H. F. Moorhouse', in *Social History*, Vol. 3, No. 3, October 1978.

Reid, A., 'Response', in *Social History*, Vol. 4, No. 3, October 1979.

BOOKS

Alexander, M., *Guildford. A Short History* (Godalming, 1986).

An Outline of Salvation Army History (London, 1932).

Avery, G., *Victorian People in Life and in Literature* (London, 1970).

Armytage, W. H. G., *HEAVENS BELOW. Utopian Experiments in England, 1560–1960* (London, 1961).

Ayerst, O., *The Manchester Guardian* (New York, 1971).

Bailey, V., 'Salvation Army Riots, the 'Skeleton Army' and Legal Authority in the Provincial Town', in Donajgrodzki, A. P. (Ed.), *Social Control in Nineteenth Century Britain* (London, 1977).

Barnes, C. J., *Any Questions, answered by Colonel Cyril J. Barnes* (London, 1981, sixth edition).

Barnes, C. J., *With Booth in London* (London, 1986).

Bateman, C. J., *Everybody's Life of General Booth* (London, *c.* 1914).

Bebbington, D. W., *The Nonconformist Conscience. Chapel and Politics, 1870–1914* (London, 1982).

Begbie, H., *William Booth, Founder of the Salvation Army*, Vols. I, II (London, 1920).

Bellamy, J. M., 'Occupation Statistics in the Nineteenth Century Censuses', in Lawton, R. (Ed.), *The Census and Social Structure* (London, 1978).

Benham, W. and Davidson, R. T., *Life of Archbishop Campbell Tait. Archbishop of Canterbury* (London, 1891).

Bennett, D., *William Booth and the Salvation Army* (Basingstoke, 1987).

Betteridge, C., *Trained For War* (London, n.d.).

Bishop, E., *Blood and Fire. The Story of William Booth and the Salvation Army* (London, 1964).

Booth, B., *Echoes and Memories* (London, 1925).

Booth, C., *Aggressive Christianity* (London, 1881).

Booth, C., *Life and Labour of the People of London. Third Series: Religious Influences* (London, 1902–3).

Booth, C., *The Salvation Army in Relation to Church and State* (London, 1885).

Booth, W., *Faith-Healing. A Memorandum* (London, 1902).

Booth, W., *How to Reach the Masses with The Gospel* (London, 1872).

Booth, W., *In Darkest England and the Way Out* (London, 1890).

Booth, W., *Orders and Regulations for the Salvation Army* (London, 1878).

Booth, W., *Orders and Regulations for Field Officers* (London, 1885).

Booth, W., *Orders and Regulations for Salvation Soldiers* (London, 1891).

Booth, W., *Orders and Regulations for Soldiers* (London, 1899).

Booth, W., *The Doctrines and Disciplines of the Salvation Army* (London, 1881).

Booth, W., *The Training of Children* (London, 1888).

Booth-Tucker, F. De L., *The Life of Mrs. Booth,* Vols. I, II (London, 1892).

Booth-Tucker, F. De L., *Catherine Booth*, Vols. I, II (London, 1924).

Bramwell-Booth, C., *Bramwell Booth* (London, 1933).

Bramwell-Booth, C., *Catherine Booth* (London, 1970).

Briggs, A., *Victorian Cities* (London, 1977 edition).

Briggs, A., *Victorian People* (London, 1965 edition).

Briggs, A., *Salvation Army Riots: 1884* (unpublished paper, n.d., photocopy in author's possession).

Brook, D., *Foundations of Methodism* (London, 1927).

Brown, K. D., *A Social History of the Nonconformist Ministry in England and Wales 1800–1930* (Oxford, 1988).

Bullock, C., *The People's Archbishop* (London, 1891).

Burtner, R. W. and Chiles, R. E. *A Compendium of Wesley's Theology* (New York, 1954).

Carpenter, M. L., *Commissioner Lawley* (London, 1924).

Census of England and Wales. Population. 1801–1901. Occupation. 1861–1881.

Census of England and Wales. 1851. Religious Worship.

Chadwick, O., *The Victorian Church*, Part I (London, 1966); Part II (London, 1970).

Chamberlain, E. R., *Guildford. A Biography* (London, 1970).

Champness, E. I., *Frank Smith, M.P. Pioneer and Modern Mystic* (London, n.d.).

Checkland, S. G. *The Rise of Industrial Society in England 1815–1885* (London, 1964).

Clark, G. K., *The Making of Victorian England* (London, 1975).

Coates, T. F. G., *The Prophet of the Poor. The Life Story of General William Booth* (London, 1905).

Cole, G. D. H., *A Short History of the British Working-Class Movement 1789–1947* (London, 1948 edition).

Cole, G. D. H. and Postgate, R., *The Common People, 1746–1946* (London, 1964 edition).

Collier, R., *The General Next to God* (London, 1965).

Coppock, J. T., 'The Changing Face of England 1850–circa 1900', in Darby, H. C. (Ed.), *A New Historical Geography of England* (Cambridge, 1973).

Cornish, F. W., *The English Church in the Nineteenth Century* (London, 1910).

Court, W. H. B., *British Economic History* (Cambridge, 1965).

Coutts, F., *No Discharge in this War* (London, 1974).

Coutts, F., *The History of the Salvation Army*, Vol. VI (London, 1973); Vol. VII (London, 1986).

Cranfield, G. A., *The Press and Society* (London, 1978).

Crossick, G., *An Artisan Elite in Victorian Society: Kentish London 1840–1880* (London, 1978).

Crowther, M. A., *The Workhouse System, 1834–1929* (London, 1981).

Currie, R., Gilbert, A. D. and Horsley, L., *Churches and Church Goers* (Oxford, 1977).

Davies, H., *Worship and Theology in England. From Newman to Martineau, 1850–1900* (London, 1962).

Davies, R., *Rosina Davies, Evangelist. The Story of my Life* (Llandyssul, 1942).

Davies, R. E., *Methodism* (London, 1963).

Directory of Guildford for 1882 (Guildford, 1881).

Disraeli, B., *Sybil or the Two Nations* (London, 1845).

Douglas, E. and Duff, M., *Commissioner Railton* (London, 1920).

Dyos, H. J. and Wolff, M. (Eds.), *The Victorian City,* Vol. II (London, 1973).

Engels, F., *The Condition of the Working-Class in England* (London, 1892).

Ervine, St. J., *God's Soldier. General William Booth,* Vols. I, II (London, 1934).

Fairbank, J., *Booth's Boots. Social Service Beginnings in the Salvation Army* (London, 1983).

Fishman, W. J., *East End 1888* (London, 1988).

Fleming, G., *Hidden Fire. Plymouth, its Christian Heritage* (Plymouth, 1987).

Fraser, D., *The Evolution of the British Welfare State* (London, 1973).

Freeman, T. W., Roger, H. B. and Kinvig, R. H., *Lancashire, Cheshire and the Isle of Man* (London, 1966).

Friederichs, H., *The Romance of the Salvation Army* (London, 1908).

Fryer, P., *Mrs. Grundy. Studies in English Prudery* (London, 1963).

Gay, J. D., *The Geography of Religion in England* (London, 1971).

George, H., *Progress and Poverty* (London, 1881).

Gilbert, A. D., *Religion and Society in Industrial England* (London, 1976).

Gray, R. Q., *The Aristocracy of Labour in Nineteenth-Century Britain c. 1850–1914* (London, 1981).

Gravesend Centenary Corps Brochure, n.d. (In the possession of the Commanding Officer of Gravesend Corps.)

Greenwood, H.,*General Booth and his Critics* (London, 1891).

Guide to Census Reports — Great Britain. 1801–1966 (London, 1977).

Guildford in the Queen's Reign. 1837–1897 (Guildford, 1897).

Haggard, H. R., *Regeneration. Being an Account of the Social Work of the Salvation Army in Great Britain* (London, 1910).

Haggard, H. R., *Report to Her Majesty's Government on the Salvation Army in the United States with Scheme of National Land Settlement* (H.M.S.O. Cd. 2562, 1908).

Halevy, E., *Imperialism and the Rise of Labour* (London, 1929).

Hansard, Third Series, 1882, Vols. 267–271, 353–356; Fourth Series, 1892, Vol. 2.

Hardy, T., *The Mayor of Casterbridge* (London, 1886).

Harrington, B. W., *The London Irish: A Study in Political Activism, 1870–1910.* (Thesis presented for the Degree of Doctor of Philosophy, Princeton University, U.S.A., 1976.)

Harrison, R. and Zeitlin, J. (Eds.), *Divisions of Labour* (Brighton, 1985).

Heasman, K., *Evangelicals in Action* (London, 1962).

Heasman, K., *Army of the Church* (London, 1968).

Herklots, H. G. G., *These Denominations* (London, 1946).

Hobsbawm, E. J., *Labouring Men* (London, 1964).

Hobsbawm, E. J. and Ranger, T. (Ed.), *The Invention of Tradition* (Cambridge, 1983).

Hobsbawm, E. J., *Worlds of Labour* (London, 1984).

Honiton and District Official Guide (Honiton, 1983).

Horridge, G. K., *The Growth and Development of a Family Firm, Chivers of Histon. 1873–1939* (Cambridge, 1983).

Hoskins, W. G., *Devon* (Newton Abbot, 1972).

Hughes, W., *A New County Atlas of Great Britain and Ireland* (London, 1873).

Hume, C. H., 'The Public Health Movement', in Ward, J. T., *Popular Movements c. 1830–1850* (London, 1978).

Hunt, E. H., *Regional Wage Variations in Britain. 1850–1914* (Oxford, 1973).

Index of Salvation Army Corps 1905.

Inglis, K. S., *The Churches and the Working-Classes in Victorian England* (London, 1963).

Isichei, E., *Victorian Quakers* (Oxford, 1970).

Jones, V., 'The Salvation Army', in *Merthyr Tydfil — A Valley Community* (Cambridge, 1981).

Kelly's Directory of Devonshire and Cornwall, 1883, 1884.
Kelly's Directory of Lancashire, 1878, 1881.
Kelly's Directory of Cheshire, 1878, 1883.
Kent, J., *Holding the Fort. Studies in Victorian Revivalism* (London, 1978).
Lawton, R., 'Rural Depopulation in Nineteenth Century England', in Steel, R. W. and Lawton, R. (Ed.), *Liverpool Essays in Geography* (London, 1967).
Lax, W. H., *LAX, HIS BOOK. The Autobiography of Lax of Poplar* (London, 1937).
Liberty Booklets. *Salvation Army Biographies* (London, 1943–1957).
Longmate, N., *The Workhouse* (London, 1982).
Lovell, J., *Stevedores and Dockers* (London, 1969).
Lunn, B., *Salvation Dynasty* (London, 1938).
Mackenzie, F. A., *The Clash of Cymbals* (London, 1929).
Mackenzie, F. A., *Booth-Tucker* (London, 1930).
Mackenzie, N. and J., *The First Fabians* (London, 1977).
Manchester VIII Corps Centenary Brochure, 1983. (In the possession of the Commanding Officer of Manchester VIII.)
Manson, J., *The Salvation Army and the Public* (London, 1906).
Martin, D., *A Sociology of English Religion* (London, 1967).
Mathias, P., *The First Industrial Nation* (London, 1969).
Mayhew, H., *London Labour and London Poor* (London, 1851).
Mearns, A., *The Bitter Cry of Outcast London. An Enquiry into the Condition of the Abject Poor* (London, 1883).
Mews, S., 'The General and the Bishops: Alternative Responses to Dechristianisation', in Gourvish, T. R. and O'Day, A., *Later Victorian Britain, 1867–1900* (Basingstoke, 1988).
McLeod, H., *Class and Religion in the Late Victorian City* (London, 1974).
McLeod, H., *Religion and the Working Class in Nineteenth-Century Britain* (London, 1984).
Midwinter, E. C., *Victorian Social Reform* (London, 1968).
Mitchell, D. C. *The Darkest England Match Industry*, Part I (private printing, n.d.); Part II (private printing, 1973). (Copies in author's possession.)
Morgan, R. C., *Richard Weaver* (London, n.d.).
Morris, R. J., *Class and Class Consciousness in the Industrial Revolution, 1780–1850* (London, 1982).
Mudie-Smith, R., *The Religious Life of London* (London, 1904).
Nicol, A. M, *General Booth and the Salvation Army* (London, n.d.).
Obelkevich, J., *Religion and Rural Society: South Lindsey, 1825–75* (Oxford, 1976).
Orr, J. E., *The Second Evangelical Awakening* (London, 1949).
Parry, W. D., *Gwaed a Than* (Caernarfon, 1986).
Pearson, G., *Hooligan. A History of Respectable Fears* (London, 1983).
Phillips, P. T., *The Sectarian Spirit: Sectarianism, Society and Politics in Victorian Cotton Towns* (Toronto, 1982).
Pike, E. R., *Human Documents of the Age of the Forsytes* (London, 1969).
Plowden, A., *The Case of Eliza Armstrong* (London, 1974).
Porter, E., *Cambridgeshire Customs and Folklore* (London, 1969).
Preece, C., *Woman of the Valleys. The Story of Mother Shepherd* (Port Talbot, 1988).
Railton, G. S., *The Salvation Army. Heathen England* (London, 1883, fifth edition).
Railton, G. S., *The Salvation Navvy. The Life of John Allen* (London, 1878).
Railton, G. S., *Twenty-One Years Salvation Army* (London, 1886).
Railton, G. S., *Commissioner Dowdle, The Saved Railway Guard* (London, 1912, second edition).
Reid, A., 'Intelligent Artisans and Aristocrats of Labour. The Essays of Thomas Wright', in Winter, J. (Ed.), *The Working Class in Modern British History. Essays in Honour of Henry Pelling* (Cambridge, 1983).

Richman, G., *Fly a Flag for Poplar* (London, 1975).

Roberts, R., *The Classic Slum* (Manchester, 1971).

Robertson, R., 'The Salvation Army: the Persistence of Sectarianism', in Wilson, B. R. (Ed.), *Patterns of Sectarianism* (London, 1967).

Royle, E. *Radical Politics 1790–1900. Religion and Unbelief* (London, 1971).

Ryan, P. A., ' 'Poplarism' 1894–1930', in Thane, P., *The Origins of British Social Policy* (London, 1978).

Ryan, P. A., 'Politics and relief: East London unions in the late nineteenth and early twentieth centuries', in Rose, M. E., *The poor and the city: the English poor law in its urban context, 1834–1914* (Leicester, 1985).

Salvation Army Song Book (London, 1879).

Salvation Army Music, Vol. 1.

Salvation Army Music, Vol. II.

Sandall, R., *The History of the Salvation Army*, Vol. I (London, 1947); Vol. II (London, 1950); Vol. III (London, 1955).

Saywell, J. R., *The History and Annals of Northallerton* (Northallerton, 1885).

Scott, T. E., *Poplar In Days Gone By* (private printing, 1910).

Shaw's Local Government Manual, 1881.

Shiman, L. L., *The Crusade against drink in Victorian England* (New York, 1988).

Simmons, A., *The History of the Parish of All Saints, Poplar* (London, 1870).

Sims, G. R., *How the Poor Live in Horrible London* (London, 1889).

Smales, B. J., *Economic History* (London, 1975).

Smith, F., *The Betrayal of Bramwell Booth* (London, 1929).

Smith, G., *Gipsy Smith, His Life and Work. By Himself* (London, 1903).

Smith, R. M., *The History of the Salvation Army in Wales up to the Year 1900.* (Thesis presented for the Degree of Master of Theology, University of Cardiff, April 1982.)

Souvenir Brochure for the Opening and Dedication of the New Suite of Buildings. Guildford Salvation Army (Guildford, 1977).

Stead, W. T., *General Booth. A Biographical Sketch* (London, 1891).

Stedman Jones, G., *Outcast London* (Oxford, 1971).

Stevenson, J., *Popular Disturbances in England 1700–1870* (London, 1979).

Stock, E., *History of the Church Missionary Society* (London, 1899).

Street, H., *Freedom, Individual and the Law* (London, 1977, fourth edition).

Thane, P. (Ed.), *The Origins of British Social Policy* (London, 1978).

The Chronicle of Convocation, 1882–1885.

The Guildford Almanac and Directory for 1882 (Guildford, 1881).

The Official Index to The Times (London, 1860–1891).

The Present Position of the Salvation Army (London, 1888).

The Salvation Army. Its Origins and Development (London, 1945 edition).

The Salvation Soldier's Pocket Book for 1884 (London, 1883).

The Salvation War. 1882 (London, 1883).

The Salvation War. 1883 (London, 1884).

The Salvation War. 1884 (London, 1885).

The Salvation War. 1885 (London, 1886).

The Victorian History of the County of Lancaster, Vol. 2 (London, 1908); Vol. 4 (London, 1911).

The Warrior's Library (London, 1901–1913).

Thomson, D., *England in the Nineteenth Century* (London, 1950).

Thompson, D. M., *Nonconformity in the Nineteenth Century* (London, 1973).

Thompson, F. M. L., *The Rise of Respectable Society. A Social History of Victorian Britain, 1830–1900* (London, 1988).

Townsend, W. J., Workman, H. B. and Eayrs, G., *A New History of Methodism*, Vols. I, II (London, 1909).

Tracy, R., *Marianne Pawson. The Zulu Queen* (London, 1944).

Trevelyan, G. M., *Illustrated English Social History: 4* (London, 1960).

Troutt, M., *The General was a Lady* (Nashville, 1980).

Wallis, H., *The Happy Warrior. The Life-Story of Commissioner Elijah Cadman* (London, 1928).

Walsh, J., 'Methodism and the Mob in the Eighteenth Century', in Cuming, G. T. and Baker, D. (Eds.), *Studies in Church History*, No. 8 (Cambridge, 1972).

Ward, C., *The Social Sources of the Salvation Army*. (Thesis presented for the Degree of Master of Philosophy, University of London, January 1970.)

Watts, A. W., *Lion Hearts. Memoirs of the Christian Mission, Afterwards Known as the Salvation Army* (London, n.d.).

Weightman, G. and Humphries, S., *The Making of Modern London, 1815–1914* (London, 1983).

Weylland, J. M., *These Fifty Years* (London, 1885).

White's Directory for Devonshire, 1890.

Whyte, F., *The Life of W. T. Stead* (London, 1925).

Wiggins, A. R., *The History of the Salvation Army*, Vol. IV (London, 1964); Vol. V (London, 1966).

Williams, D. G. T., 'The Principle of Beatty v. Gillbanks: A Reappraisal', in Doob, A. N. and Greenspan, E. L. (Eds.), *Perspectives in Criminal Law* (Ontario, 1985).

Williams, S., *Punching Pride of Ancoats* (London, 1957).

Wilson, A., 'Chartism', in Ward, J. T. (Ed.), *Popular Movements c. 1830–1850* (London, 1978).

Woods, R. A., *English Social Movements* (New York, 1895, revised edition).

Yeo, S., *Religion and Voluntary Organisations in Crisis* (London, 1976).

PAMPHLETS

Booth, W., *All about the Salvation Army, 1882* (London, 1882).

Boudier, J. H., *A Sequel to "Darkest England"* (London, 1890).

Corbridge, W., *The Salvation Mine. Down to Death, Up to Heaven* (London, 1881).

Corbridge, W., *The Up Line to Heaven and the Down Line to Hell* (London, 1883).

Ex-Staff Officer, *The New Papacy. Behind the Scenes in the Salvation Army* (Toronto, 1889).

Faucher, L. J., *Manchester in 1844; its present condition and future prospects* (Manchester, 1844).

Fishbourne, Admiral, *A Calm Plea for the Enlargement of Salvation Army Work* (London, 1883).

Foote, G. W., *Salvation Syrup or Light in Darkest England. A Reply to General William Booth* (London, 1891).

Gasparin, La Comtesse Agenor de, *Read and Judge the (So Called) Salvation Army* (Paris, n.d., English translation London, 1883).

Hancock, T., *Salvation by Mammon* (London, 1891).

Kay, J. P., *The Moral and Physical Condition of the Working Classes Employed in the Cotton Manufacture in Manchester* (Manchester, 1832).

Luff, G. R., *Edward Street Literature* (Brighton, 1890).

Newton, B. W., *Address Respecting the Methods of the Salvation Army* (London, 1924).

O.W.L.A., *Some Reasons why I do not Sympathize with the Salvation Army* (London, 1882).

Redstone, J. J. R., *An Ex-Captain's Experience of the Salvation Army* (London, 1888, second edition).

Salvation Socialism, Supplement to the *War Cry*, 25 December 1889.

Taylor, J. P., *Fighting and Conquering in Lancashire and Cheshire* (Manchester, 1884).

Tristan, F. C. T. H., *Promenades Dan Londres* (Paris, 1840).

NEWSPAPERS, MAGAZINES AND PERIODICALS

All the World, 1884–1890, 1910 (Salvation Army, London).
Bristol Times and Mirror, 1882.
British Weekly, 1888.
Church Times, 1881, 1882.
Daily News, 1903.
Daily Telegraph, 1881.
Gorton, Openshaw and Bradford Reporter, 1878–1885.
Honiton and Ottery Gazette and East Devon Advertiser, 1883, 1884.
Manchester City News, 1878–1880.
Manchester Evening News, 1878–1880, 1979.
Merthyr Express, 1881.
Nottingham Express, 1881.
Pall Mall Gazette, 1885.
Pictorial World, 1880–1887.
Review of Reviews, 1890, 1891.
Sheffield Independent, 1879.
The Caernarvon and Denbigh Herald, 1886.
The Christian, 1875, 1882.
The Christian Mission Magazine, 1870–1878.
The Church Reformers' Magazine for England and Ireland, 1832 (London).
The Devon Weekly Times, 1882.
The East End News, 1875.
The East London Advertiser, 1866, 1868, 1964.
The East London Evangelist, 1868, 1869.
The East London Leader, 1885.
The East London Observer, 1865–1880, 1894.
The Keep. The Quarterly Magazine of the Guildford Institute, 1912, 1913.
The Local Officer, 1905 (Salvation Army, London).
The Manchester Guardian, 1884.
The Methodist Times, 1881, 1890.
The Revival, 1860–1868.
The Salvationist, 1879.
The South Wales Daily News, 1879.
The Surrey Advertiser and County Times, 1860–1890, 1981.
The Textile Manufacturer (Manchester), 1870s–1880s.
The Times (London, 1860, 1865–1891).
The Treasury, 1879.
War Cry, 1879–1900.
The Western Times, 1882–1884.
The West Middlesex Herald, 1885.
The Wrexham Advertiser, 1883.
Y Gad Lef, 1888.

INDEX

Italicized page numbers refer to illustrations

Otter, River, 195
Ottery St Mary, Devon, 200
outposts, 172
Over Darwin, 73
Overend and Gurney Bank, 129
Owen, Merton and Co., 133
Owen, Mr., 133
Owen, S., Miss, 214
Oxford, Bishop of, 115

Pall Mall Gazette, The, 117, 122
pamphlets, 121, 123, 126
Parkin, H., 210–11
Parliament, 34, 105, 111–2, 123, 188–9,
    202–3, 205
Parliamentary committees, 112
Particular Baptists, *see also* Baptists, 5
pawn broking, 12–3, 143
Paynter, F., Rev., 185ff, 193
Pearson, Major, 175
Pearson, W., 78, 157
Peck, A., 175
Peek, F., 123
Pembroke Dock, 214
Penge, 20
penitent form *see also* mourners' bench, 21,
    177
Penrhyndeudraeth, 217
Pentre, 212–3, 220
People's Mission hall, 23, *24*
Pepper, Lt-Col., 105
Perkins, Cpt., 176
persecution, *see* opposition
petition, 111
pew-rents, 2, 5–6, 49, 184
"phossy jaw", 147
pit disaster, 221
Plaistow, 19
Plymouth, 174
Police, 92, 95–7, 104–6, 111, 137, 142–3,
    160, 163, 165, 167, 169, 173, 185–6,
    188–92, 194, 196, 198–205, 209–10, 212
Poole, 104, 107
Poor Law Rate, 130
Poor Law Unions, London, 130
Poor Man's Palace, Manchester, *179*
Poplar, 17, 128, 185, 212, 227
Poplarism, 131
Poplar Union, 130
Porth, 220–1
Portsmouth, 19–20, 31
postcards, 169
posters, 34, 45, 50, *51,* 99, *118,* 163, 171,
    185–6
potato famine, *see also* Ireland/Irish, 7
pottery, 196, 207
prayer, *see also* theology, 100, 141, 211
Presbyterians, *see also* English Presbyterians,
    64, 66, 216

press, *see also* individual newspapers, 121–4,
    141–2, 148, 159, 186–8, 191, 198, 201,
    203–5, 209, 215–6
Price, I., 211
Primitive Methodists, *see also* Methodists, 4,
    40, 74–6, 78, 86, 135, 180, 187, 222,
    224–5, 228
prison, Belle Vue, *see also* imprisonment, 163,
    171
processions *see* marches
Progress and Poverty, 149
promotion to glory, *see* funerals
prostitution, 117, 119, 135, 157, 167, 210
prostitution, child, 126, 147, 226
protection, Police, 123, 165, 167, 200, 203
Protestant Work Ethic, 79
publicans, *see also* drink trade/interest, 95–6,
    102, 104, 113, 142, 156, 159–60, 165,
    173, 183, 189, 193, 201, 203, 205, 210
public houses, *16,* 77, 96, 113, 134–5, 160,
    191, 201, 210, 214, 226
publicity, 122, 126, 186, 206

Quakers, 6, 15, 93, 116, 231
Queen's Bench, 107ff, 127, 189, 203, 226
Queensberry, Marquis of, 121
Queen Victoria, 119
Queen Victoria Road, 53

Rabbits, E., 13
Radcliffe, R., 8, 15
ragged schools, *see also* social schemes, 133,
    136, 223
Railton, G., 27–9, 31, 33–4, 53, 116, 127,
    140, 208
railways, 85, 128, 131, 156, 175, 183, 191,
    196, 198, 208, 214–5
rallies, *see also* marches, welcome home
    rallies, 45, 48, 217
Reading, 40
reading rooms, 133, 136
reconnaissance, 39, 41, 185
recruits, 41, 197, 212
Red Nose Army/Red Ribbon Army, 94, 192
Redstone, Capt., and Mrs., 142–3
Reed, H., 25–6
Reformers, 13–5, 23, 222–3
refuse collection, 119
Regent Hall, London, 215
Registration Districts, 128, 132, 138, 182–3,
    195–6
Religious Accommodation, 74
Religious Census, 1851, 1–2, 7, 132, 157, 183,
    222
Renshaw, T., 174, 181, 227
Review of Reviews, 122
Revival, The, 8, 15, 95
revivalism/revivals, 7–9, 90, 161, 165, 168,
    171, 208, 213–4, 217–8, 221–2

297